HOLMAN
Old
Testament
Commentary

HOLMAN
Old Testament Commentary

Genesis

GENERAL EDITOR
Max Anders

AUTHORS
Kenneth O. Gangel
and Stephen J. Bramer

HOLMAN
REFERENCE

Nashville, Tennessee

Holman Old Testament Commentary
© 2002 Broadman & Holman Publishers
Nashville, Tennessee
All rights reserved

ISBN 0–8054–9461–8
Dewey Decimal Classification: 222.11
Subject Heading: BIBLE. O.T. Genesis

Genesis/Kenneth O. Gangel and Stephen J. Bramer
        p.   cm. — (Holman Old Testament commentary)
    Includes bibliographical references. (p.).
    ISBN
    1. Bible. O.T. Genesis—Commentaries.   I. Title.   II. Series.

—dc21

2 3 4 5 6 06 05
R

o my daughter Julie,
just because I love you.

Kenneth O. Gangel
2002

o my firstborn daughter
Sarah Grace Bramer.
Your Christian love and life
(as well as suggestions for this
commentary)
make a dad proud.

Stephen J. Bramer
2002

Contents

Contents

Editorial Preface

Today's church hungers for Bible teaching, and Bible teachers hunger for resources to guide them in teaching God's Word. The Holman Old Testament Commentary provides the church with the food to feed the spiritually hungry in an easily digestible format. The result: new spiritual vitality that the church can readily use.

Bible teaching should result in new interest in the Scriptures, expanded Bible knowledge, discovery of specific scriptural principles, relevant applications, and exciting living. The unique format of the Holman Old Testament Commentary includes sections to achieve these results for every Old Testament book.

Opening quotations stimulate thinking and lead to an introductory illustration and discussion that draw individuals and study groups into the Word of God. "In a Nutshell" summarizes the content and teaching of the chapter. Verse-by-verse commentary answers the church's questions rather than raising issues scholars usually admit they cannot adequately solve. Bible principles and specific contemporary applications encourage students to move from Bible to contemporary times. A specific modern illustration then ties application vividly to present life. A brief prayer aids the student to commit his or her daily life to the principles and applications found in the Bible chapter being studied. For those still hungry for more, "Deeper Discoveries" take the student into a more personal, deeper study of the words, phrases, and themes of God's Word. Finally, a teaching outline provides transitional statements and conclusions along with an outline to assist the teacher in group Bible studies.

It is the editors' prayer that this new resource for local church Bible teaching will enrich the ministry of group, as well as individual, Bible study, and that it will lead God's people truly to be people of the Book, living out what God calls us to be.

Acknowledgments

When Dr. Kenneth Gangel contacted me with the opportunity to share in authoring this commentary of Genesis I was both excited and sobered. I was excited to be able to share in writing what I have taught in classes previously at Briercrest Bible College in Caronport, Saskatchewan, Canada and now at Dallas Theological Seminary in Dallas Texas. Both these fine Christian schools have allowed me the opportunity to grow and develop as a Bible teacher. But I was sobered when I realized again that is serious business to put into writing explanations and applications concerning the Word of God. My thanks to Kenn Gangel for his offer that allowed me to contribute to this commentary and to editors Max Anders and Steve Bond for their help and oversight in making this volume what it is in its final form. My wife Sharon, daughters Sarah and Charity, and son Joshua all deserve my grateful appreciation for living with a husband and father consumed this past year with finishing "the book."

Stephen J. Bramer, author of chapters 1–11 and 37–50

As the dedication notes, I express loving appreciation to my daughter, Julie. In addition, I must thank my wife, Betty, for assisting with proofreading, and my manuscript manager, Mrs. Ginny Murray, for impeccable handling of the commentary text.

Kenneth O. Gangel, author of chapters 12–36

Holman Old Testament Commentary Contributors

Vol. 1, Genesis
ISBN 0-8054-9461-8
Kenneth O. Gangel and
Stephen J. Bramer

Vol. 2, Exodus, Leviticus, Numbers
ISBN 0-8054-9462-6
Glen Martin

Vol. 3, Deuteronomy
ISBN 0-8054-9463-4
Doug McIntosh

Vol. 4, Joshua
ISBN 0-8054-9464-2
Kenneth O. Gangel

Vol. 5, Judges, Ruth
ISBN 0-8054-9465-0
W. Gary Phillips

Vol. 6, 1 & 2 Samuel
ISBN 0-8054-9466-9
Stephen Andrews

Vol. 7, 1 & 2 Kings
ISBN 0-8054-9467-7
Gary Inrig

Vol. 8, 1 & 2 Chronicles
ISBN 0-8054-9468-5
Winfried Corduan

Vol. 9, Ezra, Nehemiah, Esther
ISBN 0-8054-9469-3
Knute Larson and Kathy Dahlen

Vol. 10, Job
ISBN 0-8054-9470-7
Steven J. Lawson

Vol. 11, Psalms 1–75
ISBN 0-8054-9471-5
Steven J. Lawson

Vol. 12, Psalms 76–150
ISBN 0-8054-9481-2
Steven J. Lawson

Vol. 13, Proverbs
ISBN 0-8054-9472-3
Max Anders

Vol. 14, Ecclesiastes, Song of Songs
ISBN 0-8054-9482-0
David George Moore and Daniel L. Akin

Vol. 15, Isaiah
ISBN 0-8054-9473-1
Trent C. Butler

Vol. 16, Jeremiah, Lamentations
ISBN 0-8054-9474-X
Fred M. Wood and Ross McLaren

Vol. 17, Ezekiel
ISBN 0-8054-9475-8
Mark F. Rooker

Vol. 18, Daniel
ISBN 0-8054-9476-6
Kenneth O. Gangel

**Vol. 19, Hosea, Joel, Amos,
Obadiah, Jonah, Micah**
ISBN 0-8054-9477-4
Trent C. Butler

**Vol. 20, Nahum, Habakkuk,
Zephaniah, Haggai, Zechariah, Malachi**
ISBN 0-8054-9478-2
Stephen R. Miller

Holman New Testament Commentary Contributors

Vol. 1, Matthew
ISBN 0-8054-0201-2
Stuart K. Weber

Vol. 2, Mark
ISBN 0-8054-0202-0
Rodney L. Cooper

Vol. 3, Luke
ISBN 0-8054-0203-9
Trent C. Butler

Vol. 4, John
ISBN 0-8054-0204-7
Kenneth O. Gangel

Vol. 5, Acts
ISBN 0-8054-0205-5
Kenneth O. Gangel

Vol. 6, Romans
ISBN 0-8054-0206-3
Kenneth Boa and William Kruidenier

Vol. 7, 1 & 2 Corinthians
ISBN 0-8054-0207-1
Richard L. Pratt Jr.

**Vol. 8, Galatians, Ephesians,
Philippians, Colossians**
ISBN 0-8054-0208-X
Max Anders

**Vol. 9, 1 & 2 Thessalonians,
1 & 2 Timothy, Titus, Philemon**
ISBN 0-8054-0209-8
Knute Larson

Vol. 10, Hebrews, James
ISBN 0-8054-0211-X
Thomas D. Lea

Vol. 11, 1 & 2 Peter, 1, 2, 3 John, Jude
ISBN 0-8054-0210-1
David Walls and Max Anders

Vol. 12, Revelation
ISBN 0-8054-0212-8
Kendell H. Easley

Holman Old Testament Commentary

Twenty volumes designed for Bible study and teaching to enrich the local church and God's people.

Series Editor	Max Anders
Managing Editor	Steve Bond
Project Editor	Dean Richardson
Product Development Manager	Ricky D. King
Marketing Manager	Stephanie Huffman
Executive Editor	David Shepherd
Page Composition	TF Designs, Mt. Juliet, TN

Introduction to

Genesis

Genesis—what a great place to start! For centuries Jews and Christians have started to read their Bibles right here. For well over a century, Genesis has been a battlefield for biblical scholars. One interpreter has compared Genesis 1–11 with a minefield that has to be crossed with great care.

In this commentary designed for teachers and preachers, we won't rehearse the history of these conflicts in great detail. There are many fine commentaries that have extensive treatments on introductory and critical matters. Here we will practice the "inoculation approach." We will present just enough information to prevent a person from coming down with a case of "doubts" or "I've never heard of that." Those who wish to study more on introductory matters may wish to consult the evangelical standards such as Gleason Archer's *A Survey of Old Testament Introduction* or R. K. Harrison's *Introduction to the Old Testament*.

AUTHOR

Two names that one hears most often in connection with the authorship of Genesis are Moses and Julius Wellhausen! Moses is the traditional author of Genesis and was considered to be the author of the entire Pentateuch (first five books of the Old Testament) by the Israelites of the Old Testament, by the Jews since the return from Babylonian exile, and by almost all Christians until well into the eighteenth century. Wellhausen's name is associated with the authorship of Genesis, not as author but as the biblical critic who popularized a theory that has come to be known as the "documentary hypothesis" or the "JEDP theory."

The "documentary hypothesis" is but a part of Wellhausen's project to account for Israel's religion within an evolutionary framework. This hypothesis maintains that the Pentateuch was a compilation of selections from several different written documents composed at different places and times over a period of five centuries, long after Moses lived. A redactor or redactors (editors) joined portions of these documents into the form that we have now. The major documents came to be known as J, E, D, P, which represent a Yahwistic (Jehovah) tradition, an Elohistic tradition, a Deuteronomic tradition, and a Priestly tradition.

1

Evidence that must be taken into account on the so-called "authorship controversy" of the Pentateuch is multifaceted. Internal literary evidence in each book of the Pentateuch supports the view that a single author wrote each. For Genesis this will be discussed below under the literary features of Genesis. Moreover, a unity exists among the first five books of the Bible that would argue for the same author for all five. Numerous references within the Pentateuch indicate Moses was told by God to write down specific material that critical scholars want to assign to other authors centuries after Moses (e.g., Exod. 17:14; 24:4; 34:27; Num. 33:1–2; Deut. 31:9).

Because Genesis ends approximately four hundred years before Moses lived, the material of this first book must have been "compiled" by Moses based on direct revelations, family tradition, and with reference to existing historical records. Nevertheless the resulting book is to be considered inspired by God and trustworthy in all that it affirms (cp. Matt. 19:4–5). In addition to material from the Pentateuch, there is much evidence from the rest of Scripture, especially Christ's own words in the New Testament, that indicate Moses wrote the Pentateuch (e.g., preexilic references—Josh. 8:31; 23:6; 1 Kgs. 2:3; 2 Kgs. 14:6; 21:8; exilic reference—Dan. 9:11–13; postexilic references—Ezra 6:18; 7:6 [cp. 7:10–11]; Neh 8:1; 13:1; 2 Chr. 25:4; 35:12; Mal. 4:4; New Testament references—Matt. 19:8; Mark 7:10; Luke 20:37; 24:27; John 5:46–47; 7:19). While the specific Book of Genesis is not singled out, during the entire Old Testament period up to and including the time of Jesus, the Jews regarded the Pentateuch as a unit. Consequently, the hearers would have understood what Jesus or an Old Testament writer said about any of the five books of Moses as an endorsement of the Mosaic authorship of them all.

In addition to direct testimonies to Mosaic authorship, evidence from within the Pentateuch suggests that the author (and readers) had little or no firsthand acquaintance with Canaan, but the lands of Egypt and Sinai were well-known to them. References to agriculture (Exod. 9:31–32), to trees (Exod. 25:5; the shittim or acacia tree is native to Egypt but rare in Canaan), to animals (Exod. 25:5; the sea cow or dugong is foreign to Canaan but available in the seas around Egypt and Sinai), to geography (Gen. 13:10 compares the Jordan River to the land of Egypt), to the creation of the tabernacle in a desert setting (Exod. 25–40) all point clearly to an author and recipients who had lived in Egypt and Sinai but were still not in Canaan.

The biblical stories about Moses' upbringing, training, and adult experiences (Exod. 1–2) combine to demonstrate that Moses had the right qualifications to write just such material as we find in Genesis.

In 1990 Harold Bloom, an eminent Yale University literary critic, argued for a woman author for the most memorable sections of Genesis and Exodus, as well as bits of Numbers and Deuteronomy. His book, *The Book of J,* used such arguments as: Genesis contains the only known account from the ancient Middle East of the creation of woman and this account is six times longer than that of Adam's advent; the women of the Pentateuch (Eve, Sarah, Rebecca, Rachel, Tamar, Zipporah) are strong, but none of the men (Abraham, Jacob, Moses) are particularly good-looking! Bloom sees "J" as a single individual who wrote after Solomon's reign in the tenth century B.C. but who displays a modern skepticism and worldliness. He believes she cherished neither love nor awe of God but rather portrayed God as impish and arbitrary.

The authors of this commentary still find the evidence for Mosaic authorship of Genesis more compelling than any other theory on the authorship of Genesis. Therefore, we assume that frame of reference.

DATE OF WRITING

If one accepts Mosaic authorship of Genesis, the date of composition of the book must be within the lifetime of Moses (about 1525–1405 B.C.) and specifically during the time of the wilderness wanderings of the Israelites (1446–1406 B.C.).

DATE OF MATERIAL PRESENTED

The events recorded in Genesis stretch historically from creation to Joseph's death. If the genealogies in Genesis are taken as "closed" (that is, with no gaps), then the minimal period from the end of creation to Israel's entry into Egypt would be some 2,328 years, dating the creation of the world at some 6,176 years ago.

This figure is arrived at by adding the 2,002 years of the Christian era, plus the 1,446 years (taking an early date for the exodus) back to the exodus, plus the 400 years of slavery in Egypt, plus the 2,328 years from the entry into Egypt back to Adam. If there are gaps, then the time period could be extended considerably and made to fit more closely with the more commonly accepted belief among conservatives that mankind has been on the earth some 10,000 years (Egyptian history appears to go back to 3,500 B.C.). The period covered by the creation account itself is, of course, subject to much controversy.

TITLE

Each book of the Pentateuch originally received its title from the first word or two in the book. For Genesis the first Hebrew word is *beresit*, translated "in the beginning." The English title *Genesis* is a transliteration of a Greek word (*geneseos*) used in the Septuagint translation for the key Hebrew term (*toledot*) which means "the generations of/the histories of/the account of."

RECIPIENTS

Although the recipients are not named, if one accepts the Mosaic authorship of Genesis as most evangelicals do, then the book was written initially either for the Israelites who were part of the group that left Egypt and hoped to enter the promised land from Kadesh Barnea. Or, if Genesis was written later in Moses' life, the Israelites were part of the group looking forward to entering the promised land from the plains of Moab. For either group, the book would have encouraged the Israelites to trust their faithful, omnipotent God.

But this initial group of Israelites was not the exclusive group for whom the material of Genesis was written. It is clear that various teachings in Genesis were to be the basis of how mankind and specifically God's people were to think of themselves, of sin, and of their relationship to God. It remains relevant information for all people. Without Genesis much teaching in subsequent Scripture, including the New Testament, would be unclear or unintelligible. In his commentary on Genesis 1–11, Kenneth Mathews says, "If we possessed a Bible without Genesis, we would have a 'house of cards' without foundation or mortar" (Mathews, 22).

LITERARY FEATURES

The material in Genesis, as in all biblical historical books, is a composite, interpreted history that has settings, characters, plots, dialogues, and narrators. The author has included and excluded materials to make his point. But the selection of material was not random, as this commentary will demonstrate. Neither was it arranged in a haphazard manner.

Genesis has a wonderfully developed literary structure that will be explored in greater detail throughout the commentary. In brief, it is structured around the Hebrew term *toledot* ("the generations of/the histories of/the account of").

The literary structure of Genesis based on the use of *toledot* would be as follows (the initial introductory section is not introduced by *toledot*):

1. Introduction: the story of creation (1:1–2:3)
2. What became of creation (2:4–4:26)
3. What became of Adam (5:1–6:8)
4. What became of Noah (6:9–9:29)
5. What became of Noah's sons (10:1–11:9)
6. What became of Shem (11:10–26)
7. What became of Terah (11:27–25:11)
8. What became of Ishmael (25:12–18)
9. What became of Isaac (25:19–35:29)

10. What became of Esau (36:1–37:1)
11. What became of Jacob (37:2–50:26)

While such a structure reflects the literary feature of *toledot*, it does not reflect all the topical emphases that are found in Genesis. For example, the significant change between the prepatriarchal history and that of Abraham, Isaac, and Jacob is not reflected. Neither is the very extensive treatment of Joseph anticipated by this structure. This commentary will acknowledge both the structure created by the *toledot* and structure created by topical-theological concerns. Chapters of this commentary will vary in amount of material covered as the writers anticipate concerns of the readers and also recognize that some material is easier to cover in large sections but still with good understanding than are other sections.

PURPOSE

The general purpose of Genesis is to provide an accurate record of the history of God's sovereign establishment of his covenant of blessing with his people. In Genesis we see God establishing his relationship with Abraham as a means of blessing the entire world.

The context of the Abrahamic covenant includes: the beginning and establishment of the earth and the human race, the fall of humans into sin, the resulting judgments and the means by which God, through his created beings, would seek to reestablish his rule over creation, the previous judgment of all corrupt humans and the blessing of obedient Noah (and his family), and then the choosing of Abraham through whom God's blessing would come to all nations. This material was designed to instruct Israel about its heritage of promise as well as to remind the nation of the absolute faithfulness of its God.

Genesis 1:1–2:3

Creation

I. **INTRODUCTION**
The Big Bang from God's Perspective

II. **COMMENTARY**
A verse-by-verse explanation of this passage.

III. **CONCLUSION**
What a World and What a God!

An overview of the principles and applications from this passage.

IV. **LIFE APPLICATION**
"The Heavens Declare the Glory of God"

Melding this passage to life.

V. **PRAYER**
Tying this passage to life with God.

VI. **DEEPER DISCOVERIES**
Historical, geographical, and grammatical enrichment of the commentary.

VII. **TEACHING OUTLINE**
Suggested step-by-step group study of this passage.

VIII. **ISSUES FOR DISCUSSION**
Zeroing this passage in on daily life.

Quote

"*A* house testifies that there was a builder, a dress that there was a weaver, a door that there was a carpenter; so our world by its existence proclaims its Creator, God."

R a b b i   A k i b a   B e n   J o s e p h

Genesis 1:1–2:3

IN A NUTSHELL

G od created the world in six days, speaking everything into existence. The creation account in Genesis shows us that God existed before all, God has made all, and therefore God deserves all our obedience and adoration. This creation account is foundational for our understanding of who God is and what place we as humans occupy in this plan.

Creation

I. INTRODUCTION

The Big Bang from God's Perspective

*P*erhaps no other chapter in the Scriptures is quite as well-known, yet less agreed upon, as the very first chapter of the Bible. From what appears to be a fairly simple, brief, chronological account of how creation came into being comes an array of complicated, extended explanations of what "really" happened. To some people the creation account in Genesis is nothing more than a fairy tale, a myth, or an attempt to explain the beginning of the universe from a prescientific perspective. The scientific method is used by many people to try to explain this event in history that no one saw and which cannot be repeated.

Various attempts have been made to reconcile the theology presented and the "assured" results of science. Believers who are committed to the inspiration and authority of the Scriptures come up with mutually exclusive points of view. How can this be? What theory best explains the evidence we see in our world and the truth we read in the Scriptures? What was the purpose of the author as he recorded this historical event that must have been revealed to him by the Lord God?

Sometimes, tongue in cheek, I announce to my Genesis class that I am about to play a recording from one of the great theologians of our day. Imagine their surprise when they hear the voice of comedian Bill Cosby. On his tape titled *Those of You with or Without Children, You'll Understand,* Cosby has a live monologue called "Genesis." While I don't appreciate all that Cosby has to say on this tape, he does have an excellent depiction of the quality of God's work in creation.

> Let there be trees. And God saw that it was good, said it was good, and it was good. Trees, let the trees stand. Good, quality of God's work, good, that God was satisfied, good, just good. Man invents, God creates. Man invented an automobile. Called it fantastic! God did a tree. Said it was good, you see. Man did a refrigerator. Said amazing! God did a rabbit. Said good. The wheels fell off the car and the refrigerator broke down. Tree's still up, the rabbit's still running. Good!

Genesis 1 depicts God as creating this world. And he did it well and all by himself! You might say the "big bang" was really the voice of God!

II. COMMENTARY

Creation

> **MAIN IDEA:** *Although Christians may disagree on some aspects of the creation story, we agree that God created this world, he created it by himself, and he created it "very good."*

A Creation in Summary (1:1)

> **SUPPORTING IDEA:** *God is the Creator of matter and space.*

1:1. The words **in the beginning God created the heavens and the earth** show that the existence of God is assumed right from the start. There are no arguments or evidence given since creation itself will declare the truth of the existence of God (Ps. 19:1–4). Using the term *Elohim*, which in Scripture is both a generic term for god (or gods since it is plural in form) and the proper name God (the context will need to determine the proper translation), the author declares that both space (**the heavens**) and matter (**the earth**) were created by him. This name for God (*Elohim*) will be used throughout the creation account of Genesis 1:1–2:3.

The term **created** is a Hebrew verb that always has God as its subject. No preexisting material is mentioned or implied here (this type of creation is often called by the Latin term *ex nihilo*), although the Hebrew verb does not have to have this meaning in all its uses. The New Testament makes clear that all things created came from God (John 1:3; Rom. 4:17; Heb. 11:3). This is a theological affirmation that all believers can agree on.

In the beginning speaks of the beginning of the universe—not of all things, since God is eternal (John 1:1; Eph. 1:4; Col. 1:15–17). Genesis, and the rest of Scripture, will not give us an exhaustive view of all that happens but an interpreted, theological history so we can understand God's plan to establish—and after the fall to reestablish—his rule over all creation through the beings he has created. Genesis will start with a universal picture of creation but will soon narrow to God's choice of a man and his family through whom he will work out his plan.

The heavens and the earth is a figure of speech that describes the totality of creation (like Revelation's use of *alpha* and *omega* to denote everything between). The Hebrew word for **heavens** is plural and is used here to describe everything that is above the surface of the earth. Later, "heavens" will refer to the home of the sun, moon, and stars, or the universe (Ps. 19:1), the home of the birds and the clouds, or the atmosphere (Dan. 4:12). Finally, in 2 Corinthians 12:2 "heaven" will refer to the home of the angels and departed saints. Specifying **the heavens and the earth** means that God created everything.

B Initial Conditions of Creation (1:2)

SUPPORTING IDEA: *What we see now in the physical universe once existed in a condition of chaos and emptiness.*

1:2. This verse tells us that **the earth was formless and empty, darkness was over the surface of the deep, and the Spirit of God was hovering over the waters.** The fact that the Spirit of God was present must caution us not to espouse an interpretation that would present this condition as either antagonistic to or outside of God's control. Not only was the Spirit of God present, but the second person of the Trinity, the incarnate Word, was also present and active in creation (see John 1:3).

The creative Word will turn chaotic matter into that which has structure and order. This ancient interpretation does not conflict with the biblical concept that God created the universe out of nothing. This would only be a stage in the great plan of God. Isaiah 45:18 states, "For this is what the LORD says—he who created the heavens, he is God; he who fashioned and made the earth, he founded it; he did not create it to be empty, but formed it to be inhabited—he says: 'I am the LORD, and there is no other.'" The first couple of days of creation will bring order to this matter, while the next several days will bring fertility and fullness.

C The Six Days of Creation (1:3–31)

SUPPORTING IDEA: *God fills his universe with productive matter and places mankind in a position of authority.*

1:3–5. God had only to speak and things came into being. This demonstrates the sovereignty of God in a marvelous manner. It reminds us of the importance and authority behind all of God's words.

The fact that creation occurred at the word of God (cp. Ps. 33:9; Heb. 11:3) is significant theologically in a couple of ways. For example, Jesus Christ, who in John's Gospel is called the Word of God, was active in creation (John 1:3). Also God's word is sufficient authority to have matter and life come into being in a way that was decreed for them. The Latin term *fiat* is a translation of *let there be*. This is a technical term for creation that occurred as a result of God's word. This phrase **and God said** is found in every day of creation, but it occurs twice on the third day and three times on the sixth day.

God called is a phrase that is used when God named the items he had created. Naming something, both today and in the ancient world, signifies an exercise of sovereign right. Only the parent of a child, or the inventor of an item, has the legal right and authority to name.

The light created on Day 1 of creation does not appear to be the light from the sun since this celestial body was introduced on the fourth day

(vv. 14–18). Some interpreters believe that the specific functions of the celestial bodies were assigned on the fourth day with their creation occurring here on the first day. This view does not appear to be the best explanation of the relationship of this verse and Genesis 1:14–18. Some believe that light should be understood as symbolic of energy and that it is this "force" that was created on Day 1.

Others believe that this light corresponds to that light spoken of later in Scripture as the "shekinah," the light that is a manifestation of God's glory (Exod. 40:34–35; 1 Kgs. 8:11). Such a view is supported by Revelation 22:5a, where the apostle John—speaking of the future in God's presence—declares, "There will be no more night. They will not need the light of a lamp or the light of the sun, for the Lord God will give them light."

This view would not suggest that God's glory was created on the first day but only that his manifested, visible glory was created to illuminate the creation. This understanding is also in keeping with the statement made in the prior verse that the Spirit of God was present. God's presence was now manifested in a manner (creation of **light**) that would allow God's creative works to be visible.

Darkness is the absence of light and in later Scripture will often signify evil (e.g., Exod 10:21–23; Job 3:4). But Genesis 1:2 declares that the Spirit of God was present, and no evil is mentioned.

The phrase **And there was evening, and there was morning** shows the effect of the creation of light and also implies the rotation of the earth. The Jewish people have regarded their day as beginning with the setting of the sun because the evening is mentioned first in this and subsequent verses.

The evaluation of each element of God's creation as being **good** carries the concept of approval and acceptance. Nothing resisted God's word; nothing was only partial or blemished. All that God made on this day and on each of the following days met with his positive endorsement.

1:6–8. On Day 2 of creation, God declared, **Let there be an expanse between the waters to separate water from water.** The resulting space or expanse between the waters that existed on the earth and the moisture that was now in the atmosphere is called by a Hebrew term meaning "hammered out," usually translated "firmament" (KJV) or **sky**. Into this area God later placed the sun, moon, and stars. So this space apparently included more than just the atmosphere within which the clouds were formed. "Sky" or "firmament" or "heaven" describes everything above the earth's surface.

1:9–13. God declared on the third day of creation, **Let the water under the sky be gathered to one place, and let dry ground appear.** In the gathering together of the waters on the surface of the earth, separation occurred. This separation produced both **dry ground** called **land** and a body (or "bodies," since the Hebrew term is plural) of water called **seas**. The Hebrew language used here does not demand that all waters on earth form a single ocean nor does all dry ground have to be a single continent, although the latter is certainly possible. From the now-exposed soil God brought forth vegetation, **according to their various kinds**. The concept of creation producing like-creation is emphasized by the tenfold use in Genesis 1 of the expression **according to their various kinds**. This is a refutation of most evolutionary theories.

In relation to the forming of dry land, the first evaluation on Day 3 is given: **And God saw that it was good** (v. 10). From this land man will be formed. Over this land, and over what is produced on it, man will rule as God's caretaker.

God produced vegetation: **seed-bearing plants and trees on the land that bear fruit with seed in it**. The first life-form, vegetation, was created. This life was an unconscious life, not the same as the life that animals and man would possess. The emphasis is not on all the vegetation that God created but specifically on those that would provide food for humans. The phrase **various kinds** indicates that there were several separate families of plants.

1:14–19. This fourth day of creation parallels Day 1 on which light (singular) was created. God declared, **Let there be lights in the expanse of the sky to separate the day from the night, and let them serve as signs to mark seasons and days and years, and let them be lights in the expanse of the sky to give light on the earth**. The functions of these luminaries involved: (1) a distinction between day and night; (2) the means, both solar and lunar, by which time could be measured; (3) an illumination of the earth which involved the capability of life to exist on earth; and (4) a reminder to mankind of God's creative work (Ps. 8:3; Rom. 1:19–20).

The second function above is noted by the phrase **let them serve as signs to mark seasons and days and years**. Later in the Pentateuch (first five books of the Old Testament), God will create for his nation Israel a calendar of religious festivals regulated by the movement of the earth around the sun and the movement of the moon. This function of regulating time has sometimes been misinterpreted as suggesting that the celestial bodies were created as signs to guide man in making decisions or in understanding the future (for example, the use of the horoscope). But that is never suggested and in fact is a violation of scriptural teaching on seeking guidance from none but God and through his prescribed means (Prov. 3:5–6; Deut. 18:10–13). Later in Genesis various "signs" will be mentioned as reminders of God's grace and mercy (Gen. 4; 9; 17).

While many ancient cultures worshiped the sun, in the biblical creation account the sun was not created until the fourth day after light and life had been created. God was the Creator of the sun and the stars. To consider them as gods is to engage in false worship.

1:20–23. The creation of aquatic and flying creatures occurs on Day 5, a day which parallels Day 2 when the waters and skies were created. Each creature of the sky and the water is carefully noted to be set apart from the others by species. This declaration refutes the idea that the Bible allows for macro-evolution that includes all fish or birds coming from one original form. This does not teach against mutations or the development of various breeds within a species.

The expression **God blessed them and said** is a new aspect in the creation story. God did not do this for the life called vegetation. Evidently, the life of a fish or bird is inherently different from plant life. God caused his special favor to rest upon this newly created, conscious life.

1:24–31. Life-forms that live primarily on the land were created on the sixth day. This day paralleled the third day when dry land appeared. Again the creation was according to various **kinds.**

The life that animals possessed was a conscious life in comparison to the unconscious life of vegetation. All sorts of animals were created. This is noted by various terms (**livestock, creatures that move along the ground, and wild animals**) which relate to those that man was able to tame and use and those that remained wild. The fact that certain animals such as dinosaurs have become extinct—a situation that continues to occur—does not conflict with the original creation. The creation of animals is dealt with first, but on the same day mankind was also created.

Special attention is paid to one creature who, although he could be confused with other land animals, was significantly different. Mankind became the highlight of this day and, except for the Creator himself, became the most powerful, authoritative being in all creation. His creation is treated separately from the other land creatures.

Only of this creature is it said that he was created **in the image of God.** The creation of "man" in the image of God refers to all mankind, not just Adam, as the pronoun **them** and the reference to **male and female** in verse 27 indicates. God and mankind share a likeness (the Hebrew terms for **image** and **likeness** are essentially synonymous terms) that is not shared by the other creatures. This likeness probably involves the personality, aesthetic appreciation, authority, moral, and spiritual qualities that both God and humans share, unlike the animals. Since God and humans share such likeness, it should not be surprising that a relationship between God and humans is a focus in the rest of Scripture. Mankind possesses a self-conscious life in which he is able to thank and worship the Creator.

Mankind's function included the subduing of the earth and all that was created and placed on it. Man found himself accountable to God from the beginning. The restriction on eating of the Tree of the Knowledge of Good and Evil would come later. But even here in Genesis 1, he was told to be **fruit-**

ful and increase in number; fill the earth and subdue it. Rule over the fish of the sea and the birds of the air and over every living creature that moves on the ground. The command to be fruitful and increase in number is generally recognized as a command to the heads of the human race (here to Adam and Eve and again later to Noah in Gen. 9:1). It is not usually interpreted as something required of every person. This seems clear from the fact that some humans are incapable of reproducing and others can please God by not getting married (1 Cor. 7:8).

To demand that everyone should bear as many children as he or she possibly can is unscriptural. The fact that children are produced from a divinely designed sexual union affirms that this type of sexual activity is good with no hint of evil. In God's plan both a father and mother are needed to produce children. Both are also needed to raise children. Those who are forced to raise children as single parents often struggle and need special support.

God was both gracious and generous in his provision of food for man: I give you every seed-bearing plant on the face of the whole earth and every tree that has fruit with seed in it. They will be yours for food. Man was originally created as a vegetarian. Only after the flood was he given animals to eat (Gen. 9:3). There is no indication in the New Testament that Christians are required to return to this preflood lifestyle of vegetarianism.

Ⓓ The Seventh Day (2:1–3)

SUPPORTING IDEA: *On this day there is no need for further creation, just an enjoyment of perfection.*

2:1–3. The **seventh day** was a climactic day on which God stopped his work of creation, since he **had finished the work he had been doing.** He **rested** and he **blessed the seventh day.** The mood resembled what existed in Genesis 1:1–2 (silence and calm), but the situation was totally different. The stopping of work signifies that the universe had reached a state of completion in which all required components were present. This is the only place in the Bible where God is described as resting, although rest would be held out by the author of Hebrews as a future benefit for all God's people (Heb. 4:1–11). No further creation was needed other than that which God would bring into his created order through procreation or reproduction (Gen. 1:11,22,28). The resting of God does not connote exhaustion, indifference, or lack of activity on God's part to maintain this world and everything in it (cp. Col. 1:17).

The blessing of Day 7 was that God set it apart as different from the other days—as a memorial to his creative work. While the command for mankind to observe the seventh day as a day of rest was part of the Mosaic covenant with the nation of Israel at Mt. Sinai and not with Christian believers, Scripture does teach the importance of periodic rest.

MAIN IDEA REVIEW: *Although Christians may disagree on some aspects of the creation story, we agree that God created this world, he created it by himself, and he created it "very good."*

III. CONCLUSION

What a World and What a God!

Reading the creation story causes us to declare, "What a world and what a God!" To declare this requires a step of faith based on the revealed Word of God. It is the first of many steps that we as believers must take as we listen to our Creator and Redeemer reveal truth. If we accept this great truth, many other truths will follow for us. If we refuse to accept this fundamental truth, little is left for us to be sure of or to believe. May God grant us faith even as we wonder and contemplate just how God accomplished the creation.

PRINCIPLES

- The creation story refutes atheism because it declares the existence of God; it refutes macroevolution because it states that God created all things; it refutes pantheism because it shows that God is separate from his creation; it refutes eternality of matter because there was a beginning to creation; it refutes fatalism because there is purpose to creation.
- Many humans have sought to worship the sun, but God desires people to worship him. God was there in the beginning, and he waited until the fourth day to create the sun. This was after life and light had existed.
- Creation is foundational to understanding life on this planet. It is the basis of man's responsibility to follow God's law (Rom. 1:18–20) and a reason for him to praise God (Pss. 19:1–6; 104:24–30).
- Genesis gives us the "what" of creation. The "how" is assumed by the concept of "God said . . . and it was so." This demonstrates the sovereignty of God and the fact that we as finite creatures will never know everything.
- What God does, he does with excellence.
- Man is accountable to the Creator for taking care of his creation.
- God works in a planned and orderly fashion.

APPLICATIONS

- Acknowledge God and your accountability to him.
- Recognize that God has made distinctions and divisions a part of his creation from the very beginning.
- Declare to the world through the godly life you live that God exists and is present in his creation.

IV. LIFE APPLICATION

"The Heavens Declare the Glory of God"

An atheist once complained to a friend because Christians and Jews had their special holidays. "But we atheists," he said, "have no special day, no recognized national holiday. It's just not fair." His friend replied, "Why don't you celebrate April first?"

No one wants to be known as a fool. But a person *is* a fool if he doesn't acknowledge God. The Lord has not left us without evidence of his existence. Romans 1:20 explains that "since the creation of the world God's invisible qualities—his eternal power and divine nature—have been clearly seen, being understood from what has been made, so that men are without excuse." Creation gives evidence in its order, design, and harmony that there is some cause for all this. And mankind must recognize that all creation points to the Creator. All of creation shouts that God exists and that he is a God of power and glory—a being worthy of worship. The fool may talk of "Mother Nature," but nature itself is powerless to produce life of any kind without the processes put into place by God himself. To substitute "Mother Nature" for "God" is to confuse the creature or creation with the Creator.

V. PRAYER

God of creation, majestic in power, awesome in your design, we worship you today. We acknowledge that you were before all things, that all things came into being at your word, and that everything owes its existence to you. Thank you for your constant reminder of your power and presence in this world that you created. Amen.

VI. DEEPER DISCOVERIES

A. Title for Genesis

Each book of the Pentateuch (first five books of the Old Testament) originally received its title from the first word or words in the book. For the Book of Genesis, the Hebrew word translated "in the beginning" is *bereshit.* So Jews know this book as the "In the Beginning" book. The English title "Genesis" transliterates the Greek word used in the Septuagint translation (Greek translation of the Old Testament). This Greek word *geneseos* is a translation of the key Hebrew term *toledot,* or "generations of." This Hebrew word is found in Genesis 2:4; 5:1; 6:9; 10:1; 11:10,27; 25:12,19; 36:1,9; 37:2. It is translated into the English as "account of" or "generations of" and will be more extensively treated in the next chapter.

B. Date or Length of the Creation

The period covered by the creation account is subject to much controversy. If present scientific "facts" are accepted, then the earth is about 4,500,000 years old. Interpreters who believe such "facts" are compelled to interpret the words of Scripture in light of such accepted "facts." In addition, the days of creation are seen as short, long, or unrelated to time, as can be seen in the following list.

The Hebrew word *yom* (day) is used three ways in Genesis 1 and 2:

1. Twelve-hour period of daylight (Gen. 1:5,14,16,18)
2. Twenty-four-hour day (Gen. 1:14)
3. The entire "six-day" period of creation (Gen. 2:4)

Major views about the length of the "days of creation":

1. Literal twenty-four-hour-day view
2. Day-age (or geologic-day) view
3. Literal days with intervening ages view
4. Revelatory-day view

Factors involved in making a decision:

1. The use of the word *day* in Scripture (whenever the numerical adjective is used with "day," it refers to a twenty-four-hour day)
2. The use of the word *create* (*bara*)
3. The acknowledgment of the "facts" of scientific research
4. The value placed on nonbiblical creation stories
5. The place given to other scriptural "accounts" of creation (Gen. 2; Exod. 20:11; 31:17; Pss. 33:6–9; 104; Prov. 8; Isa. 45:18)

In light of these factors, it seems best to take the creation days as twenty-four-hour days. This appears to be what the author of Genesis sought to cause his readers to understand.

Genesis 2:4–25

The First Family

I. **INTRODUCTION**
A Creation Challenge

II. **COMMENTARY**
A verse-by-verse explanation of these verses.

III. **CONCLUSION**
God's Perfect Design for Mankind

An overview of the principles and applications from these verses.

IV. **LIFE APPLICATION**
Only Worth $4.50

Melding these verses to life.

V. **PRAYER**
Tying these verses to life with God.

VI. **DEEPER DISCOVERIES**
Historical, geographical, and grammatical enrichment of the commentary.

VII. **TEACHING OUTLINE**
Suggested step-by-step group study of these verses.

VIII. **ISSUES FOR DISCUSSION**
Zeroing these verses in on daily life.

Quote

"*T*he woman was formed out of man—not out of his head to rule over him; not out of his feet to be trampled upon by him; but out of his side to be his equal, from beneath his arm to be protected, and from near his heart to be loved."

Matthew Henry

Genesis 2:4–25

IN A NUTSHELL

*T*he account of the creation of man is given again, only in more detail. This account includes the creation of Adam, a description of the garden of Eden, and the creation of Eve.

The First Family

I. INTRODUCTION

A Creation Challenge

*O*ne day a group of scientists got together and decided that man had come a long way and no longer needed God. So they picked one scientist to go and tell God that they were finished with him. The scientist walked up and said, "God, we've decided that we no longer need you. We're to the point that we can clone people and do many miraculous things, so why don't you just get lost?"

God listened very patiently and kindly. Then he replied, "Very well, let's have a man-making contest."

The scientist replied, "OK, great!"

But God added, "Now we're going to do this just like I did with Adam."

The scientist said, "Sure, no problem." Then he bent down and grabbed a handful of dirt.

God said, "No, no, no. Go get your own dirt!"

The creation of man was more than just the creation of a body. And the creation of humankind was more than just the creation of the man. It was the distinct creation of male and female who together would be God's plan for humanity. In our unisex world today, it is important that we as believers understand God's plan and purpose for humanity.

II. COMMENTARY

The First Family

> **MAIN IDEA:** *The creation of male and female reveals the fundamentals for the proper functioning of the family.*

A God's Formation of Man (2:4–7)

> **SUPPORTING IDEA:** *The author of Genesis summarizes the conditions of the world before man's creation.*

2:4. The phrase **this is the account of** translates the Hebrew word *toledot*, which will occur ten more times in the Book of Genesis. Although scholars are divided on the exact function of this expression (some believe these are colophons or summary conclusions to the preceding section), it seems most reasonable to see it functioning as a heading over what follows. Genesis 1:1–2:3 is an introductory section with all remaining sections of Genesis having a *toledot* heading. Taking *toledot* in this manner introduces the reader to what became of creation (**the heavens and the earth when they were cre-ated**) as developed in Genesis 2:4–4:26. For a more thorough discussion on *toledot*, see "Deeper Discoveries."

Genesis 1:1–2:3 was a general account of all creation. Here in Genesis 2:4–25 we have a topical account of creation as it relates to mankind. As Dyer and Merrill explain, "If the former account of creation can be labeled the 'cosmic account,' this should be considered the 'anthropological account,' because humankind, not the heavens and the earth, is now central" (Dyer and Merrill, 8).

The expression LORD **God** uses two different names for the Creator. As noted in Genesis 1:1, *Elohim* (God) in Scripture is both a generic term for god (or gods since it is plural in form) and the proper name *God.* The name LORD (or *Yahweh*) usually denotes deity in personal relationship (see Exod. 3:15). Now that the focus is primarily on Adam and Eve, this name appropriately accompanies the more generic "God." It will be used eleven times in twenty-two verses as the LORD relates to humankind.

When is the translation of the Hebrew word *yom,* normally rendered "day."

2:5–6. "When the LORD God made the earth and the heavens" (v. 4b) **and no shrub of the field had yet appeared** describes the global conditions before man's creation. The NIV tries to show that the material of verses 5 and 6 are like a parenthetical comment that serves as a flashback to the conditions before Genesis 1:26 by its use of the dash at the end of verses 4 and 6. There was no agriculture at this time because there was no one to tend the fields.

Note the statement, **for the LORD God had not sent rain on the earth . . . but streams came up from the earth and watered the whole surface of the ground.** Some scholars have speculated from these statements that there was a "vapor canopy" that covered the earth until the time of the flood in Noah's day. Such a canopy and the resulting benefits of reducing destructive rays and distributing heat are credited with allowing antediluvian man (man before the flood) to live longer and allowing vegetation to grow throughout the earth. While such speculation does provide answers to some questions about early man and the earth, it must be noted that this is a theory and not a required biblical belief. In addition, such a theory is based upon the condition that is described when as yet **there was no man to work the ground** (v. 5). What was needed was a created being powerful and authoritative enough to act as God's steward.

2:7. This verse says that God **formed the man from the dust of the ground.** The Hebrew verb for "formed" is commonly used of the work of a potter with clay (e.g., Job 33:6; Isa. 45:9; Jer. 18:6). It conveys the idea of molding and shaping with careful, loving care. It is a new word for Genesis. The Hebrew words used in the first account to describe the creation of man and animals include "make" (*asah*) and "create" (*bara*) (Gen. 1:26–27). Here God acts as the potter taking clay or soil and forming man. The **dust of the ground** shows that the physical part of man was made from the elements common to this world. In one sense it reflects man's lowly, common origin.

But man was not merely of this earth. He is a combination of dust and divinity. Genesis 2:7 goes on to say that the Lord God **breathed into his nostrils the breath of life, and man became a living being.** It was God who gave man a life unique to mankind. Animals had life too, but man had a portion of deity within him because he was made "in the image of God." Merrill notes, "Especially noteworthy is the fact that man did not *get* a soul but he *became* one, that is, he became a person" (Dryer and Merrill, 8).

Ⓑ Man's Placement on the Earth (2:8–14)

> **SUPPORTING IDEA:** *The author gives further details about the premankind world, noting especially two major trees of the garden: the tree of life and the tree of the knowledge of good and evil.*

2:8. Some of the vegetation created on the third day that would require man's cultivation and care was placed in a specific spot called **Eden.** This proper name could be related to the Hebrew word for "bliss" or "delight." The Septuagint uses the Greek word that is translated into the English "paradise." It might also come from a Mesopotamian word that means "plain." By announcing it was **in the east,** the author of Genesis must have been speaking from his perspective of the Sinai area. He will further note in Genesis 2:10–14 that the area was around a river that subsequently divided into four rivers named Pishon, Gihon, Tigris, and Euphrates and that the area contained many valuable things.

2:9. In these verses the author clearly describes that what the Lᴏʀᴅ **God** had prepared for man was generous and sufficient for his welfare. It is stated that **in the middle of the garden were the tree of life and the tree of the knowledge of good and evil.** These two trees that would have such subsequent significance are noted early in this creation account. What is meant by both **life** and **knowledge of good and evil** will be described in greater detail in Genesis 3.

2:10–14. The river that arose and then flowed through Eden seems to have produced four headwaters that created rivers named **Pishon, Gihon, Tigris,** and **Euphrates.** These rivers provided irrigation to the region since there was an absence of rain at this time (Gen. 2:5–6). The fact that the names of two of these rivers still exist today in the area of Iraq (the Tigris and Euphrates) has caused many interpreters to suggest that the garden was in what today is southern Iraq. But the rivers of the preflood era may not be related to the postflood rivers of the same name. It is possible that when the survivors of the flood saw some major rivers, they named them after ones they had known in the preflood time.

Not only are the rivers named, but the land of these rivers is noted as being an area where **gold**, **aromatic resin** (or pearls), and **onyx** were found. This shows how wonderful and **good** was the place that God had prepared for man.

C The Responsibilities Given to Man (2:15–17)

SUPPORTING IDEA: *Adam was placed in the garden to carry out his responsibilities as the chief representative of God on earth.*

2:15–17. As God's supreme creation Adam was given great honor as well as important responsibilities. The concept of placing man in the garden is done with a Hebrew word that is often used to mean "rest." The concept of a Sabbath rest will be developed later in Scripture (see Heb. 3:7–4:11) and is probably to be related back to this presinful world where mankind was placed ("rested") with responsibilities.

The concepts of **work it** and **take care of it** involve two Hebrew verbs that are used later in the Pentateuch for spiritual service—for both worshiping and keeping the commandments of God. "Whatever activity the man was to engage in in the garden (and there is no reason to doubt that physical activity was involved), it was described in terms of spiritual service of the Lord" (Ross, 124).

Man was not created to be lazy or to be a workaholic. His work was to involve a fulfillment of God's mandate to him in a place where he could find true rest and accomplishment. Before the female appeared on earth, the male of the human race had been given authority over creation and responsibility toward God.

D Man's Incompleteness Is Solved (2:18–23)

SUPPORTING IDEA: *The creation of the woman benefited the man.*

2:18. Up to now a reiterated statement in Genesis is "it was good." Now it comes as almost a shock to read that **it is not good for the man to be alone**. It was not good for the male of the human species to be alone, to remain uncomplemented as were all the other creatures God had made. It was not that man was in some manner bad but that God had made him to exist in relationship with others.

The creation of the female was for the welfare of the male. But she was to be a **helper**, not a slave! The Hebrew term *ēzer* is used to describe the function of the female to the male. The use of this term elsewhere in the Old Testament confirms that this was not a demeaning term. It is used of God himself

(Exod. 18:4; Deut. 33:7; 1 Sam. 7:12; Pss. 20:2; 46:1) who is described as the **helper.** The term denotes one who can provide what is lacking in another. God created man in such a way that he needed the help of a partner to fulfill God's plan for him. He would not be able to procreate by himself. Neither would he find the intimacy he desired if he remained in isolation. The phrase **suitable for him** or "corresponding to him" is from the Hebrew expression *kenegdo* that literally means "according to his opposite." The woman would share the same nature as man (unlike animals among which there was found "no suitable helper"; v. 20).

2:19–20. The phrase **now the LORD God had formed** implies, in both English and in the Hebrew construction, that what is said in verses 19 and 20 occurred before the statement given in verse 18 about man's aloneness. The Lord had formed and then brought the various animals to man so he could name them. The assignment of names was an act of dominion and authority. When Adam named the animals, he noticed that all other species had a match but that he was unique—no other creature corresponded or complemented him. But Adam could do nothing about this situation. It was the Lord God who first stated the predicament and then remedied it.

2:21. A couple of important points are made in this verse. First, the creation of the woman was accomplished by God without the help of the man he had created. Man was not even conscious (**while he was sleeping**) at the time of woman's creation. The gift of the woman was an act of grace. Genesis 15:12 and 28:11 reveal two other times when God put people to sleep as he initiated a new relationship.

Second, the creation of woman was not a totally distinct creation since she was made from preexisting material—from man's side. She would share much in common with the male. She was not made from the dust of the earth but from Adam. The apostle Paul interpreted this action in 1 Timothy 2:12–13 as applying to functions of the male and female. Traditionally the word **rib** is used, although the Hebrew is literally "took part of the man's side."

The use of the rib from man does not indicate that man "lost" something. The differences of a female are not the "preowned" aspects of the male. God made her different so she might complement the man in his need of companionship. Her creation would also allow procreation so man could multiply and fill the earth. The fact that procreation is obviously God's method for offspring in the animal world indicates that woman was never an afterthought in the mind of God. She was created after man so man might first experience loneliness and then recognize her great value to him.

2:22–23. When the Lord brought the woman to the man, you might say he was "beside himself"! **This is now bone of my bones and flesh of my flesh** is a way of stating that the woman was of the same essence as the man.

Adam then named her: **She shall be called "woman," for she was taken out of man**. The term **woman** would be a constant reminder that woman had her origin in man. Later the apostle Paul affirmed the truth of the seniority of the male but reminded believers, "In the Lord, however, woman is not independent of man, nor is man independent of woman. For as woman came from man, so also man is born of woman. But everything comes from God" (1 Cor. 11:11–12).

E The Institution of Marriage (2:24–25)

SUPPORTING IDEA: *Here in embryonic form is the essence of marriage.*

2:24. Based on the origin of the human genders, the author of Genesis makes an evaluative statement. Marriage is described as both "leaving" and "cleaving." For Adam, of course, there were no parents to leave. But for the rest of mankind, a leaving of what up to now was the most precious relationship—that of a child to a parent—is needed for a marriage to work. This is not to imply that a man is no longer a child from his parents' union. But it underscores the priority of the new relationship and the authority that is no longer there from the parent-child relationship.

The uniting or cleaving is not simply physical, although all cultures recognize the necessity of a sexual consummation of a marriage for it to be valid. The man and woman are to become **one flesh** as they were before she was created. Ephesians 5:28–29 also speaks of the oneness when Paul writes, "In this same way, husbands ought to love their wives as their own bodies. He who loves his wife loves himself. After all, no one ever hated his own body, but he feeds and cares for it, just as Christ does the church."

2:25. This verse emphasizes the innocence, openness, and trust that existed between the man (husband) and woman (wife). While in our contemporary world many people want to criticize the Genesis creation story as being less than ideal or good, the Scripture presents it differently. The relationship between man and woman is seen as complementary and "without shame." The intimacy that existed between Adam and Eve is something that most couples desire in their relationship.

MAIN IDEA REVIEW: *The creation of male and female reveals the fundamentals for the proper functioning of the family.*

III. CONCLUSION

God's Perfect Design for Mankind

There is much discussion today about the nature of male and female and what this means for the marriage relationship. In some states the very definition of marriage is under revision. From the extreme right where man is king and woman is an object, to the effeminate left where man is emasculated and woman is defeminized, the very nature of male and female is under assault. But the Lord God has not left the believer without revelation on this subject.

Genesis 2 reveals to the Bible-believing disciple some basic tenets of God's process and design for the male and female of his creation. God created both the male and female. Together they would have the privilege and responsibility of responding to God's commands and creating the human race. It was to Adam that certain instructions were first given. Adam recognized his lack of a partner with whom he could accomplish God's plan.

Marriage was God's idea. Through a monogamous, heterosexual relationship God planned the procreation of children. The family, based on the creation foundation, was God's plan for a human race that would obey his commands and glorify him.

PRINCIPLES

- Distinctions in masculine and feminine roles are ordained by God as part of the created order and should find an echo in every human heart.
- Marriage was instituted by the Lord and is part of his design for human society. While there are exceptions to this general design because of unusual circumstances (Matt. 19:11–12; 1 Cor. 7:26), the institution of marriage is never to be belittled.
- Marriage as originally designed by God is intended to be heterosexual and monogamous.
- Marriage involves both a physical *and* a spiritual union (Gen. 2:24; cp. Matt. 19:4–5).
- The order and function of creation is to be carefully noted. Adam's headship in marriage was established by God before the fall and was not a result of sin.
- Since the woman's original function was to complement her husband, a marriage can be complete without the bearing of children. Normally, a marriage will produce children, but God did not specify how early in marriage this must be done or to what extent a couple had to go in their "multiplication"!

APPLICATIONS

- Thank God for his wonderful creation of the human race, both male and female.

- Even a believer in perfect fellowship with the Lord needs others. Remember, Adam, who had never sinned, needed Eve to accomplish all that God had for him to do.

- If you are married, don't try to make your spouse a replica of yourself but "enjoy the differences" God has produced in the different sexes.

- Recognize the necessity of both "leaving" and "cleaving" if a marriage is to work in a biblical fashion.

- Males must affirm the truth that it is not good for man to be alone. Allow your spouse and other believers to minister to your needs.

IV. LIFE APPLICATION

Only Worth $4.50

From a Web site named *uselessknowledge.com,* I obtained some interesting information about the human body. When the monetary value of the elements in our bodies and the value of the average person's skin are totaled, the net worth, as of 2002, is $4.50! We are reminded on the Web site that "this value is, however, subject to change, due to stock market fluctuations."

The U.S. Bureau of Chemistry and Soils invested many tax dollars calculating that the chemical and mineral composition of the human body amounted to less than $1.00 at today's prices!

Our most valuable asset, according to scientists, is our skin because of its possible use as a leather substitute. The Japanese invested their time and money in measuring this part of our bodies. Basing the skin's value on the selling price of cowhide, the value of an average person's skin is about $3.50. This amount, along with the approximately $1.00 value of the chemicals and minerals, makes your body worth about $4.50! Don't you feel precious?

But really, you're worth more than you can imagine! As Genesis teaches, mankind is more than minerals and chemicals. God breathed into man "the breath of life." This immaterial part of man is that part which will exist for all eternity. Ecclesiastes 3:11 declares, "He [God] has also set eternity in the hearts of men." It is that part that allows us to communicate with God.

In fact, you're so valuable that God sent his own Son, the Lord Jesus Christ, to come to earth and die on your behalf so you might spend eternity in relationship to your Creator. You really are priceless in the sight of God!

V. PRAYER

Lord, we come to you as our Creator to thank you for your gracious act in giving us life. Thank you for breathing into us your breath so we might live forever. And thank you for what Jesus has done for us. Amen.

VI. DEEPER DISCOVERIES

A. The Hebrew Word *Toledot*

Toledot ("the account of") occurs throughout Genesis and when taken as a heading introduces a new section each time except for its use in Genesis 36:9 (Gen. 2:4; 5:1; 6:9; 10:1; 11:10,27; 25:12,19; 36:1; 37:2). The person mentioned after *toledot* is not usually the focus of the section but rather the person who originated what follows.

R. K. Harrison follows P. J. Wiseman and argues for this word to be taken as a colophon that offers a summary conclusion to the preceding section (Harrison, 548). While this approach is conceivable, it seems better to take *toledot* as a heading for what follows. This approach is based on the fact that the use of *toledot* in Genesis as a heading is the only consistent system that works, and the fact that in every other place in the Scriptures where *toledot* is used it clearly refers to content that precedes. This will be the approach followed in this commentary.

B. Two Creation Accounts in Genesis 1 and 2

The differences between these two accounts have convinced many scholars that there must be two different authors for these sections. However, "doublets" in Scripture by the same author are not unusual, as will be seen in the Book of Genesis as well as in the rest of Scripture. Such a presentation should not be unexpected, especially in the poetic parallelism feature in Hebrew.

Francis Schaeffer notes:

> More light is shed on the relationship between Genesis 1 and Genesis 2 by a consideration of a literary structure that occurs throughout the entire Book of Genesis: First, less important things are dealt with rapidly, and then the things more important to the central theme of the Bible are returned to and developed more fully (Schaeffer, 40–41).

The differences can be explained in light of the focus of each account, as is done in this commentary.

C. The Location of Eden

It is possible to regard all descriptions of Eden as completely useless since the flood changed much of the topography of the earth. But Moses appears to be using these descriptions so that those of his generation could have a general idea about where Eden once was located.

The names of the Tigris and Euphrates rivers are still used today. Perhaps the Pishon and Gihon, whose location remains unknown today, were smaller rivers of Mesopotamia known to the author at the time of the writing of Genesis.

The Pishon is said to wind through the entire land of Havilah where there is gold, aromatic resin, and onyx (Gen. 2:11). Havilah is probably to be distinguished from the Havilah of Genesis 10:7 which was in Egypt (part of the genealogy of Japheth), a long way from Mesopotamia. However, the region of Havilah mentioned in Genesis 10:29 is in the Semite genealogy and is mentioned right after Ophir, from where Solomon obtained much of his gold (1 Kgs. 9:28; 10:11).

The Gihon River is said to wind "through the entire land of Cush" (Gen. 2:13), while the Tigris River is recorded as running along the east side of Asshur (Gen. 2:14). Surely the author was using Cush and Asshur as he would have known them; Cush is normally identified with the upper Nile River region, south of Egypt, but this location seems distant from the other four. Perhaps Cush here may be a reference to the Kassites located east of the Tigris River. Asshur was an ancient capital of Assyria, but the word is sometimes used of the entire Assyrian Empire.

VII. TEACHING OUTLINE

A. INTRODUCTION

1. Lead Story: A Creation Challenge
2. Context: This chapter explains in greater detail the creation of mankind as male and female. It gives a topical presentation of creation centered on mankind.
3. Transition: Chapter 3 will introduce the first sin and resulting fall of mankind. Genesis 2 has introduced the creation of mankind in greater detail since man will be the focus in the next chapter. Such principles as headship, moral responsibility, and authority need to be established in chapter 2 in order to understand the following chapter.

B. COMMENTARY

1. God's Formation of Man (2:4–7)
2. Man's Placement on the Earth (2:8–14)

3. The Responsibilities Given to Man (2:15–17)
4. Man's Incompleteness Is Solved (2:18–23)
5. The Institution of Marriage (2:24–25)

C. CONCLUSION: ONLY WORTH $4.50

VIII. ISSUES FOR DISCUSSION

1. How would you respond to the claim that there is really no difference in value, in creation, in roles, in needs, between male and female (see Gen. 2)?
2. In our world today many people treat pets as if they were people while others treat people as if they were animals because of gender or race. How does Genesis 2 contribute to an answer for this predicament?
3. Should a marriage work for the type of intimacy Adam and Eve experienced, or is this an impossibility in our world today?
4. What does it take to make marriage more than just a close relationship between two people?

Genesis 3:1–24

Sin and the Fall

I. INTRODUCTION
The Malfunctioning Human Being

II. COMMENTARY
A verse-by-verse explanation of the chapter.

III. CONCLUSION
Eternal Consequences

An overview of the principles and applications from the chapter.

IV. LIFE APPLICATION
Conscious Sin

Melding the chapter to life.

V. PRAYER
Tying the chapter to life with God.

VI. DEEPER DISCOVERIES
Historical, geographical, and grammatical enrichment of the commentary.

VII. TEACHING OUTLINE
Suggested step-by-step group study of the chapter.

VIII. ISSUES FOR DISCUSSION
Zeroing the chapter in on daily life.

Genesis 3:1–24

Q u o t e

"*T*his chapter is the pivot on which

the whole Bible turns."

G r i f f i t h   T h o m a s

I N   A   N U T S H E L L

*D*eceived by the serpent, Eve disobeyed God's command not to eat of the tree of the knowledge of good and evil. Adam followed her example. As a result God placed a curse on them, Satan, and creation, and drove Adam and Eve out of the garden. All of God's creation will find itself coping with less-than-perfect conditions because of the disobedience of Adam and Eve.

Sin and the Fall

I. INTRODUCTION

The Malfunctioning Human Being

*S*tudents often send me E-mails containing jokes that are relevant to the Scriptures. Someone sent the following simulated notice that humorously illustrates the effect of sin.

> The Maker of all human beings is recalling all units manufactured, regardless of make or year, due to the serious defect in the primary and central component of the heart. This is due to a malfunction in the original prototype units code named Adam and Eve, resulting in the reproduction of the same defect in all subsequent units. This defect has been technically termed, "Subsequential Internal Nonmorality"—or more commonly known as SIN, as it is primarily expressed. Some other symptoms are the loss of direction, foul vocal emissions, amnesia of origin, lack of peace and joy, selfish or violent behavior, depression or confusion in the mental component, fearfulness, idolatry, and rebellion.

> The Manufacturer, who is neither liable nor at fault for this defect, is providing factory authorized repair and service free of charge to correct this SIN defect. The Repair Technician, Jesus, has most generously offered to bear the entire burden of the staggering cost of these repairs. The number to call for repair in all areas is: P-R-A-Y-E-R.

> Once connected, please upload your burden of SIN through the REPENTANCE procedure. Next, download ATONEMENT from the Repair Technician, Jesus, into the heart component. No matter how big or small the SIN defect is, Jesus will replace it with love, joy, peace, patience, kindness, goodness, faithfulness, gentleness, and self-control.

> Please see the operating manual, HOLY BIBLE, for further details on the use of these fixes. As an added upgrade, the Manufacturer has made available to all repaired units a facility enabling direct monitoring and assistance from a resident Maintenance Technician, the Holy Spirit. Repaired units need only make him welcome and he will take up permanent residence on the premises.

II. COMMENTARY

Sin and the Fall

MAIN IDEA: *The fall of mankind into sin produces conditions of alienation from the Creator God, from fellow human beings, and from the created world.*

A The Temptation to Sin (3:1–5)

SUPPORTING IDEA: *Temptation occurs when Eve questions the word and the character of God.*

3:1–4. A serpent is introduced both as a created being *and* as one who spoke against the revelation of God. He is said to be **more crafty than any of the wild animals the LORD God had made**. The word *crafty* indicates that this creature was subtle in its actions. One might ask why Eve was not disturbed by an animal who spoke to her. But everything was new to her. Perhaps before the alienation that would come with the fall, mankind and animals could communicate. While the serpent is not identified here as Satan, he spoke against the word of God. Later revelation referred to "that ancient serpent called the devil, or Satan" (Rev. 12:9; cp. Rev. 20:2; Rom. 16:20), which shows a close connection between this serpent and Satan.

The serpent caused Eve to question the word of God. He planted doubt in her mind when he asked, **Did God *really* say, "You must *not* eat from *any* tree in the garden"?** (emphasis added). What God had said to the man was, "You are free to eat from any tree in the garden; but you must not eat from the tree of the knowledge of good and evil, for when you eat of it you will surely die" (Gen. 2:16–17). Notice how the Evil One, through the serpent, focused on the negative, the prohibition, rather than on the generosity of God. The serpent did not dare suggest that perhaps if God had withheld this tree from humanity, it was not needed by humans. God's prohibition was really his line of protection.

Notice too that the Evil One through the serpent addressed the woman and not the man. It was the man to whom God had originally given his revelation about the food that they were to eat (Gen. 2:16–17). Apparently Adam had passed on to Eve what God had declared to him before she was created. It may be that the Evil One knew that stipulations given through someone else might be easier to ignore or disobey than that received as a direct revelation from God.

Eve's response shows that the Evil One succeeded in getting her to question the word of God or at least to get her phrasing it in such a way that it didn't seem so restrictive. Her response reveals a number of subtle shifts in thought. First, she disparaged her privileges. God said, "You are free to eat from any tree." But Eve said, **We may eat fruit from the trees**. God just didn't seem as generous in Eve's phraseology.

Second, she overstated the restrictions. God said, "You must not eat from the tree of the knowledge of good and evil." But Eve said, **You must not eat fruit from the tree that is in the middle of the garden,** *and you must not touch it* (emphasis added).

Third, Eve underrated her obligations. God said, "For when you eat of it you will *surely* die" (emphasis added) while she merely stated, **Or you will die**.

Eve would come to understand that God's word is not just generally true; it's absolutely and precisely true. God says what he means—and he means what he says. This understanding of the absolute authority of God's word is necessary for mankind to acknowledge so he might respond in a God-honoring manner.

Satan's response to Eve's somewhat less-than-accurate understanding of God's word was to deny that God's word was true: **You will not surely die**. This contradicted God's revealed word to Adam. The very first doctrine in Scripture that Satan denied is that sin results in death (or to put it another way, Satan declared that God would not punish sin). If he could have God's created human beings believing this, then sinning would not seem too serious.

3:5. In this verse the Evil One questioned the *goodness* of God when he declared, **God knows that when you eat of it your eyes will be opened, and you will be like God, knowing good and evil**. Satan had already hinted that God must not be good if he had restricted mankind in any way. His next attack was consistent with what he had already implied. God reveals his character through his Word. When the serpent questioned God's word, he questioned God's goodness. When he questioned God's goodness, he questioned God's word.

The serpent was not totally lying. There was a half-truth here, which was acknowledged by God in verse 22. They would gain an insight that they did not presently have, but what the Evil One didn't explain was that this insight would come at a high price. His teaching contradicted the main points of Genesis 1 and 2—that God has provided what is good for man. God's true motives and actions were in the interest of man, but Satan implied it was God's welfare at man's expense.

B The Fall into Sin (3:6)

SUPPORTING IDEA: *Humanity makes the worst decision in the history of the world.*

3:6. Notice the threefold temptation experienced by Eve: **When the woman saw that the fruit of the tree was good for food and pleasing to the**

eye, and also desirable for gaining wisdom, she took some and ate it. Eve allowed her God-given desires to be wrongly satisfied. This threefold temptation is similar to the various means of temptation detailed in 1 John 2:16: "For everything in the world—the cravings of sinful man, the lust of his eyes and the boasting of what he has and does—comes not from the Father but from the world." The difference is that Eve did not have a sinful nature within her. These appetites that Eve had were *before* sin entered the world. They were hers as a created being.

These desires—to satisfy herself with food, to appreciate the beauty of the fruit, and to gain knowledge and wisdom—were all legitimate and God-given and could be satisfied in a God-ordained manner. The problem for Eve, however, was in how these desires would be fulfilled. No doubt there was a lot of fruit she could eat, lots of beauty to appreciate, and much about which she could learn and gain wisdom. There was a whole new world for her to explore and master.

Ignorance, disregard, or deception about God's word makes a person vulnerable to temptation. Psalm 119:11 declares, "I have hidden your word in my heart that I might not sin against you."

Failure to appreciate God's goodness leads to distrust of his goodness. Distrust leads to dissatisfaction and finally to disobedience. God's prohibitions as well as his provisions are for our good. But mankind wants to be independent, to go his own way, to be subject to no one. God has always asked people to believe and trust his word. God has always asked people to believe that he is sovereign and good. His desire is that we trust him so we will live abundantly (John 10:10; 17:3). God has always asked people to believe that true satisfaction comes by obeying him and respecting his prohibitions—to live by faith, not by sight.

Not only did Eve eat, but her partner participated in the sin as well: **She also gave some to her husband, who was with her, and he ate it.** Sinners have a way of involving others and then validating one another in their sinning. Romans 1:32 says, "Although they [sinners] know God's righteous decree that those who do such things deserve death, they not only continue to do these very things but also approve of those who practice them." Adam was not deceived (1 Tim. 2:14); he sinned with understanding.

It is important to understand that it was not when Eve sinned but when Adam sinned that the entire human race fell. Eve had not been created independently but was made from Adam. Adam had been created first, and from him came the whole human race, including Eve. The apostle Paul makes it clear in Romans that everyone born into the human race will be a sinner, for it was as head of the human race that Adam sinned. All participate in this "original sin." Romans 5:12 declares, "Just as sin entered the world through one man, and death through sin, and in this way death came to all men, because all sinned."

Results of the Fall into Sin (3:7–13)

> **SUPPORTING IDEA:** *When Adam and Eve sinned, it affected not only their relationship with God but also their relationship with each other and with the rest of creation.*

3:7. As a result of their sin, Adam and Eve felt shame about their physical bodies. Before the fall, Genesis 2:25 declared, "The man and his wife were both naked, and they felt no shame." But now they were no longer virtuous. They had a new awareness of themselves and of each other; they now knew that their bodies could be viewed and used with evil lusting. They sensed a need for concealment: **They sewed fig leaves together and made coverings for themselves.** They tried to change these conditions by their own effort. But these leaves from the fig tree were neither long-lasting nor effective.

3:8–10. But not only was there shame; there was also guilt. Their relationship with God was broken. They fled from God's presence out of fear: **They hid from the LORD God among the trees of the garden.** Isn't this amazing—hiding from the God who had the power to make them? But God came looking for them. The question, **Where are you?** was a rhetorical question asked for their benefit. God, in his mercy, was giving them a chance to acknowledge their wrong.

3:11–13. Both Adam and Eve blamed others for their sin. Rather than confessing personal responsibility, they tried to put the blame on someone else. As sinners we find it so hard to say, "I did it and I was wrong." We blame our environment, genetics, upbringing or lack thereof, and so on. Our original parents were no different. First, Adam blamed the woman and indirectly God himself. Second, the woman blamed the serpent. And as the old joke goes, "Adam blamed Eve, Eve blamed the serpent, and the serpent was left without a leg to stand on!"

Judgments of the Fall into Sin (3:14–19)

> **SUPPORTING IDEA:** *Each of the earthly participants receives just but gracious discipline from their Creator God.*

3:14–15. Several judgments were pronounced by the Lord on the participants in this original sin. The word *bless* was used three times in the account of creation (Gen. 1:22,28; 2:3), but now the word *curse* is used three times in the account of what happened to creation. It is used twice in this section (3:14,17) and once in the section on Cain and Abel (4:11).

The first recipient was the serpent: **So the LORD God said to the serpent, "Because you have done this, Cursed are you above all the livestock and all**

the wild animals!" The curse would result in the physical condition of the snake changing (**you will crawl on your belly**) and the manner in which he would obtain food (**and you will eat dust all the days of your life**). The symbol of death (Gen. 3:19) became the food of the serpent. But all animals would die, and snakes do not actually eat dust. It is better to regard this phrase as referring to the place where the snake would eat (i.e., among the dust) rather than the substance of his meal.

But the second part of the judgment made clear that the one behind the deception was also to be judged. God declared, **And I will put enmity between you and the woman, and between your offspring** [seed] **and hers; he will crush** [strike] **your head and you will strike his heel**. Some interpreters see nothing more than an ongoing hatred between mankind and snakes in this phrase. But more than this is implied. We find out that there will be an ongoing hatred between the woman along with her descendants and the serpent and the ones who would be the offspring of the serpent. This could refer to the one who possessed the serpent—that is Satan, the Evil One. The term **offspring** can be a collective singular referring first to all who would come from the serpent and then to all who would come from the woman.

But it does not need to be a collective noun (cp. Gal. 3:16). It could refer to a single being, one from the serpent and one from the woman, who would do battle. **Hers** (literally "her seed") may infer the virgin birth of Jesus, since it is not "their" seed. In this verse there is the use of the third-person, masculine, singular "he" in the expression **he will crush your head**. A seed of the woman would crush the head (a fatal blow), not of the descendants of the serpent (we don't expect all snakes to be killed by mankind) but of the one who had started all of this, Satan himself.

Here we have the first prophetic word of promise that gives a glimpse of hope to those who are dying. This identity of the one behind the serpent is confirmed in the last book of the Bible. Revelation 20:2 describes how "the dragon, *that ancient serpent,* who is the devil, or Satan" (emphasis added) was thrown into the Abyss and finally in Revelation 20:10, into the lake of burning sulfur.

In Romans 16:20 Paul writes, "The God of peace will soon crush Satan under your feet." This refers to the ongoing struggle between God's people and Satan. This continual struggle may signify that although there will be a final and decisive victory of Christ over Satan, down through history this battle has been fought in each generation. Various individuals (offspring of the woman) will seek to conquer the attempts of evil people (offspring of the serpent) to dominate the godly. But no one will be victorious until the Messiah, our Lord Jesus Christ (the Seed of the woman) finally triumphs (Rev. 20:10).

The reference to the offspring of the woman reflects God's opinion that the world should go on. It also reflects God's plan for victory over Satan. We sometimes wonder how we can bring children into such an evil world. But God's desire is that there should be children. These offspring of the woman should be prepared to resist the Evil One until finally Jesus Christ accomplishes his victorious work.

3:16. The physical condition of the woman as well as the relationship between the wife and her husband was changed. Judgment fell on what was uniquely hers as a woman, the function of childbearing. God said to the woman, **I will greatly increase your pains in childbearing; with pain you will give birth to children.** Although death has come into this world, life is possible. The **pain** that accompanies childbirth would be a reminder to woman of Eve's part in bringing trouble and suffering into this world. The same word for **pain** is found (in only a slightly different spelling in the Hebrew) in the curse to the man (Gen. 3:17).

But God also told the woman, **Your desire will be for your husband, and he will rule over you.** There are at least three different interpretations of the meaning of this sentence: (1) A woman's desire would not be her own. Her desire would be subject to her husband's desire, for her husband would rule over her. (2) A woman, in spite of the pain that would be involved in bearing children, would develop an attraction, a longing, for her husband so that she would enter into relationships with him that would result in children. (3) A woman would desire to dominate the relationship with her husband, but God declared that the man would rule as head.

A decision on interpretation must involve not only the meaning of specific words and the immediate context but include factors such as: the use of the word for *desire* in Genesis 4:7 and Song 7:10; the teaching of the New Testament on the difficulties in the husband-wife relationship; and the realities we observe in married life. Based on these factors, it appears that the wife will now desire to dominate the relationship and no longer intuitively submit as her husband's "helper" (see "Deeper Discoveries").

3:17–19. Adam's curse was based on two factors stated by God: **Because you listened to your wife and ate from the tree about which I commanded you, "You must not eat of it."** Adam listened to his wife about an evil action, and he also disobeyed the command of God. Adam was the head of the human race and had the responsibility and authority to act independently of his wife when she suggested disobedience. But he chose to listen and then to disobey.

The physical condition of the man was changed because his environment was altered, and physical death would be his lot: **Cursed is the ground because of you; through painful toil you will eat of it all the days of your life.** The ground over which he was to have dominion would now be less than ideal. Great effort would be required to accomplish his task. The land would produce thorns and thistles . . . by the sweat of your brow you will eat your food.

This indicates the start of what has become known as "the fallen world." Romans 8:20–22 declares, "For the creation was subjected to frustration, not by its own choice, but by the will of the one who subjected it, in hope that the creation itself will be liberated from its bondage to decay and brought into the glorious freedom of the children of God. We know that the whole creation has been groaning as in the pains of childbirth right up to the present time."

Apparently not only would plants now grow as weeds without any benefit for man, but the entire creation was affected. No doubt such disasters as volcanoes, earthquakes, and tornadoes can be traced to this cursing of the ground. At death man's body would return to dust rather than experience physical immortality.

But each of the curses also involved grace. The cursed ground would still yield food for man. The woman would still be able to have children. The serpent would still exist. And some day victory would come.

■ Naming of the Woman (3:20)

SUPPORTING IDEA: *Adam, by calling his wife not merely woman but Eve, declares his faith that the human race will continue.*

3:20. In Genesis 2:23 Adam declared that his wife would "be called 'woman,' for she was taken out of man." Now, after the fall, and hearing the elements of judgment, Adam named the woman Eve. This verse should be seen as indication of Adam's acceptance of and faith in God's decrees that had just been given. The name *Eve* means "living" or "life producer." By the personal name he gave his wife, Adam declared that he believed she would conceive and produce offspring for **she would become the mother of all the living**. He accepted God's judgments but believed God's word about children and perhaps implicitly proclaimed his faith that some day an offspring of his would conquer the Evil One.

■ Clothing for Mankind (3:21)

SUPPORTING IDEA: *A sacrifice of animals is made to cover what brought shame to mankind.*

3:21. Man's nakedness had caused him shame and had forced him to seek a covering of his own creativity. God, in an act that appeared to require the death of an animal, provided **garments of skin for Adam and his wife and clothed them**. It may not be possible to speak dogmatically of these skins or hides as representing atonement. But it is clear that God had concern and compassion for mankind. He provided them clothing but at the expense of life. This may foreshadow the sacrificial system that would provide for fellowship with God. Man's attempt to cover himself with fig leaves was appropriate but not adequate. God recognized that human nakedness would now need to be covered if life was to go on in God's way. God expressed his grace in the face of sin and judgment.

G Expulsion from the Garden (3:22–24)

SUPPORTING IDEA: *Adam and Eve's expulsion from the garden is for their own good.*

3:22–24. As a result of eating from the tree of the knowledge of good and evil, man became more like God in obtaining knowledge of good and evil. While this statement may be hard to accept, it is clearly stated in God's Word that **the man has now become like one of us, knowing good and evil.** While there is much debate of the meaning of this verse, it is apparent that man had gained a kind of knowledge both like and unlike divine knowledge. Much like a doctor and patient both know the illness yet differ in their understanding, both God and mankind knew that something could be used for good or for evil yet differed in the way they had reached that knowledge.

God had not done evil, as man had, in order to know what was good and evil. But God, in his omniscience, knows what is good and evil and makes decisions accordingly. Man however, had obtained this knowledge by committing evil. Now man would seek to act like God in making decisions based on his inadequate knowledge of good and evil. He would no longer accept God's word as the final authority.

But man had also become less like God because he was no longer innocent of sin and would now die. And so **he must not be allowed to reach out his hand and take also from the tree of life and eat, and live forever.** If man were to decide that the good thing to do would be to eat from the tree of life, he would forever experience a living death. Man's knowledge was not accurate or sufficient, but he might think it was. God, in grace, would not allow fallen man to make a temporal decision that would prevent him from accepting God's provision for his predicament. In the future, when man's sin would be dealt with through redemption, the tree of life would be placed in the new earth for man to eat (Rev. 22:2).

MAIN IDEA REVIEW: *The fall of mankind into sin produces conditions of alienation from the Creator God, from fellow human beings, and from the created world.*

III. CONCLUSION

Eternal Consequences

When Adam and Eve decided to disobey the word of God, they made a decision that changed not only their whole life but the history of the human race. It was a decision that should have been easy to get right. It came down to deciding whose word should be trusted—the word that came through the serpent or the word that came directly from God.

The Evil One, speaking through the serpent, caused Eve to question the word of God by putting doubts in her mind about the goodness and generosity of God. This matter of responding authoritatively to God's word is still a vital matter and one that continues to have varied responses to this very day.

PRINCIPLES

- God's Word must be obeyed by humans just as all of the rest of creation has done in the creation narrative.
- Most Christians believe that the Old and New Testaments constitute the inerrant Word of God. If this is true, then we must receive the Bible as the complete revelation of his will for salvation and the only unfailing rule of faith and practice for Christian life and doctrine.
- The Evil One denies the truth of the Word of God.
- The first doctrine in Scripture that Satan denied is that God will judge sin. This is still the truth that he tries to get people to deny.
- Sin is not an isolated action; it always has social consequences.
- A distorted view of the character of God can cause a person to sin against a holy God.

APPLICATIONS

- Don't accept Satan's lie that God's prohibitions are a limitation rather than a gracious provision from a loving God.
- The Evil One still tempts those who do not read the Word of God for themselves. Read your Bible!
- Realize that victory over temptation and sin begins with exposing the deceptions that Satan uses.
- Understand that not everything that happens to us can be related to an act of disobedience or foolishness on our part. We live in a fallen world that will not be made right until God establishes his eternal kingdom.

IV. LIFE APPLICATION

Conscious Sin

After the fall, Adam was walking with his sons Cain and Abel. They passed by the garden of Eden. One of the boys asked, "Dad, why did you ever leave such a beautiful place?"

Adam replied, "Well, you might say your mother and I ate us out of house and home!"

Why did Eve and then Adam eat from the forbidden fruit? For some of the same reasons that you and I commit sin! Sometimes, like Eve, we are deceived into believing an opinion or idea that is not true. This can come about by not paying close attention to revealed truth, by not believing revealed truth, and finally by rationalizing that we know best. We sin because we use our rational minds to make a decision in an area for which our minds were never made to function. We don't decide what is sinful. God does!

But sometimes we sin because we are like Adam. Adam was not deceived (1 Tim. 2:14), but he sinned anyway. We might like to think that Eve was the most culpable or liable, but in reality it was Adam. Adam had heard God's voice directly. Adam knew he was responsible for Eve since she had been taken from him. He knew that the other creatures were to be in submission to him. He knew all this yet still ate from the fruit that Eve gave him.

Just how long the man was with the woman during the temptation is not revealed. He put the offer of his wife above that of the Lord. He may have done this because he didn't want to be alone again, since he may have assumed his wife was going to die. He may have sinned because he was jealous of her experience that he had not yet had. He may have eaten because he knew he had not exercised the leadership required of him. Adam should have told his wife that she was not allowed to eat from the tree of the knowledge of good and evil. He may have sinned for some other reason. But the reality is that he consciously and deliberately violated God's command.

Like Adam and Eve, we too, in the words of the old hymn, "are prone to wander . . . prone to leave the God I love." We must not depend on our own logic, our own rational thinking, our own perception of what we must do. Our goal should be to please the God who made us and who has redeemed us at great cost.

V. PRAYER

Lord, make us alert to the temptations introduced into our lives. Make us discerning when your Word is treated as less than genuine. Give us the grace and desire to live a life that brings honor to you. Amen.

VI. DEEPER DISCOVERIES

A. The Problem of Evil

Evil appears in human history, not associated with or caused by God or introduced by the serpent, but as a result of Adam and Eve's action. Genesis 3 does not explain the presence of evil acting in the serpent. Man has put forth many different theories to explain the presence of evil. But they all fall short. The origin of evil in the world remains a mystery.

B. Satan and the Snake

Some interpreters do not take the position advocated in this commentary that there was someone behind the serpent. Rather, they see the serpent as acting with craftiness to deceive the woman. As a result, the curse uttered to the serpent would be seen as limited to the earthly creature alone. Genesis 3:15 uses "offspring" ("seed")—a masculine singular noun with a third feminine singular suffix—in reference to the offspring of the woman (a hint of the virgin birth?). It goes on to use the "he"—a personal pronoun, third masculine singular (Christ?)—to describe the one who would crush the serpent's head.

It is possible to take "seed" or "offspring" as a collective noun. For example, the NET Bible contains the following footnote on Genesis 3:15:

> The singular pronoun and verb agree grammatically with the collective singular noun "offspring." To clarify the collective sense of the pronoun, the translation uses the English plural pronoun "they." For other examples of singular verb and pronominal forms being used with the collective singular "offspring," see Gen. 16:10; 22:17; 24:60. The word "head" is an adverbial accusative, locating the blow. A crushing blow to the head would be potentially fatal.

Many interpreters see Genesis 3:15 as the first glimpse of the gospel in the Bible. The use of "seed" or "offspring" in such verses as Genesis 22:18, 2 Samuel 7:12, and Psalm 89:4,29,36 gives credence to the offspring being ultimately the Messiah. But it is true that the seed or offspring of the woman might have first been thought to be Cain and then Seth and then perhaps Enoch or Noah. These are all offspring of the woman, and all those who oppose righteousness and reject God's word could be considered the offspring of the serpent. Christ, as recorded in John 8:44, declared that the unbelieving Jews belonged to "your father, the devil." The struggle between good and evil has always gone on. But no one had crushed the head of evil until Christ appeared. His final victory, although secure, is still to come.

C. Submission of a Wife to Her Husband

Woman was created to be man's helper. She was created from man and for man (1 Cor. 11:8–9). Submission to his leadership came before the fall (1 Tim. 2:11–13) and continued after the fall even in the Christian church and home (Eph. 5:22–24; 1 Cor. 11:3). The curse directed to the woman in Genesis 3:16 includes the sentence, "Your desire will be for your husband, and he will rule over you." It is important to recognize that the rulership of the man over the woman should not be taken as a newly introduced concept. God reiterated this principle as applicable after the fall, after woman had exercised leadership apart from her husband. This submission is also reiterated to Christian women in the New Testament (Col. 3:18; 1 Pet. 3:1).

It is important to recognize how "desire" is used in Genesis 4:7 by the same author and in near context (the use in Song 7:10 is by a different author and hundreds of years later). This desire, which can be interpreted as a longing to dominate, is a response of the fall. However, the New Testament will deal with this issue in a number of places as it counsels submission for the wife. For the man who was charged to be the leader, the apostles counseled against unloving domination or abuse (Eph. 5:25–33; Col. 3:19; 1 Pet. 3:7).

This teaching in the New Testament indicates the most probable meaning of Genesis 3:16. It also attests that becoming a believer does not undo the creation teachings in this regard. Willing submission and Christlike leadership are not "natural" but are required by God and must be developed by responding to God's Word and using the grace that he supplies.

VII. TEACHING OUTLINE

A. INTRODUCTION

1. Lead Story: The Malfunctioning Human Being
2. Context: This chapter explains what happened to the beautiful world that God had created. It explains much of what we refer to as the "fallen" world in which we live.
3. Transition: The material in this chapter is crucial for understanding not only the rest of Genesis but for understanding why the entire Bible will present a needed salvation plan.

B. COMMENTARY

1. The Temptation to Sin (3:1–5)
2. The Fall into Sin (3:6)
3. Results of the Fall into Sin (3:7–13)

4. Judgments of the Fall into Sin (3:14–19)
5. Naming of the Woman (3:20)
6. Clothing for Mankind (3:21)
7. Expulsion from the Garden (3:22–24)

C. CONCLUSION: CONSCIOUS SIN

VIII. ISSUES FOR DISCUSSION

1. How can studying the temptation of Eve prepare us for temptations we face?
2. Do you see God's judgments on the man and woman also containing a measure of blessing for them? How?
3. Why is it so important to believe this account of the fall if we are to believe the redemption story of Christ, the Savior of the world?
4. How has the fall affected marriage, work, family, and our relationship with God?

Genesis 4:1–6:8

Cycles of Birth and Death

I. **INTRODUCTION**
   Is There Anything "Spiritual" About a
   Genealogy?

II. **COMMENTARY**
   A verse-by-verse explanation of this passage.

III. **CONCLUSION**
   Choose God and Godliness

   An overview of the principles and applications from
   this passage.

IV. **LIFE APPLICATION**
   Passing the Faith to the Next Generation

   Melding this passage to life with God.

V. **PRAYER**
   Tying this passage to life with God.

VI. **DEEPER DISCOVERIES**
   Historical, geographical, and grammatical enrichment of the commentary.

VII. **TEACHING OUTLINE**
   Suggested step-by-step group study of this passage.

VIII. **ISSUES FOR DISCUSSION**
   Zeroing this passage in on daily life.

Genesis 4:1–6:8

Quote

"*Every man must do two things alone; he must do his own believing and his own dying.*"

Martin Luther

IN A NUTSHELL

These chapters give us the first birth, the first death, and then lots more birthing and dying and living in sin until God determines to begin human society again! Adam and Eve had two sons, Cain and Abel. Cain killed Abel and subsequently experienced God's judgment. After Abel's death, Adam and Eve had a third son, Seth.

Cycles of Birth and Death

I. INTRODUCTION

Is There Anything "Spiritual" About a Genealogy?

A few years ago I offered my son Joshua a sum of money if he would read through the entire Bible. I remember after a few weeks that he came to ask me if it was necessary to read through all "the names." I told him that it wasn't required that he pronounce all the names (even I have a difficult time doing that) or that he remember all the ages! But I mentioned that he should look through the list and observe when there was an incident developed in the middle of a list of names. I told him that there is usually something very special going on at that time. And in our section of Scripture for this chapter, we will see this truth.

When we read through these genealogies, we are amazed at the longevity of these people. Methuselah lived to 969 years of age. Just think if you were the life insurance agent who sold him his annuity! Or what if you were the insurance company that provided his long-term care. Today people are living longer than they have in many centuries. According to the *Guinness Book of World Records*, Maud Farris-Luse was the oldest living person whose age (115 years, 56 days) could be verified when she died in March 2002. Mary Thompson of DeWitt, Arkansas, was said to be 119 years old when she died on October 8, 2001, but her age could not be officially verified.

Various reasons have been given for why people today do not live as long as in the preflood times:

1. Environmental changes in the postflood era: perhaps the vapor canopy that some speculate was around the earth protected mankind from the sun's harmful rays

2. The accumulated effect of sin on human genetics

3. The absence of disease on preflood earth

4. Man's altered diet: postflood man was no longer a strict vegetarian but was now a meat eater as well

5. The possibility of God's blessing being removed from mankind because of his continual sin

Many companies advertise that they can postpone the aging process. Others claim that they can reverse the process. But what no company claims is that they can prevent death. As George Bernard Shaw stated, "The statistics on death are quite impressive. One out of one people die." These chapters in

Genesis will deal with the reality of death. But they will also reveal that it is possible to receive God's grace and please him while we live.

II. COMMENTARY

Cycles of Birth and Death

MAIN IDEA: *The human race can be divided into two classes: the godly who listen to God and the ungodly who reject God.*

A Problems Between Cain and Abel (4:1–16)

SUPPORTING IDEA: *Each descendant of Adam and Eve must choose whether he or she will listen to God or rebel against him.*

4:1–2a. The firstborn of Adam and Eve was a son whom Eve called **Cain**. This name in Hebrew sounds like the Hebrew verb that means "to acquire, to get." While in Scripture it is usually the father who names the child, Eve did the naming in this case. Perhaps she did so because she believed this boy was the seed or offspring that God had promised would crush the serpent's head (see Gen. 3:15). She recognized that it was **with the help of the LORD** she had acquired him. **Later she gave birth to his brother Abel,** whose name means "breath" or "temporary." The name may have been an indication that she recognized the temporary nature of life on earth. Abel's name came to have meaning in the abrupt shortening of his life.

4:2b–5a. When they grew up, the boys engaged in different vocations. Cain worked the soil while Abel kept flocks. When the time came for a sacrifice to be made, each brought to the Lord the product of his vocation. Adam's family must have received God's revelation about the necessity of sacrifice to create and maintain fellowship with God. The background to this was probably the sacrifice that God performed to provide the clothing to cover Adam and Eve's shame (see Gen. 3:21).

The LORD looked with favor on Abel and his offering, but on Cain and his offering he did not look with favor. The reason for this contrast is never stated. Perhaps the issue was the *attitude* of the respective worshipers rather than the *nature* of the offering. Some interpreters suggest that the attitudes expressed were faith versus nonfaith (cp. Heb. 11:4). Others suggest that the contrast was between a careless, miserly offering and a choice, generous offering (cp. Lev. 3:16; 1 John 3:12).

But if the Lord had given prior revelation about sacrifice, it is likely that he would have included some specifics about the nature of the sacrifice as well. Although later sacrifices could include grain (i.e., bloodless), this was usually given in conjunction with another sacrifice (e.g., Lev. 2). The Book of Hebrews speaks of the "better sacrifice" of Abel (Heb. 11:4a) and that God "spoke well of his offerings" (Heb. 11:4b). Later the author of Hebrews wrote of "Jesus the mediator of a new covenant, and to the sprinkled blood that speaks a better word than the blood of Abel" (Heb. 12:24).

The contrast here is not between the death of Abel and the blood Cain spilled (this blood did not create fellowship) but the acceptable blood sacrifice of Abel and the better sacrifice of Jesus. The contrast then is not primarily about faith, although faith is absolutely required, but between offering what the Lord had declared was acceptable and what Cain decided was admissible.

Like Adam and Eve in the garden of Eden, the word of God must be accepted as precise and authoritative. If the Lord declared that Cain's sacrifice was unacceptable, then this was true. What was now required of Cain was to offer what was acceptable to God.

4:5b–12. The poor attitude of Cain is demonstrated by his response to correction from God. He was unwilling to accept God's decision on the matter. After sulking and then becoming angry, he proceeded to kill his brother.

The Lord confronted Cain with the question, **Where is your brother Abel?** Cain's response, **I don't know. . . . Am I my brother's keeper?** was both a lie and a revelation of his callous indifference toward a family member. Cain was his brother's keeper in the sense that he had a responsibility to honor and protect him, not to despise and murder him. Cain became a seed or offspring of the serpent (see Gen. 3:15), who desired the death of God's creation. In the very first story about fallen humanity, we have a man choosing to be ungodly.

Cain, like his parents before him, tried to avoid admitting his guilt. But the Lord God knew exactly what he had done. For the second time in this chapter, the Lord confronted Cain: **What have you done? Listen! Your brother's blood cries out to me from the ground. Now you are under a curse and driven from the ground, which opened its mouth to receive your brother's blood from your hand. When you work the ground, it will no longer yield its crops for you. You will be a restless wanderer on the earth** (Gen. 4:10–12).

Cain's punishment was filled with grace, since he could easily have been punished with death. He would become a nomad, having difficulty making a living from the ground. Again the ground from which man had been taken and over which man was to rule was affected by man's actions (Gen. 4:10; 3:17).

4:13–16. Cain responded to God's gracious discipline with self-pity: **My punishment is more than I can bear.** God put a sign of protection on Cain so **no one who found him would kill him.** This idea of an identifying mark on a person is the first of many in Scripture (see "Deeper Discoveries").

The expulsion from the Lord's presence is confirmed by the statement that **Cain went out from the LORD's presence and lived in the land of Nod, east of Eden.** Nod means "wandering" or "homelessness." It was located as east of the place where the tree of life was located and the home where God had first placed sinless mankind.

B The Genealogy of Cain (4:17–24)

SUPPORTING IDEA: *A genealogy shows the direction that the descendants of Cain took in their rejection of the revelation that God had given.*

4:17–18. The mention of Cain's wife always raises the question of the identity of the wives of the first men. She must have been a sister or possibly a niece.

Cain's wife gave birth to a son **Enoch** at the time Cain was building a city. This city also received the name *Enoch*. The fact that Cain was involved in city-building seems to be an attempt to defy the reality that he was to be homeless and a wanderer (Gen 4:12,16). But this fact also demonstrated that anyone away from the Lord's presence was a wanderer. This comment about a city also tied together Cain and the godless people at the Tower of Babel (Gen. 11:1–9).

4:19–24. The line of descent of Cain through Enoch culminated in Lamech. This man was a bigamist whose three sons were the founders of herding, music, and metallurgy. The fact that culture, including various arts and sciences, is recorded in the genealogy of the rebellious, ungodly line demonstrates that much of the image of God remained in these fallen creatures. These unbelievers still had the ability to discover and invent. Believers should not equate ungodliness with a lack of culture or intelligence.

C The Genealogy of Seth (4:25–26)

SUPPORTING IDEA: *The abbreviated genealogy of Seth shows the godly direction that a descendant of Adam and Eve took in his submission to the Lord.*

4:25–26. The name *Seth* probably means "granted," since Eve declared that God had granted her **another child in place of Abel, since Cain killed him.** It was after Seth had a son whom he named Enosh that the Scripture records, **at that time men began to call on** [or to proclaim] **the name of the LORD.** This statement stands in sharp contrast to the statements made by Lamech in verses 23–24. Seth showed dependence on God. Just how this is demonstrated in Seth's life is not detailed. But it probably included proper sacrifice like the model of the now-dead Abel. Seth became a descendant of the woman who would respond to the Lord God in calling upon him and thus proclaiming him to society at large.

This completes the *toledot* (the account of) of the creation (Gen. 2:4–4:26). Here is a sordid picture of what had happened to the beautiful, good creation of

God. It had become cursed through disobedience. There was violence among people and decay in the natural world. There was a line through Cain, who rejected God's word but espoused violence and polygamy. There was another line through Seth, who called on the name of the Lord.

Ⅾ The Genealogy of Adam Through Seth to Noah (5:1–32)

SUPPORTING IDEA: *This genealogy helps us understand God's plan for the world. The corruption of the human race threatens the godly line.*

5:1a. This *toledot* describes what became of Adam's line through his godly offspring. It stands in contrast to the development of the ungodly line of Cain. But the godly line will conclude with a single godly man.

5:1b–2. Before detailing the genealogy of Adam through Seth down to Noah, the author of Genesis reviews the fundamentals about the creation of man. Similar to the genealogy of Luke 3:23–37 that ends "the son of Seth, the son of Adam, the son of God," the genealogy of Genesis 5 begins with God who created mankind. **When God created man, he made him in the likeness of God. He created them male and female and blessed them. And when they were created, he called them "man."** It is important to recognize that man is unique in all creation because he alone was made in the **likeness** of God (see Gen. 1:26–27). It is also important to recognize that mankind was created both male and female and that God blessed them as distinct genders (see Gen. 1:28). There is nothing inferior about either man or woman. This information serves as a crucial background to the mixed marriages of Genesis 6.

5:3–20. The names in Genesis 5 (as well as in Gen. 10) give a historical record of descent. They also demonstrate that there was the potential of a "seed" or offspring in each generation to do battle with evil. There is therefore a continuing presence of various descendants who could produce "the" seed. Later, after Abraham was designated as a chosen one, there were no numbers in the genealogies, although the names of Abraham's descendants were carefully recorded. The numbers that are given before Abraham seem to be there for the sole purpose of determining the length of time from Adam to Abraham (see "Deeper Discoveries").

The number ten is significant in Genesis. Not only is the entire book divided by the author into ten *toledots,* but the number of names appearing in the genealogies of Genesis 5 (from Adam to Noah) and Genesis 11:10–26 (from Noah to Abram) are both ten.

There is a clear emphasis on death in this chapter (cp. Gen. 2:17) and yet grace as well. Sons and daughters were being born, and people were living to an old age. Both of these were evidence of God's grace.

5:21–24. Just as Lamech in the ungodly line of Cain was seventh from Adam (when Adam is included), so Enoch was seventh from Adam in the godly line of Seth. The contrast is obvious. Scripture tells us Enoch was one of two men who **walked with God** prior to the flood (the other was Noah; Gen. 6:9). Previously, Seth and his descendants are said to "call on the name of the LORD" (Gen. 4:26b). To "walk with God" could literally be translated "walk about (i.e., live) with God." This is a figure of speech that, like Seth's calling of the name of the Lord, signifies that Enoch had a close relationship and fellowship with God.

Enoch's belief in God produced actions in words of witness. Jude 14–15 declares, "Enoch, the seventh from Adam, prophesied about these men: 'See, the Lord is coming with thousands upon thousands of his holy ones to judge everyone, and to convict all the ungodly of all the ungodly acts they have done in the ungodly way, and of all the harsh words ungodly sinners have spoken against him.'" Enoch spoke of the second coming of Christ centuries before his first coming!

Enoch is an exception to the dismal refrain ("then he died") of this chapter. Hebrews 11:5 declares, "By faith Enoch was taken from this life, so that he did not experience death; he could not be found, because God had taken him away. For before he was taken, he was commended as one who pleased God." Enoch was one of two people in the Bible who left this life without undergoing physical death (see also Elijah in 2 Kgs. 2:11; the same Hebrew word used of Enoch is used for the translation of Elijah in 2 Kgs. 2:3,5).

How can this be, in light of God's pronouncement of death coming upon sinful humanity? First, the death that God spoke about in the garden of Eden (Gen. 2:17) was primarily spiritual death since Adam and Eve did not experience physical death upon sinning, at least not for 930 years in the case of Adam (Gen. 5:5). Second, both of these examples (Enoch and Elijah) foretell the experience of millions of believers at the time of the rapture (1 Thess. 4:16–17; 1 Cor. 15:51–52).

5:25–27. The death of Methuselah, son of the godly Enoch, coincided with the date of the flood (see "Deeper Discoveries"). Methuselah died at 969 years of age. Methuselah was 187 when Lamech was born. Lamech was 182 when Noah was born. Noah was 600 when the flood came. These figures add up to 969 years. It is possible that Methuselah died in the flood, but it is more likely that he died just before the flood.

Unlike some extrabiblical genealogies which have unrealistic numbers and which result in impossible dates (e.g., three kings in a Sumerian list are said to have reigned 72,000 years each!), the Bible is logical in the genealogies in spite of the great ages. In spite of the longevity of this era, no one lived past the flood except Noah and his sons. Adding up the ages of the fathers when they fathered the listed sons yields 1,556 years. Attached to this must be the 100 years until the flood (Gen. 7:6). This gives a total of 1,656 years from creation to the flood if there are no gaps in these genealogies.

5:28–32. We must be careful not to confuse the Lamech of Seth's line with the ungodly Lamech of Cain's line. This Lamech in Genesis 5 was the ninth in Seth's line and the father of Noah. He gave his son the name *Noah* prophetically, or at least expectantly, stating he would **comfort us in the labor and painful toil of our hands caused by the ground the LORD has cursed**. This reminder of the curse in the garden of Eden also ties Noah to the promise of a descendant who would deliver mankind from the Evil One. While Noah would not be "the" seed (i.e., the Messiah), he would serve as a great deliverer (by the use of an ark) in the midst of the evil world.

After Noah was 500 years old, he became the father of Shem, Ham and Japheth. A couple of points should be noted here. First, descendants of Noah were not numerous, and they apparently were not born early in Noah's life. This is in keeping with other marriages in Genesis that end up producing a significant descendant but only after notable time (e.g., Sarah and Abraham, Rebekah and Isaac). Second, since Noah was six hundred years old when the flood came (Gen. 7:6), this may imply that the building of the ark took up to one hundred years.

E Conflict Between the Godly and the Ungodly (6:1–8)

SUPPORTING IDEA: *This historical narrative provides the background to God's decision to curse the earth with a flood.*

6:1–2. After recording population growth in keeping with God's plan (Gen. 1:28), the author Moses records a type of marriage and resulting society that would bring judgment on almost all humanity. The first condition stated about humanity after the genealogies have been given (Gen. 4:17–5:32) is that the **sons of God saw that the daughters of men were beautiful, and they married any of them they chose**. Just exactly who the sons of God and the daughters of men were has been a debate throughout much of history. (See Deeper Discoveries.) The answer is complicated by the statement found in verse 4: "The Nephilim were on the earth in those days—and also afterward—when the sons of God went to the daughters of men and had children by them. They were the heroes of old, men of renown."

This statement has been taken either as describing the result of the union (but notice the Nephilim were on earth not only before the flood but also afterwards; Num. 13:33) or as the time when this type of marriage was taking place. It was a time when well-known heroes chose whoever they wanted to marry without considering the spiritual conditions of their marriage partner. It was improper, mixed marriage that was the catalyst for creating such an ungodly society that God was forced to act in judgment.

6:3. The 120 years referred to here have been taken as either the longevity of mankind's life from now on (taking the alternate translation that man's life would be limited to 120 years) or the period of time God granted to mankind so he could repent to avoid judgment. There is no indication in Scripture that man began to live only 120 years. In fact, there is just the opposite evidence until after Abraham (Gen. 11:10–26). Psalm 90:10 states, "The length of our days is seventy years—or eighty, if we have the strength." So it is best to take this period of time as opportunity for repentance. Either translation of the expression **My Spirit will not contend** or "my spirit will not remain in" can fit this interpretation, since all but Noah's family would disappear during the flood.

But this provision of 120 years shows God's great patience. The apostle Peter, immediately after writing about the flood (2 Pet. 3:5–6), stated in 2 Peter 3:9, "The Lord is not slow in keeping his promise, as some understand slowness. He is patient with you, not wanting anyone to perish, but everyone to come to repentance."

It appears that Noah had one hundred years from the birth of his sons until the flood (Gen. 5:32; 7:6). God must have warned humanity and then, after there was no repentance for at least twenty years, began to make plans with Noah.

6:4. This material on the **Nephilim** has been taken as either descriptive of the descendants of this mixed union or as an indication of time. Nephilim (literally, "fallen ones") is used later in Numbers 13:31–33 to describe a people of great size and strength. In men's eyes in the preflood era, these were **heroes of old, men of renown** (military leaders with wealth or power). But they were not godly people, since they were destroyed in the flood. Since Nephilim are mentioned after the flood, it does not appear that they are the offspring of a certain type of marriage. It seems best to take this reference as an indication that the 120 years started at the time of the rule of the Nephilim.

6:5–7. The conditions that resulted from such marriages were **wickedness** and violence that were universal and without precedent. Jesus Christ warned that the last days would exhibit the same disregard for God's standards and concerns when he said:

> As it was in the days of Noah, so it will be at the coming of the Son of Man. For in the days before the flood, people were eating and drinking, marrying and giving in marriage, up to the day Noah entered the ark; and they knew nothing about what would happen

until the flood came and took them all away. That is how it will be at the coming of the Son of Man (Matt. 24:37–39).

He specifically mentioned marriage in such a manner as to indicate that not only was it routine but that it was done without much thought.

The LORD was grieved that he had made man on the earth, and his heart was filled with pain. This is one of some thirty expressions in the Scriptures that express God's response using human emotions. God's creation had ceased to reflect his glory in almost every way (see Rev. 4:11), so he was no longer pleased or comforted by it. God stated, **I will wipe mankind, whom I have created, from the face of the earth . . . for I am grieved that I have made them.** God changed his previous manner of dealing with humanity, which had been one of patient endurance even when there was no positive response (see Cain's response in Gen. 4:13,24). Now he would deal with them in temporal judgment.

6:8. Noah was introduced in Genesis 5:29–32. He was in the line of Seth and Enoch (the line of the godly), and he was chosen by God to be a redeemer of the human race (to allow for "the" seed to come). His provision of salvation would preserve the human race, although not most of preflood humanity.

To find **favor** is to obtain grace. Although there have been many examples of God's grace in Genesis (especially in the context of judgment; Gen. 3:14–24), this is the first specific mention of the term. Although Noah's faith evidenced itself by righteous living (Gen. 6:9), he also needed God's favor.

> **MAIN IDEA REVIEW:** *The human race can be divided into two classes: the godly who listen to God and the ungodly who reject God.*

III. CONCLUSION

Choose God and Godliness

"You and God are a majority" is an expression most of us have heard. In fact, God all alone is a majority! He doesn't need us to be dominant, powerful, or right. But God in his grace allows us to choose to become part of a line of people who find grace and live righteously before him. People like Seth and his son Enosh, Enoch, and Noah are examples who influence us to live for God.

Although we often find ourselves being drawn by the majority of society to a belief or action, we must resist when it is not of truth. John Calvin wrote in "The Appeal to 'Custom' against Truth" in the Prefatory Address to King Francis in his *Institutes*:

Even though the whole world may conspire in the same wickedness, he has taught us by experience what is the end of those who sin with the multitude. This he did when he destroyed all mankind by the flood, but kept Noah with his little family; and Noah by his faith, the faith of one man, condemned the whole world (Gen. 7:1; Heb. 11:7). To sum up, evil custom is nothing but a kind of public pestilence in which men do not perish the less though they fall with the multitude.

The whole of the human race can be divided into the godly and the ungodly. Ultimately, the only correct choice is to identify with God. In him you are never alone, and you will be kept safe just like Noah.

PRINCIPLES

- Our relationship with the Lord affects our relationship with other people.
- God's Word, whether satisfying to us or not, is still the authoritative Word of God and is to be obeyed.
- All Scripture is inspired and useful, even the genealogies. Certain Scripture is not as applicable to contemporary life as other Scripture, but all Scripture is valuable for the author's intended purpose.
- God is patient, not wanting anyone to perish.
- God is concerned about proper marriage, because godly marriages are the foundation of a righteous society.
- Only God's grace enables us to escape his judgment on the wicked.
- God is sovereign, and he decides the duration of life for the people whom he loves.

APPLICATIONS

- Be careful of your reaction to God's blessing on others. Abel's blessing didn't take anything away from Cain.
- Don't let pride prevent you from obeying God.
- Be careful whom you marry. Marriages that do not take into consideration the spiritual condition of the marriage partner can cause considerable heartache (see 1 Cor. 7:39; 2 Cor. 6:14–18).
- Seek, accept, and live by God's grace and favor.

IV. LIFE APPLICATION

Passing the Faith to the Next Generation

It is obvious from reading Genesis 4:1–6:8 that life moves on from one generation to the next. How can a generation live on? Someone suggested that parenting is hereditary—if your parents didn't have any children, you're not likely to have any either! But having a physical child is only the first step in a generation living on. Only by following the Lord and passing this faith on can a generation live on.

You must have a faith before you can pass it on. So take a moment and make sure you believe God's Word. Once that answer is firmly positive, then decide to live in such a way that the next generation in your family and in your church will have reason to believe because of you. Never underestimate the power of living out your faith. The next generation needs to see people with a living faith in a living God.

V. PRAYER

Lord, may you find us like Noah, righteous and walking with you. But even more, Lord, may we find favor in your eyes, like Noah did, because of your grace. Amen.

VI. DEEPER DISCOVERIES

A. The Mark on Cain

In Genesis 4:15 God placed a mark on Cain "so that no one who found him would kill him." The concept of a mark for identification is found throughout Scripture. In Exodus 13:16 the redemption of the firstborn son was "like a sign on your hand and a symbol on your forehead that the LORD brought us out of Egypt with his mighty hand." Deuteronomy 6:8 instructed God's people to take his commands and "tie them as symbols on your hands and bind them on your foreheads." Many Jews took this statement literally and tied phylacteries to their foreheads and left arms (cp. Matt. 23:5). But it is best to take this figuratively as stating that the Word of God should control our thinking and actions. Exodus 13:9 treats the consecration of the firstborn this way when it says, "This observance will be for you like a sign on your hand and a reminder on your forehead that the law of the LORD is to be on your lips."

In the Book of Revelation, a number of passages deal with a mark or seal that is placed on the forehead or the right hand. God places his mark on the

144,000 (Rev. 7:2–4) as a sign of protection. This mark is described in Revelation 14:1 as the name of the Lamb and his Father's name (see also Rev. 22:4).

B. "Sons of God"

The identification of the "sons of God" is an age-old biblical-theological challenge that has been answered in various ways. The position taken in this commentary is that the marriages involving the "sons of God" and the "daughters of men" were between the godly and ungodly lines of humanity based on the literary context and resulting judgment on the human world.

The more traditional explanation is that the "sons of God" were fallen angelic beings, based upon such evidence as the later use of this term in Job and Psalms, the apocryphal Book of First Enoch 6-7 which says they were angels, and possible reference to this sin in 1 Peter 3:18-20 and 2 Peter 2:4.

Other explanations have included dynastic rulers who were seeking to rule all humanity and non-elect despots under demonic influence.

Whatever position one takes on the identification of "sons of God," the truth remains that there was a sin of improper, mixed marriage that resulted in great sin and eventually necessitated God's world-wide judgment.

C. Numbers in the Genealogy of Genesis 5

Gaps are usually assumed in biblical genealogies. This is based on at least four factors: First, the Hebrew word for "the father of" is comprehensive and can mean a more generic "ancestor." Second, evidence from Seth not being the firstborn of Adam (Gen. 4:25) as well as the arrangement of Noah's three sons (Shem, Ham, and Japheth) in Genesis 5:32 suggest to some interpreters that this is not a complete or chronological listing. Third, the genealogies of Genesis 11 and Matthew 1 are not complete (when compared to the genealogies in 1 Chr. 1–4). So some interpreters assume the genealogy in Genesis 5 must not be complete either. Fourth, the correspondences between Cain's genealogy of Genesis 4 and Seth's of Genesis 5 (specifically the obvious contrast between ungodly Lamech who is seventh and godly Enoch who is also seventh) is suggestive to some of a selective listing.

In addition, the long ages given are sometimes seen as having some conventional literary function (for example, Enoch's 365 years refers to the 365 days in a year and so represents a full life for Enoch) rather than serving as literal numbers.

Before one too readily accepts the common notion that there are gaps in the genealogies and therefore the ages are useless to indicate the length of time back to Adam, consider the following:

- The position of a child in the family does not change the age of the father when this particular son is born (i.e., it does not matter whether Seth was the third-born or hundredth-born; Adam was still 130 years of age when Seth was born).

- The number of siblings in the family does not change the age of the father when he gave birth to a particular son or when he died.
- The relationship between the people does not change the age. If Lamech was the grandson rather than the son of Methuselah, the Scripture still states that Methuselah was 187 years old when he became the father (or grandfather, or great-grandfather) of Lamech.

Notice too, the following indications that there cannot be gaps (generations that have been left out) in the following relationships in the genealogy from Adam to Enoch:

- Adam as the first man (Gen. 5:1–2; cp. Gen. 2–4; 1 Cor. 15:45; 1 Tim. 2:13)
- Seth as an immediate descendant from Adam (Gen. 5:3–4; cp. Gen. 4:25)
- Enosh as an immediate descendant of Seth (Gen. 5:6; cp Gen. 4:26)
- Enoch as the seventh from Adam (Gen. 5:18; cp. Jude 14)

The genealogy of 1 Chronicles 1:1–3 does not give any additional names for this period of history.

The numbers must be given for a reason. Later genealogies, essentially from after the time of Abraham, do not contain ages for the people in the genealogies. After Abraham we are able to date the biblical history and correlate it with secular history. It is true that when the Bible refers back to pre-Abrahamic events or people, it never adds up these numbers. But this does not mean that they can't be added up. Perhaps they were not added up for the very reason that people could if they desired to do so.

VII. TEACHING OUTLINE

A. INTRODUCTION

1. Lead Story: Is There Anything "Spiritual" About a Genealogy?
2. Context: These chapters give the historical-theological narrative from Adam to Noah. The contrast between the ungodly line and the godly line gives the needed background to the coming flood.
3. Transition: Before the flood God promises to make a covenant with Noah. The anticipation is now there for just what this new arrangement between God and man will involve.

B. COMMENTARY

1. Problems Between Cain and Abel (4:1–16)
2. The Genealogy of Cain (4:17–24)
3. The Genealogy of Seth (4:25–26)
4. The Genealogy of Adam Through Seth to Noah (5:1–32)
5. Conflict Between the Godly and the Ungodly (6:1–8)

C. CONCLUSION: PASSING THE FAITH TO THE NEXT GENERATION

VIII. ISSUES FOR DISCUSSION

1. There are only four methods in Scripture that God has used to bring a human being into this world: (1) Adam was "born" without a mother or father, being a direct creation of God from the dust of the earth; (2) Eve was "born" without a mother, being a creation by God out of Adam; (3) Christ was "born," that is conceived, without a father in the unique virgin birth; and (4) all others are "born" with a father and mother. What does this have to say about the present dilemma of "test-tube" babies and cloning?
2. What are the dangers of marrying a person who does not have the same commitment of faith as you?
3. What do you think the intent of the author of Genesis was in giving the ages of the various men when they died?
4. What in Noah's heritage may have influenced him to decide to live for God?

Genesis 6:9–7:24

Noah and the Flood

I. INTRODUCTION
Excuses

II. COMMENTARY
A verse-by-verse explanation of the passage.

III. CONCLUSION
Does Your Faith Produce an Umbrella?

An overview of the principles and applications from the passage.

IV. LIFE APPLICATION
Persevering Faith for the Family

Melding the passage to life with God.

V. PRAYER
Tying the passage to life with God.

VI. DEEPER DISCOVERIES
Historical, geographical, and grammatical enrichment of the commentary.

VII. TEACHING OUTLINE
Suggested step-by-step group study of the passage.

VIII. ISSUES FOR DISCUSSION
Zeroing the passage in on daily life.

Genesis 6:9–7:24

Quote

"*G*od's darkest threatenings are always accompanied with a revelation of the way of escape. The ark is always along with the Flood."

A l e x a n d e r   M a c l a r e n

I N   A   N U T S H E L L

*T*his passage gives us a review of the necessity for the flood, the divine plans for the ark, the account of the building of the ark, and its maiden voyage.

Noah and the Flood

I. INTRODUCTION

Excuses

I am not sure if we can imagine what an undertaking the ark was to a man over five hundred years old, living long before the industrial revolution, and without the support of public funds! Perhaps a conversation such as the following occurred between the Lord and Noah:

And the Lord said unto Noah: "Where is the ark which I have commanded thee to build?"

And Noah said unto the Lord, "Verily, I have had three carpenters off ill. The gopher wood supplier hath let me down—yea, even though the gopher wood hath been on order for nigh upon twelve months. What can I do, O Lord?"

And God said unto Noah: "I want that ark finished even after seven days and seven nights."

And Noah said: "It will be so." And it was not so.

And the Lord said unto Noah: "What seemeth to be the trouble this time?"

And Noah said unto the Lord: "Mine subcontractor hath gone bankrupt. The pitch which Thou commandest me to put on the outside of the ark hath not arrived. The plumber hath gone on strike. Shem, my son who helpeth me on the ark side of the business, hath formed a pop group with his brothers Ham and Japheth. Lord, I am undone."

And the Lord grew angry and said: "And what about the animals, the male and female of every sort that I ordered to come unto thee to keep their seed upon the face of the earth?"

And Noah said: "They have been delivered unto the wrong address but should arrive on Friday."

And the Lord said: "How about the unicorns, and the fowls of the air by seven?"

And Noah wrung his hands and wept, saying: "Lord, unicorns are a discontinued line; thou canst not get them for love or money. And fowls of the air are sold only in half-dozens. Lord, Lord, Thou knowest how it is."

And the Lord in his wisdom said: "Noah, my son, I knowest. Why else dost thou think I have caused a flood to descend upon the earth?"

But the story as presented in the Scriptures never has Noah making excuses. It only presents him as obeying. I wonder how we might have responded if we were presented with the same challenge? I wonder how we will respond when the next challenge comes to us to obey a word from God in the midst of an unbelieving, ungodly, unsympathetic world?

II. COMMENTARY

Noah and the Flood

> **MAIN IDEA:** *Godly Noah acted in faith in the midst of a faithless, ungodly society.*

A The Man Noah (6:9–10)

> **SUPPORTING IDEA:** *Noah's godly life stands in contrast to ungodliness throughout the world.*

6:9. The phrase **this is the account of Noah** introduces one of the best-known stories of the Old Testament. It is the third *toledot* of Genesis. The following narrative describes what happens to Noah.

The Bible describes Noah as **a righteous man, blameless among the people of his time, and he walked with God** (cp. Job 1:1 for a similar description of Job). Noah's reputation was impeccable even among his peers. This description is not to suggest that Noah was sinless, which is impossible for anyone living in this life except for the Son of God. Noah lived a life of obedience and fellowship with God. **Righteous**, in context, stands in opposition to the description of society as corrupt and violent (Gen. 6:5,11–12).

In Scripture a righteous person is one who honors God and seeks to follow his commands. **Blameless** contrasts with the blame that God placed on society because of its corruption and violence (Gen. 6:6–7,13). The phrase **walked with God** was used of Enoch in Genesis 5:22. It distinguishes Noah from the rest of society who were not in fellowship with God since "every inclination of the thoughts of his [man's] heart was only evil all the time" (Gen. 6:5).

6:10. The information that **Noah had three sons: Shem, Ham and Japheth** reiterates that of Genesis 5:32. It connects our narrative back to the end of chapter 5 before the interlude of the "sons of God" and "daughters of men" narrative.

The listed arrangement of these sons is not their birth order. Rather, Japheth was the oldest son of Noah (Gen. 10:21), Shem was the middle child, and Ham was the youngest (Gen. 9:24). They are listed here in order of importance for biblical history.

B Reasons for the Flood (6:11–13)

SUPPORTING IDEA: *Society is described in terms that show most people had no belief in the Lord God.*

6:11–13. The cause and effect of the flood are detailed in the two important words, **corrupt** and **violence**. In contrast to Noah who "walked with God" (v. 9), the rest of society was **corrupt** and **full of violence**. These words show the outworking of the fact that "every inclination of the thoughts of his [man's] heart was only evil all the time" (Gen. 6:5). Man does not earn God's grace, but he is to respond to it appropriately. The vices of violence and corruption are natural consequences of sinful mankind. Similar vices permeate our society today. Their presence shows a lack of godliness in much of civilization.

This corruption had affected **the earth**, a comprehensive term for the entire world of nature as distinct from man. It will be defined in verse 13 as that which was **filled with violence because of them** (i.e., corrupt people), and that God was **surely going to destroy both them** (i.e., corrupt people) **and the earth**. The flood would not only wipe out corrupt mankind but also the rest of nature over which mankind was to rule (Gen. 1:28). Nature is intimately connected with mankind. This has been seen in the previous Scriptures. Adam was made from the earth (Gen. 2:7), the earth was cursed because of Adam's sin (Gen. 3:17–19), and the blood of Abel cried out from the earth (Gen. 4:10). Now the depravity of mankind had so corrupted the earth that it must also be destroyed.

God's decision as announced to Noah was **to put an end to all people, for the earth is filled with violence because of them**. While the virtues of God's patience and long-suffering are not mentioned here, these can be assumed from the context and from other Scriptures. Was this flood to be local, regional, limited, or was it to be universal? All mankind that was corrupt and all the earth in which he lived was destined for destruction (see "Deeper Discoveries").

C Instructions to Noah (6:14–21)

SUPPORTING IDEA: *God is specific in his instructions about both the ark and the coming watery judgment.*

6:14–16. The term **ark** is used elsewhere in the Scriptures only in reference to the papyrus basket that saved Moses from the waters of the Nile River (Exod. 2:3,5). A different Hebrew word is used for the ark of the covenant in the tabernacle. The construction details include both material and dimensions. The material required was **cypress wood** and **pitch** that would be used to **coat it . . . inside and out**. Cypress wood is used for a Hebrew term whose meaning is uncertain. Both the KJV and the NASB use the term "gopher wood."

Pitch refers to some substance that would make the ark waterproof. Since Mesopotamia today is home to a vast supply of the world's oil, it is possible that in the preflood era, if this oil reserve was already in place, some of this underground reserve might have made its way to the earth's surface. It is interesting that Moses' mother made his basket watertight by using similar material (Exod. 2:3), although the word for "pitch" in that event is a different Hebrew word.

The dimensions of the ark are given in the Hebrew in cubits—300 cubits long by 50 cubits wide by 30 cubits high. A cubit is usually thought to be about 18 inches or 0.5 meter (see "Deeper Discoveries"). So the ark was to be **450 feet long, 75 feet wide and 45 feet high**. It was to be made with a roof and finished to **within 18 inches of the top**. This space between the ark sides and the roof must have consisted of a series of small windowlike openings that Noah would use to release and recapture birds (see Gen. 8:6). The function of this space is never specified, but it might have been used to admit light and circulate air. The ark was also to be made with three decks and a door in its side.

The actual shape of the ark is not cited, but it may have been much like a rectangular box. According to Ramm, such a boat uses space efficiently, could float comfortably, and not capsize easily (Ramm, 230–31). Modern ocean liners and military aircraft carriers have a similar shape.

The specific, propositional revelation of the ark is a forerunner of what was given to Moses about the tabernacle (Exod. 25:9–40). In both cases it was a first-time construction project that demanded exact conformity to the divine commands.

6:17–21. After declaring his intention to destroy the world by means of a watery flood, God informed Noah of his intention to enter into a special relationship with Noah and his family. Noah would be like Adam in some respects. All humans trace their lineage to him.

In this context, the word **covenant** (Heb. *berith*) is used for the first time in Scripture (see "Deeper Discoveries"). Noah would understand the features of this covenant after the flood receded (Gen. 9:8–17). Since Noah had three sons, a total of eight persons would be saved by the ark. First Peter 3:20 also gives this detail: "In it [the ark] only a few people, eight in all, were saved through water." Some baptismal fonts are eight-sided as a reminder of this fact.

Noah's sons are known by their names, but the names of the wives are not recorded. This should not cause undue concern, although in our contemporary society such an oversight is considered thoughtless. In the biblical record an untold number of details are left out. The names of the men are given because the genealogical record goes through the male in keeping with his position from Eden. This does not teach any lesser value for the mothers who bore these sons but does suggest the theological truth that Adam was the head of the human race.

The covenant was made with Noah and his family. But God commanded that Noah **bring into the ark two of all living creatures, male and female, to keep them alive with you.** After the flood the covenant would also be made with "every living creature that was with you" (Gen. 9:10). These were ones over whom mankind was to have dominion and for whom mankind was to care (Gen. 1:28). The number of species of animals alive at that time is not known, but it could not be less than the number alive today and those known to have succumbed to extinction (see "Deeper Discoveries"). Later this command will be expanded to require that certain clean animals and birds be taken by seven or seven pairs (Gen. 7:2).

Ⓓ Noah's Obedience (6:22–7:9)

> **SUPPORTING IDEA:** *Noah responds to the word of the Lord with obedience.*

6:22. Noah's response to God's word is simply noted as **Noah did everything just as God commanded him.** What wonderful words to read in the context of the actions of his contemporary culture! Godly obedience is simple but profound. This concept of obedience will be seen again and again in the flood narrative (e.g., Gen. 7:5,7,9).

7:1–9. These words appear to come to Noah once he had completed the ark. God reminded Noah to **go into the ark, you and your whole family** (cp. Gen. 6:18), and then God gave his commands about the animals. No longer was it merely "two of all living creatures, male and female" (cp. Gen. 6:19), but now Noah was to take **seven of every kind of clean animal, a male and its mate, and two of every kind of unclean animal, a male and its mate, and also seven of every kind of bird, male and female.** The introduction of more than two of each kind of clean animal and bird (apparently the fish were not destroyed since they did not live on the land with mankind) is accompanied by the purpose statement, **to keep their various kinds alive.**

The term **seven** may infer "seven pairs." For the first time in Scripture, the terms **clean** and **unclean** are used. These terms will become common especially in reference to foods and to acceptable and unacceptable sacrifices (cp. Lev. 10–11). In Genesis 8:20 these terms are used in reference to the initial postflood sacrifices of Noah. If clean animals were to be used immediately in the postflood sacrificial system, more than a single pair would need to be preserved from the flood.

Noah was given a seven-day advance notice of the start of the flood as well as additional details such as the coming of **rain on the earth** and the fact that this rain would last **forty days and forty nights**. This mention of rain is significant since in the garden of Eden there was a river to provide water (Gen. 2:10). The expression in Genesis 2:5, "for the LORD God had not sent rain on the earth . . . but streams came up from the earth and watered the whole surface of the ground," is contained in the passage which is describing the earth in its pre-Adamic state.

It may imply that rain began once Adam was created. But it is often taken as suggesting that before the flood no rain fell from the sky. If the latter is the case, then this announcement of rain introduced a new phenomenon which Noah had not yet experienced but would need to believe by faith.

The period of **forty days and forty nights** introduces the reader to a length of time that will come to characterize a number of critical periods in history (e.g., time of testing for Christ). This lengthy period was given to Noah to assure him that God would do a thorough job of flooding the earth.

Some final details are stated before the flood event begins. First, Noah was six hundred years old when the flood came. This seems to indicate he had up to one hundred years to build the ark. Second, the ark was clearly designated as the means **to escape the waters of the flood**. Obviously, no other means was available. The ark is presented as the only, God-designed, God-sanctioned means of deliverance. Third, the animals **came to Noah and entered the ark**. Whether this was a miraculous gathering of animals is not clear. But before the flood the animals may have been more obedient to the voice of a man than afterwards when they would be hunted for food.

⒠ The Flood (7:10–24)

> **SUPPORTING IDEA:** *God brings about the promised destruction of the earth by water.*

7:10–12. Specific temporal designations for the preflood inhabitation of the ark (**seven days**), for the initiation of the flood (**in the six hundredth year of Noah's life, on the seventeenth day of the second month**) as well as specific details about the source of the flood waters (**springs of the great deep burst forth, and the floodgates of the heavens were opened**) are given. These facts demonstrate the literalness of the flood. They also allow us to determine the exact duration of the flood.

7:13–16. These verses serve as a flashback to verse 7 and Noah's entrance into the ark. The fact that animals **came to Noah and entered the ark** is repeated. This flashback contains one unusual piece of reassuring information: **Then the LORD shut him in**. Noah did not make the decision about the means of deliverance, and neither did he make the decision about when the provision would no longer be available. God himself shut the door to signify that the days of grace (Gen. 6:3) were over.

7:17–24. The rain lasted for forty days. By the end of this time, the entire earth including **all the high mountains under the entire heavens** were covered **to a depth of more than twenty feet**. This demonstrates that no living creature could possibly survive by escape to a high place. But not only was everything covered by water; this water remained in place for **a hundred and fifty days**. The implication of this is that no living creature, even clinging to a floating piece of debris or existing in some air pocket on earth, could live through such a deluge.

Only Noah was left, and those with him in the ark. This is both reassuring and heartbreaking. All the rest of humanity perished, not for lack of a means of deliverance but because of their unwillingness to believe God's word. "He [Christ] was put to death in the body but made alive by the Spirit, through whom also he went and preached to the spirits in prison who disobeyed long ago when God waited patiently in the days of Noah while the ark was being built" (1 Pet. 3:18b–20a). While there are a number of interpretations of these verses, it is possible to understand that the people of Noah's day were warned by God through Noah. Even without this Scripture, surely Noah's example and attestation of God's revelation to him would have been a significant testimony to the people of his day.

MAIN IDEA REVIEW: *Godly Noah acted in faith in the midst of a faithless, ungodly society.*

III. CONCLUSION

Does Your Faith Produce an Umbrella?

A drought threatened crops in a village in Crete. The priest told his flock: "There isn't anything that will save us, except a special litany for rain. Go to your homes, fast during the week, believe, and come on Sunday for the litany of rain." The villagers heard him, fasted during the week, and went to the church on Sunday morning. But as soon as the priest saw them, he was furious. He said, "Go away, I will not do the litany. You do not believe."

"But Father," they protested, "we fasted and we believe."

"Believe? And where are your umbrellas?"

Noah believed. He worked for years on an ark that God told him to build. Perhaps he had never experienced rain. Certainly he had never built a boat before that would be large enough to rescue a representative pair of all the birds and animals that lived on the earth. He didn't know the answer to most questions he had when he started. What he did know was what God told him to do, and he believed. He believed in the midst of a faithless, godless society—and he was saved!

PRINCIPLES

- Impending doom can be avoided by responding positively to God's plan of deliverance.
- All humanity lives in a moral universe under a moral God who will respond to immorality at his chosen time.
- The means of deliverance, as well as the length of the days of grace that are part of God's patience, are decided by God and God alone.
- Peter reminds us in his epistle that God's judgment will come because it has been promised. God's "delays" are his patience at work giving time for repentance.
- In Scripture it is generally a minority that responds positively to God's revelation.

APPLICATIONS

- Don't count on the majority being right. Always seek to be part of the minority who respond in faith and obedience to God's voice.
- Obedience is required, heroism is optional. Just obey God's commands, whether you feel like it or not.
- Take advantage of God's deliverance from sin through the means of Christ while there is still time.

IV. LIFE APPLICATION

Persevering Faith for the Family

On June 4, 1940, Sir Winston Churchill delivered a speech to the British House of Commons that has been titled "We Shall Fight on the Beaches." At the time of this speech, the British had just evacuated most of the British forces that were at the Dunkirk bridgehead. But Churchill, seeking to check the mood of national euphoria and relief at the unexpected deliverance and wanting to make a clear appeal to the United States, delivered one of his most famous speeches:

> I have, myself, full confidence that if all do their duty, if nothing is neglected, and if the best arrangements are made, as they are being made, we shall prove ourselves once again able to defend our Island home, to ride out the storm of war, and to outlive the menace of tyranny, if necessary for years, if necessary alone. At any rate, that is what we are going to try to do. That is the resolve of His Majesty's Government—every man of them. That is the will of Parliament and

the nation. The British Empire and the French Republic, linked together in their cause and in their need, will defend to the death their native soil, aiding each other like good comrades to the utmost of their strength.

Even though large tracts of Europe and many old and famous States have fallen or may fall into the grip of the Gestapo and all the odious apparatus of Nazi rule, we shall not flag or fail. We shall go on to the end, we shall fight in France, we shall fight on the seas and oceans, we shall fight with growing confidence and growing strength in the air, we shall defend our Island, whatever the cost may be, we shall fight on the beaches, we shall fight on the landing grounds, we shall fight in the fields and in the streets, we shall fight in the hills; *we shall never surrender,* and even if, which I do not for a moment believe, this Island or a large part of it were subjugated and starving, then our Empire beyond the seas, armed and guarded by the British Fleet, would carry on the struggle, until, in God's good time, the New World, with all its power and might, steps forth to the rescue and the liberation of the old.

How could Noah have kept building an ark for perhaps as long as one hundred years? Did he need God to come down and reassure him over and over in order to keep on building? Hebrews 11:7 declares, "By faith Noah, when warned about things not yet seen, in holy fear built an ark to save his family."

Believers today need a little more of this type of faith and a little more of this type of fear and a little more of this type of familial motivation. Noah's faith was a faith in the promises of God. The Lord had declared to him what was coming, and Noah believed God. He had a holy fear that developed a motivation to protect his family, and *he never surrendered* this belief. He determined to believe God and live out that belief in the coming decades so he and his family would experience God's deliverance.

V. PRAYER

God, give us the faith to believe and the courage and dedication to live out our faith in the midst of a corrupt and violent world. Amen.

VI. DEEPER DISCOVERIES

A. Historicity of the Flood

The historicity of Noah's flood can be answered in four ways. First, the evidence from Genesis presents the flood as a historical event in space and time by its many references to people, events, and the specifics of timing and construction. From all appearances the author Moses desired those reading this narrative to believe it as history.

Second, other Scriptures refer to this event. The Lord asserts in Isaiah 54:9, "To me this is like the days of Noah, when I swore that the waters of Noah would never again cover the earth." The New Testament also regards this event as historical (see Matt. 24:36–39; Heb. 11:7; 1 Pet. 3:20; 2 Pet. 2:5).

Third, scientists often acknowledge a historical flood based on geological flood evidence, although there is debate over whether this evidence should be equated with the flood of Noah's time.

Fourth, anthropologists talk of the flood sagas that are found almost universally in various cultures of the world. Among common myths or stories, none is so widespread as a story about a flood and a boat. The figure of over 270 flood stories from various people groups has been suggested. The Babylonians had in their Gilgamesh Epic a man comparable to Noah named Utnapishtim, the Sumerians had Ziusidru, the Greeks had Deucalion, the Hindus had Manu, the Chinese had Fah-he, the Hawaiians had Nu-u, the Mexican Indians had Tezpi, the Algonquins had Manabozho. The one significant difference between the Genesis account and all the other flood sagas is that only the biblical record indicates the exact time and duration and other details of the flood. These details suggest an account that goes back to Noah himself.

B. Universal or Limited Nature of the Flood

Phrases such as "mankind," "all the people of earth," "every living creature," "all the high mountains," "everything on dry land that had the breath of life in its nostrils," "every living thing on the face of the earth," and "all life" are found in Genesis 6:7,12–13; 7:4,19,21–23; 8:21; 9:11,15.

A decision on whether the flood was local (limited to Mesopotamian) as opposed to worldwide must be based on the clear intent of the passage. But the universal interpretation is further substantiated by the laws of physics. Water seeks its own level. So if "all the high mountains under the entire heavens were covered" (Gen. 7:19) for a period of almost a year, then the whole world would have been under water. Since the earth is covered on approximately five-sixths of its surface by water, and since the oceans are deeper than the highest mountains, there is plenty of water to cover the surface of the earth if in the preflood era the oceans were not as deep and the mountains not as high.

The apostle Peter spoke of the universal nature of the flood when he declared, "By these waters also the world of that time was deluged and destroyed." Peter was speaking of a universal judgment on the day of the Lord.

There seems to be no room within the biblical account to accommodate a local flood if words are taken at face value, although this is the most common modern scientific opinion when faced with the possibility of contemplating an ancient universal flood. In fact, there are many conservative scholars who interpret the flood as a Mesopotamian regional flood.

C. Length of a Cubit

An inscription found in 1880 near the mouth of the Siloam tunnel built by King Hezekiah (2 Chr. 32:30) describes the building feat and notes the length as 1,200 cubits long. Since the tunnel measures 1,777 feet, the resulting calculation puts a cubit at approximately 18 inches.

The dimensions of the ark used in this commentary are based upon this calculation with the assumption that a cubit remained a standard, unchanged measurement.

Gleason Archer apparently assumes that a cubit is the measurement between the elbow and the tip of the figure. Noting that men were probably bigger in Noah's day than they were after the flood (cp. Gen. 6:4), he suggests that a cubit measured twenty-four inches (Archer, 84). If this measurement is correct, then the carrying capacity of the ark suggested below would be almost doubled to 3.6 million cubic feet.

D. The Holding Capacity of the Ark

The Ryrie Study Bible contains the following interesting information about the ark. Based on the dimensions of 450 feet by 75 feet by 45 feet it is estimated: "[The ark would have] a displacement of about 20,000 tons and gross tonnage of about 14,000 tons. Its carrying capacity equaled that of 522 standard railroad stock cars (each of which can hold 240 sheep). Only 188 cars would be required to hold 45,000 sheep-sized animals, leaving three trains of 104 cars each for food, Noah's family, and 'range' for the animals. Today it is estimated that there are 17,600 species of animals, making 45,000 a likely approximation of the number Noah might have taken into the ark" (*The Ryrie Study Bible*, note on Gen. 6:15).

Gleason Archer suggests a different number of species. His figures are that at the present time there are approximately 2,405 main species of animals, including only 290 species of land animals larger than a sheep, 757 more ranging in size from sheep to rats, and 1,358 species smaller than rats (Archer, 84). What Archer refers to as "main species" may be better identified as "genus," which is a category or class of animals marked by certain common characteristics, usually comprising several species.

Apparently the average size of a sheep has been chosen to take into account the largest animals (elephants, giraffes) and also the smallest (mice, insects). It may be that God brought some of the younger and smaller members of each species into the ark. Many of the smaller animals could have lived among the larger without conflict in the almost 101,250 square feet and 1,518,750 cubic feet of space. It is possible the animals existed peacefully with one another before the flood and would not need to have been separated on the ark.

In terms of the amount of food needed, it is also possible that God caused many of the animals to go into a deep sleep or hibernation by using the sudden lack of light and cool temperature. All of this is only speculation, but it does give a possible scenario.

E. Concept of "Covenant"

In the Ancient Near East there were two basic types of covenants or agreements that could be made. First, the parity covenant was an agreement between equals. Examples of this type can be found in Genesis 21:22–32 (Abraham and Abimelech), Genesis 26:26–33 (Isaac and Abimelech), and Genesis 31:44–54 (Jacob and Laban).

Second, the suzerainty covenant was an agreement made between a superior (often a king) and an inferior (vassal). Examples found in the Old Testament include the Abrahamic covenant in Genesis 15:18 (God and Abraham), and the Mosaic covenant in Exodus 19 (God and the nation of Israel). The covenant made with Noah in Genesis 9 but first referred to in Genesis 6:17 is obviously of the suzerainty-vassal form.

VII. TEACHING OUTLINE

A. INTRODUCTION

1. Lead Story: Excuses
2. Context: The flood narrative comes right after the material on the mixed marriages between the "sons of God" and the "daughters of men" and the resulting ungodly society.
3. Transition: Early in the instructions to Noah, there is a divine promise of a covenant that God would make with Noah. This covenant, known as the Noahic covenant, will be made after the flood has receded from the earth and Noah has debarked from his floating home.

B. COMMENTARY

1. The Man Noah (6:9–10)
2. Reasons for the Flood (6:11–13)
3. Instructions to Noah (6:14–21)
4. Noah's Obedience (6:22–7:9)
5. The Flood (7:10–24)

C. CONCLUSION: PERSEVERING FAITH FOR THE FAMILY

VIII. ISSUES FOR DISCUSSION

1. The close connection between man's corruption and the earth is specifically noted in the flood narrative. What is the connection between humankind and the earth, according to the Scriptures?
2. How would you respond if someone suggested that the flood narrative teaches that children can be saved on the basis of a father's faith?
3. What is the difference between faith and mere presumption?

Genesis 8:1–9:29

Rainbow and Peace

"*M*ajorities mean nothing; during the Flood, only one man knew enough to get out of the rain."

U n k n o w n

Genesis 8:1–9:29

I N   A   N U T S H E L L

*T*hese two chapters present the culmination of the flood and the new agreement that God makes with Noah as head of the human race.

Rainbow and Peace

I. INTRODUCTION

All I Really Need to Know I Learned from Noah's Ark

*O*n my office door I recently placed a cartoon drawing of Noah's ark with the following statements printed underneath:

- Don't miss the boat.

- Don't forget that we're all in the same boat.

- Plan ahead. It wasn't raining when Noah built the ark.

- Stay fit. When you're six hundred years old, someone might ask you to do something REALLY big.

- Don't listen to critics; just get on with what has to be done.

- Build your future on high ground.

- For safety's sake, travel in pairs.

- Two heads are better than one.

- Speed isn't always an advantage; the snails were on board with the cheetahs.

- When you're stressed, float a while.

- Remember that the ark was built by amateurs; the Titanic was built by professionals.

- Remember that woodpeckers inside are a larger threat than the storm outside.

- No matter the storm, when God is with you, there's a rainbow waiting.

While we may smile at these statements, what God apparently wanted Noah and his descendants to know isn't mentioned in this list. God spoke directly to Noah after he left the ark and told him exactly the conditions under which he was to live. Most Sunday school lessons never deal with any of these stipulations. So it is no wonder that Christian people know the sign of this covenant—the rainbow—but they don't know the content of the covenant.

II. COMMENTARY

Rainbow and Peace

> **MAIN IDEA:** *Mankind is given a new chance to live a life pleasing to God. But it is not long before the "cancer" of sin conquers man again.*

A Docking on Dry Land (8:1–14)

> **SUPPORTING IDEA:** *God intervenes in the watery judgment and acts with favor toward Noah.*

8:1a. But God remembered Noah is how the eighth chapter of Genesis begins. Allen Ross developed the entire flood narrative in a chiastic (sometimes called inversion parallelism) structure (Ross, 191). In his arrangement the climax of the entire narrative comes at Genesis 8:1a: **But God remembered Noah**. God, of course, had not forgotten Noah! To "remember," as it is used in Scripture, is not merely to recall to mind. It is to express concern and care for someone. For example, in the postexilic period Nehemiah desired that God "remember" him and act "with favor" (Neh. 5:19; 13:31). In Genesis 19:29 God "remembered Abraham, and he brought Lot out of the catastrophe." In Genesis 30:22 God "remembered Rachel; he listened to her and opened her womb." God is gracious when he remembers his people. So again the grace of God is emphasized when the waters begin to recede to allow the earth to dry out so mankind might live once again on the land.

God not only remembered Noah; he also remembered **all the wild animals and the livestock that were with him in the ark**. The living creatures with Noah were also the objects of God's favor.

8:1b–5. The receding of the waters occurred for two reasons. First, **the springs of the deep and the floodgates of the heavens had been closed, and the rain had stopped falling from the sky**. This had actually happened after the first forty days and nights (Gen. 7:17), but the resulting flood remained on the earth for 150 days. Now God **sent a wind over the earth, and the waters receded**. This wind could have caused some evaporation but not enough to cause mountains to appear on the earth. Somehow God caused pressure from water to buckle the crust of the earth to create the large oceans we have today. Apparently he did so by causing a huge tidal surge created by a divine wind.

As the waters pressed down the crust of the earth in other places, the crust must have thrust upwards to create the mountains we have today. This entire process took another 150 days. So **at the end of the hundred and fifty days the water had gone down, and on the seventeenth day of the seventh** month the ark came to rest on the mountains of Ararat. The mountain that today is known as Mt. Ararat (over 17,000 feet above sea level) lies on the north-central border of modern Turkey and Soviet Armenia.

8:6–14. This extensive narrative in Genesis describes the method Noah used to ascertain that the waters had receded enough for his family to leave the ark. Forty days after "the tops of the mountains became visible," he sent out a raven. Today ravens are omnivorous, that is, they will eat anything edible (and many things that aren't). Their usual diet consists of insects, seeds, berries, carrion (the bodies of animals killed by creatures other than the raven), the eggs and young of other birds, and occasionally small mammals. When living near humans, ravens will also eat human garbage. The ravens of Noah's era were strictly vegetarian. But compared to the dove, the raven seemed to be willing to rest on wet surfaces.

The forty days that the raven remained outside the ark equals the time from when it was released until the time when the water **had dried up from the earth**. The phrase **it kept flying back and forth** should not be taken to mean continuous flight for forty days but a constant flying around the ark. In contrast, the dove which was released (probably seven days after the raven since for the second dove Noah **waited seven more days**) returned because **the dove could find no place to set its feet because there was water over all the surface of the earth**. The earth was still wet from the flood, although the waters were receding.

The second dove returned with **a freshly plucked olive leaf**. So **Noah knew that the water had receded from the earth** at least to the level where plants once grew and for a long enough duration that plants could begin to grow again. The modern symbol of peace, represented by a dove carrying an olive branch in its beak, has its origin here. The dove with the olive branch did not represent peace between any people but only that the earth was becoming a place where man could live once again.

The third dove never returned. This indicated that the earth was so dry that the bird could make a nest and find food.

B Leaving the Ark (8:15–19)

SUPPORTING IDEA: *God designed mankind and the animals to live on the dry land of the earth, so once again he provides that environment for them.*

8:15–19. The disembarkment occurred after Noah and the other inhabitants of the ark had been confined there for more than a year (Gen. 8:13). This disembarkment took place, not only because there was dry land available, but also because God commanded it: **Then God said to Noah, "Come out of the ark, you and your wife and your sons and their wives. Bring out every kind** of living creature . . . so they can multiply on the earth and be fruitful and increase in number upon it." This reiterates the creation mandate of Genesis 1:26–28. Obviously this is not the complete fulfillment of Genesis 6:18, "But I will establish my covenant with you," since the Adamic covenant had already been established with mankind.

[C] God's Covenant with Noah (8:20–9:17)

> **SUPPORTING IDEA:** *In response to Noah's worship and in ful-fillment of the Lord's declared purpose, God makes a covenant with Noah as head of the human race.*

8:20. Noah's act of worship in sacrificing burnt offerings using the **clean animals and clean birds** was probably done both as an act of gratitude and of anticipated covenant ceremony. The form and size of the **altar** is unknown since this is the first mention in Genesis of an altar. Later the Lord gave the nation Israel specific details about the form and size of an acceptable altar (Exod. 27:1–8; 38:1–7) as well as prohibitions about an altar (Exod. 20:24–26; Deut. 27:5–6). The purpose of the large number of **clean animals** and **birds** taken on the ark is made clear here. It was necessary that more than one pair of these particular animals and birds be preserved so sacrifice could be made after the flood.

8:21. The phrase **the LORD smelled the pleasing aroma** (or "smell of sat-isfaction") is a figurative way of saying that the Lord took notice of Noah's sacrifice. It was smoking and smelling like a backyard barbecue! Early on in my ministry I had a young person give a devotional to a small group. When she announced that her title was "Stink for God!" I was a bit apprehensive about what she would express as biblical truth. While the title was perhaps lacking in delicacy, she proceeded to challenge the group to live a life that God would take notice of because of our total commitment to him.

As a result of Noah's gratitude and sign of commitment, the Lord **said in his heart: "Never again will I curse the ground because of man, even though every inclination of his heart is evil from childhood. And never again will I destroy all living creatures, as I have done."** Not until Genesis 9:8–9 would God speak directly of establishing the covenant with Noah and his descendants. But the first pledge by God is made here. It deals with the promise not to curse the ground any further because of man's sinfulness.

The Hebrew verb for *curse* is different from the one used in Genesis 3:17 when the ground was originally cursed. This pledge can be taken in two pos-sible ways—that the ground would no longer be subject to continual cursing because of mankind's sin (as happened because of Cain's sin; Gen. 4:12), or that the ground would never again experience the type of cursing by water that had just occurred in the flood. The second explanation is in keeping with

Genesis 9:11b: "Never again will all life be cut off by the waters of a flood; never again will there be a flood to destroy the earth." This did not prevent God from disciplining mankind because of sinful actions (for example, scattering the nations as a result of the Tower of Babel; Gen. 11:8).

While many of the changes in nature after the flood are not stated, they include: length of life was decreased; oceans were more extensive and therefore habitable land was reduced; there was a greater variation in climate; the crust of the earth was now unstable and subject to seismic activity; hurricanes, tornadoes, and thunderstorms would now buffet the earth; and local floods and ocean surfs would also cause destruction. This curse upon the earth would be lifted in the future.

Romans 8:21 says, "The creation itself will be liberated from its bondage to decay and brought into the glorious freedom of the children of God." Isaiah 65:20 speaks of a time when a man dying "at a hundred will be thought a mere youth." When Christ returns and rules, the effect of sin on this world will be changed dramatically.

The reference to **childhood** in the clause **every inclination of his heart is evil from childhood,** emphasizes the fact that sin contaminates a person from his earliest conscious moments. Psalms 51:5; 58:3 indicate that sin is part of us from conception.

8:22. The pledge of no universal flood in the future is further developed in a passage that guarantees uninterrupted seasons: **As long as the earth endures, seedtime and harvest, cold and heat, summer and winter, day and night will never cease.**

The need for such a promise may result from the changes in climate that would now occur after the flood. Times and seasons were created by God in the beginning (Gen. 1:14), but the more drastic changes of cold and heat, summer and winter may be a new innovation. Now when it began to get colder and to rain, Noah's descendants were not to build an ark hurriedly. This promise would not prevent local floods.

Any drastic change in climate from preflood climatic conditions may be a reason why certain species like the dinosaur became extinct. Even today when a scarce animal's environment changes, the possibility of extinction exists.

9:1–3. The Noahic covenant was a reiteration of much of the original Adamic covenant but now with modifications caused by man's sin and the resulting judgments. One of the clearest aspects of the original covenants was the command to multiply. **Be fruitful and increase in number and fill the earth** is repeated from Genesis 1:28a. But God stopped before repeating his original command: "Subdue it. Rule over the fish of the sea and the birds of the air and over every living creature that moves on the ground" (Gen. 1:28b). Now **the fear and dread of you** [mankind] **will fall upon all the**

beasts of the earth and all the birds of the air, upon every creature that moves along the ground, and upon all the fish of the sea; they are given into your hands.

There was a significant change in the way animals would now respond to mankind. Before the flood the animals "came" to Noah (Gen. 7:9,15); now they would tend to flee from him. This was a means of survival for the animals since the Lord declared that everything that lives and moves will be food for you. Just as I gave you the green plants, I now give you everything. An animal diet would cause mankind to kill various creatures. To prevent the annihilation of many species, the Lord provided animals with a fear of mankind.

The declaration that the fear and dread of you will fall upon all beasts of the earth does not mean that pets and domesticated animals are a violation of God's revelation. Man has been able to overcome the natural fear of man by animals through a process of behavioral modification. The rare and surprised "wild" reaction by trained animals reminds us that animals have an innate fear of man.

9:4–6. The provision of animals for food is further evidence of the grace of God to mankind. Now that the seasons would involve the extremes of cold and heat, there would be a need in some cases to supplement the vegetarian diet with animal flesh. But even in this gracious provision was a prohibition that would test humanity's obedience: You must not eat meat that has its lifeblood still in it. Leviticus 17:14 emphasizes the connection between life and blood by declaring that "the life of every creature is its blood." Man might be tempted to increase the length or quality of his own life by drinking the "lifeblood" of another creature, but this was not God's design. It is interesting that many cultures throughout history have attempted this very thing. The opposite extreme are religious groups that refuse the intravenous taking of blood to save a life.

Life is a gift of God, and he is the great defender and preserver of life (Gen. 4:9–12). As such he has the right to put a value on life. His declaration is that whoever sheds the blood of man, by man shall his blood be shed. The introduction of capital punishment (both of humans as well as the destruction of an animal that takes man's life; Gen. 9:5b; Exod. 21:28–32) must be carefully observed.

Capital punishment introduces a measure of societal government since there must be an accounting for the loss of the life of a human. The resulting death, because it is done in response to a command of God, is considered the proper result, not a second murder. This is a divine command that was established before the Mosaic covenant was introduced to the nation of Israel (Exod. 21:12–14; Num. 35:16–32). This covenant with Noah was made with him as the new head of the human race. Unless God chose to change this requirement in a future covenant made with mankind, this should remain in effect for all people in all nations (cp. Rom. 13:1–4; 1 Pet. 2:13–14). Of course, Christians must submit to governmental laws. Individual believers have no right to take this judgment into their own hands if a properly recognized government refuses to enact such a punishment.

The reasons given for capital punishment are not merely to serve as a deterrent to others, or so that the criminal could not commit murder again, or that it is impossible to rehabilitate a murderer, but because **in the image of God has God made man**. Man has an innate nobility. To murder someone is to extinguish a revelation of God and to display contempt for God who has made mankind with the highest value in all of creation. The senseless killing of animals, while wrong, is not on the same scale as the murder of a human.

The murder of Abel by Cain did not result in capital punishment (Gen. 4:11–12) nor did Lamech's murder of an unnamed young man (Gen. 4:23). The reasons that God now required capital punishment to signify the value of human life seem to be twofold: First, it would help prevent the violence that existed before the flood. Second, the stigma against taking life would be blunted because of the killing of animals. Now that humans would hunt for food, the weapons used for killing would be available. God must ensure that humans will not take human life carelessly and thoughtlessly.

9:7. After the instructions about capital punishment, God repeated the creation mandate about procreation. Like the promise of childbirth given after the fall, this repetition serves as a declaration that life should go on. Humans, even with the possibility of giving birth to someone who could commit murder, must procreate and carry out the divine commands.

9:8–11. God declared that he would **establish my covenant with you and with your descendants after you and with every living creature**. This covenant was made between the sovereign Lord and Noah, his descendants, and every living creature on the earth. He promised again that a flood would never again destroy all life. Capital punishment would function to keep life on earth in check so such a drastic universal judgment would not be needed again.

9:12–17. The sign of the Noahic covenant was the rainbow that forms in the clouds, especially after a rain. This was probably a new phenomenon as a result of the changed atmospheric conditions. This sign would be observed by mankind, but it would be a sign that would bring remembrance of the covenant on God's part. This covenant is of the nature of an unconditional royal grant type (see "Deeper Discoveries") because the substance of the covenant was what God promised to do. Mankind has no responsibility in ensuring that God would not flood the earth again. The sign was for God since he had obligated himself and made the promise to man.

D Noah's Curse on His Grandson Canaan (9:18–29)

> **SUPPORTING IDEA:** *Canaan, the son of Ham, will be cursed with slavery because of the disrespect shown by Ham to his father Noah.*

9:18–19. The material in verse 18 is similar to the material in Genesis 5:32; 6:10 except that now we learn that **Ham was the father of Canaan.** This is done in preparation for the following narrative. The description given in verse 19 anticipates Genesis 10–11.

9:20–24. Just as Adam's son Cain violated God's moral law and murdered his brother Abel, so now Noah's son Ham violated God's moral law and sinned against his father. The nature of the crime remains under considerable debate. It is clear that Noah got drunk. Verse 21 contains the first use of the Hebrew word for **wine.** Some interpreters suggest that Noah may not have been aware of fermentation and the effects of alcohol. But the reference in Matthew 24:38 to "eating and drinking" may imply that alcoholic drink was available before the flood and that Noah would have known the effects of drinking. Certainly, fermentation could take place even if climatic conditions were somewhat different before the flood.

While Noah's actions may have been wrong or at least unwise, this is the only negative event in Genesis 3–11 in which God does not say a word. However, both here and in Genesis 19:30–38 where drunkenness again occurs, the results show the devastation that can result from drunkenness.

In addition to being drunk, Noah **lay uncovered inside his tent.** Since this is connected with his drinking, his nakedness may have occurred because Noah became warm from the alcohol or because he lost his inhibitions from being drunk. The shame of nakedness has already been recorded in the case of Adam and Eve. But **Ham, the father of Canaan, saw his father's nakedness and told his two brothers outside.** In contrast to Ham's actions, Shem and Japheth **took a garment and laid it across their shoulders; then they walked in backward and covered their father's nakedness. Their faces were turned the other way so that they would not see their father's nakedness.**

There are at least six interpretations about the nature of this crime:

1. It was an act of incest between Ham and his mother. This is based on the later use of the phrase **father's nakedness** to refer to the mother as translated word for word in the NASB (e.g., Lev. 18:8). This interpretation sometimes suggests that Canaan was the result of this act of incest.

2. It was an act of homosexuality between Ham and his father. This is based on taking the phrase **what his youngest son had done to him** (Gen. 9:24) as referring to a physical act.
3. It was an act of trespassing by Ham into his father's tent.
4. It was an act of castration. This view is found in the *Talmud*, a Jewish collection of rabbinical law, law decisions, and comments on the Laws of Moses. It is seen as a power struggle in the family.
5. It was an act in which Ham attempted to achieve authority over his father by "blackmailing" him with his indecent exposure. Ham, in this view, desired to be head of the family.
6. It was a viewing (accidental or purposeful) in which Ham did not treat his father with respect because he spoke about his condition to his brothers.

The last interpretation seems the most natural, when all the circumstances are considered. Any improper action can be seen as an attempt to embarrass the father and as a result possibly to take leadership from the father. The actions of the brothers Shem and Japheth seem to contrast with the actions of Ham. Since they actually covered Noah's nakedness, Ham apparently saw and left his father in a compromising position and then gossiped about it. Since Canaan has been mentioned previously (Gen. 9:18,22) and Noah's curse on Canaan appears immediate, Canaan is best seen as living at the time of this incident.

9:25–27. Noah's reaction came in the form of a curse oracle: **Cursed be Canaan! The lowest of slaves will he be to his brothers**. This reaction was similar to the curse oracles of God after the sin of Adam and Eve in the Garden of Eden.

The question about why Canaan, probably Ham's youngest son (Gen. 10:6), was cursed instead of Ham who was Noah's youngest son (Gen. 9:24) has had many suggested answers, including the following:

1. Canaan was the result of an incestuous act, and therefore the judgment fell on him.
2. Canaan was present with his father when the act was committed (see Gen. 9:22 which notes that "Ham, the father of Canaan, saw his father's nakedness"). But this is an argument from silence except for this one brief comment that actually does not state that Canaan was present.
3. Canaan was punished for his father's sin, but this would not be allowed later in the law (e.g., Deut. 24:16; Ezek. 18:4; but see Exod. 34:7) except in the case of "those who hate me" (Exod. 20:5).
4. The name *Canaan* is used, but the text is actually speaking of Ham. But the curse would not fall on all Ham's descendants. There are

some, interpreters, however, who notice that Ham's descendants become dwellers in Africa and because of prejudice desire that all of Ham's descendants be made slaves.

5. Ham was actually the one being punished by having his youngest son Canaan bring shame to him just as he, the youngest son, brought shame to his father Noah. The reason the son can be cursed for the father is that Noah, by observation or revelation, knew that Canaan and his descendants would be even worse than Ham (Lev. 18:2–3), especially in sexual matters. The literary discoveries from the fifteenth century B.C. at Ras Shamra (ancient Ugarit) have revealed just how evil many Canaanite religious and social practices were. This may be the reason God lists sexual prohibitions (Lev. 18:6–30) immediately after stating, "You must not do as they do in the land of Canaan" (Lev. 18:2).

The judgment that Canaan would be **the lowest of slaves . . . to his brothers** is not evident early in the Scriptures. Joshua's subjection of the Gibeonites (Josh. 9:11,27), who were descendants of Canaan through the people called the Hivites (Gen. 10:17; Josh. 9:7), may be the first clear example (see also Josh. 16:10; Judg. 1:28,30,33,35; 1 Kgs. 9:20–21). But the entire conquest of Canaan can also be regarded in the light of the Canaanites exhibiting forced subjection to the descendants of Shem.

The biblical Canaanites became extinct (their last colony at Carthage in North Africa was destroyed by the Romans in 146 B.C.). Therefore, any attempt to apply this curse to so-called "Canaanites" today is unwarranted. Any attempt to place this curse on all of Ham's descendants, many of whom settled in Africa and became the majority of the black race, is also unwarranted.

But the curse oracle contains more than just the initial stanza that focuses on Canaan. Noah also said, **Blessed be the LORD, the God of Shem! May Canaan be the slave of Shem. May God extend the territory of Japheth, may Japheth live in the tents of Shem, and may Canaan be his slave.** The Lord is to be blessed because he is the God of Shem. Shem was given precedence over his nephew Canaan by the word of Noah, but this was apparently approved by the God whom Noah served. This reference to the Lord demonstrates that this was not a vengeful individual who was out of fellowship with God. Although this curse oracle came from the mouth of Noah, the implications are that God would stand behind Noah's words. For the first time God is a God of the individual.

The wish **may Japheth live in the tents of Shem** uses "Japheth" for the subject of the Hebrew verb that is third masculine singular, typically translated "may he live" (the NASB translates this clause "and let him dwell in the tents of Shem"). A second translation that this construction allows is "may God live in the tents of Shem" (Kaiser, 114). This fits the parallelism that can be seen in verses 26 and 27. Scripture does not develop the idea that Japheth lived in the area or dwellings of Shem, but it does develop the concept that Shem's line would be the chosen line through Abraham.

9:28–29. These verses have the same form as the genealogical material of Genesis 5. Noah was the tenth member of the genealogy of Seth. The report of his death brings the *toledot* of Noah (Gen. 6:9) to an end.

MAIN IDEA REVIEW: *Mankind is given a new chance to live a life pleasing to God. But it is not long before the "cancer" of sin conquers man again.*

III. CONCLUSION

Even a New Start Cannot Guarantee a Good Journey

God gives human society a chance at a new start by destroying all that was evil and corrupt and starting with a blameless, righteous man named Noah. But even Noah and his sons were descendants of Adam, who had sinned in the garden of Eden. They inherited the tendency to sin, and they chose to act on that tendency.

Noah sinned by getting drunk. Ham failed by disrespecting his father and then by gossiping. As a result of these sins, a portion of this new society would find itself on a bad journey.

PRINCIPLES

- The prohibition against eating blood has not been changed. While all meat contains some blood, the prohibition is against the eating of meat that has had its blood preserved for consumption through killing by strangulation or the direct drinking of blood. The symbol of blood not only represents life but the sacrifice of our Lord Jesus Christ (Matt. 26:28).
- God blesses those who act righteously, but he curses those who abandon moral restraint.
- Civil government is ordained by God to protect human life and dignity.
- God often takes his time in offering repentance as well as in preparing his people for a new opportunity.
- Respect for our parents is always appropriate, no matter how old they may be or how unwise they may have been in the past.

APPLICATIONS

- Give sacrifices of praise (Heb. 13:15), good works (Heb. 13:16), financial giving (Phil. 4:18), and commitment of your body (Rom. 12:1).
- Smell like a "pleasing aroma" to your Lord.
- Live a life of love, "just as Christ loved us and gave himself up for us as a fragrant offering and sacrifice to God" (Eph. 5:2).
- Don't gossip. If you see something you shouldn't have observed, respect the people involved enough not to say anything to anyone.

IV. LIFE APPLICATION

Protecting All Life

One thing that comes through clearly in the conclusion to the flood narrative is that God expects human beings to place the highest value on human life. He does this by requiring that the highest payment be made for it. God took the lives of thousands of preflood people because of their sin. God gave them life and he took it away because they were treating others with violence out of a corrupt heart. Mankind is required to demonstrate that life is made in the image of God.

In our world today many people see the financial or emotional well-being of a mother as more important than that of the life of an unborn child. Some people see the jobless or homeless as "throwaways."

Jesus called us to protect the inner life of fellow human beings. Many people do not recognize that the anger they show toward others is a form of murder. Jesus declared:

> You have heard that it was said to the people long ago, "Do not murder, and anyone who murders will be subject to judgment." But I tell you that anyone who is angry with his brother will be subject to judgment. . . . Therefore, if you are offering your gift at the altar and there remember that your brother has something against you, leave your gift there in front of the altar. First go and be reconciled to your brother; then come and offer your gift (Matt. 5:21–24).

It is easy to talk about capital punishment as a theory and regard serial murder as something equal to evil itself. But we should ask ourselves, "Have I given or taken life today in the way I have treated my brother?"

V. PRAYER

Lord, give us the desire to be life-givers rather than life-takers in how we treat others. Remind us that life is from you and that fellow humans bear your image. Amen.

VI. DEEPER DISCOVERIES

A. The Search for Noah's Ark (8:4)

Many Christians believe that Noah's ark has been found, or that it will be found, while others scoff at such an idea. It is important to keep the following facts and ideas in mind:

1. Noah's ark came to rest on the "mountains" (plural) of Ararat, not merely Mt. Ararat.

2. God never promised that the ark would be preserved or discovered. Although such a discovery would be a significant confirmation of the biblical story, believers should keep in mind that many unbelievers would remain unconvinced. In response to the Pharisees, Jesus said, "An evil and adulterous generation seeketh after a sign; and there shall no sign be given to it, but the sign of the prophet Jonas" (Matt. 12:39 KJV).

3. When the bronze snake that Moses had made as a means of deliverance (Num. 21:9) was preserved, it later became an object of worship and had to be destroyed (2 Kgs. 18:4). Could the same thing happen if we were to discover the ark?

B. Royal Grant Treaty or Covenant (9:16)

A royal grant was a covenant made between a superior (such as a king) and a loyal servant. It was usually made because of some longtime faithful or exceptional service. Such a grant was perpetual and unconditional, but the heirs of the person to whom it was originally given could benefit from it only as long as they continued in the type of faithful service that characterized their ancestor (see 1 Sam. 8:14; 22:7; 27:6; Esth. 8:1).

The Noahic covenant was made with "righteous" Noah and would continue with his descendants and every living creature on earth.

Other types of treaties or covenants found in Scripture are the parity covenant, a covenant between equals, and the suzerainty-vassal treaty, a conditional covenant that regulated the relationship between a king and a subject. This latter type of treaty regulated the relationship between the Lord and his people Israel.

VII. TEACHING OUTLINE

A. INTRODUCTION

1. Lead Story: All I Really Need to Know I Learned from Noah's Ark

2. Context: These chapters conclude the story of Noah's flood and the resulting covenant that God made. It prepares us for the question, How will God be the God of Shem? The next genealogy will lead to Abraham, the father of the nation Israel.

3. Transition: Genesis 9:19 records, "These were the three sons of Noah, and from them came the people who were scattered over the earth." Genesis 10–11 will describe the people and the scattering in greater detail.

B. COMMENTARY

1. Docking on Dry Land (8:1–14)

2. Leaving the Ark (8:15–19)

3. God's Covenant with Noah (8:20–9:17)

4. Noah's Curse on His Grandson Canaan (9:18–29)

C. CONCLUSION: PROTECTING ALL LIFE

VIII. ISSUES FOR DISCUSSION

1. Is there any biblical reason to insist on mankind, in the Christian era, returning to vegetarianism as he knew it before the flood?

2. How would you respond to someone who insisted that capital punishment is taking revenge and is therefore outlawed in both the Old Testament law and Christ's law of love?

3. It is clear that whatever Ham did, he did not respect his father. Why is respect for parents emphasized in the Scriptures? What results can be expected for obeying this command (Deut. 5:16; Col. 3:20; cp. 2 Tim. 3:2)?

Genesis 10:1–11:32

Generations and Language

I. INTRODUCTION
The Tower of Babel and New York's World Trade Center

II. COMMENTARY
A verse-by-verse explanation of these chapters.

III. CONCLUSION
Man's Choice Versus God's Choice

An overview of the principles and applications from these chapters.

IV. LIFE APPLICATION
Growing Proud in Our Achievements

Melding these chapters to life with God.

V. PRAYER
Tying these chapters to life with God.

VI. DEEPER DISCOVERIES
Historical, geographical, and grammatical enrichment of the commentary.

VII. TEACHING OUTLINE
Suggested step-by-step group study of these chapters.

VIII. ISSUES FOR DISCUSSION
Zeroing these chapters in on daily life.

Quote

"*T*he original language in which Adam in Paradise had named all the animals was, as it were, a great mirror in which the whole of nature was accurately reflected. But now God shattered this mirror, and each people retained only a fragment of it, the one a larger, the other a smaller piece, and now each people sees only a piece of the whole, but never the whole completely."

Erich Sauer

Genesis 10:1–11:32

IN A NUTSHELL

*T*he corporate rebellion of the human race expressed itself in their trying to make a name for themselves and so God disperses them. God continues to ensure godly offspring in Shem's line.

Generations and Language

I. INTRODUCTION

The Tower of Babel and New York's World Trade Center

*G*ary Gere, an actor and photographer, claims to have found a page from the Bible in the rubble of the World Trade Center in New York City. This particular page, from the Book of Genesis, describes a tower that reached into the heavens. "After more than 93 days of fire, a skinny little frail page from the Bible survived. I find it quite unbelievable," he told *New York Post* reporter Maria Alvarez, who reported this discovery in the February 11 edition of the newspaper.

When Gere found this portion of Scripture, the *New York Post* reported he said it was "a sign from God that he is still watching over us."

Michael Bellone, a safety director with the New York City Fire Department, was accompanying Gere when the page was found near the place where the south tower once stood. "It was amazing," Bellone said. "We can't rebuild fast enough. We can start all over again."

But is this the message that should be taken from the story of the Tower of Babel found in Genesis 11? Obviously, someone has not done his or her research on the context and meaning of this narrative. The World Trade Centers were not a Tower of Babel built in defiance of God. So any correspondence between the two is based solely on a physical similarity.

The discovery of a piece of Scripture is not necessarily a sign that God "is still watching over us." Nor should the fact that Scripture spoke of a tower be interpreted that God wants us to build a new tower. The World Trade Centers were destroyed by Islamic terrorists because of their hatred toward the United States of America and all that it stands for. Many human lives were lost in this terrible tragedy. In contrast, the Tower of Babel dispersion occurred because God himself was upset with mankind. So he scattered humans by confusing their language. It's a fascinating story that applies to our generation.

II. COMMENTARY

Generations and Language

MAIN IDEA: *God prevents humanity from organizing a widespread rebellion against him by confusing their language and scattering the people.*

A Japheth's Descendants (10:1–5)

SUPPORTING IDEA: *The descendants of Japheth, Noah's oldest son, are listed without comment since they are the ones with the least involvement with the rest of the Old Testament narrative.*

10:1. Japheth was the oldest son of Noah (Gen. 10:21), Shem was the middle child, and Ham was the youngest (Gen. 9:24). And yet the *toledoth* (or account of) is put in the introductory order of **Shem, Ham and Japheth**. But the author of Genesis will deal with their descendants in reverse order from this initial introduction: first Japheth, then Ham, and finally Shem, although Shem will be dealt with both before and after the Tower of Babel event. The latter order seems to be connected with the importance for the remainder of the Pentateuch. Japheth's descendants will be involved the least. Ham because of the curse on his son Canaan will be of greater significance. Finally, Shem through whom Abraham, Isaac, and Jacob will descend is of the most importance and is the line that will be extensively developed.

10:2–4. Fourteen nations are listed as coming from Japheth (his name means "enlargement"), seven from his sons, and another seven from his grandsons. Gomer (the later Cimmerians) and his three sons lived near the Black Sea. Magog was possibly the father of a Scythian people who lived in the Caucasus and adjacent regions southeast of the Black Sea. Madai was the father of the Medes, while Javan inhabited southern Greece and perhaps western Asia Minor. Tubal and Meshech along with Magog are mentioned in later Assyrian inscriptions. Their exact area of habitation is not certain, but Tubal was probably in Pontus and Meshech in the Moschian Mountains. Finally, Tiras was possibly the Thrace of a later era. Ezekiel 38:1–6 uses the names of Magog, Meshech, Tubal, and Gomer to indicate geographical area (cp. Ezek. 27:13; 32:26).

10:5. The descendants of Japheth spread across Eurasia from the Black Sea and the Caspian Sea to Spain. This area spreads north and west of the land later promised to Abraham and his descendants. The mention of **each with its own language** assumes chapter 11 and the Tower of Babel.

ⓑ Ham's Descendants (10:6–20)

SUPPORTING IDEA: *The descendants of Ham are listed in greater detail (thirty different nations), since many of them will be in conflict with God's chosen people throughout the Old Testament era.*

10:6. After listing Ham's four sons (**Cush, Mizraim, Put and Canaan**), each, except Put, receives a more detailed explanation in the following verses, listing various sons and certain characteristics of significant descendants. The general territory that Ham's descendants occupied was southwestern Asia and northeast Africa. This is determined by the following: the later identification of Cush with the upper Nile region, the meaning of Mizraim which is "two Egypts" (i.e., Upper and Lower Egypt), the identification of Put with the land which the ancient Egyptians called Punt (modern Somalia), and the well-known land of Canaan later called Palestine after the Philistines.

10:7. The sons of Cush included **Seba, Havilah, Sabtah, Raamah and Sabteca**. The sons of Raamah were **Sheba and Dedan**. Although Cush, as mentioned above, is identified with the upper Nile River region, his seven sons and grandsons mentioned in verse 7 are identified as locating in Arabia.

10:8–12. A man named Cush is given extensive treatment in verses 8–12 because of where his son built his kingdom that eventually included **Babylon . . . in Shinar**. Whether this Cush was actually Noah's son or another later descendant of the same name is debated. His son's name was **Nimrod**. The Scripture describes him as **a mighty warrior on the earth**. Many secular historians identify him as Sargon I, an early ruler of Akkad, with Nimrod being his Hebrew name. He is further depicted as **a mighty hunter before the LORD**.

The relevance of this expression is not clear. Nimrod was in the line of Ham, not Shem through whom Abram would descend. Perhaps this statement about the Lord was included to signify that not all of Ham's descendants would be under the curse of Canaan (Gen. 9:25), or it could signify that this was done in God's presence, as Genesis 11:5 points out.

Nimrod was a mighty ruler. This is indicated by the fact that the **first centers of his kingdom were Babylon, Erech, Akkad and Calneh, in Shinar** (that is, the land later known as Babylonia). Erech is the Hebrew name for the ancient city of Uruk (modern Warka). But this was not all of his rulership. **From that land he went to Assyria, where he built Nineveh, Rehoboth Ir, Calah and Resen, which is between Nineveh and Calah; that is the great city.** The last expression may refer to Calah but most likely to Nineveh as later depicted by Jonah (Jon. 1:2; 3:2; 4:11). Assyria was depicted by the prophet Micah in parallel to "the land of Nimrod" (Mic. 5:6). All of this depicts Nimrod as a mighty, motivated warrior who established his rulership over the region of Mesopotamia.

10:13–14. The descendants of Mizraim are identified with an important comment about the Casluhites. It was from the Casluhites that **the Philistines came**. This information will be important for future material in the Pentateuch.

10:15–19. The most important information in Ham's genealogy is revealed last. Canaan, of whom much has already been revealed in Genesis 9, is identified as **the father of Sidon his firstborn, and of the Hittites, Jebusites, Amorites, Girgashites, Hivites, Arkites, Sinites, Arvadites, Zemarites and Hamathites.** All of these various peoples were Canaanites. Most of them occupied small city-states in and around the land of Canaan (v. 19). The Jebusites founded Jebus, afterwards known as the city of Jerusalem (Josh. 15:63; Judg. 1:21). The nation of Israel would come into conflict with them as these Canaanite peoples resisted what was predicted by Noah about Canaan's descendants (Gen. 9:25–27).

10:20. This verse points out that all of these various peoples were descended from Ham but were divided by **clans and languages, in their territories and nations.** Again, like Genesis 10:5, this statement anticipates the Tower of Babel in Genesis 11.

Shem's Descendants Through Joktan (10:21–32)

SUPPORTING IDEA: *The descendants of Shem through Joktan are listed to introduce the ancestor of the Hebrews and to present the timing of the Tower of Babel event.*

10:21. As Moses, the author of Genesis, introduces the Shem genealogy, he does something quite different than he did with Japheth and Ham. First, he identifies Shem by the fact that he was not the firstborn (**whose older brother was Japheth**). This divine choosing of the blessed one (Gen. 9:26–27) from other than the firstborn will be repeated a number of times in Genesis. Second, an individual, distant descendant **Eber** is identified as being important before that individual is even listed in the genealogy. Previously Nimrod was noted to be significant, but he was not included in the title verse of Ham's genealogy.

Here it is recorded that **Shem was the ancestor of all the sons of Eber.** Eber is the origin of the Hebrew word for "Hebrew." It is interesting that the Ebla tablets, Sumerian texts from the mid-third millennium B.C., refer to a king named Ebrium, who ruled Ebla (northern Syria) for twenty-eight years. Some scholars have speculated that Ebrium and Eber were in fact the same person. Abraham is the first person in the Scriptures referred to as a "Hebrew" (Gen. 14:13).

10:22–24. The descendants of Shem would occupy the area north of the Persian Gulf. The five sons of Shem are listed as **Elam, Asshur, Arphaxad,**

Lud and Aram. The Elamites (from Elam) settled east of Mesopotamia. Asshur is related to the name *Assyria* and is probably the ancient name for the region of Assyria (cp. Gen. 2:14). Arphaxad is often thought to be a compound form of the Hebrew word for Chaldea, a region in southern Mesopotamia. Arphaxad is developed in this genealogy as well as the following one in Genesis 11:10–13. Lud is probably the Lydians of Asia Minor, while Aram is identified with the area northeast of the promised land, known today as Syria. The sons of Aram are listed in verse 23 (notice Uz, which will be referred to again in Job 1:1), while the son and grandson of Arphaxad are identified in verse 24. The descendants of Elam, Asshur, and Lud are not enumerated.

10:25–30. The division of the earth in the days of Peleg has been interpreted in at least a couple of different ways. Some interpreters want to take the word **earth** as referring to the physical planet. They see this division as pertaining to the dividing of the dry land into continents. In the commentary on Genesis 8–9, it was suggested that such a remaking of the earth probably occurred during the 150 days when the water was receding and the earth's crust was responding to the tremendous pressure of the water. The time of Peleg seems late to have such a significant division and movement of continents take place.

Most interpreters regard the division spoken of in verse 25 as the result of the scattering of nations because of the confusion of language as detailed in Genesis 11:9. The author follows the brother **Joktan** and will come back to follow the descendants of **Peleg** after the Tower of Babel incident.

10:31–32. The descendants of Shem were later called the "Semites," as the term "Shemites" was modified through use. The genealogy appears to be complete as Moses states, **these are the clans of Noah's sons, according to their lines of descent, within their nations. From these the nations spread out over the earth after the flood.** The significance of the phrase "in his time the earth was divided" (v. 25) will become more prominent in light of the statement of the next verse.

Ⓓ The Tower of Babel (11:1–9)

> **SUPPORTING IDEA:** *At Babel, for the first time, humanity introduces corporate idolatry in an attempt to build their own kingdom rather than God's kingdom.*

11:1–9. The incident of 11:1–9 occurs chronologically earlier than some of the material in chapter 10. This section on the Tower of Babel provides the reason for the scattering of the people and the necessity for the confusion of human language.

The structure of Genesis 11:1–9 is often referred to as an hourglass or *chiasm*. The narrative portions are found in verses 1–2 and 8–9, while the discourse material is in verses 3–4 and 6–7. Verse 5 acts as the transition between the first and second parts.

11:1–2. The survivors of the flood (the whole world) **had one language and a common speech**. This would change as a result of their rebellion and God's judgment. They **moved eastward** and **found a plain in Shinar and settled there**. Since there were mountains and then the Caspian Sea to the east of Ararat, humanity's movements must first have been south and then eastward as they settled in the Mesopotamia region. It is clear that humanity settled in a plain called Shinar. The city will be called Babel, which sounds very similar to the Hebrew word *Babylon*. Nimrod (Gen. 10:10) had one of the centers of his kingdom at Babylon. All these facts indicate that the area was somewhere in Mesopotamia, probably very close to the later city of Babylon.

11:3–4. A portion of humanity decided to build **a city, with a tower that reaches to the heavens**. Just how much of the population of the world was involved in this enterprise is not known. But the results would affect the entire world.

The purpose of this building was **so that we may make a name for ourselves and not be scattered over the face of the whole earth**. Genesis 11 does not teach, as many interpreters have suggested, that the builders were trying to build a tower that would reach to outer space or to God's dwelling place of heaven. Nor is the novel idea that the builder's hope was that the top of the tower would provide a place of refuge in the event of another flood. These explanation have no textual basis. Even if this had been their hope, the number who could have enjoyed a place of refuge would have been few. Besides, another ark would have been a more suitable haven.

The Scriptures teach that there were two purposes for their building. First, they were seeking immortality based on achievement. The **name** they desired probably refers to the reputation or fame they were seeking. Their action was a manifestation of their independence from God. The term *name* has been used this way in Genesis 6:4. Later God would promise Abram that "I will make your name great" (Gen. 12:2). By embarking on a massive building project, rebellious mankind hoped to create such a reputation that future generations would remain in the region and continue to honor the original builders. Humans want to make a difference in the world in some way so they will be remembered.

Second, they wanted to assure themselves of a strength that would come with unity. As a unified group they could be powerful—even without God's help. The tower was to prevent the goal that they should **be scattered over the face of the whole earth**. God wanted humanity to "be fruitful and increase in number; fill the earth and subdue it" (Gen. 1:28). The Lord repeated this to Noah and his family in Genesis 9:1. Theologically, he had caused Cain to be separated from godly mankind. Cain protested, "Today you are driving me from the land, and I will be hidden from your presence; I will be a restless wanderer on the earth" (Gen. 4:14). Now mankind was rebelling against God, but they were anxious to stay together.

They used bricks instead of stone and tar for mortar, because stone was scarce in Mesopotamia. Tar could have been available from the oil resources that have been discovered in this region. Using what was available, they sought to create a monument that would be majestic enough to keep mankind in the surrounding area.

11:5–9. The Lord is described as coming **down to see**. This is a figure of speech, known as "anthropomorphic," when God is decribed as having a human form or attributes that belong to humans. The presence of the Lord is said to be on earth in order to obtain information. Certain theologians insinuate that this was required because God is not an all-knowing God but must seek out information. But the God of creation is an eternal, all-powerful, all-knowing God. This figure of speech is better taken as informing the readers that the transcendent God is also the imminent God who responds to man's actions.

God's evaluation was that **if as one people speaking the same language they have begun to do this, then nothing they plan to do will be impossible for them**. The Lord recognized the powerful nature of peer pressure and the great appeal immortality has to mankind. Humans would be able to create a society in which they would control the community at large.

God's solution was to agree to **go down and confuse . . . the language of the whole world**. Although all of Noah's descendants were probably not gathered in this one area, the effect of God's judgment seems universal. Perhaps each division or clan descended from Noah's family began to speak a specific language among themselves. The effect, in order to accomplish the cessation of building, seems to be immediate rather than a gradual development of separate languages over hundreds or thousands of years. Someone has stated that the Tower of Babel became a din of iniquity.

It is obvious that the present world speaks different languages. Many rooms in the United Nations buildings in New York require earphones and translation booths so that modern, civilized mankind can have a measure of communication. SIL International (a service organization that works with people who speak the world's lesser-known languages) reports that their Ethnologue system of language identification has assigned a three-letter code to each of the more than seven thousand known living and recently extinct languages of the world. Their Web site (*www.ethnologue.com/codes/*) has a listing of the 6,800 main languages.

This gives powerful testimony to the incident at Babel. The fact that some modern languages are developments from other main languages is obvious.

However, the number of original languages must have been significant to develop the array of languages that have evolved in the modern world.

E Shem's Descendants Through Peleg (11:10–26)

SUPPORTING IDEA: *The descendants of Shem, this time through Peleg, are listed to introduce Abraham, the father of the Jewish nation.*

11:10–17. This genealogy follows the same line up to Peleg as the earlier one in Genesis 10:21–25, except that in addition to names it also gives ages similar to the genealogy of Genesis 5:3–32. Unlike Genesis 5, this genealogy omits the age at a man's death and the phrase "and then he died" and therefore emphasizes life and expansion rather than death. The age of man became progressively shorter in the postflood era up to the time of Abraham.

11:18–26. These verses list ten generations from Noah, through Shem, through Peleg to Lot, Abraham's nephew. The total time, if no gaps are permitted, is about 352 years from the flood to Abraham. Abraham's birth year is usually considered to be 2166 B.C., based on the coordination of biblical and extra-biblical events that can be backdated from a known time.

The phrase **Terah . . . became the father of Abram, Nahor and Haran** may not give the three sons in chronological order by age (cp. Noah's sons in Gen 9:24; 10:1,21). Haran died while their father Terah was still alive (Gen. 11:28). Again, the first-listed son, not necessarily the firstborn son, would become the most significant in the following narratives.

F Terah and His Son Abram (11:27–32)

SUPPORTING IDEA: *This recounting of Abram's family will introduce us to many characters who will play important roles in the coming narrative.*

11:27–32. The phrase **this is the account of Terah** is the sixth *toledot* of Genesis. It describes what became of Terah, especially through his son Abram. Each individual named becomes important in the succeeding stories, with the exception of Iscah, Abram's nephew through his brother Haran. Abram's name means "exalted father," but it would later be changed to Abraham, which means "father of a great number" (Gen. 17:5).

Besides the mention of the names of individuals, certain relationships are recorded that are necessary for understanding succeeding stories. Lot was Abram's nephew by means of Abram's now-dead brother Haran. Haran's daughter Milcah became the wife of her uncle, Abram's brother, Nahor. Abram married Sarai, whose name means "my princess." Later her name was changed to Sarah, which means "princess" (of the nation; Gen. 17:15–16).

In addition to names and relationships, certain historical facts are recorded that prove important later on. Haran **died in Ur of the Chaldeans, in the land of his birth.** Perhaps because of the death of Haran, his son Lot was sheltered first by his grandfather Terah (Gen. 11:31) and after his death by Abram (Gen. 12:5), while the daughter Milcah was married by her uncle Nahor (Gen. 11:29).

While it is impossible to be dogmatic about the location of **Ur of the Chaldeans,** it was likely a site on the Euphrates River in modern southern Iraq (some 220 miles southeast of Baghdad) rather than a location in northern Mesopotamia that is sometimes suggested. Ur was a place of idol worship in which Abram and his family participated (Josh. 24:2,14). Judging from archeological remains, this city's most prosperous and literate time was during Abraham's sojourn there. King Ur-Nammu, who may have lived at the same time as Abram, is famous for a law code.

It is also recorded that **Terah took his son Abram, his grandson Lot son of Haran, and his daughter-in-law Sarai . . . and together they set out from Ur of the Chaldeans to go to Canaan. But when they came to Haran, they settled there.** The apparent contradiction between Terah's leadership and Abram's response to the Lord's call (Gen. 12:1) will be dealt with in the next chapter. In English the term **Haran** is not only the name of Terah's now-dead son but the name of a place. But in Hebrew the initial letter of the two names is different, the first being a common *h* while the place starts with a letter with a *ch* sound.

Haran, the place, was located in northwestern Mesopotamia between the main Euphrates River and a tributary to the east known as the Habor River. It was a well-known caravan city in the nineteenth century B.C., but by the next century the Amorites ruled it. **Haran,** like **Ur,** was a place of idolatry, especially worship of the pagan moon god.

Also to be noted is the fact that **Sarai was barren; she had no children.** Because procreation was expected and even demanded in this society, the sterility of Sarai will be the focus of a couple of later narratives, especially in light of the promises Abram will receive about his descendants.

Finally, **Terah lived 205 years, and he died in Haran.** The next recorded event will be God's call of Abram and the promises from God to Abram. This chapter begins with man's attempt to unify humankind and ends with God's provision to unify all humans in blessing with Abraham's descendants.

MAIN IDEA REVIEW: *God prevents humanity from organizing a widespread rebellion against him by confusing their language and scattering the people.*

III. CONCLUSION

Man's Choice Versus God's Choice

Making a choice at a restaurant or clothing store is a time-consuming process for some people. It's hard sometimes to choose between a steak and a salad or between a red dress and a blue dress. But some choices should never be hard to make. In the Tower of Babel incident, we have seen human beings contending with God when they decide to make a name for themselves and resist the plan of God to spread out and fill the earth. Mankind makes an evil choice.

But throughout these chapters we have also seen portrayed a choosing of a different kind. Some genealogies have led from Adam to various persons whom we might have chosen to be "our man." Take Nimrod, for instance. He was a "mighty warrior on the earth." Or Canaan, who had eleven different nations originate from him. But the last genealogy presents a listing of names that led from Shem, son of Noah, to Abram. This anticipates the next chapter where God chooses a man named Abram to bring blessings to the world. In the midst of seeming endless birthing and listing of names, God demonstrated his sovereignty. He was making wise choices that resulted in blessings for his people.

PRINCIPLES

- Ungodly mankind will always seek to create immortality based on achievement rather than favor with God based on grace and obedience.
- The Lord God is gracious in his willingness to act and speak to a sinful society. Nations that defy God will be humbled.
- The world's languages serve as a reminder to believers that humankind has long sought to rebel against God and to create immortality for themselves.

APPLICATIONS

- Avoid being part of any group that has proud, egotistical plans.
- Create a legacy, not by egotistical human enterprises, but by faithfully obeying the Lord and laying up "treasures in heaven, where moth and rust do not destroy, and where thieves do not break in and steal" (Matt. 6:20).
- Beware of uniformity that doesn't allow for God's creativity in your life.

IV. LIFE APPLICATION

Growing Proud in Our Achievements

When Napoleon set out to conquer Russia at the head of the Grand Army of Europe, someone reminded him that "man proposes but God disposes." The conqueror of Europe replied, "I am he that both proposes and disposes." Napoleon would have fit right in as the leader of the people at Babel. But God has always resisted the proud and given grace to the humble.

C. S. Lewis wrote:

> The essential vice, the utmost evil, is Pride. Unchastity, greed, drunkenness, and all that are mere flea biters in comparison; it was through Pride that the devil became the devil: Pride leads to every other vice: It is the complete anti-God state of mind. . . . As long as you are proud you cannot know God. A proud man is always looking down on things and people: and, of course, as long as you are looking down, you cannot see something that is above you (Lewis, 94,96).

As we find ourselves in the midst of "the Great American dream," we must not develop the attitude of those whom God found so despicable at Babel. An ungodly, independent attitude, a rejection of God's mandates for humanity, a desire for earthly immortality—all these are signs that we are descendants of Babel. As we hear the languages of the world being spoken around us, we should be motivated to stay humble and true to the Lord.

V. PRAYER

Father, show us that our security is not in others or in our possessions or in our status. Remind us that the only true security is found in humble dependence and obedience to your word. Amen.

VI. DEEPER DISCOVERIES

A. Towers in Mesopotamia (11:4)

Towers in ancient Mesopotamia were known as ziggurats. They were often temple towers with a square base and sloping, stepped sides. The worship shrine was placed at the top. Archaeologists have discovered among the ruins of ancient Babylon a building 153 feet high with a 400-foot base. The construction material was dried brick, and there were seven stages to its structure. Some suggest that these seven stages correspond to the seven known planets at that time and that a lofty tower on top contained the signs of the Zodiac. This would suggest that such a tower was for astrology and perhaps the worship of the sky and stars.

VII. TEACHING OUTLINE

A. INTRODUCTION

1. Lead Story: The Tower of Babel and New York's World Trade Center
2. Context: These chapters explain in a broad outline what became of the descendants of Noah. They also explain why the world we live in today is so scattered in terms of geography and the ability to communicate.
3. Transition: The stage is now set for Abraham and for God to provide a descendant of Adam to do battle with evil and to "crush" the serpent's head.

B. COMMENTARY

1. Japheth's Descendants (10:1–5)
2. Ham's Descendants (10:6–20)
3. Shem's Descendants Through Joktan (10:21–32)
4. The Tower of Babel (11:1–9)
5. Shem's Descendants Through Peleg (11:10–26)
6. Terah and His Son Abram (11:27–32)

C. CONCLUSION: GROWING PROUD IN OUR ACHIEVEMENTS

VIII. ISSUES FOR DISCUSSION

1. When, where, and how do you think the distinct racial characteristics of modern humanity began?
2. Why aren't the Chinese, Japanese, or American Indians mentioned in the Scriptures?
3. Do you think the demand from some people for a universal modern language has implications for believers?

Genesis 12:1–13:18

Journeys of Faith

I. INTRODUCTION
The Bifocals of Faith

II. COMMENTARY
A verse-by-verse explanation of these chapters.

III. CONCLUSION
"Get Me Out of Here!"

An overview of the principles and applications from these chapters.

IV. LIFE APPLICATION
Trafalgar Square

Melding these chapters to life with God.

V. PRAYER
Tying these chapters to life with God.

VI. DEEPER DISCOVERIES
Historical, geographical, and grammatical enrichment of the commentary.

VII. TEACHING OUTLINE
Suggested step-by-step group study of these chapters.

VIII. ISSUES FOR DISCUSSION
Zeroing these chapters in on daily life.

Quote

"*O*ften God's will for our lives is revealed gradually, and the most difficult part of obedience can be waiting."

Bill T. Arnold

GEOGRAPHICAL PROFILE: HARAN

- Located in the Fertile Crescent 450 miles northeast of Beersheba
- Located on the banks of the Balih River, a tributary of the Euphrates
- Important Amorite center during the first half of the second millennium B.C.

GEOGRAPHICAL PROFILE: SHECHEM

- Place where God promised to give Abraham the land of Canaan for his descendants
- Temporary home of Abraham's grandson, Jacob
- Located near the modern city of Nablus in what was known later as Samaria

GEOGRAPHICAL PROFILE: NEGEV

- Desert land stretching south from Canaan
- Hebrew name means "the dry land"
- Generally located between the southern hills of Judea and Kadesh Barnea

GEOGRAPHICAL PROFILE: SODOM AND GOMORRAH

- Possibly located under what is now the southern part of the Dead Sea
- Both were among the ancient "cities of the plain"
- Cities of the plain were highly populated and economically prosperous at the time of Abraham

GEOGRAPHICAL PROFILE: ZOAR

- Only one of the five cities of the plain not destroyed in God's judgment on Sodom and Gomorrah
- Called *Bela* in Genesis 14:2
- Appears again in Deuteronomy 34:3, Isaiah 15:5, and Jeremiah 48:34
- Served as an important travel point between Elath and Jerusalem in the Middle Ages

PERSONAL PROFILE: SARAI

- Also appears as *Sara* and *Sarah* which mean "princess"
- Abraham's wife, first mentioned in Genesis 11:29
- Also Abraham's half sister (Gen. 20:12)
- Mentioned in the New Testament in Romans 4:19; 9:9; Galatians 4:21–5:1; Hebrews 11:11; 1 Peter 3:6

PERSONAL PROFILE: LOT

- Abraham's nephew (Gen. 11:31; 12:5)
- Man of questionable morality and integrity (Gen. 19:8–9,15–22)
- Identified by Peter as "a righteous man" (2 Pet. 2:7–8)

Genesis 12:1–13:18

I N   A   N U T S H E L L

*G*od reached down and plucked Abram out of his situation with only the promise that Abram would become a great nation. From this godly man we learn to "step out on faith."

Journeys of Faith

I. INTRODUCTION

The Bifocals of Faith

In his devotional booklet *On This Day*, Robert J. Morgan tells about one of the most beloved Senate chaplains in American history, Peter Marshall. A Scottish immigrant who came to the United States in 1927, Marshall served as a pastor first in Georgia and then at the New York Avenue Presbyterian Church in Washington. He was named senate chaplain on January 5, 1947, just nineteen years after he entered the country.

Shortly before he died, Marshall offered one of the greatest public prayers ever heard in this country. Those familiar with such matters call it "The Bifocals of Faith Prayer" that Marshall delivered before the Senate on November 24, 1947. Here is the text:

> God of our fathers and our God, give us the faith to believe in the ultimate triumph of righteousness, no matter how dark and uncertain are the skies of today.
>
> We pray for the bifocals of faith—that see the despair and the need of the hour but also see, further on, the patience of our God working out his plan in the world he has made.
>
> So help Your servants to interpret for our time the meaning of the motto inscribed on our coins. Make our faith honest by helping us this day to do one thing because Thou hast said, "Do it," or to abstain because Thou hast said, "Thou shalt not."
>
> How can we say we believe in Thee, or even want to believe in Thee, when we do not anything Thou doest tell us? May our faith be seen in our works. Through Jesus Christ our Lord. Amen.

Abram may have been the first man since Noah to wear the bifocals of faith. His story, which formally begins in chapter 12, actually starts at 11:27 where Moses writes briefly about Abram's family tree. He had been raised by his father Terah in Ur of the Chaldeans, in the land of his birth along with his two brothers Nahor and Haran (not to be confused with a town of identical spelling).

When Abram headed northwest out of Ur, he took along his wife Sarai and Nahor's son Lot. Probably Terah headed this expedition which settled at Haran in northern Syria where Terah lived to the age of 205. Arnold refers to Haran as "the patriotic homeland, the area where Abram's extended family originated," and notes that "Haran is probably the unknown city of Nahor, Laban, and Rebekah in Genesis 24" (Arnold, 78).

II. COMMENTARY

Journeys of Faith

> **MAIN IDEA:** *The key to describing the leadership of Abram is the word "faith." We see parallels between Abram and Moses, but surely the most distinctive is their commitment to the God who had called them.*

A Journey to Canaan (12:1–9)

> **SUPPORTING IDEA:** *Abram forsook everything he had known all his life to begin all over again in a new world, a challenge that probably required greater faith than that of Moses.*

12:1. The story of Abraham, recorded in Genesis 12–25, begins with the first three verses of chapter 12. We need to understand the geography involved in Abram's call. He was born in Ur about 2166 B.C. as the "Old Akkadian" age had just finished and the Sumerians, former rulers of the Mesopotamian world, had come back into power. This offers us one of those important historical pegs on which to hang our understanding of Abram's era since we can link him with the famous Hammurabi.

William Sanford LaSor fits Abraham into the old "Babylonian civilization at a time when it was at one of its peaks of cultural and political splendor. . . . Abraham came out of an area which for a long period of time—for four, five, or six hundred years—had had a high level of civilization with writing, with fine cities, with highly developed arts, beautiful gems and carvings and very well-established law codes and legal systems; *all* of these things were his, *plus* a highly developed religious system" (LaSor, 16–17).

This is quite different from our understanding of a desert nomad who made his way across the wide spaces of the Fertile Crescent. But we notice the past tense of the first verb in chapter 12, **the LORD had said**. According to Acts 7:2, Abram's call came while he was still in Mesopotamia, before the family trip to Haran. We must assume, therefore, that he always knew that the years he spent in that cradle of northern Syria were only a temporary stop in God's ultimate plan for his life.

We can see why God had to separate this new leader from his cultural surroundings. He had designed a new nation apart from the Sumerians and the Babylonians, opposed to their idol worship and cultural practices bathed in paganism. To make that possible, God selected one man and his family and took them away. Let's not forget that Abram was seventy-five years old when he responded to the call of God and left Haran.

12:2–3. Abram stepped out in faith as Hebrews 11:8 clearly reminds us. But when God calls us to personal sacrifice, he compensates by great promises of blessing. These verses offer God's promise to Abram which broadly unfolds into three general areas—land, descendants, and blessing. These two verses center on the blessing and offer a sevenfold promise. Although they are clear in the text, it may be worth listing them separately.

1. I will make you into a great nation.
2. I will bless you.
3. I will make your name great.
4. You will be a blessing.
5. I will bless those who bless you.
6. Whoever curses you I will curse.
7. All peoples on earth will be blessed through you.

This blessing theme began in Genesis 1:28, appeared again in 9:1, and we shall see it throughout the narrative of Abraham and his descendants (12:1–3; 13:15–16; 15:5,18; 17:6–8; 22:17–18; 25:11; 26:2–4; 27:27–29; 49:28). Peter used the seventh promise in his great sermon in Acts 3, and Paul wrote about it in Galatians 3. Griffith Thomas captured the principle in two brief sentences: "God never places burdens on His people's shoulders without giving them power to respond. God's biddings are His enablings" (Thomas, *Genesis*, 116).

12:4–5. We cannot tell from the text whether Lot continued with Abram because he sensed something of God's vision for the future or whether Abram had simply become a new father figure in the absence of Lot's father, Nahor. Possibly Lot was traveling on Abram's faith, a faith that responded immediately.

At seventy-five Abram was still a middle-aged man. Nor was he from a poor family, since we gather that this move involved a great deal of luggage (tents, garments, flocks, herds) and many people (children, relatives, slaves). The text shows us a pilgrim who refused to be bound to a comfortable lifestyle simply because he had **acquired** and **accumulated** the things of this world.

12:6–7. Abram headed east and south through Syria into Canaan. So Abram came south to Shechem and stopped at **the site of the great tree of Moreh**. Canaanite peoples worshiped a local deity at this famous shrine developed around a large tree mentioned again in Genesis 35:4 and Judges 9:6,37.

Geography is always important as we follow Abram. But in these verses we begin to sense the pagan opposition he would face. Maybe Abram felt a sense of his minority faith in alien surroundings, so God stated: **To your off-spring I will give this land**. This is the second of four references to the land in this chapter.

Here Abram built his first altar **to the Lord, who had appeared to him**. Here we have the first witness to the true God in the land of Canaan that was inhabited by the sons of Ham. We are not told how God appeared to Abram, but this was not an unusual experience for the patriarch of faith.

Notice that God gave the land not just to Abraham but to his **offspring**. Galatians 3:16 provides a fascinating commentary on this promise: "The promises were spoken to Abraham and to his seed. The Scripture does not say, 'and to seeds,' meaning many people, but 'and to your seed,' meaning one person, who is Christ." Obviously the gift included Isaac, Jacob, and thousands of others who possessed the land in Abraham's name and to a limited extent, still do. But the link between Abram and Christ forms the very foundation of the Jewish nation and its relationship to God.

12:8–9. Apparently Abram lived two other places in Canaan before his next international trip—first at Bethel and then down in the southern regions of the Negev. Bethel lay just north of Jerusalem, and it became a very important town in the history of Israel. In fact, only Jerusalem is mentioned more often than Bethel in the Old Testament. Continuing to establish God's claim on the land, Abram built a second altar in Shechem, a location that will reappear frequently throughout the Old Testament.

Why Canaan? LaSor offers a plausible answer.

> It was a land in association with the rest of the world of its day; it was the land bridge connecting the world of that day, namely: Asia Minor and the Hittite Empire, Mesopotamia and the Babylonian and Sumerian civilizations, and Egypt. To get from one to the other, you had to go through Canaan (LaSor, 23).

B Journey to Egypt (12:10–20)

SUPPORTING IDEA: *Even godly people are tempted to tell less than the truth. Such deceit is always dangerous.*

12:10–13. Why did Abram leave the land to which he had clearly been called by the Lord and head for Egypt? Since Moses mentions the famine twice, indicating the second time that **the famine was severe**, we conclude that Abram headed south and west, driven by the natural human instinct for survival. He went with God's permission rather than by the kind of direct call that took him to Canaan.

Commentators have offered numerous reasons why Abram took this trip: he was lonely in Canaan, he was depressed by Canaanite idolatry, his wife was barren. But the text only allows one—survival. The people of Canaan realized that Egypt was the breadbasket of the world at that time (see "Deeper Discoveries"). Griffith Thomas criticizes Abram for this decision and adds, "It would certainly seem that Abraham was now thinking solely of the land and its famine, and forgetting God and His promises" (Thomas, 119). Kidner adds, "His craven and tortuous calculations are doubly revealing, both of the natural character of this spiritual giant and of the sudden transition that can be made from the plane of faith to that of fear" (Kidner, 116).

But the text never faults Abraham for making the trip, only for lying about Sarai. Certainly this was a human scheme from the beginning, but *the sin lay in the deceit—not the journey.* Verse 10 tells us that Abram went to Egypt **to live there for a while**. He was not leaving the promised land for the glitter of the big city.

I prefer Allen Ross's handling of this passage:

> One cannot fault him [Abram] for this, except that there is no indication Abram was operating in faith. The Bedouin scheme he concocted was to speak a half-truth about his sister-wife. This was a subtle way to salve his own conscience. She was indeed his *sister* (actually a half-sister; cp. 20:12), so he conveyed to the Egyptians only what he wanted them to know. His motive was undoubtedly based on fratriarchical society laws (cp. Laban, 24:29–61). In enemy territory a husband could be killed for his wife. But if Abram were known as her brother, someone wanting her would have to make marriage arrangement with him, which would possibly give him time to react in his own interest (Ross, 49).

12:14–16. Abram had not counted on Sarai's being approached by the one man in Egypt who needed no special permission to take a woman. Abram's selfish concern of verse 13 ("so that I will be treated well") may have stuck in his throat, for Moses writes of Pharaoh, **he treated Abram well**. Wealth in the ancient Middle East was not measured in gold but in animals, slaves, and land.

12:17–20. Abram's sin brought God's judgment on Pharaoh's house. But in a true demonstration of biblical grace, God overcame Abram's sin, forgave his lie, and sent him back to the land. Egyptian ethics insisted on absolute truthfulness, so Abram's behavior offended his hosts. Abram probably learned two important spiritual lessons from this side trip to Egypt—*truth* and *trust*. The lesson of trust he exemplified throughout the rest of his life. The issue of truth, unfortunately, gave him difficulty on at least one other occasion.

C Journey to Bethel (13:1–7)

> **SUPPORTING IDEA:** *Prosperity can bring great peril to spiritual health, as in the case of Lot.*

13:1–2. Expelled from Egypt, Abram headed northeast back to the Negev **with his wife and everything he had.** These verses also tell us that Abram **had become very wealthy in livestock and in silver and gold.** Twice now Genesis has emphasized Abram's wealth (12:5,16). But both God and Abram knew that the Negev was only a temporary rest area on the interstate highway of his life.

13:3–4. As he had done earlier (12:8), Abram came to **Bethel** as if on a pilgrimage. **Bethel** was about sixty miles north of Beersheba and just ten miles north of Jerusalem. The area is known as Beitin or sometimes Beit El. During the days of the judges, the ark of the covenant rested here for a while (Judg. 20:26–28). **Bethel** literally means "house of God." In later years Hosea called it *Beth-aven,* referring to it as a house of wickedness.

13:5–7. We get a wider understanding of the wealth Abram's family had accumulated when we read, **the land could not support them while they stayed together, for their possessions were so great that they were not able to stay together.** How easy it would have been for Abram to say to his nephew, "Look, you are just along for the ride here. God gave me the vision and God gave me the land, so settle your people down or you are history." But Abram had matured a bit since his Egyptian fiasco. At the risk of losing what God had already promised him, he stood aside to allow Lot first choice.

In addition to the family squabble, Abram and Lot were surrounded by pagan peoples in the land. To the **Canaanites,** the text now adds the **Perizzites.** Some commentators suggest that the Perizzites were rural peoples while the Canaanites lived in the cities. We have no nonbiblical references to the Perizzites. There is some similarity between the name and the ancient word for people who live out in the open, that is, not inside a walled city. This tribal group appears again in Genesis 34:30 and throughout Exodus (3:8,17; 23:23; 33:2; 34:11), Deuteronomy, Joshua, and Judges.

D Journey to Hebron (13:8–18)

> **SUPPORTING IDEA:** *Trust in God's promises allows his people the goodness of generosity that brings blessing to the giver.*

13:8–9. With verse 5 a new section begins in the record of Abraham. Geography now gives way to adventure. We find the opening key in the words **part company,** a focus on separation that appears again in verses 11 and 14. John Sailhamer says:

Just as the first statement of the "promise" was preceded by Abraham's separation from among the nations (10:31) and his father's house (12:1), so the second statement of the "promise" is put in the context of Abraham's separation . . . from his closest kin, Lot (13:14). It is not without purpose that the final statement of the "promise" to Abraham comes immediately after he has demonstrated his willingness to be separated from his only son and heir, Isaac (22:15–18) (Sailhamer, 118).

No longer making his own choices without consulting God, Abram left this dispute in heaven's hands. Lot could have made a choice that moved Abram out of the promised land area. But if that should happen, the problem was God's.

13:10–11. Lot could not resist collecting the best for himself: **the whole plain of the Jordan**. This describes a southern point where the Jordan River runs into the Dead Sea and moves north about twenty-five miles. There lay the cities of the Canaanites.

What are we to make of the descriptive similes, **like the garden of the Lord, like the land of Egypt**? The Jordan River certainly cannot match the Nile as one of the great rivers of the world, but Abram and Lot had seen what abundant water could do for a land and its people. Here was a microcosmic opportunity to relive that opulence in Canaan.

13:12–13. Lot based his decision on appearances, and it turned out to be his undoing; Abram now had the entire **land**. We should not assume that Lot chose Sodom because of its wickedness; likely he had no idea of the behavior in those cities. The passage actually focuses on his shallow selfishness. Phillips offers an outline that helps us understand Lot's spiritual condition at this point in his life: He "was weak in his devotions, worldly in his desires, and wrong in his decisions" (Phillips, 123).

13:14–17. The Lord told Abram to **look north and south, east and west**. Lot missed the fact that when Abram looked east he actually saw what Lot had already chosen. This meant that Lot's temporary acquisition of the whole plain of Jordan had no impact on Abram's ultimate ownership! Notice also the word **forever**. Griffith Thomas says of these verses: "They are to be interpreted literally and spiritually. They are already having their primary fulfillment in the Church of Christ as Abraham's spiritual seed (Gal. iii. 7–9,16), but there will surely be a literal fulfillment in the future to the Jewish nation (Rom. xi. 26–29)" (Thomas, 125). Not only did Abram receive deed and title insurance; he was sent on the first-ever Holy Land tour with the Lord as his guide.

13:18. Time for another move. Abram relocated south to Hebron, several miles west of the center of the Dead Sea in the Judean mountains about half-way between Jerusalem and Beersheba. He settled **near the great trees of Mamre**, a town named for one of Abram's allies in battle whom we will meet in chapter 14. This would become Abram's center of operations for many years—site of the family estate and the burial ground of Sarai in the cave of Machpelah.

Two words in this verse characterize the life of Abram from the time he had first arrived in Canaan—**tents** and **altar**. This great man of faith became the prototypical spiritual pilgrim, a model we should all follow. Even the names are symbolic: *Mamre* means "vision," and *Hebron* comes from the verb "linked together" and could be called *communion* or *fellowship*. A new calm and maturity settled over Abram's life. He was learning obedience and patience. His communications with God were no ordinary religious experience. He had no alternative but to follow the word of the Lord. Where would it lead? What sacrifices would he be required to make? What would happen to his family in this strange land?

God did not answer any of these questions, nor did Abram ask them. God promised; Abram believed. God commanded; Abram obeyed.

MAIN IDEA REVIEW: *The key to describing the leadership of Abram is the word "faith." We see remarkable parallels between Abram and Moses, but surely the most distinctive is their commitment to the God who had called them.*

III. CONCLUSION

"Get Me Out of Here!"

Thinking about Abram's call reminds me of my first call to pastoral ministry. I was twenty-two years old and serving a little church in Indiana while attending seminary full-time. Because of my own immaturity and lack of experience, the problems seemed unbearable. I walked those gravel roads crying out to God for strength and courage to face yet another day. Actually my prayer was considerably more negative: "God, get me out of here!" One thing sustained me during those years—the awareness that God had called me and he would provide whatever I needed until he called me elsewhere.

Among Christians we often see a willingness to begin and a hesitancy to finish. It is one thing to leave Haran and dash off after a dramatic experience of God's call. It is quite another to keep going through famines, wars, and a variety of tests and struggles. How many times Abram must have been tempted to quit. But the key to his consistency was that he believed in God's consistency. Christians can be faithful because we believe in the faithfulness of Christ.

All of us face major tests of faith. In those tests we must hold to the original understanding of call and to the belief that God will see us through to the achievements he wants. The record of Abram's life is one of the most interesting narratives in the Bible. He remained faithful to God's call.

PRINCIPLES

- God seeks human beings, and he initiates the call to relationship with him.
- God's call doesn't make us immune to difficult situations and tests.
- Lying may seem successful for a while, but it will eventually bring embarrassment and disaster.
- Persons who are confident they belong to God don't have to prove their worth by being greedy and grasping.

APPLICATIONS

- Obey God even when you don't understand why he asks what he does.
- Never make an important decision without considering the possibility that God might have better options than the ones you have considered.
- Never lie, even in a good cause.
- Be a peacemaker. Peacemakers have always received God's blessing.
- Wherever you are, call upon the name of the Lord.

IV. LIFE APPLICATION

Trafalgar Square

Trafalgar Square, named in honor of Admiral Horatio Nelson, commemorates the victory of the British fleet at Trafalgar on the southern coast of Spain. The great naval battle was won on October 21, 1805. It gave England undisputed control of the sea, although Nelson was killed during the battle.

The backdrop was the British war against Napoleon Bonaparte, who tried to draw the fleet away to the West Indies so his armies could invade England. But Napoleon's admiral, Villeneuve, decided on his own to attack the British fleet in concert with a combined French and Spanish fleet. This seemed a good strategy, since his ships outnumbered Nelson's 33 to 27.

But Nelson's ships cut through the line and destroyed or captured over half the French and Spanish ships without losing a British ship in the process. That battle gave rise to one of those interesting stories that come out of military lore. Nelson came on deck and found two British officers quarreling. He grabbed them by their shoulders, turned them around to face the French fleet, and shouted, "Gentlemen, there are your enemies!"

Abram spent a lot of time in his early years learning who his friends and enemies were. Lot could not be categorized in either camp since he was a relative with whom Abram had to deal. Nevertheless, a quarrel between them could have pulled Abram out of God's design for the land and the covenant. He would face more enemies along the way, but Abram had learned the important fact that God was his friend.

V. PRAYER

Father, may we learn the lessons of these chapters—a willingness to leave whatever we consider dear in order to follow your call and to be your pilgrim people in the alien lands of our time. Amen.

VI. DEEPER DISCOVERIES

A. The Patriarchs

After his life span of 950 years, Noah was followed in the godly line by Shem, Arphaxad, Cainan, Shelah, Eber, and Peleg. During Peleg's time it is possible the Tower of Babel judgment occurred (Gen. 10:25). Following Peleg we trace Abram's lineage through Reu and Serug down to Nahor. This brings us to the final verses of Genesis 11. A good deal of dispute takes place over the birth of Abram, with dates between 2200 and 2000 B.C. commonly chosen (the NIV Study Bible selects 2166). None of this should be viewed as exacting chronology, but an attempt to give us a feel for the kind of world into which Abram was born.

The period between 3300 and 2000 B.C. is called the Early Bronze era, a time that included the invention of writing, the birth of human civilization as we know it, the development of the ancient Egyptian kingdom, and the domination of Sumerian, Akkadian, and Canaanite cultures. The year 2000 serves as the pivotal stone that moves history into the Middle Bronze era for the next 450 years (2000–1550), the time of the patriarchs. Amorites and other ethnic groups arrived in Mesopotamia while the old Babylonian Empire (along with the Egyptian Middle Kingdom) more or less ruled the world. During the Late Bronze period (1550–1200) we can place the bondage in Egypt, the birth of Moses, the exodus, the wilderness wanderings, and the time of Joshua and the conquest of Canaan.

B. Ancient Egypt (12:10)

Egypt's history was shaped by two great forces—the Nile River and the surrounding desert. The river provided life with its annual overflow and deposits of rich soil across the flood plain. The desert became a natural barrier that protected Egypt from invading armies and potential enemies. Abram was probably born some time during the late Old Kingdom (2575–2150 B.C.). Historians know this period as Dynasties 7 through 11, although it is impossible to identify the pharaoh of chapter 12.

Since Egypt went through a time of internal conflict, poverty, and famine during the first intermediate period, we lean toward placing Abram's visit in the Middle Kingdom, perhaps during the reign of Mentuhotep II, the first pharaoh who was able to regain control of the entire country. His fifty-year reign initiated a renaissance of culture and wealth that seems to characterize the nation during Abram's visit. This was the Eleventh Dynasty, known as the period of reunification.

VII. TEACHING OUTLINE

A. INTRODUCTION

1. Lead Story: The Bifocals of Faith
2. Context: The genealogical review at the end of chapter 11 sets the stage for the entrance of the main character—Abraham, father of the chosen people.
3. Transition: Chapter 13 leaves Abram in peace, pondering God's promises and worshiping. Now we will see something of the neighborhood into which he has moved.

B. COMMENTARY

1. Journey to Canaan (12:1–9)
2. Journey to Egypt (12:10–20)
3. Journey to Bethel (13:1–7)
4. Journey to Hebron (13:8–18)

C. CONCLUSION: "GET ME OUT OF HERE!"

VIII. ISSUES FOR DISCUSSION

1. Describe how Abram exemplifies the type of faith we should live out today.
2. In what ways might Abram's brief visit to Egypt parallel the journey of Jacob some years later?
3. What kind of choices do we make today that place us in the situation of Lot's opportunity to select the plain of the Jordan River?

Genesis 14:1–15:21

Covenant with God

I. INTRODUCTION
Pilgrim Promises

II. COMMENTARY
A verse-by-verse explanation of these chapters.

III. CONCLUSION
When Pilgrim Confronts Pagan

An overview of the principles and applications from these chapters.

IV. LIFE APPLICATION
A Different John Henry

Melding these chapters to life.

V. PRAYER
Tying these chapters to life with God.

VI. DEEPER DISCOVERIES
Historical, geographical, and grammatical enrichment of the commentary.

VII. TEACHING OUTLINE
Suggested step-by-step group study of these chapters.

VIII. ISSUES FOR DISCUSSION
Zeroing these chapters in on daily life.

Quote

"I have a key in my bosom, called Promise, that will, I am sure, open any lock in Doubting Castle."

John Bunyan

GEOGRAPHICAL PROFILE: VALLEY OF SIDDIM

- A location in the southern part of the plain of Jordan
- Close to the Dead Sea, possibly at the north or south end
- Mentioned only in Genesis 14:3

GEOGRAPHICAL PROFILE: KADESH

- Also known as En Mishpat or Kadesh Barnea
- Located in the Negev about fifty miles south of Beersheba
- Mentioned first in Genesis 14:7 but also in 16:14; 20:1, and frequently throughout the Pentateuch
- The sending point for the twelve spies

Genesis 14:1–15:21

IN A NUTSHELL

*G*od's promises are certain and eternal. In times of warfare or peace, sickness or health, believers can depend on God's power and care.

Covenant with God

I. INTRODUCTION

Pilgrim Promises

*O*n his first Sunday in adult church, Andrew, age three, wanted to participate in the prayer time. His daddy happened to be the pastor. During an opportunity for prayer requests, Andrew rose to his feet and asked the congregation to pray for his brother Bart, who lived in a castle in London and, strangely, was a dragon. Andrew intended no spiritual symbolism; he was just engaging in typical childhood fantasy that all parents are familiar with.

Another dreamer named John Bunyan wrote *Pilgrim's Progress,* the story of a wanderer named Christian and his journey from the City of Destruction to the Celestial City. In one scene Christian finds the road difficult and enters an area of soggy ground covered with poisonous vines. The rain beats mercilessly all night as Christian huddles at the foot of an oak tree. Giant Despair stumbles upon him, kidnaps him, and imprisons him in Doubting Castle. Christian's plight frightens him so that he nearly ends his misery in suicide.

At that time of his struggle, Christian utters the words from which our quote for this chapter is taken: "What a fool am I, thus to lie in a stinking dungeon, when I may as well walk at liberty! I have a key in my bosom, called Promise, that will, I am sure, open any lock in Doubting Castle." Christian used the key of God's promise to escape, never encountering Giant Despair again.

Abram was a pilgrim as well—a pilgrim who depended on the promises of God. From two thousand years before Christ, to 1678 when Bunyan wrote *Pilgrim's Progress,* on into the twenty-first century, God's pilgrim people wander on earth, sustained and delivered by his promises.

II. COMMENTARY

Covenant with God

> **MAIN IDEA:** *Through a war, a mysterious visit, a personal discussion with God, and a vision of fire, Abram learns what all Christians must know: God takes his promises and ours very seriously.*

A Tribal Warfare (14:1–17)

> **SUPPORTING IDEA:** *The ultimate cause for war can be found in the sinful heart of humanity.*

14:1–7. Abraham may be the most important character in Genesis. The Bible mentions him 115 times outside of Genesis and presents him in the New Testament as the outstanding Old Testament example of justification by faith. Many people have observed that his life was characterized by two things—tents and altars. Together these symbols reflect his pilgrimage in the world, controlled and energized by his constant worship of God.

But Abram was also characterized by crisis after crisis. The battles of Genesis 14 reflect this clearly. This is the first war mentioned in the Bible. Four powerful tribes from the northeast came to punish rebellious tribes in the south that included the five cities of the plain, including Sodom, Lot's new home.

14:8–12. This invaded land belonged to the country God promised to Abram. All this occurred on low ground that **was full of tar pits**. The Dead Sea is the lowest body of water on earth (1,300 feet below sea level). One can still see lumps of asphalt floating in the southern end of this body of water. The residents of Sodom and Gomorrah abandoned their cities before invading kings plundered **all the goods of Sodom and Gomorrah and all their food**. The account clearly tells us the battle was a rout.

Lot now lived in the city, whereas in 13:12 he had only "pitched his tents near Sodom." This offers an important key to understanding this chapter. Abram was content to let the inhabitants of the land do what they wished while he lived in peace. But now they had forcibly involved him by taking Lot away along with the captives. Barnhouse compares Lot and Abram to carnal and spiritual Christians: "The spiritual man will have to stand against all, for he stands alone with God. The moral victory of the religious world must not be confused with the spiritual victory of the man of faith" (Barnhouse, 96).

14:13–17. Notice the mention of **Abram the Hebrew**. The name "Eber" appears in 10:21 where we are told that "Shem was the ancestor of all the sons of Eber." Thus the origin of the Hebrew word for *Hebrew*, the people also known as "Shemites" or "Semites." Eber himself briefly appears in 10:24–25 but now takes on new meaning as Abram becomes the first Hebrew, the father of the Jewish nation. The root of **Hebrew** comes from a word that means "passed over," translated in the Septuagint as *passenger*. So the pilgrim theme dominates Abraham's life.

Abram also **called out the 318 trained men born in his household.** We have read several times about Abram's great wealth, but the phrase **trained men** appears only here in Scripture. Since Abram had never fought a war, we find it interesting that he had trained more than three hundred of his people as warriors. Not only that, but he had an ambush strategy that allowed him to defeat the northern kings and recover **all the goods** and captives.

But Abram didn't do it alone: **Mamre the Amorite . . . Eshcol and Aner . . . were allied with Abram.** This alliance of neighbors receives negative mention later in the Old Testament description of Hebrews fighting Amorites. Ross explains: "When the term 'Amorite' is used alone, it refers to western Semitic peoples living in Trans-jordanian kingdoms and the hill country of Palestine. These Amorites were a small ethnic group, not the large wave of Amorites who poured into both ancient Sumer and the West" (Ross, 53).

So Abram came marching back victoriously after defeating Kedorlaomer and his four friends. There to meet him were two kings. The first mentioned is **the king of Sodom.** At this point we expect the narrative to move immediately to verse 21 where the king of Sodom speaks. But Moses chose to interrupt the story by introducing one of the most mysterious and interesting characters of the Old Testament—Melchizedek.

𝔹 Unexpected Blessing (14:18–24)

> **SUPPORTING IDEA:** *Christians are often confronted by two types of representatives—those of wickedness and those of righteousness. So it was with Abram. Like Abram, we must know which plaudits and gifts to accept and which to deny.*

14:18. Bible scholars can't agree about this narrative. Some say that Melchizedek was the king of Jerusalem, merely abbreviated as **Salem** here in Genesis. That site would have been approximately twenty-five miles north of Abram's home in Hebron (Ps. 76:2). But the name *Melchizedek* means "king of righteousness." How unusual to learn that this Canaanite king was also a **priest of God Most High.** We will explore Melchizedek more thoroughly in "Deeper Discoveries," but here we recognize this unusual encounter. Its treatment in the New Testament (Heb. 7) does not allow us to link Melchizedek with Adoni-Zedek, the king of Jerusalem mentioned in Joshua 10:1, although their names are similar in meaning, merely a switch from "king of righteousness" to "lord of righteousness."

Many interpreters believe this was another Christophany, a demonstration of the preincarnate Christ. Anyone reading the Bible carelessly could easily pass over this strategic and spiritual man who demonstrates that God's work in the world did not rest entirely upon the shoulders of Abram the Hebrew.

14:19–20. It would be easy to see in Melchizedek's blessing nothing but ancient incantations of a Canaanite king-priest invoking the name of the chief Canaanite deity. But that would ignore the context of the rest of the Bible as well as this chapter. Melchizedek was speaking of Yahweh, **Creator of heaven and earth.** How interesting that Melchizedek should emphasize that God's blessing comes from the Creator.

Was the victory the result of Abram's 318 trained warriors fighting alongside the supportive Amorites? Not a chance. Melchizedek laid it on the line: **God Most High . . . delivered your enemies into your hand.**

The brief Melchizedek narrative ends with another astonishing line: **Then Abram gave him a tenth of everything.** In view of the major emphasis in many churches today on "tithing," I find it puzzling that so many commentaries pass over this statement. Consider Hebrews 7:4, "Just think how great he was: Even the patriarch Abraham gave him a tenth of the plunder!" And then just a few verses later, "One might even say that Levi, who collects the tenth, paid the tenth through Abraham, because when Melchizedek met Abraham, Levi was still in the body of his ancestor" (Heb. 7:9–10). Later in the text of the Old Testament, we learn that a tenth was the king's share (1 Sam. 8:15,17) and it becomes significant in the law of Israel. But the symbolism of Abram's act here seems to emphasize the importance of the mysterious Melchizedek.

14:21–24. Old Testament scholars call the construction of this passage a *chiasm.* The text falls into four parts in which Bera (king of Sodom) meets Abram; Melchizedek meets Abram; Melchizedek blesses Abram; Bera offers Abram all the loot. But Abram showed no interest. He was surely basking in the spiritual high of Melchizedek's blessing, and Bera's money meant nothing to him. Barnhouse says, "The worldly king is offering a fellowship that would be understood by all as participation with him in all that was possessed. But Abram has eaten the bread and drunk the wine which Melchizedek has given him, and strong in that strength he resists" (Barnhouse, 102).

Notice that Abram did not force his spiritual standards on other people. He seemed perfectly happy to have Bera distribute **the share that belongs to the men who went with me—to Aner, Eshcol and Mamre** and to accept sufficient funds to pay his expenses for the battle. He distanced himself in every other way from King Bera lest anybody think that his dependence rested anywhere other than upon **God Most High.**

Kidner applies it for us:

> For Abram the harder battle begins. For there is a profound contrast between the two kings who come to meet him. Melchizedek,

king and priest, his name and title expressive of the realm of right and good (c. Heb. 7:2), offers him, in token, a simple sufficiency from God, pronounces an unspecified blessing (dwelling on the Giver not the gift), and accepts costly tribute. All this is meaningful only to faith. The king of Sodom, on the other hand, makes a handsome and business-like offer; its sole disadvantage is perceptible, again, only to faith. To these rival benefactors Abram signifies his Yes and his No, refusing to compromise his call (Kidner, 120–21).

Promised Descendants (15:1–6)

SUPPORTING IDEA: *All the victories and wealth in the world seem insignificant without a family, particularly a son.*

15:1. When we read that **the word of the LORD came to Abram in a vision**, we think of prophetic language. Indeed, Abraham is later called a prophet. But in these verses his credentials are established **in a vision**, offering a word that appears only here and in Numbers 24. Sailhamer says:

> Such an introduction to the events of this chapter is intended to show that the events recorded in chapter 15 are, in fact, those that Abraham saw in the vision (Jacob, in loc.). Thus, like prophetic visions elsewhere in Scripture, there may be more than a little symbolic value to the events. This is especially likely to be true of the visual display that Abraham saw in v. 17 (Sailhamer, 127).

Was Abram shaken by the events of chapter 14? Certainly, fighting a battle and dealing with two very different kings was a variation from sitting under the oaks at Hebron, but this vision seems to be preparatory rather than therapeutic. The phrase **do not be afraid** is a major message throughout the Scriptures (Luke 1:13,30). Elsewhere in Scripture, **shield** represents the guardianship of a king (Deut. 33:29; 2 Sam. 22:3; Ps. 7:10), so God solidified his promise to protect Abram and to make him even more prosperous than he already was.

15:2–3. Abram pleaded with God about the emptiness of his life: **What can you give me since I remain childless?** He had been in Canaan for ten years but still had seen no evidence of the promise of offspring (12:2,7). Abram had already made plans for his estate and, in accordance with the laws of his time, determined to bequeath his inheritance to **Eliezer of Damascus . . . a servant in my household**. Ross says:

> His concern was expressed by a marvelous word play on his household servant's origin: this Eliezer of Damascus (*Dammeseq*) is the possessor-heir (*ben meseq*, lit., 'son of possession') of my estate

(15:2). It is as if Abram were stressing to God that 'the omen is in the nomen'—a mere servant would become his heir (Ross, 55).

15:4–5. But Abram's impatience was cut short by the Lord's response. Eliezer would not be the heir. God promised that Abram would have **a son coming from your own body.** Even if Abram had already adopted Eliezer in some official ceremony, the servant's rights would be negated by the birth of a son.

Not one son, but thousands upon thousands. Imagine the pitch-black darkness of a desert night. Abram could have seen thousands of stars. Isaac would be the son of promise (Gal. 4:28), and his descendants would multiply in Egypt. But ultimately, every believer in Jesus Christ fits into this promise to Abram (Gal. 3:29). This promise appears twice again, in Genesis 22:17 after the offering of Isaac and in Deuteronomy 1:10 at the entrance into Canaan. Paul mentions it in Romans 4:18, and Hebrews 11:12 tells about its fulfillment.

15:6. Abram's response in this verse forms the centerpiece of the gospel. Here we see the first use of the verb *believe* in the Bible. It teaches us what faith means—believing God. So Paul could say that Abram was the father of all who believe (Rom. 4:11). Some interpreters even suggest that Genesis 15:6 records Abram's conversion experience.

Genesis 15:6 is so important that the New Testament writers quoted it several times. It appears in whole or in part three times in the fourth chapter of Romans (4:3,22–23), as well as in Galatians 3:6 and James 2:23. In Romans 4:23–25, Abram's faith is compared with our faith in the death and resurrection of Christ. In other words, his faith in what God had told him up to that point is placed on the same level as our faith in what God has told us and revealed to us through Christ. In Galatians 3:6–7 we learn that believers in general are children of Abraham. James 2:23 also quotes Genesis 15:6 as proof that faith apart from works is dead. If we do not prove our faith by working for Christ and living as he wants us to live, our faith is not worth much. It is as good as dead (see Lightfoot, 161).

𝕯 Covenant Ritual (15:7–11)

SUPPORTING IDEA: *God speaks again, affirming Abram's call and reestablishing the promise of the land.*

15:7–11. Abram appealed for some guarantee, some human way of knowing that God would deliver on his promise. He managed to accept the promise of a son, but the land still seemed questionable. God's program for Abram was on schedule, but at the age of 85, the patriarch was getting a little nervous about the fulfillment of the promises. We have no previous Old Testament record of this ritual, although sacrifices were common. The experience foreshadows a variety of sacrificial procedures that Israel would practice after the deliverance from Egypt. Some interpreters also see in these verses an early foundation for the cross.

Ⓔ Geographical Dimensions (15:12–21)

SUPPORTING IDEA: *Sometimes we experience delays in the fulfillment of God's promises, but this only reflects our finite understanding of the divine plan.*

15:12–14. As the sun set, **Abram fell into a deep sleep**. His discussion with God had been tiring and demanding. But what do we make of this **thick and dreadful darkness**? Some interpreters suggest Abram still had emotional turmoil over the predatory birds that attacked the carcasses of his sacrifice. Others look ahead in the text and see the dreariness of Egypt. Abram had not yet held his first son, and he learned that his offspring would be slaves for four hundred years. The word **mistreated** appears again in Exodus 1:11–12 to describe Egyptian oppression.

We best count the four hundred years from the time of Jacob's entry into Egypt (c. 1876 B.C.) to the exodus dated c. 1446 B.C. Ross observes, "Apparently, then, Genesis 15:13 and Acts 7:6 with their references to 400 years, are using rounded figures and that makes a good bit of sense" (Ross, 55). When Abram's nation did end its term of slavery, they would **come out with great possessions**, a reminder of the way Abram himself had left Egypt (13:2,6). Egypt learned through history that when the Israelites paid a visit, the taillights were always more attractive than the headlights.

15:15–16. Abram would not be a part of this slavery since he would be **buried at a good old age**. This is the first time Abram had heard that he would not participate personally in God's promise of the land. Since his fathers were not buried in Canaan as Abram was, we assume he would be at peace with them in Sheol, the place of departed righteous spirits. His people would return **in the fourth generation**, a reference back to the four hundred years of slavery. By that time **the sin of the Amorites** would have **reached its full measure**.

From Canaanite literature, we have learned that the worshipers of many of the Canaanite deities participated in such degraded practices as atrocities in warfare and promiscuity in sexual matters—all in the name of religion. God is merciful, but his long-suffering and forbearance are not granted to people indefinitely. When stubborn disobedience passes the point of no return, God punishes the sinner.

15:17–21. During all this, presumably after God had revealed the future of Israel in relation to Egypt and Canaan, **a smoking firepot with a blazing torch appeared and passed between the pieces**. This symbolized the presence of

God (Exod. 3:2; 14:24; 19:18; Acts 2:3–4). Then the Lord cut a covenant with Abram that identified the precise boundaries of the **land**.

The western boundary would be an Egyptian river just south of the Gaza strip, possibly near the present site of El Arish (assuming the Mediterranean Sea as well), and the eastern boundary, the Euphrates. This included all the land that belonged to ten people groups (10:15–18), signifying completeness of God's gift to Abram. Scholars have calculated this territory in different ways, most agreeing that it exceeded 300,000 square miles.

> **MAIN IDEA REVIEW:** *Through a war, a mysterious visit, a personal discussion with God, and a vision of fire, Abram learns what all Christians must know: God takes his promises and ours very seriously.*

III. CONCLUSION

When Pilgrim Confronts Pagan

One of the most difficult evenings of my life was spent in a cramped television studio in Miami, Florida. In the fall of 1977, I was pitted in a ninety-minute live television debate with the atheist Madalyn Murray O'Hair. All across the city Christians had gathered in prayer that Sunday evening, many in fellowship halls of churches around a television set.

I had done my best to avoid the event—suggested other evangelical leaders in the city, excused myself because I had just spent the previous week lecturing at Dallas Seminary, and whatever other reasons sounded plausible. In the end the station made one of those offers one cannot refuse: "If you don't come and debate, we will give her the full ninety minutes to say whatever she wishes." By God's grace I made it through the evening, thanks to the help of those praying friends. But I experienced again the battle of the ages—truth versus error, biblicism versus atheism, God versus the ideologies of earth.

But Mrs. O'Hair was not the first atheist to gain public attention on the American scene. Decades earlier Robert Ingersoll drew large audiences for his lectures, shocking his readers by taking out a big pocket watch and announcing, "I give God—if there is one—five minutes to strike me dead."

Someone told the English evangelist Joseph Parker about Ingersoll's little trick since Parker was conducting evangelistic meetings in the United States at that time. Parker responded with a typical British line: "And did the gentleman presume to exhaust the patience of the eternal God in five minutes?"

These two chapters depict the conflict between good and evil—Abram the pilgrim against the kings of this world. That battle continues to the present hour in spite of great interest in spiritual matters across the Western world. Infatuation with angels, demons, prayer, and meditation cannot hide the blatant paganism on display in our modern culture. Like Abram we are also pilgrims in a world occupied by the kings of Sodom and Gomorrah. And, like Abraham, we must learn to depend on God alone for the strength to carry on the battle.

PRINCIPLES

- Seeking selfish advantage and ignoring God's will have consequences.
- Faith living is possible and profitable when we keep our eyes on God's promises.
- God brings blessing to us through unexpected people.
- Struggles in our Christian lives that occurred during earlier days do not preclude God's great blessing in later years.

APPLICATIONS

- Never doubt God's protection, even in the most difficult and dangerous hours.
- When given the choice, deny selfishness and choose generosity.
- Look for the Melchizedeks in your life—people who represent God and can offer blessing on his behalf.
- Never take gifts from the world that make you subject to it in any way; trust God for what you need.

IV. LIFE APPLICATION

A Different John Henry

We all know the old folk song about John Henry, the steel-driving man who tried to beat a steam drill with his hammer—and lost. But not many know about John Henry Yates, a shoe salesman born in Batavia, New York, in 1837. God called him to preach, and he was licensed as a Methodist preacher. But later in life he served as pastor of West Bethany Freewill Baptist Church for seven years. Yates maintained an ongoing association with the famous Ira Sankey, and he wrote a number of poems for which Sankey composed tunes.

We rarely know what Scripture passage a poet may have had in mind when composing a hymn text. But the refrain of *Faith Is the Victory* directs our attention to the passage in 1 John 5:4: "This is the victory that has overcome the world, even our faith." Our spiritual warfare depends upon the same kind of faith Abraham exercised in fighting pagan kings. John the apostle reminds us that "everyone who believes that Jesus is the Christ is born of

God" (1 John 5:1), affirming the role of faith in salvation as well as its power for spiritual victory.

John Henry Yates put it this way:

His banner over us is love, our sword the Word of God;
We tread the road the saints above with shouts of triumph trod.
By faith they, like a whirlwind's breath, swept on o'er every field;
The faith by which they conquered death is still our shining shield.

V. PRAYER

Father, grant us faith for life eternal and faith for living this day. May we victoriously press on for Jesus in all the spiritual battles of our lives. Amen.

VI. DEEPER DISCOVERIES

A. Melchizedek (14:18)

Views on the identification of this person gallop across the exegetical map. Critical commentator Westermann doubts the historicity of Melchizedek, at least in the context of Genesis 14, when he says:

What is presented here is the sedentary cult of which priests, cultic institutions, and tithes are part. None of these belonged to the worship of the patriarchal period. It is certain that this scene was only later linked with the Abraham of the patriarchal period (Westermann, 203).

Most evangelicals place no credence in Westermann's conclusions, seeing a reasonable combination of priest and king in Melchizedek, who became something of an ideal ruler in Israelite thought during later centuries. Leupold observes:

This is a name of Yahweh, found indeed only in Ps. 78:35 but in many similar combinations quite frequently. We are compelled to regard this venerable king-priest as a worshipper and public adherent of the true religion of Yahweh as handed down from the sounder tradition of the times of the flood. That this was the actual course of development of religions, and that monotheism definitely preceded polytheism may now be regarded as fully demonstrated (Leupold, 463).

There seems to be little reason to support the idea of a Christophany here, but certainly the text of Hebrews confirms *typology*. Speaking of Jesus, that writer declared, "He became the source of eternal salvation for all who obey him and was designated by God to be high priest in the order of Melchizedek" (Heb. 5:9–10). Then two chapters later, in a discussion of the priesthood, the typology is elaborately developed throughout most of the chapter. The first three verses take on particular importance.

> This Melchizedek was king of Salem and priest of God Most High. He met Abraham returning from the defeat of the kings and blessed him, and Abraham gave him a tenth of everything. First, his name means, "king of righteousness"; then also, "king of Salem" means "king of peace." Without father or mother, without genealogy, without beginning of days or end of life, like the Son of God he remains a priest forever (Heb. 7:1–3).

Scripture teaches that Christ is greater than the law and a high priest far above anyone in the levitical line because he "has become a priest not on the basis of a regulation as to his ancestry but on the basis of the power of an indestructible life" (Heb. 7:16). Then the writer draws on Psalm 110:4 to emphasize the eternal priesthood of Christ: "You are a priest forever, in the order of Melchizedek."

Of all this Thomas Lea writes:

> Historically, Melchizedek appears to have belonged to a succession of priest-kings and had both predecessors and successors. In comparing the priesthood of Melchizedek to that of the Son of God, Hebrews makes the priesthood of Jesus the standard. Melchizedek is like Jesus, the Son of God. The record about Melchizedek was arranged so that it demonstrated some truths which applied more fully to Jesus than to Melchizedek. Melchizedek was a figure of Christ, but Christ was the reality (Lea, 129).

B. Creator (14:19,22)

Although we have dealt with the concept of creation in earlier chapters, we can never overemphasize the significance of the doctrine of creation throughout the Book of Genesis and the entire Bible, as well as its foundational role in Christian theology. Sometimes the highly scientific and equally complex accounts of bones, rocks, and fossils leave us cold, groping for some practical reality in all the arguments. Creationism seems too impractical, confusing, and even superfluous to a pragmatic society.

But God's creation was meant to be a revelation of himself, a reflection of the beauty and orderliness of the Creator. Through sin humanity has perpetuated its own wickedness upon the magnificence of God's creation and perverted the truth of natural revelation. That's why the Melchizedekian account with its emphasis on God as Creator is so refreshing, falling as it does between the battles of the pagan kings and the approach of the king of Sodom.

Since Melchizedek is a type of Christ, we would expect him to mention God as Creator since one of the foundational truths about the person of Jesus is his role as Creator (John 1:3; Col. 1:16; Heb. 1:1–3). In fact, Jesus himself confirmed creation on numerous occasions in his teaching; to believe Jesus is to believe the biblical account of creation.

My beloved theology teacher at Grace Seminary many years ago told the story about a town drunk who had become a believer and had his life changed by the power of God. One day they found him standing in the park with his arms around a tree, weeping. At first everyone thought he had gone back to his former life. But as they got closer, they heard him whispering amid the tears with a smile on his face, "Jesus made it; Jesus made it."

So it is with all the material and spiritual creation. All sound theology begins with the recognition that "Jesus made it"—the universe, the reality of human life, and the eternal hope offered in the gospel.

C. Credited as Righteousness (15:6)

Every Christian can quote Romans 3:23: "For all have sinned and fall short of the glory of God." That brief verse falls right in the middle of Paul's discussion of righteousness through faith, an argument he builds on the premise that religious practice or genetic connection cannot produce a genuine relationship with God. Then he opens Romans 4 with a section that quotes our passage here in Genesis 15:6.

> What then shall we say that Abraham, our forefather, discovered in this matter? If, in fact, Abraham was justified by works, he had something to boast about—but not before God. What does the Scripture say? "Abraham believed God, and it was credited to him as righteousness" (Rom. 4:1–3).

When God credited Abram's faith for righteousness, the patriarch had kept no laws, rendered no great service to Yahweh, and, apart from his occasional altars, had performed no religious ritual. God made a promise and Abram believed it. The result was Abram's justification.

D. Abrahamic Covenant

Although God's covenant with Abram began in chapter 12, it builds throughout the patriarch's experience, always emphasizing offspring and land. Chapter 15 focuses on the geographical boundaries established for the land. Some interpreters believe the covenant was conditional. Since both Abram and Israel disobeyed God, the covenant was nullified and is now being fulfilled spiritually in the church. But even Westermann says:

> It was supremely important for the later period that the promises to the patriarchs were unconditional. Later generations, under immi-

nent threat, could reawaken the promises adapted to their situation and dealing with preservation of the people and the retention of the land, so as to cling to God's assurance when both were in jeopardy (Westermann, 230).

Many evangelical scholars believe that this covenant will yet be fulfilled when Jesus returns again and sets up his kingdom and reigns over Israel. Boice describes the promises of God.

> First, they are unilateral; they are established by God alone. Second, they are eternal and irrevocable. Third, they are based on grace; no people or individual deserves the promises that God makes. These three points are seen in the life of Abram, just as they were also seen in the account of the making of God's covenant with Noah (Boice, 117).

Genesis 15 offers a foundation stone for the development of the gospel throughout the Scriptures. Salvation is based on God's promises—promises that cannot and will not change. We have studied the eternally valid covenant of grace given to a man whose name will soon be changed, though at this point he still represents God's dim light in pagan surroundings. The centerpiece of the covenant is grace. For that reason Erich Sauer can say, "Genesis 15 is thus far the most basic chapter of the Old Testament" (Sauer, 98).

VII. TEACHING OUTLINE

A. INTRODUCTION

1. Lead Story: Pilgrim Promises

2. Context: Although we have not dealt with it, there is a great deal of discussion among higher critics about the flow of events in this part of Genesis. We picked up some of that in Westermann, but this is not even the tip of the iceberg. But one who reads the Bible naturally and with an open mind should find no difficulty dropping this war narrative right into the middle of the events of Abram's life in Hebron. In fact, brief mention of the covenant in 13:14–17 sets up its fuller development in chapter 15. Both chapters begin with natural lead lines one might expect from a historical author: "at this time" (14:1) and "after this" (15:1).

3. Transition: Next we will see how Abram handles the promise of offspring. These promises have already appeared in chapters 12, 13, and 15.

B. COMMENTARY

1. Tribal Warfare (14:1–17)
2. Unexpected Blessing (14:18–24)
3. Promised Descendants (15:1–6)
4. Covenant Ritual (15:7–11)
5. Geographical Dimensions (15:12–21)

C. CONCLUSION: A DIFFERENT JOHN HENRY

VIII. ISSUES FOR DISCUSSION

1. In what practical ways do we trust God?
2. Describe a contemporary parallel to the covenant ceremony of chapter 15.
3. How do you believe God's covenant with Abraham affects you?

Genesis 16:1–18:15

The First Arab

I. INTRODUCTION
Christmas in April

II. COMMENTARY
A verse-by-verse explanation of this passage.

III. CONCLUSION
The Prayer of Jabez

An overview of the principles and applications from this passage.

IV. LIFE APPLICATION
How Firm a Foundation

Melding this passage to life.

V. PRAYER
Tying this passage to life with God.

VI. DEEPER DISCOVERIES
Historical, geographical, and grammatical enrichment of the commentary.

VII. TEACHING OUTLINE
Suggested step-by-step group study of this passage.

VIII. ISSUES FOR DISCUSSION
Zeroing this passage in on daily life.

Genesis 16:1–18:15

Quote

"*G*od never made a promise that was too good to be true."

D . L . M o o d y

GEOGRAPHICAL PROFILE: BEER LAHAI ROI

- Means "the well of the living one who sees me"
- Probably near Kadesh
- An area where Isaac lived for some time (Gen. 24:62; 25:11)

GEOGRAPHICAL PROFILE: BERED

- Means "to be cold"
- Located in the vicinity of Kadesh-Barnea
- This location formed a connecting link between Palestine, Kadesh, and the Sinai

PERSONAL PROFILE: HAGAR

- Sarai's Egyptian servant girl
- Name means "flight"
- Mother of Ishmael
- Last mentioned in the Old Testament in Genesis 21:21
- Appears in the New Testament (Gal. 4) in Paul's allegory of the difference between law and grace

I N   A   N U T S H E L L

*G*od's promise stands at the center of his relationship with Abraham and his relationship with us. Both rely upon God's faithfulness in keeping his word. We have already seen God's promise of the land (12:1), descendants (12:2), and the blessing (12:3). References to these aspects of the promise have been repeated several times. We also know the promise is literal (13:14–16), eternal (13:15), and unconditional (15:9–18).

The First Arab

I. INTRODUCTION

Christmas in April

*R*obert Morgan chose the title "Christmas in April" to describe the ministry of Christmas Evans, a Welsh evangelist born on December 25, 1766, to a poor shoemaker and his wife. When Evans was nine, his father died in the cobbler stall. Christmas ended up in the home of an alcoholic uncle. Through the preaching of David Davies, Christmas gave his life to Christ and began to learn Scripture by candlelight at a barn in Penyralltfawr. The wild gang he had been running with was so upset by his conversion and calling to preach that they beat him and gouged out his right eye.

As Morgan tells the story, "The young man resolved nonetheless to preach, and preach he did. Wherever he went—churches, coal mines, open fields—crowds gathered and a spirit of revival swept over the listeners. Unable to afford a horse, he started across Wales by foot, preaching in towns and villages with great effect."

On April 10, 1802, Evans, having burned out in ministry and lost the joy of the Lord, climbed into the Welsh mountains to pray until God brought revival to his heart. "He made a covenant with God that day, writing down thirteen items, initialing each one. The fourth said, 'Grant that I may not be left to any foolish act that may occasion my gifts to wither.' The eighth said, 'Grant that I may experience the power of thy Word before I deliver it" (Morgan, "April 10," *On This Day*).

Evans came down from the mountain like Moses and rumbled through Wales and the neighboring island of Angeles for the next thirty-six years. Some historians still refer to him as "the Bunyan of Wales."

Abraham is about to face a similar spiritual crisis. He will not burn out in ministry, but he will lose patience in waiting for God's promise to be fulfilled.

II. COMMENTARY

The First Arab

> **MAIN IDEA:** *God sometimes seems to be slow in fulfilling his promises. This causes us to implement our own plans, which inevitably leads to trouble. In these chapters Abram feels threatened and also fears for his loved ones. Most believers go through experiences like these at one time or another.*

A Servant in the Desert (16:1–16)

> **SUPPORTING IDEA:** *God's program for Abram was right on schedule, but in finite human thinking, neither Abram nor Sarai could grasp that truth.*

16:1–6. The front pages of newspapers across the world are filled with stories of war and turmoil in Palestine, of suicide bombers and retaliations, of television scenes displaying mob violence with screams of "Death to the Arabs" or "Death to the Jews." The conflict is not over religion; it centers in the land.

In spite of the human logic that supports the Arab claim, God's plan has not changed. Palestine was given to Israel and will be theirs entirely some day as fulfillment of God's promise to Abraham. We must remember the promise was given while Abram was still childless. According to all standards of Jewish and Oriental inheritance, Ishmael, the firstborn, would become the heir of Abram's wealth and the descendant of a promised line. But God's plan of a chosen nation did not include the son of Hagar the Egyptian.

As the events of this chapter unfold, Abram was eighty-six years old and still had **no children**. The aging couple had probably discussed the promised child many times. Human impatience drove them to adopt a cultural pattern common at their time and in their part of the world. Sarai suggested that Abram could father a child through her servant girl Hagar.

Since this ancient Oriental practice seems so foreign to our system of ethics, we wonder with Youngblood:

> How could the wives of the patriarchs suggest such a thing? Once again, it was the legally authorized custom of that time for a man who had no son to take measures that would insure the orderly disposition of his inheritance when he died. He could adopt a son, as Abram had apparently already done (c. 15:2–3). Or . . . he could produce a son by cohabiting with one of the servant girls in his household. If a son were born as a result of such cohabitation, the inheritance rights of that son would supercede the rights of any previously adopted son.

In a polygamous society, where men commonly had a wife and one or more concubines (as Abram did; see 25:6), sleeping with a servant girl was not nearly so strange or shocking as it might seem to us (Youngblood, 166).

But the plan went awry from the beginning. Like Peninnah and Hannah (1 Sam. 1:6), Hagar despised Sarai, Sarai blamed Abram, Abram gave permission for whatever Sarai wanted to do, Sarai mistreated Hagar . . . and the horrors continued. Griffith Thomas points out that Abraham "was, of course, powerless in the matter as Hagar was her mistress' absolute property. He could not interfere, and was compelled to accept the inevitable, and say that Sarai must do 'as it pleased her'" (Thomas, 148).

No doubt for Hagar this was a door of opportunity. To become the first concubine of the great Abram was a considerable step up from being the slave of Sarai. All of Abram's camp knew his wife was barren, and word of Hagar's fertility probably traveled fast. But Sarai was not quite ready to be replaced as the mistress of the house. She never cared to see the child of that union which she herself had suggested. Sarai's jealousy eventually drove Hagar into the wilderness to escape bondage in Abram's tent because of the child she carried.

16:7–12. The stage was now set for the birth of the Arab nation. Their ancestress, driven by a love of freedom, sat alone by a spring in the wilderness of Shur. There she was met by **the angel of the LORD**. This designation is found with some frequency in the Old Testament (Gen. 19:1,21; 31:11,13; Exod. 3:2,4; Judg. 2:1–5; 6:11–12,14; 13:3,6,8–11,13,15–17,20–23). Many interpreters find a Christophany here, a preincarnate appearance of the second person of the Trinity. But this is hardly the only explanation, since angels of the Lord appear throughout the Bible as his messengers on important occasions.

The angel asked two specific questions. Hagar told about her experience and why she was in the wilderness alone. The angel encouraged her to return to Sarai **and submit to her**, and then offered her a promise from God as well: **I will so increase your descendants that they will be too numerous to count**. And then the message from the Lord continued with increasing specificity. These verses contain three distinct promises about Hagar and three about her son.

The angel promised that her descendants would be multiplied, that she would bear a son, and the son would be called Ishmael, which means "God hears." About this son the angel said he would be **a wild donkey**, would be fighting constantly with other people, and would live on the margin of civilization **in hostility toward all his brothers**.

Sailhamer observes, "The key term throughout the chapter is 'misery' . . . which occurs as a noun in v. 11b and as a verb in v. 6 [mistreated] . . . and v. 9

[submit]. Hagar was afflicted by Sarai (v. 6); she was told to put herself back under that affliction (v. 9); and the Lord heard her affliction (v. 11)" (Sailhamer, 135).

16:13–16. The appearance of the angel taught the runaway servant a lesson she probably never forgot. She discovered that God is *El Roi*—the seeing God. She learned what many people today have never learned—that they cannot run away from the Lord whose eyes are everywhere seeing the evil and the good. Like Samuel, Ishmael received his name from events in his mother's life and not his own. All this happened at a well **between Kadesh and Bered**, a place where Isaac later lived (Gen. 25:11).

How happy Abraham must have been at the return of Hagar from the desert. Her testimony must have reminded him of his own experiences with God's promise. Surely it was plain to Abraham that Sarai's slave girl had met God in a personal way, and the pregnancy must have taken on new meaning until the birth.

B The Sign of the Covenant (17:1–14)

SUPPORTING IDEA: *God's promises throughout his Word are true, and we can trust them.*

17:1–2. Thirteen years passed between the end of chapter 16 and the beginning of chapter 17. Ishmael was now a teenager, and Abram received a visit from El-Shaddai, the Almighty. This was God's special name for confrontation with the patriarchs. God asked Abram to continue walking in righteousness and confirmed the covenant of the seed. This chapter raises Abram to a new level of spiritual experience. Apparently his continuing need for confidence and reassurance occasioned this fresh revelation from God.

17:3. God again emphasized to Abram that this promise was **my covenant with you**. Bible scholars consider this the third covenant of the Old Testament. This covenant took the form of a suzerainty-vassal conditional pledge in which both parties played a role. This was significantly different from the unconditional promise of chapter 15.

17:4–8. The name change from Abram ("exalted father") to Abraham ("father of many") indicates the sovereign authority of El-Shaddai and an additional pledge that God would fulfill his promise. Every time Abraham and Sarah heard their new names, they would be reminded of God's promise and encouraged by his faithfulness. In these verses Abraham was quiet before God, who did all the talking.

Five promises appear in the passage, beginning with **I will make you very fruitful**. How interesting that one of the blessings God gave to Abraham was the joy of children, the joy of fathering Ishmael and Isaac, initially in his own family and then through other descendants as the nation grew. The second promise, **I will make nations of you**, expanded the first. The word **nations** appears in the plural. We think of Abraham as the father of the Jewish nation, but he was also the father of all Arabs. This promise that God would make Abraham into great nations reminds us of chapter 12 where the initial promise was given (12:1–3).

God also promised Abraham that **kings will come from you**. For years Israel did not have kings because they did not need them. But when Saul rose from the tribe of Benjamin (Abraham's great-grandson), God fulfilled these words of 17:6. Later the great warrior and hymn writer David came from the line of Judah, another great-grandson of Abraham. So we trace the heritage of the kings back to the patriarchs and ultimately back to Abraham.

In verse 7 God told Abraham, **I will establish my covenant** with you. There are different ways of looking at this passage. Some people see only one covenant extending through the Old and New Testaments; others see two, and some see several. In making this promise to Abraham, God was saying he wanted to bind to himself a very special group of people: covenant people of the Old Testament and covenant people of the New Testament.

Finally, God told Abraham, **The whole land of Canaan . . . I will give you as an everlasting possession**. This was Palestine—a little strip of land east of the Mediterranean Sea and the focal point of history. The spotlight of current events in the twenty-first century shines on this strip of real estate that God promised to an old man several thousand years ago. The land was the focal point of the covenant, and the conflict of the ages will find its culmination on the sun-baked plains of Palestine.

17:9–14. In verse 9 we learn that this covenant, everlasting though it may be from God's perspective, required a response from Abraham and his **descendants**. God also provided a symbol of this human response: **You are to undergo circumcision**. This was not some new physical sign that God created just for this occasion. In fact, circumcision was well-known in ancient times and was practiced by many of the nations among which Abraham lived.

God transformed this social custom into an act with religious significance. Rather than instituting a totally new ritual to signify the covenant, he adapted and transformed an ancient and familiar custom, investing it with new meaning.

Abraham responded with obedient faith and carried out the stipulations that God announced. Unlike the "uncircumcised Philistines," a typical symbol of a pagan nation, Abraham's descendants would be separated, pure, and loyal to the covenant.

Paul picked up on this symbol in the New Testament and talked about the spiritual parallel. Does a person receive forgiveness of sins and a relationship with the eternal God only through ethnic connections with Abraham? Absolutely not.

Abraham's faith was credited to him for righteousness. Under what circumstances was it credited? Was it after he was circumcised, or before? It was before. And he received the sign of circumcision, a seal of the righteousness that he had by faith while he was still uncircumcised. So then, he is the father of all who believe but have not been circumcised, in order that righteousness might be credited to them. And he is also the father of the circumcised who not only are circumcised but who also walk in the footsteps of the faith that our father Abraham had before he was circumcised (see Rom. 4:9b–12).

So we have been circumcised as well—new covenant believers whose hearts have been transformed. God has given us a new identity in Jesus Christ and two new covenant signs (baptism and the Lord's supper) to help us remember our relationship with him.

Perhaps the spiritual inclusion of believing Gentiles is implied as early as Genesis 17 when God included people **who are not your offspring**. Abraham's camp included many slaves. Were they also participants in the rite of circumcision and somehow incorporated into the nation?

Leupold points out:

> We believe that the answer must be, "Yes." Israel certainly never had a separate slave class, who were deemed inferior beings and mere chattels. What then became of the slaves that originally were part of the household establishment and went down into Egypt at Jacob's time? The answer seems to be: "They were naturally absorbed by the Israelites and blended with the Israelite stock, adopting the Israelite religion." So with all its necessary exclusiveness Israel was at the same time broader in its attitude than many assume. But there certainly could be little hesitation about letting circumcised slaves be merged with the chosen race (Leupold, 524).

C Son of Promise (17:15–27)

> **SUPPORTING IDEA:** *God's promises today are no less capable of fulfillment than they were in Abraham's day.*

17:15–22. A third section of the chapter begins with, **God also said to Abraham**. Like the first section, it also begins with a name change. Both **Sarai** and **Sarah** mean "princess." The change is considerably more subtle than Abram ("exalted father") to Abraham ("father of many"). Both name changes emphasize that these parents would be the founders of a whole new race.

As for Ishmael replacing Eliezer, that would not happen. Sarah would have a son, and she would be **the mother of nations**. At these words **Abraham fell facedown**. The word **laughed** is actually a pun on the name *Isaac* ("he laughs"). Notice Abraham's rejoinder: **If only Ishmael might live under your blessing**. Abraham had almost lost Ishmael once. But God's response indicated there was no substitution necessary here. Ishmael would be blessed, he would be **fruitful**, and he would become **a great nation**. But he was not to become the covenant child.

Verse 21 specifically rules out Ishmael from the covenant. In spiritual terms he portrays works, a clever design that Abram and Sarai had concocted. But Isaac would be a child completely of grace. And all of this would happen within a year.

17:23–27. God broke off his discussion with Abraham as quickly as he had initiated it. Now it was Abraham's turn to act. Beginning with Ishmael, he circumcised **every male in his household**. Like a father-son baptism in the same pool on the same day, Abraham and Ishmael underwent circumcision at the same time.

Ⅾ Sojourners from Heaven (18:1–15)

> **SUPPORTING IDEA:** *Abraham's growth and faith and his response to God's covenant are testimonies to God's power and purpose.*

18:1–2. As we enter chapter 18, we cross a divide from a section that has focused on the Abrahamic covenant to four chapters which are concerned mostly with Abraham's family. After the events of chapter 17, Abraham settled again by his beloved oaks. Suddenly he **saw three men standing nearby**. These were no ordinary visitors, since the chapter begins with the words **the LORD appeared to Abraham**, and two of them are called angels in 19:1. Many scholars identify the third person of this group as the Lord himself (another Christophany).

According to Leupold, "the assertion of this first verse, that it was 'Yahweh' who appeared to Abraham here, must be held fast in determining the identity of the three visitors. This first verse furnishes the basic statement. This statement cannot be meant in the rather loose sense that Yahweh made his appearance by sending some three men. If that sense were to be conveyed, v. 1 would have made a very unsatisfactory statement of the case" (Leupold, 535).

18:3–8. The first half of Genesis 18 reflects hospitality shown by courtesy and respect. Strangers appeared at the tent. Without giving a second thought to who they might be, Abraham bowed before them, got water for their feet, and offered them rest and a meal. This incident finds its way into the New Testament where we read in Hebrews 13:2, "Do not forget to entertain strangers, for by so doing some people have entertained angels without knowing it."

Abraham spared no expense in the hospitality that he extended. Sarah used **fine flour**, and Abraham **selected a choice, tender calf**. Notice also the interesting phrase at the end of verse 8: **While they ate, he stood near them under a tree**. This was the posture of a servant—standing just far enough away from guests to avoid the appearance of intrusion, yet close enough to be summoned to meet their needs.

18:9–15. As Abraham stood under a tree ready to serve his guests, they asked him where Sarah was. He immediately told them she was **in the tent**. Then **the LORD said** that within a year the son of promise would be born to Sarah. All the talk about offspring in general terms and the specific promise of a son by Sarah (17:16) now came down to a specific prophecy about when this event would occur. This miraculous event would come about because the Lord himself would bring it to pass.

Sarah heard the words, thought immediately about how old she and Abraham were, and **laughed to herself**. This is precisely what Abraham had done in 17:17. Abraham may have spoken to Sarah of the promises he had received, but this was Sarah's first direct contact with the Lord's promise. This was no cruel divine joke.

Although Sarah's laugh was probably not heard outside the tent, the Lord asked Abraham, **Why did Sarah laugh**? Sarah denied that she had laughed. But in the difficulty of this moment, one of the great rhetorical questions of the Bible is stated: **Is anything too hard for the LORD?**

Boice directs the practical question to today's generations.

> "Is anything too hard for the Lord?" Is there any sin for which the blood of the Lord Jesus Christ, God's Son, cannot atone? Moses was a murderer but he was saved. David was an adulterer and a murderer, and he was saved. Peter denied Christ. Paul killed Stephen. These and countless other sinners have been saved by the merits of Jesus Christ alone. Their salvation was not too hard for God. Why should yours be impossible? God says to you, "Come now, let us reason together . . . though your sins are like scarlet, they shall be as white as snow; though they are red as crimson, they shall be like wool" (Isa. 1:18) (Boice, 155).

MAIN IDEA REVIEW: *Sometimes God seems to be slow in fulfilling his promises. This causes us to implement our own plans, which inevitably leads to trouble. In these chapters Abram feels threatened and also fears for his loved ones. Most believers go through experiences like these at one time or another.*

III. CONCLUSION

The Prayer of Jabez

A little book entitled *The Prayer of Jabez* was one of the top ten books on the *New York Times* best-seller list for several months in 2001. Millions of copies have been sold, and pastors have bought the book by the thousands to give to their church members.

The book expounds on one verse, 1 Chronicles 4:10, which rises like an oasis in the desert of the first nine chapters of 1 Chronicles. Jabez is speaking about military victory and increasing his ownership of land. J. Barton Payne offers two lines: "Yet Jabez' prayer of faith became an occasion of grace, so that God kept and blessed him, rather than *osbi*, literally, 'causing me pain'" (Payne, 341).

Abraham did not need to pray for God to bless him or widen his boundaries since God had already made clear that was what he intended to do. But Abraham still needed to learn total dependence on God, a posture that does not appear until the great testing of chapter 22. Both Abraham and Sarah also needed to continue praying that God would keep them from evil—the evil pressing all around them in Canaan; the evil of their own hearts which caused them to doubt God and, in Sarah's case, to sin by lying. In spite of all that had been accomplished thus far, Abraham's biggest challenges were still ahead.

PRINCIPLES

- God doesn't need our help in fulfilling his promises.
- God sees and knows everything.
- God gives us visible reminders of what he has done within us and for us.
- God does not find it amusing when we laugh at his plans for our lives.

APPLICATIONS

- Learn patience from the impatience of Abram and Sarah.
- What difference does it make when you realize God sees every situation of your life?
- What does God bring to mind as you witness baptism and participate in the Lord's Supper?
- Are you putting limits on what God wants to do in your life?

IV. LIFE APPLICATION

How Firm a Foundation

As Abraham's faith grew and his spiritual walk with God reached new depths, he learned what David wrote so eloquently in Psalm 119:89–93: "Your word, O LORD, is eternal, it stands firm in the heavens. . . . I will never forget your precepts, for by them you have preserved my life." On texts like this Robert Keene built the great Christian hymn, "How Firm a Foundation."

This hymn became a favorite of General Robert E. Lee, who chose it to be sung at his funeral. It first appeared in 1787 under the title, "Exceeding Great and Precious Promises." On Christmas Eve of 1898, an entire corps of the United States Army encamped in the Quemados hills near Havana struck up the tune.

> The soul that on Jesus hath leaned for repose
>
> I will not, I will not desert to its foes;
>
> That soul, though all hell should endeavor to shake,
>
> I'll never, no never, no never forsake!

Is anything too hard for the Lord? Absolutely not. Our faith and our lives move forward on that firm foundation.

V. PRAYER

Father, give us the faith of Abraham to believe that anything you want for us can happen in our lives. Make us hospitable Christians who really believe that nothing is too hard for you. Amen.

VI. DEEPER DISCOVERIES

A. El-Shaddai (17:1)

Abram worshiped the covenant God. Years later God would say to Moses, "I am the LORD. I appeared to Abraham, to Isaac and to Jacob as God Almighty, but by my name the LORD I did not make myself known to them" (Exod. 6:2–3). The patriarchs had a relationship with the covenant God of Israel, but their theology was still primitive. They did not understand the full implications of the God who had redeemed his people repeatedly throughout their history. The exodus would be the first great event by which Israel as a nation would see the extent to which God would go to fulfill his covenant.

The name *El-Shaddai* appears five times in Genesis (17:1; 28:3; 35:11; 43:14; 48:3). In Job it appears many times. Most experts agree that the key component *shad* cannot be identified as either "mountain" or "breast" since it could mean either. Both are applicable to the God of heaven. Barnhouse chooses "breast" and says, "I believe that the spirit or theology of the passage demands that the meaning be found in the name. God, then, is the One on whose breast His children find their rest and from whom they would draw their nourishment" (Barnhouse, 132).

Kidner disagrees. He argues:

> A better guide is the study of its use, and this confirms the famil-
> iar emphasis on might, particularly over against the frailty of man (it
> is a favourite divine title in Job). In Genesis it tends to be matched to
> situations where God's servants are hard pressed and needing reassur-
> ance (Kidner, 129).

Whether the nurturing God or the powerful God, the breast or the mountain, God used this special name particularly for the patriarchs and for Job.

B. Conditional and Unconditional Covenants (17:1–14)

The concept of covenant did not originate with Abraham but with Noah.
The covenant involved God's continuing work with people from the earliest
chapters of Genesis right on through the New Testament (new covenant). In
Genesis 17 God repeatedly recalls this relationship as "my covenant" because
God initiated, confirmed, and established it. But in Genesis 17:9 the phrase
"as for you" introduces the responsibility of the people of the covenant. Participation in all that the covenant promised rested on obedience of the people
as we shall see again in chapters 18, 22, and 26. In this sense the covenant
was conditional as well as unconditional.

All this forms the unique relationship between grace and law that charac-
terizes the entire Bible. Paul deals with this over and over, but the concept of
the covenant comes to fruition in the Book of Hebrews. There the word
diatheke appears seventeen times, and the new covenant is contrasted dramatically with the old.

By the very promise of the new covenant, the old has been declared obso-
lete by God himself, so it is ready to vanish (Heb. 8:13). This does not mean
that it has been completely ruled out but that it has been overtaken and fulfilled by the new. In Christ "the pattern" (*typos*, 8:5) and "the true form"
(*eikon*, 10:1) of the one covenant concept has become reality. According to
Brown:

> The new covenant is founded on better promises . . . but like the
> old covenant it is a covenant in blood. . . . It is not, however, the
> blood of a sacrificial animal, but the blood of the sacrificer himself,
> the high priest . . . hence the death of Christ was essential, for only
> through the death of the testator does his will become operative in
> law (Brown, 371).

If we are to err in any direction, let it be toward a greater dependence on
God while not losing sight of our own responsibilities. Grace supersedes law,
and the unconditionality of God's promises forms the foundation for our faith.
In his book *The Knowledge of the Holy*, A. W. Tozer reminds us:

The heaviest obligation lying upon the Christian Church today is to purify and elevate her concept of God until it is once more worthy of Him—and of her. In all of her prayers and labors this should have first place. We do the greatest service to the next generation of Christians by passing on to them undimmed and undiminished that noble concept of God which we receive from our Hebrew and Christian fathers of generations past. This will prove of greater value to them than anything that art or science can devise (Tozer, 12).

C. Circumcision

Israel departed from the practice of circumcision while they were wandering in the desert, so Joshua reinstituted the practice on the west bank of the Jordan River before the battle for Jericho (Josh. 5:2–9). By the time of Joshua, even Israel understood that circumcision was more than an outward sign; it represented an inward commitment. Moses had said to the people in Deuteronomy 10:16, "Circumcise your hearts, therefore, and do not be stiff-necked any longer."

Griffith Thomas picks up on the devotional implications of the text:

We are here brought face-to-face for the first time in Holy Scripture with young life in relation to God. God entered into covenant with little children, and as the covenant with Abraham was one of grace, we see the true place of little children in the kingdom of God. Circumcision was not merely a mark of the Mosaic dispensation and Jewish covenant of works; it was, as here, pre-Mosaic, associated with the covenant of grace and therefore independent, and wider than, the Jewish national life (John vii. 2). God is here seen in the attitude of Father to little children, and He has never altered that attitude (Thomas, 155).

VII. TEACHING OUTLINE

A. INTRODUCTION

1. Lead Story: Christmas in April
2. Context: Abram was born about 2166 B.C. and moved to Canaan in 2091. Ishmael was born 2080 and was thirteen at the end of chapter 17, so that puts the date of this chapter at 2093. But chapter 18 must take place at least two years later. Now the birth of Isaac is only one year away, and Ishmael was sixteen at the time Isaac was born.
3. Transition: If we keep the concepts of *land* and *offspring* in mind, we see the threads running through these chapters. Wars and struggles come and go, spiritual experiences and symbols abound, but God is

working out his plan in Abraham's life. Chapter 16 tells us about the birth of Ishmael. Now thirteen years later we are about to find another interruption in Abraham's life as his divine visitors reveal God's plan for Sodom and Gomorrah.

B. COMMENTARY

1. Servant in the Desert (16:1–16)
2. Sign of the Covenant (17:1–14)
3. Son of Promise (17:15–27)
4. Sojourners from Heaven (18:1–15)

C. CONCLUSION: HOW FIRM A FOUNDATION

VIII. ISSUES FOR DISCUSSION

1. What do you conclude about the relationship between Abram and Sarai from the early verses of chapter 16?
2. Explain in your own words the relationship between Old Testament circumcision and New Testament baptism.
3. How should we respond to promises in God's Word which seem impossible and even incredible?

Genesis 18:16–19:38

Sodom and Gomorrah

"*N*othing can so quickly cancel the frictions

of life as prayer."

William T. McElroy

PERSONAL PROFILE: BEN-AMMI

- Means "son of my people"
- Lot's son and grandson by his younger daughter
- Father of the Ammonites

PERSONAL PROFILE: MOAB

- Means "seed"
- Lot's son and grandson through incest with his older daughter
- Father of the Moabites, a tribe that caused Israel repeated problems

Genesis 18:16–19:38

IN A NUTSHELL

*L*ot's choice to live in sin brings its ultimate fruition for his family. Only three people are spared the destruction of these two cities.

Sodom and Gomorrah

I. INTRODUCTION

The Roots of Evil

*I*n June 2001, Timothy McVeigh sat in jail awaiting his execution. Because of the FBI's infamous "lost documents," the originally scheduled execution was delayed, and a nation began to ponder what causes a person to come to a willingness to destroy other people recklessly and without remorse. They also took another look at the death penalty about which Jonathan Alter said, "They have become increasingly concerned about the fairness of capital punishment. The goal should now be dedication—at all levels—to building a system that punishes the guilty without executing the innocent. If not now, when?" (*Newsweek,* May 21, 2001).

The McVeigh case stirs memories of Ramzi Yousef, who masterminded the 1993 bombing of the World Trade Center in New York City, and Ted Kaczynski the Unabomber. We could add to that list John Wayne Gacy, who raped, sodomized, tortured, and killed thirty-three boys; Ted Bundy, who killed twenty-four women and called his victims "cargo" and "damaged goods." Or Jeffrey Dahmer, who lured seventeen men and boys into his apartment, murdered them, then cannibalized his victims and stored parts of their bodies in his refrigerator. In *Newsweek*'s research its reporters discovered that 31 percent of people surveyed said that everyone has the capacity for evil; 33 percent blamed poor parenting; 53 percent said religious and moral training is the best way to fight evil.

But the real answer does not surface until the following article in the same issue—"Overcoming Sin," written by Kenneth L. Woodward. Woodward began by saying:

> We are fascinated with evil because we are fascinated with ourselves. If the Bible is to be believed, alienation from God is the natural habitat of humanity and evil its full-blown manifestation. Indeed, the word "evil" appears more often in the Christian Scriptures than "good"—and with reason. From the Biblical perspective, our natural inclination is to serve ourselves rather than God—and in the case of a man like Timothy McVeigh, to mete out retribution as if he were God himself. In this view, evil acts are born of inordinate pride, a moral weakness that manifests itself as strength. Even saints must conquer festering self-regard. "I can will what is right, but I cannot do it" the

apostle Paul confesses. "For I do not do the good I want, but the evil I do not want is what I do" (*Newsweek*, 36).

As usual, Woodward hit the target. The text before us reflects one of the great demonstrations of evil in the Bible. The story of Sodom and Gomorrah is so linked with homosexuality that *sodomy* has become a synonym for the word in our society. The scriptural passage is clear and specific. Heterosexuality certainly existed in Sodom, but sexual recreation was rampant in the city to the point that gay crowds roamed the streets demanding sexual relations with every stranger who visited town. So great was the need for God's judgment that he discussed it with Abraham first and thereby invoked one of the most familiar discussions of the Bible.

II. COMMENTARY

Sodom and Gomorrah

MAIN IDEA: *God often answers our prayers in ways we do not expect.*

A Message of Judgment (18:16–21)

SUPPORTING IDEA: *Abraham was the friend of God (2 Chr. 20:7; Isa. 41:8; Jas. 2:23), and God had chosen to bless all the nations of the earth through him. Abraham was allowed the privilege of learning something of God's principles about sin in the nations of the earth.*

18:16–19. Continuing his role as host, Abraham walked with his guests as they left. They were headed **toward Sodom.** We learn later in the Bible that Abraham was God's friend. God invoked that relationship here without using the word itself. As we read the text, we wonder whether verses 17–19 display audible words which Abraham heard. Or was the Lord "talking to himself." Leupold says, "It seems best to assume that this soliloquy of Yahweh was spoken softly yet audibly. It was truly a soliloquy. It was just as certainly intended for Abraham's ears" (Leupold, 544).

If Leupold is right, this paragraph was a reminder to Abraham of his great responsibility as well as his close relationship with the Lord. We dare not miss the parenting emphasis in verse 19. God had chosen Abraham so he would **direct his children and his household after him to keep the way of the LORD.** We see the conditional side of the promise in the words **so that.**

18:20–21. These verses seem curious. Why would God need to **go down and see if what they have done is as bad as the outcry that has reached me?** We already know Sodom's sin was well attested (Gen. 13:13). The passage typifies the image of judge that appears in Abraham's rhetorical question at the end of 18:25. The heavenly visitors would **go down** not to the earth but to the plain along the Dead Sea. God's omniscience does not fall into jeopardy when he adopts the behavior of a righteous human judge who does not act until the evidence supports his judgment.

Ⓑ Prayer of Intercession (18:22–33)

SUPPORTING IDEA: *Abraham had a solid hold on his relationship with the Lord. After the two angels headed east, Abraham approached him and the bargaining began.*

18:22–26. How many righteous people does it take to remove a sinful city from God's judgment? We know of no rule of thumb, but in this case God would agree to save the entire city if he could find fifty righteous people. What would **righteous** mean in a place like Sodom? Perhaps Abraham hoped Lot's influence in the city would have attracted additional followers of the Lord. Or maybe there were genuine seekers in these cities—people who detested the sinful surroundings and wondered whether there might be truth and goodness in the world.

Of this exchange between Abraham and the Almighty, Kidner writes:

> It would be easy to say that this prayer comes near to haggling, but the right word is "exploring": Abraham is feeling his way forward in a spirit of faith (superbly expressed in 25c where he grasps the range and rightness of God's rule), of humility, in his whole mode of address, and of love, demonstrated in his concern for the whole city, not for his kinsmen alone (Kidner, 133).

18:27–33. Receiving a positive answer in verse 26, Abraham moved on and whittled the number to 45, then 40, 30, 20, and 10. God offered to grant every one of those numbers: **For the sake of ten, I will not destroy it.** Of course, God knew exactly how many righteous people there were in the cities of the plain. Abraham's understanding of the depths of sin in those places probably increased with each decreasing number.

Why did Abraham stop at ten? He was on a roll; why not go for five or even four? Phillips suggests that Abraham had multiplied the five cities of the plain by the number of necessary witnesses in each and concluded that ten was the bottom line. He says, "There were five cities in the plain. In Scripture *two* is the number of adequate witness, so it required *ten* righteous people to be in the valley, else there would not be even the minimum witness for God" (Phillips, 157).

Abraham may have thought he had won the day and saved the city (the entire conversation deals with *city* in the singular). After all, there were two sons-in-law who might have come under Lot's influence, and perhaps even their families. Some interpreters say that Abraham walked so closely with the Lord that he could sense the discussion was over and just gave up after verse 32. But the text seems to imply that the decision belonged to God: **When the LORD had finished speaking with Abraham, he left.** Standing alone with the conversation over, **Abraham returned home.**

Warning to Lot (19:1–15)

> **SUPPORTING IDEA:** *Abraham wanted God to demonstrate his justice by delivering Lot and sparing the city. But God chooses to demonstrate justice by delivering Lot and destroying the city.*

19:1–2. At first glance these verses reflect the same kind of genuine humility and hospitality that Abraham showed these same two angels in the previous chapter. Nor is there any reason to deny his sincerity. But Lot's role in Sodom is exposed by the innocent words **sitting in the gateway of the city.** This offers more than casual reference to the place where he spent his leisure time. It specifies the official meeting place of the elders where legal matters and political affairs were discussed.

Perhaps Lot took advantage of his leadership role to serve good people who entered the wicked city; that would certainly account for his immediate response to the angels. We can only guess how concerned he must have been when they insisted on spending the night **in the square.** Let's not forget Peter's comment that Lot was "a righteous man" (2 Pet. 2:7–8). We don't see much of that in the Genesis account, but Peter's witness helps us understand Lot's concerns early in this chapter.

19:3–5. In a phrase common in our day, Lot would not take *no* for an answer. He took the strangers into his home and fed them, but just about bedtime the problems started.

Lot's strong insistence indicates that he was aware of what would happen to these strangers in his city. We wonder why Peter would call Lot "righteous" (2 Pet. 2:7–8) when he lived and served as a leader in the rotten cesspool of Sodom. Barnhouse says, "It is an amazing picture of the lust of the flesh against the drawing of the Spirit. Any man who thinks that his fleshly appetites will be stilled while he is on earth has not comprehended the baseness of Lot's desires, nor, indeed, his own" (Barnhouse, 163).

Many interpreters have raised weak protests against the historic understanding of the Sodom account on the basis that the Hebrew verb *yoda*, rendered "to know" in the KJV, does not necessarily mean sexual knowledge as the NIV has translated it. Exegetes sympathizing with the pro-gay position have suggested that perhaps the Sodomites only wanted to "get acquainted" with Lot's guests. That position might be plausible if the meaning of *yoda* were the only consideration. Given the total context, this interpretation misses the mark.

To be sure, other sins plagued Sodom as they do every city. But we know of only one episode in history where God singled out a particular sin and destroyed two entire cities because of it. The sin was homosexuality, and the cities were Sodom and Gomorrah. Gay theologians argue that Lot had angered the residents of Sodom by receiving foreigners whose credentials had not been examined. Upset by the social injustice, according to this interpretation, the men were pounding at Lot's door demanding to see those credentials.

Only the most naïve of Bible students would think that homosexuality suddenly exploded in Sodom at Lot's door. God had already declared Sodom to be grievously sinful. Its homosexuality had sent up a stench for years. Abraham had been told that the destruction would take place before the angels entered the city. Gay theologians argue that *yoda* is only used about fifteen times in the Old Testament to describe sexual understanding, but it appears over nine hundred times as mental understanding.

But serious exegetes are not impressed by such statistics, since interpretation based on the contextual argument is always stronger. Even if there were just one or two uses of *yoda* in the Bible that depict a clearly sexual sense, we would certainly conclude its sexual emphasis in this passage. As Kidner puts it, "No-one suggests that in Judges 19:25 the men of Gibeah were gaining 'knowledge' of their victim in the sense of personal relationship, yet 'know' is the word used of them" (Kidner, 137). In treating the arguments offered by gay theologians to suggest something other than homosexuality as the sin of Sodom, Kidner says, "Not one of these reasons, it may be suggested, stands any serious scrutiny" (Kidner, 137).

Indeed, *yoda* here takes us back to Genesis 4:1, a foundational passage. Genesis 19 gives us a glimpse into the unspeakable possibility of human depravity. When we look into Sodom we understand that passages like Genesis 6:1–12, Leviticus 18:24–30, and Romans 1:24–27 do not exaggerate the truth. At this time in history the spotlight focuses only on the five cities of the plain, although we assume that homosexuality thrived elsewhere. In our day, homosexuality rights and gay pride have become an international cause.

19:6–9. Contemporary Christians who are urged to show tolerance for "alternate lifestyles" would do well to note the depths of backsliding to which Lot had fallen. Apparently he could overlook the sin of the city until it affected his own house and guests for whom he was responsible. But nothing prepares us for his offer of two virgin daughters in lieu of the two guests! Here we have the classic example of trying to avoid sin by committing another sin. Some commentators argue that Lot knew in advance that his offer would be rejected. But if that were the case, how would such an offer protect his guests?

No appeals to the rigid customs of hospitality in his day; no excuses for shrewdness or cleverness—indeed, no arguments at all—can excuse Lot from this disgusting proposal. Furthermore, Lot's exalted position in the city was of no concern to this crazed mob. Suddenly he became **an alien**, and the threat of rape was applied to him as well as his two guests.

Phillips says:

> No longer were their shameful sins tolerated by a permissive society as something people had a right to practice if they pleased. It had gone far beyond that. Now the people were an open, aggressive, insistent force in the city with which none dared interfere. For their behavior was not looked upon by the Sodomites as criminal but as *constitutional*. They had the constitutional right to indulge their passion when and where they wished and any attempt to thwart them could be expected to lead to open riot in the city (Phillips, 161).

The parallel with modern Western culture should chill us to the bone.

19:10–15. Now we see that God's deliverance had nothing to do with Abraham's bargaining. The angels acted quickly, striking the mob with blindness and offering Lot deliverance. He could take with him **anyone else in the city who belongs to you.** But when Lot went to his **sons-in-law, who were pledged to marry his daughters,** his hypocrisy became evident. They never took the threat of judgment against their city seriously. In fact, they **thought he was joking.**

Ⓓ Deliverance from Sodom (19:16–29)

> **SUPPORTING IDEA:** *The Lord often forces us into righteous choices even when we are unwilling.*

19:16–20. Literally dragged from the city, Lot's family escaped because **the LORD was merciful to them.** The basis of Lot's deliverance was not his righteousness, although Peter affirms that in the New Testament (2 Pet. 2:7–8). Like spiritual salvation, this physical deliverance came about solely through God's grace.

One would think Lot would have been so overcome with gratefulness that he would have obeyed immediately the command to **flee to the mountains.** But urban life had its icy fingers around his throat. He thought the judgment of Sodom and Gomorrah would reach him in the mountains, but somehow in town his life would **be spared.** Leupold calls this "a somewhat presumptuous plea by a weak and timid man. He does not seem to realize his extremity, nor to value sufficiently the undeserved favor bestowed upon him"

(Leupold, 566). Lot's thinking was so distorted that he thought God would only punish large cities, not small ones.

19:21–22. God's grace stretched even further, but the urgency was pressing. Judgment had been declared, but it could not be delivered until Lot's family was safe. So they headed for the smallest of the five cities of the plain, Zoar, whose name means "small." An amazing thing happened here. God spared Zoar because Lot was in it. Sailhamer says:

> The effect of this short episode is to further strengthen the author's point that Lot's rescue is a result of prayer, both Abraham's and his own . . . here a reminder of the importance of Abraham's prayer in chapter 18 can be seen in the fact that with Lot's request the actual circumstances envisioned in Abraham's prayer are realized when God saved the city on account of the righteous ones in it (Sailhamer, 156).

19:23–26. Now we see the kind of judgment God intended: burning sulfur that killed every living thing. Some interpreters suggest this may have been a violent earthquake, since the plain of the Dead Sea is still known for that kind of catastrophe. But there is no support for this in the text. J. Wash Watts translates verse 24 quite distinctly: "Then Yahweh made brimstone and fire to rain upon Sodom and Gomorrah, even from Yahweh out of heaven." This also happened to three other cities in the plain including Gomorrah, but Zoar was spared.

The Lord knows how to rescue godly men from trials and to hold the unrighteous for the day of judgment, while continuing their punishment (2 Pet. 2:6,9). In a similar way, Sodom and Gomorrah and the surrounding towns gave themselves up to sexual immorality and perversion. They serve as an example of those who suffer the punishment of eternal fire (Jude 7).

The region of the southern part of the Dead Sea stands forever as a warning of God's judgment against the iniquity of Sodom and Gomorrah. The destruction of the cities offers catastrophic demonstration that God cannot tolerate such behavior. The sexual wickedness of humanity had to be dealt with later in the law. God could not form an organized nation on the shoulders of relativistic thinkers like Lot. After reading Genesis 19, we should not be surprised to find frequent references to sexual deviation in the Mosaic Law (Lev. 18:22–24; 20:13; Deut. 23:17–18).

The narrative ends as sadly as it began: **Lot's wife looked back, and she became a pillar of salt.** Did she just want to see the fire? Did this act express a longing for the possessions she left behind? We can only speculate. But as Youngblood reminds us, "The memory of Lot's wife serves as a reminder to us not to turn back, no matter how temptingly the things of this world may beckon (Luke 17:32). Her hesitation cost her everything she had, including her very life" (Youngblood, 178).

19:27–29. The narrative switches back to Abraham, who had returned home to Mamre (18:33) and then walked back east to look down on the cities of the plain. What he saw that day represented a microcosm of hell. Yet rejection of God will bring a fate worse than Sodom.

Ⓔ Incest in the Mountains (19:30–38)

SUPPPORTING IDEA: *The spiritual shallowness of parents is often duplicated and amplified in their children.*

19:30–33. Lot's inadequacy as a parent surfaces in this passage. He left the town he had begged for before the catastrophe and headed for the mountains. Actually, **he was afraid to stay in Zoar**. The only possible explanation for this is Lot's warped reasoning that Zoar would also be destroyed, even though the angel had promised, "I will not overthrow the town you speak of" (19:21). Throughout the biblical picture we have of Lot, he displays greater fear than he does faith. Fear had taken him to Zoar, and now fear chased him out.

The final drama in Lot's biblical record plays out in a cave. As Kidner puts it:

> The end of choosing to carve out his career was to lose even the custody of his body. His legacy, Moab and Ammon (37f.), was destined to provide the worst carnal seduction in the history of Israel (that of Baal-Peor, Nu. 25) and the cruelest religious perversion (that of Molech, Lv. 18:21). So much stemmed from a self-regarding choice (13:10ff.) and persistence in it (Kidner, 136).

Although he was drunk when he committed incest, Lot bears the guilt since the text does not place the fault on the daughters.

19:34–38. Nine months later Lot became a grandfather and father at the same time. Notice that the boys were named by their mothers; Lot had lost control. We should note here that lust did not seem to play a role in the incest, since they intended only to **preserve our family line through our father**. Lot's descendants are mentioned in Deuteronomy 2 in positive language. The daughters achieved their goal, even though their sons fathered tribes that would always trouble Abraham's people. So we should blame neither the girls nor the boys in this narrative but rather focus on Lot himself.

Ross observes:

> Their acts of incest show Sodom's influence on them. They gave birth to boys, Moab and Ben-Ammi, whose descendants were the Moabites and the Ammonites (vv. 36–38), perennial enemies of Israel. "Moab" sounds like the words "from father," and "Ben-Ammi"

means "son of my kinsmen." These etymologies perpetuated for Israel the ignominious beginning of these wicked enemies (Ross, 61).

MAIN IDEA REVIEW: *God often answers our prayers in ways we do not expect.*

III. CONCLUSION

Sin and the City

Half of the world's more than six billion people now live in cities. This worldwide trend will continue throughout the foreseeable future. Most of the increase will occur in the world's poor countries, but industrialized and developed nations have already seen the pressures of urbanization. By 2050 an estimated two-thirds of the world's population will live in urban areas. This could challenge the space and resources of those areas and lead to social disintegration and urban poverty.

In 1900 the world's most populous cities were all in North America or Europe. At the end of the twentieth century, Tokyo, New York, and Los Angeles were the only industrialized cities in the top ten list. By 2020 demographers predict, New York and Los Angeles will drop off the list—bumped by Dhaka, Bangladesh; Karachi, Pakistan; and Jakarta, Indonesia. Tokyo will lose its number one spot to Bombay, India, as the most highly populated city in the world.

We all understand why people choose to live in cities—convenience, job opportunities, higher salaries and standard of living, and a wide variety of entertainment. Quite possibly all of these appealed to Lot when he made his choice of Sodom. But nearly every city in America also struggles with horrific traffic problems, high crime rates, and infamous slums that breed everything from typhoid to HIV.

I'm told that one of cable television's most popular programs in 2001 was entitled *Sex and the City.* Genesis 19 certainly laid the groundwork for that. Lot was hardly headed for the Hebrews honor roll before he left Abram, but apparently everything was downhill from the time he hit Sodom to the time he became a grandfather in a mountain cave.

While we could argue from our text that Sodom corrupted Lot, we could also argue that Lot could have challenged Sodom. When we look at the magnitude of God's grace in Abram's life and his spectacular achievements, we can only imagine that he might have stopped at the request of fifty and heard God say, "No problem. Your nephew already has at least that number of people worshiping with him at his home and witnessing in the city square." Just picture Lot working the crowd, handing out copies of the Gospel of John while his two sons-in-law and daughters played guitars and sang praise choruses in the gateway of the city. Just imagine the possibilities of God calling that city to repentance through the testimony of one righteous man and his family.

PRINCIPLES

- Every father bears the responsibility to "direct his children . . . to keep the way of the LORD" (18:19).
- God is opposed to wickedness and evil.
- God can deliver his people from danger and from sin in the most unusual ways.

APPLICATIONS

- God can answer our prayers in ways that grant the object of a request without using the method of our requests.
- Beware the influence of affluence, especially in the alluring temptations of urban life.
- When God warns you to abandon sin, walk away and do not look back.

IV. LIFE APPLICATION

Buesher's Basketballs and Bibles

The front page of the sports section of *USA Today* beamed the headline on Tuesday, January 23, 2001: "Filled with the Spirit." The article told the story of Erin Buesher, who had already established herself as a major star in women's college basketball. According to reporter David Leon Moore:

> For three years, she drank from the cup of victory, leading the University of California-Santa Barbara to three consecutive NCAA Tournament births, and she dined at awards banquets, winning three consecutive Big West Conference Player of the Year trophies. But she thirsted and hungered for much more (p. C1).

Suddenly she put her finger on the emptiness in her life, packed her bags, and headed to The Masters College where the emptiness inside her was filled by God. As Erin puts it:

> I have been blown away with what the Lord is doing with me. It's not some emotional high, like a roller coaster. But it's real. I feel like I am changing every day. The Bible and the Lord are coming alive to me like they never had before. I know when I'm in the Bible every

day, somehow I'm being fed. I feel alive. I feel like I'm learning so much. I'm being filled with the Spirit.

In some ways this parallels the story of Lot with opposite conclusion. Buesher played big-time basketball in a big-time town but sensed that her surroundings contributed nothing to her spiritual life. So rather than staying there with her emptiness, she left the city and in the exact words of the article "headed into the mountains."

The news from America's colleges and universities gets worse every year—persecution and mockery of Christians; massive drinking parties often resulting in physical injury to students, sometimes even death; uncontrollable riots over the slightest provocation; and the systematic inculcation of secular humanism as a philosophy of life. Christians need to understand that the separation of God's people from constant bombardment by the temptation of sin is essential for spiritual growth. But in our day we have solidly evangelical schools at all levels. Parents don't have to send their children to "Sodom" just because of the wider choice of majors or the prestige that might attach itself to a degree from a big-time university.

V. PRAYER

Father, give us a profound sense of your ability to answer the prayer that Jesus taught his disciples, "Deliver us from evil." Amen.

VI. DEEPER DISCOVERIES

A. Homosexual Perversion Today

On New Year's Day in 1965 a group of liberal Protestant ministers and their wives turned up at a homosexual dance in the hope that their presence would discourage mass arrests among the gay community they were defending. Police, having failed to persuade the operator of California Hall to cancel the rental agreement, lined up squad cars outside and photographed each of the six hundred guests as they arrived. Six arrests resulted since homosexual acts between consenting adults were illegal at that time in California.

The next day San Francisco clergy called a news conference to denounce the police, and the nation's most concentrated homosexual community came out of the closet. Since that day the financial and political clout of gays in San Francisco has been almost beyond belief. Nor is San Francisco the only city thus marked. Key West, Florida, and numerous other locations bear similar distinction. In June 2001, three of the four nominees for the Tony Award as the best musical play of the year promoted some form of homosexual or transsexual lifestyle.

During the thirty-five years from that San Francisco event to the end of the twentieth century, homosexuality moved out of the margins of society into the mainstream. The gay rights movement began in 1969. Homosexuality now dominates numerous television programs, some of which seem dedicated to the advancement of the gay lifestyle.

J. Kerby Anderson emphasizes what every Christian should understand: the root problem of homosexuality is neither biological nor psychological, but spiritual:

> Ultimately homosexuality is a manifestation of the sin nature that strikes us all (Rom. 3:23). Because of the Fall (Gen. 3) God's creation was spoiled and human behavior has fallen into degrading passions (Rom. 1:24). Sin has spoiled every aspect of our being (spiritually, intellectual, emotional, physical, sexual). Therefore we should not be surprised that anyone (heterosexual or homosexual) could have sexual fantasies and temptations in this area. Those who choose to act on those feelings and temptations are acting outside God's plan for human sexuality (Anderson, 176).

This issue will plague the world until the Lord comes. In a society for which tolerance of everything has become a religion, only scorn and oppression can come to those who proclaim what the Bible says about the sin of homosexuality.

B. The Archaeology of Sodom and Gomorrah

The Genesis account of Sodom and Gomorrah describes the area south of the Dead Sea as a lush valley with rivers and tar pits. Abraham's nephew Lot settled at first outside the city but later moved into the mainstream of Sodomite society. According to the biblical record, God judged these cities and the surrounding area with fire from heaven.

But many interpreters have questioned whether such a judgmental catastrophe ever occurred. The present geography of the area seems to support the record of a holocaust. At the southern end of the Dead Sea, variable heights of the same rock strata on the west, east, and south ends seem to confirm the account. The fault at either side of the Dead Sea indicates an earthquake. Sulfur balls found in the faults could be related to what the Bible calls "brimstone."

The mound of salt 150 feet thick at places is called "Mount Sodom" by modern Israelites. The area surrounding this portion of the Dead Sea is useless because of salt on its surface. Israel reclaims several hundred thousand tons of potash every year from the southern part of the Dead Sea.

Archaeologist Nelson Glueck has identified over four hundred village sites in the northern Negev, most of them last inhabited about 2000 to 1800

B.C. Today archeologists are uncovering ruins of a vast civilization in the ancient Sodom-Gomorrah valley.

The Book of Genesis does speak of slime pits (*bitumen*), and some interpreters have speculated that lightning or some other God-initiated agent ignited a large pocket of gas that literally blew up the valley. Large quantities of sulfur and salt were carried red hot into the heavens and, in turn, literally rained fire and brimstone on the cities. Such a view does not minimize the miraculous destruction of Sodom and Gomorrah. We cannot know or say what precise means God used to accomplish his judgment of sin in the cities of the plain.

C. Sodom in Ezekiel 16

Proponents of gay theology and hermeneutics pounce upon Ezekiel 16:48–49 as the banner text to demonstrate that the sin of Sodom was not homosexuality but a refusal of hospitality.

> As surely as I live, declares the Sovereign LORD, your sister Sodom and her daughters never did what you and your daughters have done. Now this was the sin of your sister Sodom: She and her daughters were arrogant, overfed and unconcerned; they did not help the poor and needy.

Why didn't the prophet deal with the notorious atrocities that have made Sodom a symbol of degradation for centuries? Partly because his purpose was to compare Jerusalem with Samaria and Sodom. He selected those elements of evil common to all three, and the former two were not to be compared to Sodom in sexual perversion. Selfishness and pride obviously existed in Sodom, but the verses do not claim that those were her only sins.

Furthermore, a focus on verse 49 fails to take into consideration the total contextual argument. The proverb begins at verse 44 and continues through verse 59. Sodom is mentioned not once, but five times in the passage. In addition to pride, fullness of bread, abundance of idleness, and a failure to strengthen the hand of the poor and needy, the prophet also mentions such terms as "abomination," "shame," "wickedness," and "lewdness." Reputable commentators suggest that Sodom's primary sin was not mentioned because it was so well-known to the prophet's readers that there was no point in reviewing it.

VII. TEACHING OUTLINE

A. INTRODUCTION

1. Lead Story: The Roots of Evil
2. Context: The Sodom narrative begins at 18:20, spinning immediately out of a focus on Abraham's relationship with God. It ends with the

birth of Moab and Ben-Ammi. When chapter 20 opens, we find Abraham moving one more time back to the Negev. His journey continues both geographically and spiritually.

3. Transition: The transition of the Abrahamic story which began at chapter 12 links three concepts—*blessing, land,* and *offspring*. We have seen blessing after blessing, both physical and spiritual, showered upon this faithful servant. We've seen the land covenant established, with specific geographical boundaries included. But we have not yet seen the son of promise from whom the nation of Israel will spring. But Sarah is pregnant, and we expect him at any time.

B. COMMENTARY

1. Message of Judgment (18:16–21)
2. Prayer of Intercession (18:22–33)
3. Warning to Lot (19:1–15)
4. Deliverance from Sodom (19:16–29)
5. Incest in the Mountains (19:30–38)

C. CONCLUSION: BUESHER'S BASKETBALLS AND BIBLES

VIII. ISSUES FOR DISCUSSION

1. Why do you believe Genesis 18 gives such a large portion of its space to the dialogue between Abraham and God on the fate of Sodom?
2. Explain your position on homosexuality. Is homosexuality a legitimate alternative lifestyle, or is it sin? Can people change their sexual preference, or are they "born that way"? Can homosexuals be Christians?
3. What should evangelical churches be doing to stand against the tide of militant homosexuality on the one hand, while reaching out in grace with the other?

Genesis 20:1–21:34

Sister Act II

I. **INTRODUCTION**
Heaven Is a Local Call

II. **COMMENTARY**
A verse-by-verse explanation of these chapters.

III. **CONCLUSION**
Faith Is More Than Feeling

An overview of the principles and applications from these chapters.

IV. **LIFE APPLICATION**
A Bend in the Road

Melding these chapters to life.

V. **PRAYER**
Tying these chapters to life with God.

VI. **DEEPER DISCOVERIES**
Historical, geographical, and grammatical enrichment of the commentary.

VII. **TEACHING OUTLINE**
Suggested step-by-step group study of these chapters.

VIII. **ISSUES FOR DISCUSSION**
Zeroing these chapters in on daily life.

"*T*he world will never have lasting peace so long as men reserve for war the finest human qualities. Peace, no less than war, requires idealism and self-sacrifice and a righteous and dynamic faith."

J o h n   F o s t e r   D u l l e s

GEOGRAPHICAL PROFILE: GERAR

- Located in the Negev near the Mediterranean coast south of Gaza
- A stop on a protected inland caravan route from Palestine and Egypt
- Both Abraham and Isaac lived here at various times

GEOGRAPHICIAL PROFILE: BEERSHEBA

- Probably means "well of seven" or possibly "well of the oath," located on the southern boundary of the land later occupied by the tribe of Judah
- Commonly known by the phrase which identifies the northern and southern boundaries of Israel—"from Dan to Beersheba"

GEOGRAPHICAL PROFILE: PARAN

- First mentioned in Genesis 14:6
- Located somewhere in the central area of the Sinai Peninsula
- The home of Ishmael after he left Abraham

GEOGRAPHICAL PROFILE: SHUR

- A desert region east of Egypt
- The place where the angel of the Lord found Hagar (Gen. 16)
- Location of one of Abraham's sojourns (Gen. 20:1)

PERSONAL PROFILE: ABIMELECH

- Probably means "father of a king" or "my father is king"
- First mentioned in Genesis 20 as a Philistine king of Gerar
- Entered into a covenant with Abraham after their dispute over a well (Gen. 21)

Genesis 20:1–21:34

I N   A   N U T S H E L L

These two chapters portray Abraham's ongoing faith during a time of peace and great joy. Both the peace and the joy were interrupted, however, by the testing of chapter 22.

Sister Act II

I. INTRODUCTION

Heaven Is a Local Call

*I*n the December 2000 issue of *Reader's Digest,* Richard A. Wright tells about a researcher visiting a San Francisco cathedral and noticing a golden telephone on the wall with the sign: "$10,000 per minute." When he asked the pastor about it, he explained that the call was a direct line to heaven. For that price the speaker could address God personally. As the researcher traveled around the country, he noticed similar phones with $10,000 price tags in churches in a variety of American cities. When he got to Dallas, he saw a golden phone, but this time the sign read "Thirty-five cents per minute." So he asked the pastor, "Reverend, I have found many golden phones with direct lines to heaven, but they all cost $10,000 per minute. How come yours is only 35 cents?" The pastor replied, "Son, you're in Texas now—from here heaven is a local call" (Wright, 101–2).

The chapters we are about to study continue this conversation between heaven and earth that began in chapter 12. In chapter 20 God talks to Abimelech and Abimelech responds. At the end of the chapter, Abraham prays, apparently in the presence of Abimelech. In chapter 21 God sends an angel with a message to Hagar, and Abimelech observes to Abraham, "God is with you in everything you do" (21:22). We begin to see a basic truth unfold here in the early chapters of the Bible—*talking to God is a way of life.* As Brother Lawrence once observed, "You need not cry very loud; He is nearer to us than we think."

I doubt if Texas makes any difference. For all believers heaven is a local call.

II. COMMENTARY

Sister Act II

> **MAIN IDEA:** *In spite of all our manipulations, God's plan prevails. These chapters show Abraham following God's plan for his life and protecting the inheritance that God had promised.*

Negev Neighbors (20:1–7)

> **SUPPORTING IDEA:** *Abraham struggled with the issue of telling the truth when it was dangerous to do so. In these verses we find him pulling the same trick on Abimelech that he had used on the pharaoh in Egypt years earlier.*

20:1–3. As we read these chapters in Genesis, we think the Canaanite postal service must have struggled keeping track of this wandering nomad. Here again he changes zip codes, moving back south to the Negev. The text gives us no hint why Abraham made this move. We find it disturbing in view of what he had just been through with Sodom and his awareness that the son of promise was due within a year. In chapter 12 he went to Egypt because of the famine, but here no reason for his move is evident.

Kidner says:

> The episode is chiefly one of suspense: on the brink of Isaac's birth-story here is the very Promise put in jeopardy, traded away for personal safety. If it is ever to be fulfilled, it will owe very little to man. Morally as well as physically, it will clearly have to be achieved by the grace of God (Kidner, 137).

The Lord preserved Sarah's purity yet still held Abimelech accountable for taking Sarah into his harem. Yet again God intervened with a dream (Gen. 28:12; 31:10–11; 37:5–9; 40:5; 41:1).

20:4–7. Quite possibly *Abimelech* is not a name at all but a royal title like *Pharaoh* or *Caesar*. The name appears again in chapter 26, probably to identify the son or grandson of the Abimelech we encounter here.

But the interesting thing about these verses centers not in God's encounter with Abimelech but in the language that passes between them—words like **clear conscience**, **clean hands**, and **pray for you**. Abimelech was probably as vicious and violent a monarch as the other kings we met earlier in this record of Abraham's life. Abimelech meant, of course, that according to the customs of his land and the culture around him, he had done nothing wrong—and he was correct. Nevertheless, God held him accountable and threatened him with capital punishment.

A passage like this reminds us of Paul's warning in Romans about the importance of natural revelation as a means of understanding God's truth:

> The wrath of God is being revealed from heaven against all the godlessness and wickedness of men who suppress the truth by their wickedness, since what may be known about God is plain to them, because God has made it plain to them. For since the creation of the world God's invisible qualities—his eternal power and divine nature—have been clearly seen, being understood from what has been made, so that men are without excuse. For although they knew God, they neither glorified him as God nor gave thanks to him, but their thinking became futile and their foolish hearts were darkened. Although they claimed to be wise, they became fools and exchanged the glory of the immortal God for images made to look like mortal man and birds and animals and reptiles. Therefore God gave them over in the sinful desires of their hearts to sexual impurity for the degrading of their bodies with one another. They exchanged the truth of God for a lie, and worshiped and served created things rather than the Creator—who is forever praised. Amen (Rom. 1:18–25).

B Rationalization Redux (20:8–18)

SUPPORTING IDEA: *We need to stay alert to the influence of believers on unbelievers. Things we say and do may be interpreted in ways we do not anticipate by unbelievers.*

20:8–10. This threat from God had to be taken seriously. Abimelech brought in all his top people. When they heard the story **they were very much afraid.** Then Abimlech asked Abraham three questions. The most important appears in verse 10: **What was your reason for doing this?**

20:11–13. The three excuses given by Abraham were not reasons at all but rationalization of behavior unbecoming a giant of faith:

1. I was afraid.
2. I only told a half lie.
3. Sarah and I do this quite often.

But the opening line of verse 11 reveals a great deal: **There is surely no fear of God in this place.** How many times Christians live, work, travel, and go to school in places where there seems to be no fear of God. The word **fear** here takes on its religious sense. Abimelech did not *fear* God; he had no idea who God was. But Abraham *feared* Abimelech because the patriarch knew God well. This kind of fear has often been described as reverential trust that involves commitment and obedience.

20:14–18. By God's grace Abraham received not punishment but plunder. Wherever he went, whatever he did, Abraham stood under God's protection and blessing. Abimelech reacted very much like Pharaoh did except he threw in the land. The word **shekels** does not appear in the Hebrew text, but translators use it because it describes the most common unit of weight in ancient times.

Verse 18 indicates a portion of the punishment of which we have not yet heard. Back in verse 3 only Abimelech stood in danger; now we learn **the LORD had closed up every womb in Abimelech's household because of Abraham's wife Sarah.**

God's grace covered Abraham's ignorance. He threatened Abimelech, not Abraham. Abimelech needed prayer, and Abraham prayed. Abimelech did wrong, and Abraham was paid. The whole chapter seems off kilter unless we cover it with God's grace. This sin certainly changed Abimelech's view of Abraham, but God's view remained unshaken. He forgave Abraham.

Ⓒ Child of Promise (21:1–7)

SUPPORTING IDEA: *Even when God's plans and promises seem impossible, he fulfills them—and forgives our doubts and fears.*

21:1–5. At last the son of promise arrived when Abraham was **a hundred years old.** Both Isaac and Jesus were named before they were conceived (Gen. 17:19; Luke 1:31). Both mothers conceived through God's supernatural activity. Both sons fulfilled the Abrahamic covenant. Initially Isaac began the line and eventually Jesus, one of Isaac's descendants, became the ultimate Son of Promise through whom blessing would come to all nations of the earth.

In Isaac's case no angels appeared, but the birth was no less miraculous. Abraham and Sarah could have sung together those immortal lines from *The Messiah* taken from Isaiah 9:6: "For to us a child is born, to us a son is given, and the government will be on his shoulders." The verse does not stop there, but the latter part could only apply to the final Son of Promise not the first: "He will be called Wonderful Counselor, Mighty God, Everlasting Father, Prince of Peace." The parallelism of Genesis 21:1–2 is deliberate in the use of the word **promised.**

What great hope this verse offers not only for our salvation but for everyday living: **The LORD did for Sarah what he had promised . . . at the very time God had promised him.**

21:6–7. This miraculous birth was accompanied by a laughing revival. Who would have guessed that God would actually make good on his promise. Sarah said, "I once laughed and now **God has brought me laughter.**" In his comments on 18:12, Sailhamer notes, "Her laughter becomes the occasion to draw an important theological point from the narrative, namely, that what the Lord was about to do to fulfill his promise to Abraham was a matter 'too wonderful' . . . even for his own people to imagine" (Sailhamer, 147). Both Abraham and Sarah had laughed at the thought of having a son, so that became his name.

Of this birth Paul wrote in Romans:

> Against all hope, Abraham in hope believed and so became the father of many nations, just as it had been said to him, "So shall your offspring be." Without weakening in his faith, he faced the fact that his body was as good as dead—since he was about a hundred years old—and that Sarah's womb was also dead. Yet he did not waver through unbelief regarding the promise of God, but was strengthened in his faith and gave glory to God, being fully persuaded that God had power to do what he promised. This is why "it was credited to him as righteousness" (Rom. 4:18–22).

God never scolded Abraham for his laughter as he did Sarah. His faith may have been weak, but she had no faith at all that God would give them a son.

Desert Nomad (21:8–13)

SUPPORTING IDEA: *God does not care only for prominent people like Abraham and Sarah; he cares for banished and rejected people like Hagar and Ishmael.*

21:8–13. The weaning spoken of in verse 8 probably took place at age two or three, so we have a scene familiar to modern parents—a teenager taunting a younger child. Sarah quickly got enough of this and wanted Hagar and Ishmael thrown out. In her view Ishmael did not fit into God's plan and would **never share in the inheritance with my son Isaac**. Abraham was not quite so sure. He loved Ishmael and also faced certain cultural duties as a prominent member of society in his part of the world. So again God intervened and made an amazing statement: **It is through Isaac that your offspring will be reckoned.**

Abraham also faced legal concerns. As Youngblood notes:

> According to the legal practices of that time, she [Sarah] had no genuine cause for worry. The Nuzi documents . . . imply that just as the inheritance rights of a son born to a man and his servant girl take precedence over the rights of an adopted son, so also do the inheritance rights of a son born to a man and his wife take precedence over those of a servant girl's son. To summarize the matter in the context of Abraham's family, just as Ishmael's rights superseded those of Eliezer, so also Isaac's rights would now supersede those of Ishmael (Youngblood, 181).

We need to realize also that at no time during the fourteen years of silence between Ishmael's birth and the birth of Isaac did God put divine censorship on Abraham's paternal relationship with Ishmael. Probably Abraham was content in these years, happy to dote on his son Ishmael. Keep in mind that Abraham had little access to the kind of theological depth we find in God's Word. He found himself a recipient of progressive revelation on a number of subjects, including this matter of who would inherit the divine promise.

Ishmael was probably a very important figure in Abraham's camp, the pride and delight of his father, spoiled by everyone. We must remember also that in chapter 17 God had promised fruitfulness to Ishmael as well as Isaac.

Did God keep his promise to Ishmael? The number of Arabs today is as the sand of the desert on which they live. Descending from the twelve desert princes described in Genesis 25, the children of Ishmael represent several important nations in today's world.

What exactly did Ishmael do in his **mocking**? Commentators run the gamut on this interpretation, from jeering and poking fun to nearly killing the little boy. The RSV implies that Ishmael was just "playing," but Kidner suggests the word is "the intensive form of Isaac's name-verb 'to laugh,' its malicious sense here demanded by the context and by Galatians 4:29" (Kidner, 140). Let's look at that important Galatians text: "At that time the son born in the ordinary way persecuted the son born by the power of the Spirit. It is the same now."

Persecuting is a great deal stronger than jeering. In fact, the difference is so great that F. F. Bruce writes, "Biblical substantiation for the statement that Ishmael persecuted Isaac is not forthcoming, so far as the two individuals are concerned; there could be a reference to occasions when the descendants committed aggression against the Israelites, Isaac's descendants" (Bruce, 223). Perhaps, but Paul's wording seems quite clear, and Sarah's reaction seems to account for more than just immature taunting.

We have wandered from our focus on the phrase **through Isaac that your offspring will be reckoned**. Kidner says that this "puts God's choice beyond all doubt, bringing into the open both the fact of election, as Paul shows in Romans 7–9, and, for Abraham, the irreplaceability of Isaac. On this anvil there was no escape from the hammer-blow of the next chapter, and Hebrews 11:18,19 shows that Abraham's faith was brought to perfection by this very means" (Kidner, 140).

Whatever the behavior of Ishmael, one thing is certain: Sarah determined that the two boys could not be raised together, and she demanded the expulsion of both Ishmael and his mother. In Paul's commentary on this passage in Galatians, he deals at length with this expulsion to show that law and gospel cannot coexist (Gal. 4:21–31). Paul compares Christians to Isaac, children of promise free from the law. Yet, as Isaac was persecuted by the offspring of flesh, so in Paul's day the Galatians were beset by the Judaizers. The two mothers represented two covenants: Hagar the Sinaitic covenant of law and Sarah the new covenant of grace.

E Single Mom (21:14–21)

SUPPORTING IDEA: *In these verses we learn about God's tender care for single parents, a great Bible lesson for today's society.*

21:14–18. Abraham found it difficult to send Hagar and Ishmael away. His gentle heart loved them both. He had to be reassured by God before he gave in to Sarah's demand. He gave Hagar as many supplies as she could carry and sent her with her teenage son into the wilderness. They eventually wandered to a spot later known as Beersheba. Here a crisis occurred in the life of Ishmael when the water ran out.

Careless reading of verse 15 could lead one to contradiction in the child's age. Would a mother put a teenager under a bush? Some have argued that Ishmael was an infant at this time. But that seems improbable. A slave woman born in Egypt could go longer without water than a teenager who had probably been spoiled in the wealthy tents of Abraham.

What wonderful words we find in these verses: **God heard the boy crying**. Many commentators believe that the phrase **the angel of God** refers to an appearance of Christ who carries that title throughout Scripture.

21:19–21. The comfort of the Lord continues. In verse 17 he **heard the boy crying**; in verse 19 **God opened her eyes**, and in verse 20 **God was with the boy as he grew up**. Here we find the first record of a single mom in history. Although we do not see Hagar any more in the biblical record of Genesis, we may assume that this divine encounter called her to a life of service and perhaps even sacrifice in raising her son. Her influence continued into his adulthood as she selected a wife from Egypt for her son.

Every time we read about the Israeli-Arab conflict in Palestine, we should think about Ishmael, the first Arab. And when we think of Ishmael, we should think of this passage where God promised a great future for the Arabs to Abraham and then repeated it to Hagar. God was at work on center stage with Abraham, Sarah, and Isaac. But he was also at work behind the scenes—back in the desert, beneath a bush—for Hagar and Ishmael.

F Well of the Oath (21:22–34)

SUPPORTING IDEA: *God's people need to protect their relationships with neighbors. This is precisely what Abraham does in the second part of Genesis 21.*

21:22–24. When we last saw Abimelech, Abraham prayed that his wives and slave girls could have children again. This time Abimlech brought his enforcer along and wanted to sign a long-term peace treaty with Abraham. As he said to Abraham, **God is with you in everything you do**. Abraham had already dealt falsely with Abimelech, so he brought that up first. But the real request came at the end of verse 23: **Show to me and the country where you are living as an alien the same kindness I have shown to you**. Abimelech understood not only the size and power of Abraham's influence but the size and power of Abraham's God. He did not need an enemy like Abraham. So they shook hands and Abraham declared, **I swear it**.

21:25–31. Abraham had something more specific in mind after the treaty had been signed. Abimelech's servants had snatched a certain well away from Abraham, and he wanted it back. This gave birth to an official treaty that went beyond the handshake of verse 23. Abraham gave **seven ewe lambs** to Abimelech **as a witness that I dug this well**. The place where this occurred was **Beersheba**. This name shows up frequently in the Old Testament as an important landmark, the extreme southern boundary of Israel (2 Sam. 17:11).

21:32–34. Abimelech and Phicol (possibly a title rather than a name) headed back home to a region called **the land of the Philistines**. Our minds flood with stories of David and Goliath when we learn that **Abraham stayed in the land of the Philistines for a long time**. And, in keeping with appropriate environmental concerns, he **planted a tamarisk tree** and called on **the Eternal God** (*El olam*), a name that appears only here in Scripture. It emphasizes God's everlasting nature.

> **MAIN IDEA REVIEW:** *In spite of all our manipulations, God's plan prevails. These chapters show Abraham following God's plan for his life and protecting the inheritance that God had promised.*

III. CONCLUSION

Faith Is More Than Feeling

In an article on "Religion and the Brain," Sharon Bagley tiptoed through the tulips of Zen Buddhism, Franciscan meditation, and assorted other "neurotheologies" and decided that "for a mystical experience to occur, brain regions that orient you in space and mark the distinction between self and world must go quiet" (*Newsweek*, May 7, 2001, 54).

The conclusion of Bagley's work (written with the assistance of Anne Underwood) offers this less-than-scintillating paragraph:

> For the all-tentative successes that scientists are scoring in their search for the biological bases of religious, spiritual and mystical experience, one mystery will surely lie forever beyond their grasp. They may trace a sense of transcendence to *this* bulge in our gray

matter. And they may trace a feeling of the divine to *that* one. But it is likely that they will never resolve the greatest question of all— namely, whether our brain wiring creates God, or whether God created our brain wiring. Which you believe is, in the end, a matter of faith (Bagley, *Newsweek,* 57).

Newsweek religion editor Kenneth Woodward was alloted a one-page response. He said, "The chief mistake these neurotheologians make is to identify religion with specific experiences and feelings. Losing oneself in prayer may feel good or uplifting, but these emotions have nothing to do with how well we communicate with God" (Woodward, *Newsweek,* 58).

Our union with God through Christ is not mystical but spiritual, and a world of difference separates those two words. Since science does not deal with the immaterial, neurobiologists and neurotheologians can only describe what they think they see with their various machines and insights. But suggesting that the brain is the only source of our religious experience is extreme reductionism at best and, for the context of our present study, a blatant denial of grace.

Woodward ends his remarks by saying, "It is hard to imagine a believer in the midst of mystical transport telling herself that it is just her neuro-circuits acting up. Like Saint Augustine, who lived fifteen centuries before we discovered that the brain makes waves, the religious mind intuits that 'Thou hast made us for thyself, O Lord, and our hearts are restless until they rest in thee'" (Woodward, *Newsweek,* 58).

We have restless hearts, and in that behavior we are much like Abraham. These chapters in the Book of Genesis don't read like the Twenty-Third Psalm, nor does the Twenty-Third Psalm reflect all of David's tumultuous life. Sometimes we give the impression that people who trust Christ, read their Bibles, pray, and go to church live calm, collected, and peaceful lives amid the turmoil around them. But most biblical data do not support that conclusion. Like Abraham we find our lives a constant test of choices along our pilgrim pathway. Most of these force us back to total dependence on God. Such is the life of faith. We should recite with some regularity the words of Abimelech to Abraham: "God is with you in everything you do."

PRINCIPLES

- Even Abraham seemed to take too long to learn some important lessons. We should be encouraged that God has patience with us.

- God answers the prayers of his people on behalf of others.

- God does what he promises.

APPLICATIONS

- Pray for people in your circle of influence.
- Rejoice and praise God for miracle babies, born both physically and spiritually.
- "Live in harmony with one another . . . if it is possible, as far as it depends on you, live at peace with everyone" (Rom. 12:16,18).
- Trust and obey God in the trials and tests of life.

IV. LIFE APPLICATION

A Bend in the Road

David Jeremiah wrote a book entitled *A Bend in the Road* (Word, 2000) that details his struggle with cancer that began in September 1994, when he was diagnosed with lymphoma. He describes the dark days of "life's disruptions" and reminds us that as the Israelites traveled long distances from their homes to Jerusalem to worship and celebrate the great feasts, they often sang to express their joy and faith in God.

We don't see Abraham singing at any point in Scripture, but he certainly set the foundation for people of faith who want to handle life's disruptions and struggles with spiritual courage. Abraham exemplified Jeremiah's emphasis on how to handle the burdens of life, including the conflict with Abimelech and the agony of sending Hagar and Ishmael into the desert. Jeremiah says, "When the enemy closes in, we'll never defeat him using his own weapons. Instead, we load the weapons of our lips, our tongues, our hands, our wills . . . with the most powerful gun powder that has ever been discharged on earth—worship and praise" (Jeremiah, 126).

Jeremiah survived the first physical struggle, but his cancer reappeared in the fall of 1998. During this time he found great comfort in the Book of Psalms: "Whenever I have suffered, the psalms have provided my medicine; when I have been wounded, they have bandaged me and have pointed me toward healing. . . . I've drunk deeply of them, bathed in them, and let them wash over me until I've felt the dust of the world cleansed away by the hope and peace of God's presence in the music of the psalms" (Jeremiah, 141).

V. PRAYER

Father, our life is full of brokenness—broken relationships, broken promises, broken expectations. Help us learn to live with that brokenness by returning again and again to your faithful presence in our lives. Amen.

VI. DEEPER DISCOVERIES

A. Abraham the Prophet (20:7)

When we rush through a recitation of the major and minor prophets, Abraham's name does not appear. Yet he is the first person in the Bible to be called a prophet. This makes us wonder how that word was used at this point in the history of God's revelation. The word does not appear again in the Book of Genesis, but in Exodus 7:1 God told Moses that Aaron would be his prophet. Deuteronomy has a great deal to say about prophets, particularly in chapters 13 and 18. And, by the time we get to 1 and 2 Kings, prophets are common in Israelite culture and religion.

The English word actually combines two Greek words, *pro* (on behalf of) and *phemni* (to say). So prophets spoke on behalf of other people. In the Bible they spoke mainly on behalf of God. Most of the prophets in the Old Testament were either speaking prophets like Nathan, Elijah, and Elisha or writing prophets like Isaiah, Jeremiah, and Daniel. Deuteronomy identifies two criteria to prove the truth of a prophet: He had to speak the truth (Deut. 18:22) and he must not lead people away from God (Deut. 13:1–5).

B. Ishmael in Galatians 4

Although Ishmael is not named in Galatians, Paul's argument (Gal. 3:1–5:12) certainly focuses on the contrast between Hagar and Sarah and, therefore, Ishmael and Isaac. In both cases mother and son stand for the contrast between law and grace, flesh and Spirit. Paul slides into the issue by talking about adoption in 4:6 and begins the Old Testament metaphor at 4:22. The key to the passage pops up in verse 24: "These things may be taken figuratively, for the women represent two covenants. One covenant is from Mount Sinai and bears children who are to be slaves: This is Hagar." People who insist on the law are the children of Hagar, locked into Mount Sinai and "the present city of Jerusalem" (v. 25), where Paul more than once argued this issue of law and grace. Christians, he says, "like Isaac, are children of promise" (v. 28).

Since both Hagar and Ishmael represent an action of the flesh taken by Abraham and Sarah, any act of the flesh that leads to a view of salvation by works must be rejected. Furthermore, believers must put aside the flesh and rest completely in the Spirit by faith. To make that point Paul says, "Get rid of the slave woman and her son, for the slave woman's son will never share in the inheritance with the free woman's son" (v. 30), a loose quote from Genesis 21:10. And though Galatians 4:24 may unlock the analogy, 5:1 opens the entire epistle: "It is for freedom that Christ has set us free. Stand firm, then, and do not let yourselves be burdened again by a yoke of slavery."

So already we have the law and grace issue surfacing in Scripture, long before Moses came down the mountain with his stone tablets. Abraham would have known nothing about the contrast between law and grace. But his spiritual walk with God set the stage for the way God would deal with his people throughout history.

C. Land of the Philistines (21:34)

Before Abraham's time the Philistines had settled in the southwestern corner of Canaan, having arrived there by sea from northern Egypt. They rose to their greatest power during the reigns of Saul and David. Eventually crushed by David, they were not a major force in the latter years of the Old Testament.

We should not think of the Philistines who dealt with Abraham as the great power that Joshua and later David faced. Migrations take great periods of time. This first mention of the Philistines in Genesis 21 may describe only Abimelech's tribe, forerunner of the great Philistine lords and cities of future years.

VII. TEACHING OUTLINE

A. INTRODUCTION

1. Lead Story: Heaven Is a Local Call
2. Context: When Genesis 20 opens with the words "now Abraham moved on," it provides a geographical reference. But in reality Abraham also moved beyond the problems of Lot and Sodom and into that portion of his life that launched the Hebrew nation.
3. Transition: We find a parallel between the end of chapter 21 and the beginning of chapter 22. Abraham, content at last by his tamarisk tree in Beersheba, called on the name of the eternal God and stayed in one place "for a long time." But as all mature Christians know, we dare not settle down when God is running our lives. So after Abraham's *rest* comes Abraham's *test*. That is where we will find him in our next chapter.

B. COMMENTARY

1. Negev Neighbors (20:1–7)
2. Rationalization Redux (20:8–18)
3. Child of Promise (21:1–7)
4. Desert Nomad (21:8–13)
5. Single Mom (21:14–21)
6. Well of the Oath (21:22–34)

C. CONCLUSION: A BEND IN THE ROAD

VIII. ISSUES FOR DISCUSSION

1. In your opinion, why did God judge Abimelech for Abraham's sin?
2. Name some parallels between the experience of Hagar and the struggle of today's single mothers.
3. What role does oath-taking play among Christians in our day?

Genesis 22:1–24:67

Abraham's Senior Moments

I. INTRODUCTION
God of Our Fathers

II. COMMENTARY
A verse-by-verse explanation of these chapters.

III. CONCLUSION
Matchmaking: A Personal Perspective

An overview of the principles and applications from these chapters.

IV. LIFE APPLICATION
God Will Provide the Ram

Melding these chapters to life.

V. PRAYER
Tying these chapters to life with God.

VI. DEEPER DISCOVERIES
Historical, geographical, and grammatical enrichment of the commentary.

VII. TEACHING OUTLINE
Suggested step-by-step group study of these chapters.

VIII. ISSUES FOR DISCUSSION
Zeroing these chapters in on daily life.

"*O*f any stopping place in life, it is good to ask whether it will be a good place from which to go on as well as a good place to remain."

M a r y   C a t h e r i n e   B a t e s o n

GEOGRAPHICAL PROFILE: MOUNT MORIAH

- Located north of the city of Jerusalem, just over fifty miles from Beersheba
- The site of Araunah's threshing floor where God stopped a plague (2 Sam. 24)
- The site of the temples built by Solomon, Zerubbabel, and Herod the Great

GEOGRAPHICAL PROFILE: MACHPELAH

- A piece of property belonging to Ephron the Hittite
- The property contained a large field and a cave where Abraham buried Sarah
- Also the burial place of Abraham, Isaac, Rebekah, Jacob, and Leah
- Today a large mosque sits on the site

PERSONAL PROFILE: MILCAH

- The name means "counsel"
- Daughter of Haran and nephew of Abraham
- Sister of Lot
- Mother of Bethuel

PERSONAL PROFILE: BETHUEL

- Father of Rebekah and Laban whose name means "abode of God"
- Son of Nahor and Milcah

- Name means "fawn"
- Son of Zohar the Hittite
- Landowner from whom Abraham purchased the field and cave of Machpelah

Genesis 22:1–24:67

I N   A   N U T S H E L L

*T*hese chapters contain important events in the life of Abraham and the history of the Old Testament patriarchs. The events typify things that could happen to us—the loss of a child, the death of a spouse, and the tension-filled expectation of a wedding. Through it all, God's grace continues to guide Abraham's earthly journey.

Abraham's Senior Moments

I. INTRODUCTION

God of Our Fathers

In 1876 Daniel Crane Roberts, rector of St. Thomas Episcopal Church in Brandon, Vermont, was commissioned to write the official hymn for the one-hundredth-anniversary celebration of the Declaration of Independence. Although as late as 1892 the words were sung to the tune "Russian Hymn," the current tune "National Hymn," was composed by George W. Warren, the organist at St. Thomas. Apparently this tune appeared publicly for the first time in the *Protestant Episcopal Hymnal* in 1894.

This hymn's immediate nationwide recognition has placed it in virtually every hymnbook of our time. Its theme captures the truth of that "faith once for all entrusted to the saints" which we see dominating Abraham's life. Its prayer still cries out for recognition in today's secular world.

> God of our Fathers whose almighty hand
> Leads forth in beauty all the starry band
> Of shining worlds in splendor thru the skies,
> Our grateful songs before Thy throne arise.
>
> Thy love divine hath led us in the past,
> In this free land by Thee our lot is cast;
> Be Thou our Ruler, Guardian, Guide, and Stay,
> Thy Word our law, Thy paths our chosen way.

Probably Abraham could not sing much about the God of his fathers. But Isaac, Jacob, and the entire list of offspring whom we meet in our study of Genesis could have appreciated the general sentiment of this great hymn. Genesis 12–22 contains nearly one hundred references to conversations between Abraham and God, a relationship that grew stronger as the experiences of old age brought new and different challenges.

II. COMMENTARY

Abraham's Senior Moments

> **MAIN IDEA:** *Abraham's spiritual journey moves forward by steps of faith. Now he is about to take two giant steps forward as he ties Isaac to the altar and then faces the death and burial of his beloved Sarah.*

Moriah Meeting (22:1–8)

> **SUPPORTING IDEA:** *Spiritual growth depends on how we handle the tests and trials that come our way.*

22:1–2. Although the word does not appear in our text, *obedience* to the command of God forms the fabric of this chapter. It begins by pointing out that **some time later God tested Abraham**. Some translations use the word *tempt* and others use *prove*. In any case, Abraham's faith in God's absolute righteous judgment was put on the line. As Kidner expresses it, "Abraham's trust was to be weighed in the balance against common sense, human affection, and life-long ambition; an act against everything earthly" (Kidner, 143).

We wonder why verse 2 includes the phrase **your only son** when God had emphasized that he would bless Ishmael as well. Some commentators suggest a focus on the relationship that now existed between Abraham and Isaac. Others emphasize that this was the only son God was interested in at this point—the only one who could bring Abraham through the test that lay ahead. Certainly Abraham never questioned whom God had selected for this horrible execution.

Mount Moriah enters the text of Scriptures and grows in importance throughout the history of the Jews. It appears again in 2 Chronicles 3:1 during a crisis in David's life. It became the location for the ancient temple. Today the area holds the famous Dome of the Rock built in A.D. 691, the third most holy place of Islam (after Mecca and Medina).

Certainly the word **go** would have been familiar to this pilgrim to whom God had issued that command many times. But this time it was a special journey for a special purpose; we cringe as we read the words even thousands of years later: **Sacrifice him there as a burnt offering**.

Human sacrifice, common in ancient paganism, was wrong for the righteous people who belonged to the Lord. But here God's command took precedence over human custom. We must keep in mind that Abraham had no contrary revelation about human sacrifice.

22:3–5. Abraham began what was about three days in the valley of the shadow of death. The fifty-mile trip northeast must have brought agony of heart as the donkey walked step after painful step toward that mountain. Two servants accompanied the father and son, but Abraham told them to stay back **while I and the boy go over there**. He also told the servants he was going to **worship**.

Abraham also told the servants, **We will come back to you**. This could hardly have been wishful thinking or carefully couched language to throw off any apprehension they might have had about this event. On the other hand, there is no evidence that Abraham knew God would provide a different kind of sacrifice and Isaac would be unharmed. In fact, we have no idea what was going on in Abraham's mind unless we consult the inspired record of Hebrews 11:9: "Abraham reasoned that God could raise the dead, and figuratively speaking, he did receive Isaac back from death." When God's people act in faith, they never try to designate the method God will use to achieve the ends they believe he has promised.

22:6–8. A typology of the ultimate sacrifice began to emerge as Isaac carried the wood for his own death up the mountain while Abraham carried **the fire and the knife**. But Isaac noticed there was something wrong with this picture. He asked about the sacrificial lamb, and Abraham replied with one of the great lines of the Old Testament: **God himself will provide the lamb**.

How old was Isaac when this event took place? In verse 5 we see the English word *boy*, but the Hebrew word which it translates could mean anything from an infant (Exod. 2:6) to a young man (1 Chr. 12:28). Most scholars believe Isaac was a strong and healthy teenager at this point in his life, so he was capable of refusing or resisting the entire process. Therefore we see the faith of both father and son as this scenario played out at Moriah.

Ⓑ Sacrificed Son (22:9–19)

> **SUPPORTING IDEA:** *Abraham's God asks of his people complete trust, obedience, and surrender of all human possessions, including life itself. Just as Abraham trusted God to find a way, we stand in the same position about every challenge we face in our lives.*

22:9–12. At any point in this awful journey, God could have stopped Abraham and said, "It is enough. I see your faith is sufficient." But he did not. He allowed Abraham to go through the entire ritual of the sacrifice, including tying up the boy and placing him on the altar **on top of the wood**. Only when Abraham **reached out his hand and took the knife to slay his son** did God stop him. How did he reply when he heard his name called from heaven? Exactly as he did in verse 1: **Here I am**.

22:13–14. This passage captures the theme of the gospel of substitutionary atonement. Christ did not just die for the whole world; he died for each one of us. Isaac escaped death because God provided a **ram** that Abraham sacrificed **as a burnt offering instead of his son**. When our *timid* faith becomes *tested* faith, it can turn into *triumphant* faith. But it all begins with an acceptance of God's substitutionary atonement.

The key to the passage is verse 14. Abraham called this place *Yahweh Yir'eh*—**The LORD Will Provide**. From that moment until the time Moses wrote these words, and well beyond that historic point, the site retained that name. Ross tells us, "This is the basis of a truth often repeated in the Old Testament: the Lord was to be worshiped in His holy mountain by the nation. . . . The Lord would see the needs of those who came before Him and would meet their needs. Thus in providing for them He would be 'seen'" (Ross, 65).

22:15–19. In this chapter the first call to Abraham came directly from God in a manner that is not described. However, in verse 11 a second call came from "the angel of the LORD." Now in verse 15 **the angel of the LORD** called again. This is the seventh in the series of promises that God had given to Abraham. This is the first time God actually took an oath to fulfill the blessing of the offspring **as numerous as the stars in the sky and as the sand on the seashore**. Note the unconditional and conditional nature of God's promise to Abraham. God ended the conversation by saying that all these great things would occur **because you have obeyed me**.

Most Bible scholars see the connection between Abraham's offering of Isaac and God's offering of his own son; Isaac was a type of Christ. We see it in Romans 8:32, John 3:16, and Hebrews 11:9. One major difference is that in the New Testament there was no ram in the thicket and the Son died. As LaSor points out, "I can never think about the willingness of Abraham to offer up his son Isaac without thinking of the willingness of God to offer up His son Jesus. God provided a lamb to take the place of Isaac, but there was no lamb to take the place of Jesus. *He was the Lamb!* You and I have our life and our salvation and our hope of eternity because of what God has done for us in Christ; and the only way this world will ever come to know the salvation we know will be by way of our faithfulness. God expects us to be faithful" (LaSor, 30).

Ⓒ Canaan Cave (22:20–23:20)

SUPPORTING IDEA: *Like Abraham, we should view the death of our loved ones as a great opportunity to demonstrate faith and confidence in God and his promises.*

22:20–24. The first three words of verse 20 duplicate the first three words of verse 1. The record describes the expansion of the patriarchal family tree. Milcah, Lot's sister, now the wife of her uncle Nahor, had become the mother of **Uz** and **Buz** and six other children. The text explains this because one of those children, the last named Bethuel, **became the father of Rebekah**.

23:1–6. Upon the death of Sarah, Abraham decided not to return her to their ancestral home in Mesopotamia but to secure a burial space in this land of God's promise. She died in Hebron, and we read that **Abraham went to mourn for Sarah**. Went where? Since 22:19 tells us that "Abraham stayed in Beersheba," we assume this trip took him from Beersheba to Hebron. Abraham recited words that became characteristic of the Hebrew nation from the moment of Sarah's death to the present hour: **I am an alien and a stranger among you**. Abraham's people would wander in and out of Egypt, Assyria, Babylonia, Greece, and around the Roman Empire.

Kidner elaborates the uniqueness of Abraham's position:

> A stranger (*ger*) was a resident alien with some footing in the community but restricted rights. In Israel, for example, the *ger* would be granted no land of his own, and in this chapter the keen question under the elaborate courtesies was whether Abraham was to gain a permanent foothold or not. The flattery in v. 6 was an inducement to remain a landless dependent. Abraham's rejoinder, naming an individual, made skillful use of the fact that while a group tends to resent an intruder the owner of an asset may welcome a customer (Kidner, 145).

This point is central to the land grant of earlier chapters. If Abraham had accepted the first offer, he would have buried Sarah in the Hittite tomb—and still not owned an acre of Canaan. That would have been the wrong choice.

23:7–16. Since the Hittites had agreed that Abraham could bury Sarah in their territory, the only question was where and under what conditions. Apparently Abraham already had a spot in mind because he immediately defined with great specificity **the cave of Machpelah, which belongs to him** [Ephron] **and is in the end of his field**. Although Ephron was sitting right there, Abraham addressed the request to the entire group of Hittite leaders. This kind of specific request began the Bedouin bargaining which concludes in verse 16 as Abraham placed **four hundred shekels of silver** on the table.

23:17–20. What did Abraham buy? The text leaves nothing in doubt: **Both the field and the cave in it, and all the trees within the borders of the field**. For Abraham, Mesopotamia was now history; the new homeland would be built around this burial plot. The humble beginnings of the Abrahamic estate represent a symbol of the great geography of Israel described in earlier chapters. Sarah was the first of four generations buried at Machpelah. Only after the death of his wife did Abraham actually own any portion of the land.

Abraham was buying the field not only as a burial place for Sarah but also to express his confidence in God's promises. He had lived for sixty years in the land as a nomad. But before he himself died, he mingled the dust of his love with that of the land of promise as a sign of his expectation that God would fulfill the promise to his descendants. This purchase was a testimony to his children, since they did not possess the land for some four hundred years. And the lesson was well learned. Abraham himself, Isaac, Rebekah, Jacob, and Leah were buried there, even though Jacob died in Egypt. His sons took his body back to Canaan and buried him beside his father and grandfather.

𝔻 Master's Matchmaker (24:1–33)

SUPPORTING IDEA: *After Sarah's death Abraham lived on as a model of godly leadership, investing his life in his son. His obedience to God's call sends him to seek a wife for Isaac.*

24:1–9. Old age often brings stronger focus on our children and grandchildren, but Abraham was a late bloomer in these matters. So **advanced in years**, he searched for a wife for his son. Though not named in this chapter, Abraham's **chief servant** could be none other than Eliezer whom we met in 15:2. Abraham committed him to an oath, binding him to find Isaac's wife back in Mesopotamia. Isolated among **the daughters of the Canaanites**, Abraham felt he had no other choice.

Better no wife than a Canaanite wife; better no wife than abandonment of the newly acquired estate as a foothold in the promised land. Several things in these verses capture our attention.

If this **chief servant** was Eliezer, he showed great loyalty and grace in serving the heir who displaced him. Kidner calls Eliezer "one of the most attractive minor characters in the Bible, with his quiet good sense, his piety and faith, his devotion to his employer and his firmness in seeing the matter through" (Kidner, 146).

We also see an unusual form of an oath. Rather than dividing an animal and walking between the parts, Abraham told Eliezer: **Put your hand under my thigh**. Most scholars recognize this in its most literal sense, with a connection between future offspring and the reproductive organ. Westermann says, "The rite of touching the generative organ when taking an oath occurs elsewhere only in Gen. 47:29 where the circumstances are the same, namely, imminent death. The one who is facing death secures his last will by an 'oath at the source of life'" (Westermann, 384).

Finally, note the point of separation in this section: no wife from Canaan. Abraham did quite well among the Canaanites and could surely have bought Isaac a wife as easily as he bought Sarah a burial cave. Sailhamer says:

> Though no explanation is given, Abraham's desire that Isaac not take a wife from the Canaanites appears to be a further expression of the notion of the two lines of blessing and cursing seen in Genesis 9:25–27: "Cursed be Canaan!" but "blessed be the LORD, the God of Shem!" As has been the case throughout the narratives thus far, the

inhabitants of Canaan are considered to be under a divine curse for their iniquity (e.g., 15:16). The seed of Abraham is to be kept separate from the seed of Canaan (Sailhamer, 176).

24:10–21. Eliezer loaded up with **all kinds of good things** and headed **to the town of Nahor.** We position ourselves geographically by assuming Eliezer went to the town named for Abraham's brother, Haran, located in Aram (later Syria) and close to the Tigris and Euphrates rivers. He went to a well that served as the water source for people of that area.

But Eliezer wasn't just looking over the local female population. He had his spiritual eyes open. He asked for divine help in a prayer for God to point out the appropriate woman beyond any doubt. And typical of the way God had dealt with Abraham from the beginning, **before he had finished praying, Rebekah came out with her jar on her shoulder.** The prayer now became a plan as **the servant hurried to meet her.** He spoke, she spoke, and the sign was fulfilled.

Eliezer could have just asked for someone who was willing to give him a drink, but the prayer had specified the phrase **I'll water your camels too.** Not only that but this beautiful girl **quickly emptied her jar into the trough, ran back to the well to draw more water.** Griffith Thomas points out a spiritual lesson in this tender narrative: "Notice his perfect courtesy (ver. 17). Manner counts for a very great deal in all Christian work. We may spoil a good cause by our lack of considerateness and courtesy. We observe, too, his patience (ver. 21). He will not force matters, for there must be no hurry. The man is filled with a holy watchfulness for every indication of the will of God" (Thomas, 214).

And speaking of models, some interpreters have found an intricate typology in this chapter. A faithful servant who does his master's will, goes to find a bride, proclaims the master's message, and makes clear that the message does not originate with him certainly reminds us of our blessed Lord.

24:22–27. Now it was time to bring out the wedding presents to see whether this lovely girl might have any interest in Isaac. This servant produced a nose ring, accompanied by **two gold bracelets.** On the strength of this gleaming jewelry, he suggested that her father might want him as a houseguest. If we glance ahead to verse 47, we see that these trinkets were not just displayed but actually placed on the young woman. She identified her father and grandfather and invited Eliezer and his camels to **spend the night.**

Before he left, Eliezer offered a prayer of thanks as simple and moving as his prayer for a sign. Phillips describes the scene: "It was all so effortless, so natural and yet, at the same time, so evidently of God, the natural overlaid with the supernatural. Here was no chance meeting. Here was a meeting planned in heaven and now taking place on earth. As the servant presented the cause and claims of Isaac, Rebekah listened with all her heart and with wide-open eyes" (Phillips, 192).

24:28–33. Rebekah ran back to **her mother's household** and her brother Laban. One glance at the jewelry sent him rushing out to make friends with the new stranger in town. The usual amenities took place, and an unspoken invitation for a meal was proffered when Eliezer said, **I will not eat until I have told you what I have to say.** Things could not have looked better for Eliezer's mission. He must have been well ahead of his time schedule and bursting to pour out the purpose of his long journey from Canaan.

🇪 Willing Wife (24:34–67)

SUPPORTING IDEA: *These verses remind us of several spiritual lessons—obedience to God, sincere and simple prayer, the joy of fulfilled promises, the excitement and importance of marriage, and the value of being a good servant to our heavenly Master.*

24:34–49. Up to this point Rebekah and Laban had no idea that Eliezer had come from Abraham. So Eliezer made that clear along with information about his master's wealth and power. He poured out the story again. This time we learn two or three new details. Eliezer said that Abraham had given Isaac **everything** he owned. Abraham lived to be 175 years old, but before he died, he gave everything to Isaac. This included not only all his physical possessions, although that is obviously the primary intent of both 24:36 and 25:5, but he also gave Isaac a heritage of faith that he had carried all his life.

Eliezer also emphasized the family connection; he had come **to get the granddaughter of my master's brother for his son.** After the sermon comes the invitation in verse 49. We can certainly agree with Barnhouse: "It is wonderful to work for a cause which has been blessed by the Lord. No deficits, no failures are possible, when we are in His will. Where God guides, God provides. To know that church, home, and testimony are being blessed, causes exaltation beyond expression. And all because of His grace!" (Barnhouse, 27).

24:50–60. Now it was the family's turn to respond. Both Laban and Bethuel gave the right answer: **This is from the LORD . . . let her become the wife of your master's son, as the LORD has directed.** Eliezer worshiped God at the sound of this affirmation of his mission. Then he began to drag out **gold and silver jewelry and articles of clothing** that he provided for the bride-to-be, her brother, and her mother.

What a small role Bethuel plays in this chapter. When he did speak, he joined Laban in agreeing to release Rebekah. He did not appear to be the recipient of the gifts, yet he was the head of the house and the host. The question came down to Rebekah's wishes, and her character shines through in this chapter. She treated the stranger with great courtesy, she humbled herself to take care of his animals, and she recognized the will of God for her life.

When the relatives attempted to detain Eliezer and Rebekah for **ten days or so**, she agreed that this urgent matter must be taken care of quickly. One should not keep a 140-year-old man waiting for word about his future daughter-in-law. Boice says, "She had probably never been away from home in her entire life, but if God was sending her away, she wanted to respond to His leading immediately. So should we, when God indicates new directions for us. If we delay our obedience, little will be accomplished. Ten days will turn into ten months and then ten years, and the time for service will be gone" (Boice, 250).

24:61–67. Isaac **was living in the Negev,** and he saw the returning caravan first. When Rebekah asked Eliezer who Isaac was, Eliezer responded, **He is my master.** After Eliezer's report, Isaac took Rebekah to Sarah's tent. The story comes to a rather abrupt halt with the information that they married, **he loved her, and Isaac was comforted after his mother's death.**

Several questions arise as we read this portion of the chapter. Why did the returning caravan happen to see Isaac before Abraham? Surely the ancient patriarch was at his estate in Hebron, which would have put him first in the path. That question is complicated by Eliezer's answer to Rebekah's question about Isaac: **He is my master.** The word *master* in this chapter had only been applied to Abraham up to this point.

Those two questions give way to the disappearance of Abraham from the end of the chapter. He had been in control of this operation from the beginning; he sent Eliezer out from Hebron headquarters. Now suddenly this marriage took place with not the slightest mention of his name.

Kidner speculates:

> It could mean that Abraham had set up Isaac on his own (36), in view of his impending marriage (and possibly Abraham's own remarriage, 25:1) allotting him his chief servant. But the expression could be used of Isaac as heir, and the disappearance of Abraham from the story may be no more than the narrator's way of transferring attention to the two who are the story's growing-point (Kidner, 149).

MAIN IDEA REVIEW: *Abraham's spiritual journey moves forward by simple steps of faith. Now he is about to take two giant steps forward as he ties Isaac to the altar and then faces the death and burial of his beloved Sarah.*

III. CONCLUSION

Matchmaking: A Personal Perspective

In 1976 I had crossed the border into Canada to speak at a joint service of several Mennonite Brethren churches in St. Catharines, Ontario. During the weekend Bible conference I was housed in the home of John and Lottie Durksen and discovered a chatty and talented sixteen-year-old whom they called "B. J."—a nickname for Betty Jane, the third of four daughters. Quickly taken with the young lady's wit and wisdom, I thought of my own son, the identical age. But not having been sent on any mission other than teaching the Bible, I got hold of myself and decided that the two were separated by an international boundary as well as being only sweet sixteen.

Nevertheless, just before leaving the Durksen home, I asked B. J. for a picture of herself that she promptly provided. Somewhere between Toronto and Miami, what started as a simple gesture began to grow in importance and possibility. Upon my return home, I walked into my son's bedroom with a brashness that frightens me to the present hour, handed him the photo, and said, "Jeff, this is a picture of the girl you will marry some day."

Readers familiar with Genesis 24 know exactly where this story is headed. The next year the two met at a Bible conference in Canada (where I was also speaking). The next year they entered college as freshmen together, became friends, and married just six years after my expedition to St. Catharines. The marriage, now nearly twenty years strong, has produced two lovely grandchildren and a harmony of talents between two people who have found a ministry niche and filled it remarkably well. My son is a pastor and chaplain on a college campus, and B. J. (now known as Beth) teaches her own children at home and serves in numerous capacities at the church her husband serves as pastor.

Living the life of either Abraham or Eliezer would be sufficiently burdensome in itself, but to take upon oneself the roles of both of them in one gambit could have been embarrassing. But my mission, like that of Eliezer, was blessed of God. When his hand touches anything—mission, ministry, marriage—all's well that ends well.

PRINCIPLES

- God's orders are not the basis for discussion but for action.
- God may send tests into our lives very different from those Abraham faced, but our response must be to trust and obey.
- True faith is not selfish in its duty to God or in its willingness to serve others.

APPLICATIONS

- Like Abraham and Eliezer, we must be confident that God will go before us and carry out his will in our lives.

- Through prayer, common sense, and the power of the Holy Spirit, God will direct our lives.

- God's Word is full of promises he made to Abraham; we need to depend upon him to fulfill those promises in our lives.

IV. LIFE APPLICATION

God Will Provide the Ram

The drama of Genesis 22 offers one of the most gripping portions of the Abrahamic story. Imagine Abraham with tear-filled eyes, knife poised in the air, standing beside the body of his only son strapped to an altar! But Abraham had faith in God's *call* and God's *consistency*. He also believed in God's *continuation*. He believed that when God promised a great nation, and clearly indicated that nation would come from the son of promise, nothing could thwart God's plan.

Abraham had already reached a high level of maturity, or he would never have gone through with this unthinkable command. And God knew the maturity of Abraham's faith. This was no longer the young man who offered his wife as his sister to the king of Egypt more than a quarter of a century earlier. He had grown into the father of a nation who regularly talked with God. He had come through enormous struggles to recognize that God knows what he does and why he does it. God needed no human sacrifice, nor would he allow it. He wanted Abraham's willingness to offer up his most prized prossession. Abraham's obedience to God in the offering of his son is the greatest single act of submission in the Bible apart from the submission of the Lamb of God to the cross.

V. PRAYER

Father, thank you for the faith of Abraham, the commitment of Eliezer, and the gracious readiness of Rebekah. May we reflect these qualities in our lives. Amen.

VI. DEEPER DISCOVERIES

A. Isaac as a Type of Christ (22:9–12)

For some reason Benjamin Keach leaves his section on types of Christ to the very last chapter of his one-thousand-page book, *Preaching from the Types and Metaphors of the Bible*. Prior to Isaac he identified Adam, Noah, Melchizedek, and Abraham as types of Christ. Modern scholars might doubt some of those, or at least show less enthusiasm than does Keach. But when it comes to Isaac, the typology issue is nearly impossible to avoid. Keach makes five points: Like Isaac, Jesus was the son of Abraham, mocked by his brothers, led as a lamb to the slaughter, three days "dead" (at least in Abraham's mind), and married to Rebekah, a symbol of the church (Keach, 974).

B. Alien and Stranger (23:4)

Few themes penetrate the Bible from beginning to end like the pilgrim-alien-stranger description of the people of God. Paul talked often about not being a citizen of this world but a citizen of heaven living temporarily in the world. Of Abraham the writer of Hebrews says:

> By faith he made his home in the promised land like a stranger in a foreign country; he lived in tents, as did Isaac and Jacob, who were heirs with him of the same promise. . . . All these people were still living by faith when they died. They did not receive the things promised; they only saw them and welcomed them from a distance. And they admitted that they were aliens and strangers on earth (Heb. 11:9,13).

Vagabonds, migrants, landed immigrants—such are the people of God. Faith is being sure that our true home and hope lie in heaven, not here on earth. Lea comments:

> They endured in their faith because they had seen the promises and embraced them. They trusted God to give future generations what they only hoped for. . . . They confessed that they were aliens and wanderers on earth. They did not try to return to the comforts and ease of Ur and Haran in Mesopotamia. They looked for a heavenly city prepared by God. What was the outcome of such sterling faith? In spite of the obvious failings of all these men, God was not ashamed to be called their God. He had prepared a spiritual city for them, and he was delighted to be known as their God (Lea, 202).

VII. TEACHING OUTLINE

A. INTRODUCTION

1. Lead Story: God of Our Fathers

2. Context: In this study we find Abraham in the land of the Philistines where he had been "for a long time" (21:34). Then God shook up his life with the offering of Isaac and the last-minute redemption. He barely recovers from that when Sarah dies at the age of 127. Then, this man of faith who had been content with raising tents and building altars decides he must plan for the future. So chapter 24 ends with the marriage of Isaac and Rebekah.

3. Transition: The text of Genesis moves into the record of Abraham's death at the age of 175. Genesis 25 forms a definitive bridge from the era of Abraham to the era of Isaac in the Old Testament.

B. COMMENTARY

1. Moriah Meeting (22:1–8)

2. Sacrificed Son (22:9–19)

3. Canaan Cave (22:20–23:20)

4. Master's Matchmaker (24:1–33)

5. Willing Wife (24:34–67)

C. CONCLUSION: GOD WILL PROVIDE THE RAM

VIII. ISSUES FOR DISCUSSION

1. List several similarities and differences between Genesis 12 and Genesis 22.

2. What modern implications might we place upon Abraham's insistence that Isaac not take a Canaanite wife?

3. What can we learn about courtship and marriage from Genesis 24?

Genesis 25:1–26:35

History Repeats Itself

I. INTRODUCTION
Patriarchal Pilgrimage: The Graying
of America

II. COMMENTARY
A verse-by-verse explanation of these chapters.

III. CONCLUSION
The Word of Forgiveness

An overview of the principles and applications from
these chapters.

IV. LIFE APPLICATION
"Quiet Revolution"

Melding these chapters to life.

V. PRAYER
Tying these chapters to life with God.

VI. DEEPER DISCOVERIES
Historical, geographical, and grammatical enrichment of the commentary.

VII. TEACHING OUTLINE
Suggested step-by-step group study of these chapters.

VIII. ISSUES FOR DISCUSSION
Zeroing these chapters in on daily life.

Q u o t e

"*G*od is a peacemaker. Jesus Christ is a peacemaker. So, if we want to be God's children and Christ's disciples, we must be peacemakers too."

J o h n   R .   W .   S t o t t

GEOGRAPHICAL PROFILE: PADDAN ARAM

- Means "plain of Aram"
- Appears in Genesis 31 as the site of Jacob's exile, the home of Laban
- Located in the upper Euphrates River valley, possibly the same as Haran
- Later known as Syria

PERSONAL PROFILE: MIDIAN

- Son of Abraham by Keturah
- His descendants lived east of the Jordan River and south into the peninsula of Sinai
- Midianites bought Joseph from his brothers as a slave (Gen. 37)

PERSONAL PROFILE: ABIMELECH

- Probably means "father of a king"
- A Philistine king of Gerar, possibly the son of the Abimelech whom Abraham encountered in Genesis 20–21
- The name appears elsewhere in the Bible, but none of the other references should be connected with the Genesis Philistine kings

Genesis 25:1–26:35

I N   A   N U T S H E L L

*G*od's promise to Abraham continues after his death. The battle between good and evil plays out in both intrafamily and intertribal conflict.

History Repeats Itself

I. INTRODUCTION

Patriarchal Pilgrimage: The Graying of America

$\mathcal{W}$hen surveyed, Americans claim that physical appearance doesn't matter. But in the twenty-first century, record numbers dye their hair and get plastic surgery. Among women forty-five to fifty-four years of age, 71 percent use hair coloring to hide the gray, and nearly 15 percent of women in the fifty-five to sixty-four age group have had cosmetic surgery.

This research, typical of studies done by the American Association of Retired People, claims that thirty-eight is the age of peak physical attractiveness, but the older a person gets the older that best-looking age becomes. People under the age of thirty-five say thirty is the peak attractive age, but people over sixty-five choose the age of forty-six.

Most likely none of this ever occurred to Abraham, although at the age of 175 he might have considered 100 his peak year! In the Bible attractiveness has much more to do with the heart than the face and hair, as Samuel made plain to Jesse while looking for a new king (1 Sam. 16:7). Those of us who have reached senior citizen status understand something of Abraham's dilemma. Old age brings new trials and testings, quite possibly the death of a spouse, a strong focus on our children, and memories of earlier commitments.

If the chronology of these chapters follows logically, Abraham married his concubine Keturah when he was 140 years old. She was his companion for thirty-five more years. Abraham finally disappeared from the scene, replaced by the second of the great patriarchs, his son Isaac.

II. COMMENTARY

History Repeats Itself

> **MAIN IDEA:** *After Abraham dies, God continues his work through his son Isaac, a man of human frailty like his father and a rather quiet man like Isaac's son Jacob.*

A Finally Home (25:1–11)

> **SUPPORTING IDEA:** *Old age brings memories of earlier commitments and a strong focus on our children. This was true of Abraham.*

25:1–4. We enter a transition chapter as the new generation, Jacob and Esau, appear on the scene with Isaac presiding in the background. At the age of 140, Abraham got a new lease on life through his marriage to Keturah.

Although some argue that Keturah had been a concubine, the use of the Hebrew word for *wife* raises some question about this. If we take the text literally, Abraham married a woman who was not formerly a part of his entourage and had six more children. The idea of Keturah as a previous concubine now promoted to wife rests upon a reference in 1 Chronicles 1:32.

Among the six children Midian was unquestionably the best known of the tribes, although others occasionally appear at points in the Old Testament. On the one hand, these six children were a great blessing and a fulfillment of the promise of many nations (Gen. 12:2; 17:4). Nevertheless, like Ishmael, the descendants of Midian would come back to haunt Israel, as Gideon could tell us. Judges 6 begins with the words, "Again the Israelites did evil in the eyes of the LORD, and for seven years he gave them into the hands of the Midianites. Because the power of Midian was so oppressive, the Israelites prepared shelters for themselves in mountain clefts, caves and strongholds" (Judg. 6:1–2).

25:5–6. Although Moses introduces Abraham's second family, he leaves no doubt in his readers' minds that Isaac remained the single descendant of promise. Before his death Abraham **gave gifts to the sons of his concubines and sent them away from his son Isaac.** Kidner offers an interesting comment on these verses: "It is hard to resist a comparison between verses 5,6 and the rebuke given to some of Isaac's successors in Luke 15:31,32. In God's plan, these sons were sent away that there might be a true home, in the end, to return to! (see Isa. 60:6ff.)" (Kidner, 150).

25:7–11. Finally Abraham breathed his last breath. Although we are given no details about his death, the text elaborates the place of his burial. Remember how important this place was—Abraham's one foothold in the land of promise, a cave that would eventually become a country. Abraham's quiet death fulfilled God's promise to him in Genesis 15:15: "You, however, will go to your fathers in peace and be buried at a good old age."

Sailhamer raises a fascinating contrast between Abraham's **good old age** and Jacob's "few and difficult" years (47:9): "Thus, within the context of the Book of Genesis, Abraham and Jacob provide a narrative example of the contrast of 'good'. . . and 'evil'. . . a theme begun in the first chapters of the book and carried through to the end (cp. 50:20)" (Sailhamer, 180).

B Two Sets of Grandchildren (25:12–26)

SUPPORTING IDEA: *Most people provide no memorial other than their own children. Each of us, when gathered to glory, will leave behind a testimony on earth through our children, grandchildren, and great-grandchildren. That legacy may be a mixture of good and bad.*

25:12–18. We met Abraham's six sons from his second family in the early verses of this chapter; now we return to Ishmael and Isaac. The sound of these names should be familiar to us who live in a world in which Arabs are such a great force. Ishmael was the first Arab. The lineage we find in these verses tells us how the Arab race began. Before Jacob had his famous twelve sons, Ishmael gave birth to **twelve tribal rulers** who **settled in the area from Havilah to Shur, near the border of Egypt.** We should read nothing theological in the phrase **gathered to his people** other than that Ishmael died and was buried in the company of his family. Those who contrast verses 8 and 17 by suggesting that Abraham was headed for heaven and Ishmael for hell are guilty of abusing the text.

But the passage does reminds us of God's promise to Abraham in 17:20: "And as for Ishmael, I have heard you: I will surely bless him; I will make him fruitful and will greatly increase his numbers. He will be the father of twelve rulers, and I will make him into a great nation." Blessing, yes. Many descendants, without doubt. But don't miss the prophetic sentence at the end of 25:18: **And they lived in hostility toward all their brothers.** If we place Abraham's death somewhere around 1990 B.C., we see immediately that the hostility between his two lines of grandchildren has been going on for nearly four thousand years and may be more heated today than ever.

Although we must avoid dogmatism about the actual numbers, Ishmael may have been born approximately 2081 B.C. and died approximately 1944 B.C. Just as the explanation of Ishmael's sons fulfilled Genesis 17:20, so the brief note about **hostility** picks up the angel's words to Hagar in the desert when he said of Ishmael, "He will be a wild donkey of a man; his hand will be against everyone and everyone's hand against him, and he will live in hostility toward all his brothers" (16:12).

Kidner observes, "To some degree this son of Abram would be a shadow, almost a parity, of his father, his twelve princes notable in their times (17:20; 25:13) but not in the history of salvation; his restless existence no pilgrimage, but an end in itself; his non-conformism, a habit of mind, not a light to the nations" (Kidner, 127).

25:19–26. Meanwhile, back at Beer Lahai Roi, our historian picks up the narrative of Isaac's marriage which he began at the end of chapter 24. Now we learn that Isaac was forty when the wedding took place but sixty when the twins were born. Like Abraham, Isaac struggled with the problem of bearing children. But unlike Abraham, he rested in God's promise until **the LORD answered his prayer.** The Bible emphasizes that the promised line of the Messiah came about only through God's intervention, not by human effort. We will see this again with Rachel in 29:31.

Verse 22 is more than a biological anecdote; it picks up a major literary and theological theme of Genesis: the struggle between brothers. It begins with Cain and Abel in chapter 4; reappears again with Isaac and Ishmael in chapter 21; takes on even greater proportions with Jacob and Esau; and culminates in Joseph's struggle with his ten brothers in the latter chapters of the book.

The writer of the book patiently waits until the end to thematically express the lesson behind these struggles, using the words of Joseph to his brothers: "You intended to harm me, but God intended it for good" (50:20). Out of each of the struggles, God's will was accomplished. The point is not so much that the struggles were necessary for the accomplishment of the will of God, but rather that God's will was accomplished in spite of the conflict (Sailhamer, 182).

Furthermore, God focuses on the development of entire nations, not just children. The prophecy of verse 23 picks up another theme in Genesis: **the older will serve the younger.** Again this began with Cain and Abel, followed through with Ishmael and Isaac, arose here with Esau and Jacob, and culminated with the younger Joseph (Benjamin was born later) standing against all ten of his brothers.

Behind all this history stands the doctrine of grace. By all human understanding in the culture of the day, the older son would be favored. But just as God set aside Cain, Ishmael, and Esau, he eventually set aside Israel so the Gentiles might be grafted into the tree of salvation. Only God's sovereign grace provides any reasonable explanation for this.

The boys were different from the beginning—in appearance, personality, vocation, and spiritual values. We cannot overemphasize the role of God's sovereignty in the events of Genesis.

Griffith Thomas describes it eloquently:

The great problem of Divine sovereignty is of course insolvable by human intellect. It has to be accepted as a simple fact. It should, however, be observed that it is not merely a fact in regard to things spiritual; it is found also in nature in connection with human temperaments and races. All history is full of illustrations of the Divine choice, as we may see from such examples as Cyrus and Pharaoh. Divine election is a fact, whether we can understand it or not. God's purposes are as certain as they are often inscrutable, and it is perfectly evident from the case of Esau and Jacob that the divine choice of man is entirely independent of their merits or of any pre-vision of their merits or attainments (Rom. IX.11) (Thomas, 227).

C Sibling Rivalry (25:27–34)

SUPPORTING IDEA: *How easy and how dangerous it is to regard spiritual things of lesser value than material things.*

25:27–34. The text reminds us that the difference between Isaac's twin sons Jacob and Esau increased as they **grew up**. Esau became what we would call today an outdoorsman, a man more comfortable in the woods than around other people in the Semitic civilization at Beer Lahai Roi. Jacob, on the other hand, was a homebody. No problem so far; but when we read that Isaac **loved Esau, but Rebekah loved Jacob**, we see nothing but trouble ahead. This expectation is pronounced when we see that Isaac's affection for Esau centered in his **taste for wild game**.

To illustrate his point, our writer offers one of the most famous anecdotes of the Bible: the great **red stew** swindle. Esau's casual handing over of his birthright affirms his carelessness and his casual attitude toward family and cultural tradition. The **birthright** carried with it the inheritance rights of the firstborn. With this simple little meal the prophecy of verse 23 came to pass.

Let's not rush too quickly over the interesting parenthesis at the end of verse 30. The name *Edom* means "red." Apparently it became a nickname for Esau related not to his redness at birth (v. 25) but to his fatal choice of the **red stew**. How interesting that the **skillful hunter** came back from the woods this time with no game as chef Jacob literally boiled vegetable soup. The hunter became the hunted, trapped by the bait of his brother's menu. The result was catastrophic.

Jacob, the secondborn, then had the **birthright**. The calculating, quiet man who recognized the spiritual value in the birthright manipulated his brother into giving it up. Perhaps knowing the oracle (v. 23), Jacob had been waiting for this opportunity. But God later made Jacob realize that his promises are not acquired in this way.

D Abimelech Again (26:1–11)

SUPPORTING IDEA: *Spiritual lessons must be passed down from father to son. When they are not, sons will often repeat their father's errors even when those errors fly in the face of God's directives.*

26:1–6. History, it seems, does repeat itself. In fact, this account is so much like Genesis 12 that Moses finds it necessary to say it was not **the earlier famine of Abraham's time**. Isaac took the first step by heading to Abimelech in Gerar. We should probably assume that Isaac had in mind leaving as quickly as possible for Egypt. That's why the Lord intervened to say, **Do not go down to Egypt; live in the land where I tell you to live**. Then Isaac heard again the words that God proclaimed repeatedly to Abraham about the land, the offspring, and the blessing. We have already noted that **Abimelech** was likely a title (like Pharaoh) rather than a name, so this character was likely a son or grandson of Abraham's Abimelech.

This fascinating chapter repeats incident after incident that parallels the life of Abraham. These vignettes remind the reader that Abraham's struggles were also Isaac's struggles and that Abraham's God has now become Isaac's God.

But we wonder about Isaac's obedience. He didn't go to Egypt, but he didn't stay in Canaan either, since he settled in Gerar. Sailhamer says, "We are apparently to read this in light of the promise that 'the land' is to be given to the descendants of Abraham. Thus immediately following this word from the Lord, there is the first major reiteration of the Abrahamic covenant and of the promise that 'the land' is to be given to Isaac and his descendants (v. 3)" (Sailhamer, 186).

In other words, what we have here is a prophetic interpretation of what constituted Isaac's promised land shown particularly in the phrase **all these lands**. Although they were Abimelech-owned at the moment, they would some day belong to Isaac's descendants, so God considered it legitimate ground. To his credit **Isaac stayed in Gerar**.

26:7–11. Here it comes again. In spite of the problems this same lie caused Abraham, Isaac passed Rebekah off as his sister and for precisely the same reasons. This deception apparently went on for a while. The text says that **Isaac had been there a long time** before Abimelech saw their romantic maneuvering and really figured out what had happened. In the case of both Abraham and Isaac, repentance came only through the accusation of ungodly rulers. Only when caught in a lie did Abraham and Isaac admit the truth.

This Philistine king comes off in a better light than the Hebrew patriarch. At first glance he understood the potential moral disaster of this deception. Abimelech seems to be something of a microcosm of Cyrus, a moral and relatively righteous leader who governed a powerful pagan people. "So Isaac, like Abraham, received God's great promise, but in fear he deceived Abimelech and made a mockery of the promised blessing. Fear mocks faith; faith boldly lapses in triumph. But a person who truly believes God's promises obeys His statutes, precepts, and commands" (Ross, *Bible Knowledge Commentary*, 71).

🅴 Covenant Affirmation (26:12–25)

> **SUPPORTING IDEA:** *God's people are always at odds with the world. Sometimes conflict can arise over minor issues. In those moments, we do best to follow the example of Isaac, who was emulating his father Abraham: give ground graciously and leave the results to God.*

26:12–22. Like his father before him, Isaac **became rich, and his wealth continued to grow until he became very wealthy**. To the patriarchal icons *tents* and *altars,* Isaac added *wells*—lots of them to water **many flocks and herds**—all **stopped up** by the envious Philistines. These were not new wells, but those that had been dug originally by Abraham's servants. Isaac found more when he moved to **the Valley of Gerar.** He reopened old wells and **gave them the same names his father had given them.**

But the Philistines wouldn't give up. When Isaac found fresh water at **Esek** (a name which means "dispute"), the quarrel continued. He named another well **Sitnah** ("opposition") and lost it in the quarrel as well. Finally he dug **Rehoboth** (which means "room") and decided he had located far enough away from Abimelech's Philistines to **flourish in the land.**

26:23–25. Perhaps because of his gentle spirit and obedience, Isaac received a vision from the Lord at Beersheba. This vision focused almost exclusively on **the number of your descendants,** a promise we have come to see with great frequency since God first began speaking to Abraham in chapter 12.

At Beersheba the triple icons of the patriarchs all come together in one verse: **Isaac built an altar there and called on the name of the LORD. There he pitched his tent, and there his servants dug a well.** Beersheba lay just northeast of Gerar in the foothills north of the Negev. Abraham had made a similar treaty here when he named the city Beersheba (21:23–24,31). Now Isaac reaffirmed his father's commitments.

F Fellowship Feast (26:26–35)

> **SUPPORTING IDEA:** *"When a man's ways are pleasing to the LORD, he makes even his enemies live at peace with him"* *(Prov. 16:7).*

26:26–29. Back in Gerar, Abimelech had figured out that no matter what his troops might accomplish by vandalizing Isaac's wells, this persistent Hebrew would prosper. Time for a change in strategy. So he grabbed his **personal adviser** and his chief military attaché and headed to Beersheba for peace talks. Once again we have that strange feeling of déjà vue which takes us back to chapter 21 and the origination of this accord between Abimelech I and Abraham.

26:30–35. Surprise! Right after the party and the departure of the Gerar trio, Isaac learned about the discovery of a new well. Although *Shibah* can mean "seven," in this context it surely takes its other meaning of "oath." Nor is this name new since we read in 21:31, "So that place was called Beersheba, because the two men swore an oath there."

The Isaac narrative will soon end, and Moses wants to transition into the old man's death by returning for just a moment to "Big Red." Like Isaac, Esau married at the age of forty, buying into double trouble with Judith and Basemath, both Hittites. We learn about a third wife in chapter 28 and then find a rehearsal (with different names) in chapter 36. These wives **were a source of grief to Isaac and Rebekah**.

Sailhamer puts these two verses into perspective:

> At first glance it may appear that the short notice of Esau's marriage to two Hittite women does not play a significant role within the larger narrative context. However, when read as an introduction to chapter 27, it casts quite a different light on the events of that chapter. Just before the account of the mischievous blessing of Jacob, we are told that Esau, from whom the blessing was stolen, had married Hittite women and that they were a source of grief to both Isaac and Rebekah. These verses, then, take their place along with vv. 29–34 as background to the central event of chapter 27, the blessing of Jacob. These preliminary notices put into perspective the cunning deed of Jacob and Rebekah. They demonstrate that Esau was not fit to inherit the blessing (Sailhamer, 189).

MAIN IDEA REVIEW: *After Abraham dies, God continues his work through his son Isaac, a man of human frailty like his father and a rather quiet man like Isaac's son Jacob.*

III. CONCLUSION

The Word of Forgiveness

John Paton first saw this world in a stone cottage in Kirkmahoe, Scotland—three rooms filled with eleven children. The middle room served as father Paton's prayer room. As a young man, John responded to the Scotland Reformed Church's call for missionaries to the South Pacific. When he sought his parent's advice, they told him he had been dedicated to God for missionary service since his birth. He sailed for the islands on April 16, 1858, landing on an island inhabited only by a tribe of cannibals. His proclamation of the gospel seemed to attract no response until he dug a well thirty feet deep to provide water for the islanders—rain from the ground.

Several tribesmen trusted Christ as Savior, including Chief Mamokei. Paton conducted their first communion service on October 24, 1869, nearly eleven years after his arrival. As Morgan describes it, "Twelve converted cannibals partook of the Lord's Supper. 'As I put the bread and wine into those hands once stained with the blood of cannibalism, now stretched out to receive and partake the emblems of the Redeemer's love,' he wrote, 'I had a foretaste of the joy of Glory that well nigh broke my heart to pieces.'"

The forgiveness God offered those natives, Abraham, Isaac, and us was made possible because Jesus paid the penalty for sin on the cross when he died for all humankind. Yet this essential doctrine has been so often misunderstood. About A.D. 250 Origen claimed the cross was a ransom paid to Satan; nearly nine hundred years later, Abelard taught that Christ's death was a moral influence on society, nothing more. Even after the Reformation, Socinius referred to the cross merely as an example of sacrifice.

But the Bible headlines the subject: Jesus died to pay the price of our redemption; he alone has the authority to speak *the word of forgiveness*.

In the formal celebration of Good Friday, many churches observe *the words of the cross,* among them *the word of forgiveness.* These chapters reflect forgiveness of Abraham's sin, Isaac's imitation of that sin, and God's willingness to bless them in spite of their human failures. Too often history repeats itself because we do not remember lessons of the past. May God forgive our failing memories, our failing courage, and our failing faithfulness to his Word.

PRINCIPLES

- God's faithfulness is demonstrated from generation to generation.
- Humans are tempted to get their material and spiritual priorities out of order.
- Some children repeat the sins of their fathers.
- Those who are confident of God don't have to force their way on other people.

APPLICATIONS

- Wait patiently for God's blessings.
- Remember that God has sovereign control over his world and his people.
- Be grateful that God shows us mercy rather than justice.
- Never choose earthly possessions over spiritual birthright.

IV. LIFE APPLICATION

"Quiet Revolution"

With the title "Quiet Revolution," the American Bible Society *Record* (June/July 2001) describes the work of George Gallup Jr., who heads the firm that has become synonymous with research in American life. His research has uncovered that 96 percent of Americans believe in "God or universal spirit or life force"; 78 percent believe in heaven; and 60 percent believe in hell. By comparison those numbers for Great Britain are 61 percent, 50 percent and 24 percent.

Peter Feuerherd, writer of the article, claims Gallup harbors great promise as an American and a Christian for a turnaround in the spiritual status of this country.

> Results gleaned from the thousands polled by his firm over decades culminated in a body of research from which Mr. Gallup posits a theory as well as a hope. Americans, he says, are in a seeking mode. They are exhausted by political corruption and diatribes, the stress of keeping together home and job, and harbor an abiding sense that mere acquisition cannot equate with self-fulfillment. They are, in short, in search of spiritual meaning. And it is the duty of the Christian churches to fill that vacuum in the soul (p. 8).

As the patriarchs wandered about the ancient deserts of Canaan, they also stirred a quiet revolution. The Canaanites, Philistines, and Hittites had never seen the likes of Abraham and Isaac. Their faith in a personal God, Creator of the world and director of their destinies, challenged all the idolatry and immorality around them. They were the first of the remnant descendants of God's people, the forerunners of the same kind of quiet revolution stirred by early Christians in the first century after God came to earth in the person of his Son.

Perhaps we can learn from the patriarchs that Christian leadership in pagan surroundings should look more like Abraham and Isaac and less like Samson and Saul! Serving God by killing Philistines seems less demonstrative of a quiet spiritual revolution than moving aside to let them have your wells and living in such a way that they can say, "We saw clearly that the LORD was with you" (Gen. 26:28).

V. PRAYER

We borrow a prayer from the noted pastor Phillips Brooks: "Do not pray for easy lives; pray to be stronger people! Do not pray for tasks equal to your powers, pray for power equal to your tasks. Then the doing of your work shall be no miracle, but you shall be a miracle. Every day you shall wonder at yourself, at the riches of life which has come to you by the grace of God." Amen.

VI. DEEPER DISCOVERIES

A. Birthright (25:31)

The word *bekhouroh* generally means "priority" or "seniority." Apart from Genesis 25, it appears only in 27:36 (also a reference to Esau and Jacob) and 1 Chronicles 5:1. Towns offers a paragraph describing the importance of this strategic entitlement within the ancient culture:

Traditionally, a number of distinct privileges belonged to the first-born son in a family. Called a birthright, this gave the oldest son, the firstborn, a special claim on the inheritance left by his father and the unique privilege of carrying on the family name to future generations. In the patriarchal family, this birthright had a special spiritual significance. The possessor of the birthright was the one who (1) became heir of the covenant of God, (2) received the promises given to Abraham, and (3) offered sacrifices for the family (Towns, 164).

It may be worth noting that this was not a uniquely Jewish pattern. Similar cultural practice was known in other parts of the Ancient Near East. However, those would be devoid of the spiritual relationship with the God of promise and the inheritance of this specific covenant with Abraham. In this chapter Esau lost the birthright; in chapter 27 he will lose the blessing.

B. Hittites (25:9–10; 26:34)

The Hittites along with the Mesopotamians and Egyptians constituted the three great powers that Israel faced in its early patriarchal days. Ten thousand tablets from excavations at Carchemish and later Khattusa in Turkey confirm Joshua's description of huge tracts of land in the Fertile Crescent as "all the Hittite country" (Josh. 1:4). These descendants of Ham set up shop in what is now central Turkey about the mid-third millennium B.C. But before the time of Abraham they were overcome by Indo-European people from the north who became the ruling class in the culture that moved south into Canaan.

The Hittites appear as early as Genesis 15:20, and again in 23:7, but most prominently in their dealings with Abraham and now sixty years later, Esau. With respect to Semitic historiography, we know that the Hittites and Hebrews were among the most reliable recorders of Ancient Near Eastern history. Tablets recovered from sites such as Mari and Nuzu indicate the role of these people in ancient life, an importance that increased dramatically during the periods of the judges and the kings.

Of consequence in our passage is their Canaanite paganism. Not only did Esau break with accepted patterns of wife selection by one's father, but he married (as we might say today) "outside the faith." Waltke claims:

> Esau is without excuse in marrying Hittites who are listed among the wicked Canaanites. He should have known that God condemned these people for their wickedness and would eventually give Abraham's offspring their land (15:16–20). He must have known how solicitously his grandfather acted to prevent his father from marrying these women (24:3). By marrying these women without regard to his ancestor's initiative and benediction, Esau again signals his lack of

commitment to the Abrahamic vision of Israel's destiny and so his unworthiness to receive the blessing (Waltke, 375–376).

VII. TEACHING OUTLINE

A. INTRODUCTION

1. Lead Story: Patriarchal Pilgrimage
2. Context: These two chapters of Genesis set off the brief Isaac narrative from the much more lengthy Abrahamic and Jacobite narratives. Isaac has just married at the end of chapter 24, but as chapter 27 opens he is old, weak, and blind. Since Isaac married approximately 2027 B.C. and died in 1887 B.C., these two chapters cover nearly 140 years.
3. Transition: At the end of chapter 24 we read that "Isaac was comforted after his mother's death." Then after a brief parenthetic introduction of Keturah, we return to Isaac for the remainder of the two chapters, a narrative that portrays him as reflecting many of the experiences of his father. By the end of chapter 26 the joy of his marriage has turned to grief because of the behavior of his oldest son. The last two verses of chapter 26 prepare us for the transfer of blessing in chapter 27. Esau is out; Jacob is in.

B. COMMENTARY

1. Finally Home (25:1–11)
2. Two Sets of Grandchildren (25:12–26)
3. Sibling Rivalry (25:27–34)
4. Abimelech Again (26:1–11)
5. Covenant Affirmation (26:12–25)
6. Fellowship Feast (26:26–35)

C. CONCLUSION: "QUIET REVOLUTION"

VIII. ISSUES FOR DISCUSSION

1. What reasons might Isaac have had for committing the same sin as his father in the same place under the same conditions?
2. Name at least three lessons in godly parenting that we learn in these two chapters.
3. What do we see in Isaac that helps us in our own Christian lives and in our relationship with people outside the faith?

Genesis 27:1–28:22

The Skins Game

I. INTRODUCTION
A Man and His Choices

II. COMMENTARY
A verse-by-verse explanation of these chapters.

III. CONCLUSION
Amazing Grace

An overview of the principles and applications from these chapters.

IV. LIFE APPLICATION
Back to Basics

Melding these chapters to life.

V. PRAYER
Tying these chapters to life with God.

VI. DEEPER DISCOVERIES
Historical, geographical, and grammatical enrichment of the commentary.

VII. TEACHING OUTLINE
Suggested step-by-step group study of these chapters.

VIII. ISSUES FOR DISCUSSION
Zeroing these chapters in on daily life.

Q u o t e

"*H*appy families are all alike; every unhappy family is

unhappy in its own way."

L e o   T o l s t o y

Genesis 27:1–28:22

I N   A   N U T S H E L L

*R*eading Genesis 27 and 28 is like watching a home video of a dysfunctional family. It reminds us of our own failures and frailties. We also learn that God's blessing can come to undeserving and unlikely people, sometimes in the most unusual ways.

The Skins Game

I. INTRODUCTION

A Man and His Choices

*A*fter a few of the usual Sunday evening hymns, a pastor stood up and walked over to his pulpit. Before giving his sermon for the evening, he briefly introduced a guest minister present in the service and asked him to greet the church and share whatever he felt would be appropriate.

The elderly man stepped up to the pulpit and began to speak. "A father, his son, and a friend of his son were sailing off the Pacific coast," he began, "when a fast-approaching storm blocked any attempt to get back to the shore. The waves were high; an experienced sailor like the father could not keep the boat upright, and the three were swept into the ocean." The old man hesitated for a moment, making eye contact with two teenagers who were, for the first time since the service began, looking somewhat interested in his story.

The aged minister continued with his story. "Grabbing a rescue line, the father had to make the most excruciating decision of his life: to which boy would he throw the other end of the lifeline? He only had seconds to decide. He knew his son was a Christian, and he also knew that his son's friend was not. As the father yelled out, 'I love you, son!' he threw the lifeline to the other boy. By the time the father pulled the friend back to the capsized boat, his son had disappeared beneath the raging swells into the black of night, his body never recovered."

By this time the two teenagers sat up straight in the pew, anxiously waiting the next words to come out of the old minister's mouth. "The father," he continued, "knew his son would step into heaven with Jesus, and he could not bear the thought of his son's friend stepping into an eternity without Jesus. Therefore, he sacrificed his son to save another."

"How great is the love of God that he should do the same for us. Our Heavenly Father sacrificed his only begotten Son that we could be saved. I urge you to accept his offer to rescue you and take hold of the lifeline that he is throwing out to you in this service." With that the old man turned and sat down.

The pastor again walked to the pulpit and delivered a brief sermon, adding a brief invitation. But no one responded to the appeal. Within minutes after the service was over, the two teenagers raced to the old man's side. "That was a nice story," one of the boys said, "but I don't think it is very realistic for a father to give up his only son's life in hopes that the other boy would become a Christian."

"Well, you've got a point there," the old man replied, glancing down at his worn Bible. A big smile broadened his face as he looked up at the boys and said, "It sure isn't very realistic, is it? But I'm standing here today to tell you that this story gives me a glimpse of what it must have been like for God to give up his Son for me. You see, I was the father and your pastor was my son's friend."

This story emphasizes a major theme in these chapters—choices made by Isaac, Rebekah, Jacob, and Esau—and the consequences of those choices.

II. COMMENTARY

The Skins Game

MAIN IDEA: *Parental influence on children yields sweet or sour fruit long after the tree is grown.*

A Maternal Manipulation (27:1–29)

SUPPORTING IDEA: *In scheming families people often get hurt, and those hurts run deep and last a lifetime. Only the intervention of a gracious God can turn parental conflict and sibling rivalry into good.*

27:1–4. These verses suggest that Isaac stood at death's door, a viewpoint he himself reinforces; but he may have lived another forty-three years (35:28). We know he was sixty years older than his twin boys, so by comparing the ages of Jacob and Joseph in various texts (41:46–47; 45:6; 47:9) we arrive at the possibility that this chapter unfolded when Isaac was 137 and Jacob and Esau were seventy-seven! At no time during this narrative do we see the family together; six scenes unfold—each with two family members—but Jacob and Esau never talk, nor do Rebekah and Esau meet.

We learned in Genesis 25:28 that Isaac was consumed by a carnivorous appetite, a pattern that was still with him in his older years. But that does not surprise us as much as Isaac's disregard of the promise God made to Rebekah and his clear intention of offering a complete **blessing** to Esau before he died. Indeed, *blessing* is the key idea in this chapter—the prize for which everyone grasped. We might believe that Rebekah never shared with her husband what the Lord had told her about the twins (25:23), but we cannot believe that Isaac did not know about the bartered birthright and the red stew. Although we have compared Isaac and Abraham in previous chapters, at this point Isaac seems more like Lot, a man of the world who could think only of his stomach and his own possessions.

27:5–13. Rebekah, obviously no stranger to cunning and deception, sprang to the protection of "her son." Favoritism had been their parental pattern for many years. We expect Rebekah to confront Isaac, but that's not the way things worked in this family. She explained to Jacob how they could outwit the blind old man. Rather than recoiling at the immorality of the plot, Jacob hesitated only on the grounds that he might get caught and end up with a curse instead of a blessing! In her wild quest to achieve her goals, Rebekah uttered a fearful self-implication: **Let the curse fall on me.**

All four family members were at fault in this plot. Isaac denied what he surely knew to be true about God's plan for Jacob; Esau broke his oath of 25:33; Rebekah roped her son into deception and deceit; and Jacob, demonstrating weakness and a complete absence of faith, limply went along with the plan.

27:14–25. This lengthy section challenges our study, but the narrative flows without break. Jacob offered three lies in this encounter with his father: (1) **I am Esau your firstborn;** (2) **I have done as you told me;** and (3) **The LORD your God gave me success.**

He repeated the first lie in verse 24. Our narrator dedicates eight verses to this ugly scene. Jacob's spiritual condition shows in his answer to Isaac's question in verse 20: **The LORD your God gave me success.** Not only was this lie blasphemous in nature; it suggested that Jacob saw the Lord as Isaac's God and not his own.

Why did God not intervene in this deceptive lie? Why did he not thrust a greater spiritual responsibility upon the aging man, the joyous son of promise—Isaac? In short, why does God let people get away with things like this?

Morris offers a helpful observation: "It would seem that the only way of understanding the situation is to conclude that, whatever may have been wrong with the stratagem and deception of Jacob and Rebekah, the sin of Esau and Isaac was infinitely more grievous. God does not approve of lying, and Jacob and Rebekah well knew this. They were sensitive and spiritual people; but they had decided that, as bad as deception might be in God's sight, it had become necessary in this case in order to prevent a much worse sin, that of blasphemously presuming to convey the most holy of God's promises to a man who neither wanted it nor would honor it, and to do so directly in the face of God's commandment against it. Such an eventuality surely would have incurred God's most severe judgment on both Isaac and Esau, and this they felt they must prevent at all cost" (Morris, 435).

The closest parallel to this deception in the Bible up to this point was the plot of Abraham and Sarah to help God provide a son of promise by using Hagar. In my opinion, Morris treats Rebekah and Jacob more generously than they deserve. Nevertheless, God occasionally blesses a lie with good intent as he did with the Hebrew midwives in Egypt (Exod. 1) and with Rahab in Jericho (Josh. 2:3–6), although we dare not think of lying as acceptable behavior. The fact that God may occasionally make an exception to his divine statutes does not condone our rationalization of deception, manipulation, and false-hood to achieve what we think God should do in the lives of our families and churches.

27:26–29. The kiss may have been part of the blessing ritual, or just fam-ily affection. On the other hand, it might have been counterdeception on the part of Isaac to put this questionable son to one more test. The text reads, **When Isaac caught the smell of his clothes, he blessed him.** Kidner describes the pathetic carnality of this moment:

> The real scandal is Isaac's frivolity: his palate had long since gov-erned his heart (25:28) and silenced his tongue (for he was powerless to rebuke the sin that was Esau's downfall); he now proposed to make it his arbiter between peoples and nations (29). Unfitness for office shows in every act of this sightless man rejecting the evidence of his ears for that of his hands, following the promptings of his palate and seeking inspiration through—of all things—his nose (27). Yet God put these very factors to work for Him (Kidner, 156).

The blessing unfolds in three parts: a description of the smell in verse 27; a description of earthly bounty distinctly suited for Esau in verse 28; and a description of the national destiny and dominion which the Lord had prom-ised to Rebekah in 25:23 and verse 29. The last is significantly enhanced, however, for it passed on the blessing of Abraham recorded first in 12:3.

B Rebellious Reaction (27:30–46)

SUPPORTING IDEA: *Family failure, as ugly and destructive as it is, cannot thwart God's purposes.*

27:30–40. Sure enough, the curtain barely closes and reopens before we see Esau returning from the hunt. Everything recorded in verses 5–29 took place between Isaac's request and Esau's return. In what must have been a spooky experience, Isaac heard again: **Sit up and eat some of my game, so that you may give me your blessing.** Isaac immediately sensed the awful tragedy unfolding in his tent and he **trembled violently.** At last the old man realized that the Heavenly Hunter had caught up with him to rebuke his cod-dling favoritism of the rebellious older son in spite of God's promise to Rebe-kah, Esau's denial of the birthright, and the agony of the Hittite wives. Nevertheless, the blessing to Jacob was irrevocable: **indeed he will be blessed.**

Esau's reaction mirrored his father's as he **burst out with a loud and bit-ter cry** and begged for a blessing for himself as well. When told his blessing had already been given to the deceiver, Esau affirmed Jacob's name. The "heel-grasper" had won again. But Esau skewed the story just a bit. Jacob indeed had stolen his blessing, but Esau carelessly sold his birthright. In any case, both were now gone.

Esau cried out for some kind of blessing, but what he heard was not what he had hoped for. **The earth's richness** and **the dew of heaven** had already been given to Jacob. Only warfare and servitude to the hated Jacob remained, along with one hope: **You will throw his yoke from off your neck.**

This event comes in for review in the New Testament. The writer of Hebrews developed his argument against spiritual rebellion by bringing up the Esau narrative.

> Make every effort to live in peace with all men and to be holy; without holiness no one will see the Lord. See to it that no one misses the grace of God and that no bitter root grows up to cause trouble and defile many. See that no one is sexually immoral, or is godless like Esau, who for a single meal sold his inheritance rights as the oldest son. Afterward, as you know, when he wanted to inherit this blessing, he was rejected. He could bring about no change of mind, though he sought the blessing with tears (Heb. 12:14–17).

In treating this passage, Lea tells us:

> When Esau later sought the blessing, Isaac knew that he could not reverse his action. Esau wept when he recognized that he had squandered his birthright, but his tears were futile (Gen. 27:34). He became a memorable example of someone who failed to appropriate God's grace by wasting his opportunity. The New Testament emphasizes that spiritual repentance is possible for those who desire it. Esau's tears appeared when he recognized that he had no chance to remedy his foolish actions. We are to realize that denying Christ is a serious act. We should never count on an easy route of return at a time of our own choosing. Just as Esau's tears did not earn a return to God for him, a deliberate turning away from Christ will lead to ruin and sorrow (Lea, 221).

27:41–46. The rift between the twins, which had separated them for nearly a lifetime, now became irreparable. Esau could wait only for the death of their father to say, **I will kill my brother Jacob.** This fratricidal plan revealed that Esau, like Cain, came from the offspring of ungodliness. Enter Rebekah once more to manipulate events in Jacob's favor. Apparently aware of everything that had happened, she warned Jacob and sent him to her brother's home in Haran. This would give Esau time to calm down and forget the injustice.

But there seems to be a problem here with the wording of the text. Verse 41 says that Esau **said to himself.** Then verse 42 tells us that **Rebekah was**

told what her older son Esau had said. How could she have known? Griffith Thomas says, "Full of passion and impulse he could not keep his plan to himself, for while at the outset he only spake 'in his heart,' it was not long before the project was heard of by Rebekah" (Thomas, 255). Perhaps. Certainly that explanation works as well as any, and it would fit the character of Esau. Rebekah had no idea that Jacob's exile would last twenty years (31:41), probably because no one in the family, including Isaac himself, expected the old man to live that long.

Waltke suggests that Rebekah's rhetorical question at the end of verse 45 indicates that she expected both sons might be dead if she didn't put some miles between them.

> She probably has in mind that after Esau killed Jacob, he would be killed by an avenger of blood or by judicial decree demanding his execution for taking an innocent life. . . . Ironically, she suffers even more than she anticipates, at least socially if not physically. Her relationship (if any) with Esau must have been irrevocably damaged, and she never sends for Jacob from his exile in Paddan Aram. Finally, she even loses a memorial in Scripture (Gen. 35:8). Though Rebekah parries Esau's violent resolve, nevertheless, she must taste the bitter consequences of her deception (Waltke, 381–82).

But Jacob's departure must not be the flight of a fugitive, so Rebekah concocted a plan to secure Isaac's approval. Esau's wives had been such a nuisance to both Isaac and Rebekah that she wanted to be sure Jacob didn't marry one of the locals as well. So the chapter ends with everybody unhappy in this ancient dysfunctional family. The skins game worked, but Jacob was on the lam, Esau lost his blessing and vowed to murder his brother, Isaac became heartsick over his horrible mistake, and Rebekah divided the family and ended up keeping the son she didn't want!

Before we move to chapter 28, let's gather a few spiritual lessons from this tragedy. Hebrews 11:20 says, "By faith Isaac blessed Jacob and Esau in regard to their future." True, if one stretches the meaning of *blessing* and recognizes that the focus of the verse rests on faith that somehow God will clean up the mess Isaac created in his own family. Apparently Isaac trusted God's sovereignty in this situation in spite of the sin of his sons and his own stupidity. Turning from the past, he placed his hope in the future.

Our past failures do not negate God's future blessing. Sinfulness does not mean hopelessness. Our failures do not destroy God's promises. We must trust God for what we do not see even when we see a mess. Faith looks forward, not backward.

Suppose you were on your way to some scenic spot. Suppose on the way you took a wrong turn; what would you do? Would you turn around and return home? Would you stop the car there and not move? Would you give up all hope of ever getting to your destination? Probably none of the above. When we make a wrong turn, we backtrack to the place where we turned off, find the right path, and keep heading to our destination. When we sin or make foolish decisions, God does not rip away his promises or his blessings. If we come back on track with him, we can still experience his touch in our lives. In the end, in spite of the horrors of this chapter, both Jacob and Esau received God's blessing.

Cousin Connection (28:1-9)

> **SUPPORTING IDEA:** *The path back to righteousness from ruin requires us to acknowledge God's control and to adjust our lives to fit what he expects from us.*

28:1-2. The blessings continued as Isaac took up Rebekah's plan as his own and sent Jacob to Paddan Aram. The directions were quite specific: he must marry one of his cousins, a daughter of his uncle Laban. The text suggests that Isaac had no idea of Esau's intentions and intended only to keep the patriarchal line intact. This corresponded to the same behavior his father Abraham had taken with respect to Isaac's marriage (24:2-4). "Jacob flees from two threats in his flight to Paddan Aram: persecution and accommodation. The physical threat from his brother may have seemed most obviously harmful, but the threat of accommodating to the Canaanite lifestyle was just as grave a danger. Accommodation is as great a threat as persecution to the community of faith" (Waltke, 385).

28:3-5. With the directive came yet another blessing, this one somewhat different from the "skins game" language. It sounded like a reiteration of the blessing to Abraham in regards to descendants and the land (17:1-8).

Jacob headed north and east across the Euphrates River to Paddan Aram. We will pick this up again in the next chapter when we learn in 29:1 that Jacob "came to the land of the eastern peoples." Mesopotamia lay northeast of modern Syria on the edge of northern Arabia. Like Rebekah, Isaac understood this would be a temporary journey and that Jacob would return to **take possession of the land where you now live as an alien.**

28:6-9. After Jacob's departure Esau did something of an about-face. He understood his brother's trip according to Isaac's interpretation. He assumed that the major barrier between himself and his father lay in **how displeasing the Canaanite women were to his father Isaac.** How this information had escaped him to this point seems almost beyond belief. It shows us how marginalized Esau had become in this family. He was not aware of what was happening back at the compound.

His solution also demonstrated his misunderstanding of God's plan as he married a daughter of Ishmael, identified here as Mahalath (whether this woman is the Basemath of 36:3 seems uncertain). As Griffith Thomas puts it: "Esau has no idea of spiritual realities. All that he is concerned about is to please his parents, and if possible to win back the blessing. This again shows the real character of the man and the utter absence of any spiritual reality actuating his life. Esau is one of those who, as it has been truly and accurately said, tries to do what God's people do in the vain hope that somehow or other it will be pleasing to God" (Thomas, 258).

Esau's mind-set and lifestyle patterned those of his father-in-law. Ishmael was banned to a life of constant feuding as he led marauding bands of desert warriors in attacks on villages and traveling caravans. He became the great "desert fox" of the patriarchal period.

Ⅾ Sacred Staircase (28:10–22)

SUPPORTING IDEA: *God reveals himself to his people to promise his protection and provision. Our response must be one of obedience and worship.*

28:10–12. It was risky business traveling through Canaan alone, especially for a mild-mannered man whose life decisions up to this point had been made by his mother. His destination lay five hundred miles away, weeks of travel. About seventy miles north of Beersheba (possibly three days journey) **he reached a certain place, he stopped for the night**, put his head on a stone, and **had a dream.** Abraham had built an altar near here (Gen. 12:8; 13:3–4), although the text does not tell us that Jacob knew this or stopped for that reason. The word **place** (*maqom*) appears six times in the story. Perhaps the writer's intent is to recognize that this **place** was just that, a place, until it became *Bethel*.

But the **place** pales by comparison with the **dream**, the famous ladder that was not really a ladder but a stairway reaching from earth to heaven **and the angels of God were ascending and descending on it**. This word (**stairway**) appears only here in the Old Testament, and it connects to a verb meaning "to pile up." The Septuagint translates the word with the Greek word *klimax* that does mean "ladder" or "staircase."

Ross says, "The most that can be said is that a word used in Ziggurat settings is cognate to the word used here, a word that fits the way of communication between heaven and earth. Hebrew *sullam* is thus appropriate to the point of the story—here was a place that heaven and earth touched, where there is access to God" (Ross, 489).

The parallel with the Tower of Babel in Genesis 11 directs our attention to the difference. That pagan structure started at earth and attempted to reach heaven, while Jacob's ladder took the other direction. The words **resting on the earth** can be translated "placed toward the earth." Angels, though not yet common in the text of Scripture, have previously appeared (18:2; 19:1–22). Much speculation has been offered about the motion of the angels, but none seems helpful except to note that angels commonly travel between heaven and earth and seem equally operative in both realms.

28:13–15. But the angel escalator is not the star attraction of this dream because **there above it stood the LORD.** Before Jacob could react to any of this, he received the promise directly from God's mouth that constitutes the rest of these verses. By now we are quite accustomed to this vocabulary— **descendants, land, peoples, blessed, offspring.** Lest Jacob harbor any remaining doubt about his father's words issued earlier in this chapter, he now had direct confirmation from on high. This same self-revealing God talked to Abraham in Genesis 15:7 and later addressed Moses in Exodus 20. Verses 13 and 14 reiterate promises made to Abraham and Isaac.

Verse 15 introduces personal promises to Jacob and guarantees that his return to Canaan would indeed take place. Waltke says:

> This is the first of three personal promises made to Jacob. First, in addition to promises for the remote future, God graciously grants intimate assurances to Jacob to sustain his faith . . . second, God promises preservation and protection . . . third, God promises home-coming. The God of Abraham and Isaac, and now the God of Jacob, is hardly limited to some geographic boundary like the local deities of the surrounding Canaanites. Wherever Jacob would travel, God would be with him and eventually God would bring him back home (Waltke, 391–92).

This sacred staircase image comes again in John 1:51 where Jesus says to Nathanael, "I tell you the truth, you shall see heaven open, and the angels of God ascending and descending on the Son of Man." Although interpretations differ, it would appear that the Lord meant that his disciples would see God's direct blessing on his earthly ministry in as direct and picturesque a manner as Jacob received this revelation in Genesis 28.

28:16–19. Startled by the dream, Jacob pronounced the uniqueness and meaning of the **place.** Perhaps still carrying a guilty conscience from earlier events back home, he was afraid and proclaimed, **How awesome is this place!** Today the word *awesome* can apply to anything from sandbars to stock cars, but for Jacob it meant the presence of God. Actually the word could be translated "frightening," hardly an understatement since this was **none other than the house of God; this is the gate of heaven.**

In the morning the *pillow* stone became a *pillar* stone, a memorial of worship consecrated by oil. Jacob also named the place—or more properly, renamed it—**Bethel**, "house of God."

28:20–22. Jacob **made a vow** that took God's promises to greater specificity, covering such necessities as **food to eat and clothes to wear.** He sealed his vow by acknowledging the pillar as a substitute altar and promising God **a tenth** of all he would receive (see "Deeper Discoveries"). Certainly Jacob had known his parent's faith, and the great godliness of his grandfather. But here for the first time he came face-to-face with God—and his life would never be the same. He never became a perfect model of godliness and would still see years of heartbreak among his own children. In fact, his favoritism toward Joseph mirrored Isaac's treatment of Esau—the sins of the fathers passing on to the children.

But now Jacob belonged to God, and he would show a higher level of spiritual maturity from this point on. Kidner sums up this passage:

> This is a supreme display of divine grace, unsought and unstinted. Unsought, for Jacob was no pilgrim or returning prodigal, yet God came out to meet him, angelic retinue and all, taking him wholly by surprise. Unstinted, for there was no word of reproach or demand, only a stream of assurances flowing from the central "I am the Lord" to spread from the past (13a) to the distant future, from the spot where Jacob stood (13b) to the four corners of the earth (14) and from his person to all mankind (14b). It was also immediately opposite, meeting his solitary, homeless and precarious condition by assuring him of the covenant with his forebears, allotting him a landed inheritance, and promising him safe conduct (Kidner, 158).

MAIN IDEA REVIEW: *Parental influence on children yields sweet or sour fruit long after the tree is grown.*

III. CONCLUSION

Amazing Grace

In his popular book *What's So Amazing About Grace?* (Zondervan, 1997), Philip Yancey relates a story that I loosely paraphrase here. Newsman Bill Moyers decided to produce a documentary film about John Newton's great hymn ("Amazing Grace") and included some footage shot at Wimbley Stadium in London. He made arrangements to have opera singer Jessye Norman sing the song at the end of a rock concert which had been scheduled to celebrate the political upheaval in South Africa.

For some twelve hours rock groups blasted the walls of the stadium, and finally Norman rose to sing. With no backup band or any other kind of instrumentation, she offered a simple *a cappella* version of those magnificent words:

> Amazing grace, how sweet the sound,
> That saved a wretch like me
> I once was lost but now I'm found—
> Was blind but now I see.

For reasons no one has been able to explain (including Jessye Norman), seventy thousand screaming fans fell silent; by the time she reached the third verse several thousand were singing along.

What's so amazing about grace? It surprises us when we least expect it, but most people need it. It can come in a dream, by an angel's voice, through a verse of Scripture or the encouraging words of a friend. But we can always trace it back to God. The glory of it all is that we don't have to be at Bethel to make contact because the God of Bethel travels with us wherever we go.

PRINCIPLES

- Scheming and favoritism in a family have consequences that can continue for generations.
- God is able to achieve his purposes in spite of dysfunctional families.
- God takes the initiative in bringing sinners back to himself.
- God reaches out to sinners not because of any merit on their part but according to his grace and his gracious purposes.

APPLICATIONS

- Avoid favoritism in the family by loving all children equally and treating them respectfully.
- Shun the values of the world and practice separation from the pagan practices of a godless culture.
- Acknowledge the constant presence and blessing of God in your life and respond with worship and obedience.

IV. LIFE APPLICATION

Back to Basics

At Sagamore Hill on Long Island, after an evening of talk, Teddy Roosevelt and William Beebe, the naturalist, would go out on the lawn and search the skies for a certain spot of starlike light near the lower left-hand corner of the Great Square of Pegasus. Then Roosevelt would recite: "That is the Spiral Galaxy in Andromeda. It is as large as our Milky Way. It is one of a hundred million galaxies. It consists of one hundred billion suns, each larger than our sun." Then Roosevelt would grin and say, "Now I think we are small enough! Let's go to bed."

Just as reflection on God's creation brought Theodore Roosevelt back to basics, so God brought Jacob back to basics. He came to realize that the Lord is all-powerful and we are small and insignificant.

In his fine devotional commentary, Griffith Thomas projects the experience of Jacob into our lives:

> Since at our conversion we know very little of God, we and others must not be surprised if our lack of familiarity with Divine realities leads us into error; but the great things commence the true life, for as we yield ourselves to God and wait upon Him we shall find ourselves taught, upheld and blessed by the wonderful patience of His grace. Only let us be clear that when God says, "I am with thee" we do not reply with "If," but say, out of a full heart, "I believe God, that it shall be even as it was told me" and like Abraham of old, go forward "fully persuaded that what he has promised he is able also to perform" (Thomas, 267).

V. PRAYER

Father, how often we need to return to Bethel to see your revelation, bathe in your promises, and invoke your protection. May we say of every area of our lives, every place we travel, wherever we might find ourselves in the entire world, "This is none other than the house of God." Amen.

VI. DEEPER DISCOVERIES

A. Community of Peoples (28:3)

At first glance this looks just like a further expansion of the offspring promises, but it signals the first appearance in Scripture of the concept of *congregation*. Kidner says, "In the word *company*, from the root 'to assemble,' the Old Testament term for the church or congregation makes its first appearance, bringing with it the idea of coherence as well as multiplicity. It is associated with Jacob again in 35:11; 48:4" (Kidner, 158). Waltke notes, "The blessing will be reversed against Israel under judgment when she is attacked by a community of peoples (see Ezek. 23:24; 32:3) rather than being blessed

and joined by them. The fulfillment is found in Christ and his church"
(Waltke, 383).

B. A Tenth (28:22)

Tithing is one of the great yet controversial concepts of evangelical Christianity. Already Abraham has paid tithes to Melchizedek (Gen. 14:20), perhaps the inspiration for Jacob's action at Bethel. We know of no written law at this time about tithing, although that appears later in the Pentateuch. Exactly how Jacob followed through on this promise we cannot be sure. Perhaps in the building of altars or generosity to people in need; obviously he did not bring any kind of gift to a specific tabernacle or temple. Even more likely is the offering of sacrifices in the equivalent of ten percent of his belongings.

Although tithing became a definite obligation in the Mosaic Law (Lev. 27:30; Num. 18:21,24), here it is purely voluntary, a pattern which extends into the New Testament. Pastors who fall back on Genesis 28 or Malachi 3 to preach required tithing as practice for the church have missed the distinction between the old covenant and the new covenant.

As Morris puts it:

> Jacob's vow, therefore, was given in appreciation of God's promise, not because of legal compulsion or as a means of assuring God's blessings. God's promise had been unconditional and hence did not require the payment of tithes to keep it enforced. . . . This motive, of course, should be that which constrains Christians today to tithe the possessions and incomes. There is no law requiring tithing as a condition of salvation, or even of God's blessing in material things. Tithing is to be rather an expression of love and concern for the Lord and his service (Morris, 452–53).

So the spirit, not the percentage, is at issue here. We do Scripture a great disservice and we misrepresent the Word of God when we make any kind of Christian giving compulsory or coerce people to participate in what must be offerings of free choice and an open heart. Tithing still arises as a question of dispute in the Gospels (Matt. 23:23) but

> after Christ sends the Holy Spirit, however, his apostles dropped the principle of tithing for a higher spiritual standard. God's people first give themselves to God (Rom. 12:1–2; 2 Cor. 8:5). Then they return material blessings to those who bring spiritual blessing (1 Cor. 9:6–18; Gal. 6:6) and gave gifts to needy saints (Rom. 15:25–28; 1 Cor. 16:1–3; 2 Cor. 8:1–15; Gal. 6:10; Eph. 4:28). . . . Christians are to [give] eagerly, generously, and cheerfully, the amount depending on one's level of prosperity (Waltke, 397).

VII. TEACHING OUTLINE

A. INTRODUCTION

1. Lead Story: A Man and His Choices
2. Context: Although Isaac fades slowly off the scene of the Old Testament, fade he does in these two chapters. From now on the spotlight shines on Jacob, who has begun his spiritual pilgrimage at Bethel.
3. Transition: At the beginning of our two chapters, Isaac is old, blind, and ready to pass on. Nevertheless, he hangs on to bless his two sons and to launch Jacob back to Mesopotamia for a wife. That's where we leave Jacob at the end of chapter 28. Chapter 29 begins, "Then Jacob continued on his journey."

B. COMMENTARY

1. Maternal Manipulation (27:1–29)
2. Rebellious Reaction (27:30–46)
3. Cousin Connection (28:1–9)
4. Sacred Staircase (28:10–22)

C. CONCLUSION: BACK TO BASICS

VIII. ISSUES FOR DISCUSSION

1. What kind of parental behavior divides families and what kind unites families?
2. How does Jacob's "conversion experience" at Bethel compare with your own? What are the parallels? What are the differences?
3. What steps can parents take to control a rebellious son like Esau?

Genesis 29:1–30:43

Romance in the Workplace

I. INTRODUCTION
More Than Meets the Eye

II. COMMENTARY
A verse-by-verse explanation of these chapters.

III. CONCLUSION
Belonging to God

An overview of the principles and applications from these chapters.

IV. LIFE APPLICATION
Jacob: Precursor to Postmodernism

Melding these chapters to life.

V. PRAYER
Tying these chapters to life with God.

VI. DEEPER DISCOVERIES
Historical, geographical, and grammatical enrichment of the commentary.

VII. TEACHING OUTLINE
Suggested step-by-step group study of these chapters.

VIII. ISSUES FOR DISCUSSION
Zeroing these chapters in on daily life.

"*Marriage* is far more than an exchange of vows. It is the foundation of the family, mankind's basic unit of society, the hope of the world, and the strength of our country. It is the relationship between ourselves and the generation to follow."

Sandra Day O'Conner

Genesis 29:1–30:43

 IN A NUTSHELL

In narrative form Moses develops the foundation for the history of the twelve tribes of Israel.

Romance in the Workplace

I. INTRODUCTION

More Than Meets the Eye

*D*r. Richard A. Swenson, a Christian physician, chose these words for the title of a book that describes in amazing detail the great care God has taken in creating the universe and even the human body. Without quoting specifically from the book (NavPress, 2000), let me identify some of the statistics Swenson uses.

The human body is composed of ten thousand trillion trillion atoms—a number greater than the stars of the universe. In all of us more than a trillion of these are replaced every one millionth of a second. In a normal lifetime, our hearts beat more than two billion times and pump sixty million gallons of blood through sixty thousand miles of blood vessels. A healthy body manufactures more than two million red blood cells every second. If we could somehow place these cells side by side, they would stretch for one hundred thousand miles.

The eyes you are now using to read this page contain more than one hundred million rods and cones in the retina, cones that take continuous pictures under light conditions that can vary by a factor of ten billion. If by chance you might be reading aloud, it may be worth remembering that your ear has a million moving parts which vibrate twenty thousand times per second and can distinguish among two thousand pitches. But that is merely the intricacy of one finite human body.

The universe apparently measures between ten and twenty billion light years across and may be populated by many galaxies of which our Milky Way is just one. Some astronomers believe it contains at least one hundred billion other galaxies, each one peppered with about one hundred billion stars.

That's the God Jacob served, the God who gave his blessing to Abraham and Isaac and now protected Jacob as he wandered to the land of the eastern peoples. If Swenson's analysis is right (and I have offered only the smallest sample), the amazing and awesome wonder of God's majesty and power provide all the strength we need to live effectively in any age, whether the desert nomad life of Jacob or the fast and furious urban existence of today.

II. COMMENTARY

Romance in the Workplace

> **MAIN IDEA:** *God allows families to behave in foolish and worldly ways and then often steps in to straighten out the mess.*

Ⓐ Kissing Cousins (29:1–14a)

> **SUPPORTING IDEA:** *Perhaps the selection of a lifetime partner is second only in importance to our decision to trust Christ for eternal salvation.*

29:1–3. As we begin chapter 29, we remember God's promise to be with Jacob (28:15). We also remember that he has become a new man, changed by his dream at Bethel. Once again **a well** appears, continuing the three great symbols we have seen throughout the experience of the patriarchs (tents, altars, and wells). Not only that, but a large **stone** over the well causes us to recall the important stone in the Bethel experience.

The phrase **land of the eastern peoples** seems curious, since we are accustomed to seeing specific geographical names. Waltke suggests, "This is a general designation for the territory east of Palestine. . . . The narrator could have been much more specific, but by this designation he suggests both that Jacob is unaware of his precise whereabouts and that he is in a place of danger" (Waltke, 400). We should probably assume that Moses intends us to make a historical and mental connection with chapter 24 and Eliezer's appearance at a well in his search for a wife for Isaac.

Later in this chapter we will get a picture of Jacob's physical strength, since we learn here that **the shepherds would roll the stone away** (apparently emphasizing its size and weight). But verse 10 says that Jacob "went over and rolled the stone away from the mouth of the well."

29:4–8. Not only do we find unusual strength in this chapter but also a strangely gregarious Jacob. In earlier descriptions he more or less stands in the background, taking orders from his mother and exhibiting little leadership. But in this situation he approached the shepherds and took charge of the situation right from the beginning. In God's sovereignty, Jacob was no longer just wandering through the land of the eastern peoples; he made contact with the people he was sent to find. Presumably this conversation took place in Aramaic, the language of Haran which Abraham apparently continued with his family in Canaan.

At this point Jacob did what any red-blooded college boy would do when he gets ready to meet a coed—get people out of the way so the meeting could take place in private. But they were in no hurry. In time the flocks would be pulled together, they would move the stone, and then they would **water the sheep**. The narrative seems to put Jacob's energy and eagerness in contrast with the somewhat laid-back shepherds. Three flocks had already arrived; presumably more were on the way. How many shepherds did it take to move that big stone?

29:9–14a. Rachel was obviously a striking beauty. The moment Jacob saw her and recognized who she was, he sprang into action. Our text varies from chapter 24 where the servant of Abraham "prayed" Rebekah into caring for his watering needs. Since a kiss was customary in that culture among relatives, we should not read anything romantic into verse 11. Our historian emphasizes their family connection three times in verse 10 alone, so we understand that meeting Rachel was not really the ultimate goal since Jacob had to make contact with Laban.

Although the chronology of verse 12 seems unclear, we understand the author's intent. As soon as Rachel understood who Jacob was, she ran home to tell Laban. As soon as Laban heard the news, **he hurried to meet him**. Another kiss, a trip back to the house, a review of the whole story, and a fresh bonding of relatives—after one hundred years. Rebekah had left home a century earlier, literally without warning. It is possible that the two sections of the family had no contact over that period of time, although they could have sent messages back and forth with trading caravans.

Waltke points out that although the well scenarios of chapters 24 and 29 have some similarities, the differences may be even more significant.

> The presence of prayer and worship is a key point of comparison between the two well scenes. At each important moment the servant of Abraham prays for God's guidance and thanks God for his provision (24:12–14,26–27). Of Jacob's encounter at the well, no prayers of praise or petition are recorded. The consequence of the lack of prayer seems apparent in the following scene, with the troubled and deceitful arrangements of Jacob's marriages. The narrative values prayer in the life of the community of faith (Waltke, 402).

Was Laban's enthusiastic welcome motivated by genuine delight at meeting his sister's son or the prospect of a strong and healthy laborer? We don't know. We do not forget, however, that when Rebekah left, Laban was primarily interested in Eliezer's flashy jewelry (24:30).

🅱 Double Wedding (29:14b–30)

> **SUPPORTING IDEA:** *Jacob has met his match. He has some major deceit chalked up to his record, but when going up against Laban, Jacob comes in second.*

29:14b–20. Jacob settled in for a month and helped with the work when Laban offered a full-time and presumably permanent job. Then the labor negotiations began. Rachel had an older sister **Leah** whose name means "cow." The name **Rachel** actually means "ewe." Apparently both of Laban's daughters served as walking commercials for his business operation.

But what does the text mean when it says **Leah had weak eyes**? Various synonyms have been proposed—delicate, soft, tender—but none of them really help us understand why this descriptive note appears. The key to understanding is the contrast in the second half of the verse which suggests that Rachel had eyes that sparkled (along with the rest of her face and body) but Leah's eyes were, we might say, flat. The other possibility, of course, is that she was nearsighted or partially blind.

Jacob offered his terms: Seven years of work **in return for your younger daughter Rachel**. Verse 20 covers that seven years which to Jacob **seemed like only a few days**, language reminiscent of the Song of Songs. Morris observes, "Seven years of free service, by a man who was an exceptional worker, was surely a fine windfall for Laban, especially in view of the fact that he would have been happy to have Jacob married into the family regardless" (Morris, 460).

One key word that appears in this section is **work** (15,18,20). This would be Jacob's life pattern for the next twenty years. The word appears also in verses 25, 27, and 30. Waltke says, "Jacob has entered a dark night of slavery, a foreshadow of Israel in Egypt. Laban outwits Jacob and reduces family to an economic arrangement. . . . Significantly, this key word is the same one used with reference to Esau serving Jacob (25:23; 27:29,37,40)" (Waltke, 403).

29:21–27. Perhaps you have never noticed that Jacob said **give me my wife**, not "give me Rachel." This opened the door for the master schemer (Laban) to pull the old switcheroo. Had he planned this seven years earlier? Probably not. He had every expectation that Leah might find a husband during that time; but since she didn't, he saw an opportunity to unload his less desirable daughter on his unsuspecting nephew. The ceremony took place with the bride veiled, Jacob slept with his new wife, and in the morning he got the surprise of his life.

Kidner calls this "the very embodiment of anticlimax, and this moment a miniature of man's disillusion, experienced from Eden onwards. Yet the story reveals that God, not Laban, had the last word. The deceiver Jacob was deceived and the despised Leah was exalted to become the mother of, among others, the priestly and kingly tribes of Levi and Judah" (Kidner, 160–61).

Laban, of course, had the perfect excuse: **It is not our custom here to give the younger daughter in marriage before the older one**. Not only that, but he put forth a counteroffer Jacob couldn't refuse because of his love for Rachel: **We will give you the younger one also, in return for another seven years of work**. Why hadn't Laban mentioned this custom seven years earlier? Perhaps because it was part of the deceit from the beginning, but not likely. Since Leah and Rachel were both moving on in age, and prospects of marriage for the older daughter dimmed by the hour, Laban saw his chance to pull off a double wedding and put his hooks into a foreman for the ranch for another seven years.

What did Rachel think of all this? We have no idea, but we know that the role of women in nomadic cultures even today does not permit them to object to their father's will. Why did Jacob accept this deal instead of demanding Rachel immediately? He didn't actually have the local sheriff on his side, and he probably saw himself outfoxed, outgunned, and outmaneuvered. Besides, his love for Rachel made even the second seven years seem like a good deal.

29:28–30. So Jacob, like his grandfather, ended up with two wives, though hardly for the same reason. Along with the dowry came a couple of servant girls (Zilpah and Bilhah), who would play major roles in the narrative of the next chapter. The key phrase in this section lays the groundwork for the agonies in the patriarchal family: **He loved Rachel more than Leah**. Such language indicates that he loved Leah as well, but the Sarah-Hagar motif returns to haunt the Abrahamic line, this time for the rest of Jacob's life.

Laban became God's foil for disciplining the deceitful and sometimes frivolous Jacob. Jacob's errors in judgment were far from over, but he had fourteen years to think about what the future might hold. Jacob offered an Old Testament picture of a New Testament principle: "Do not be deceived: God cannot be mocked. A man reaps what he sows. The one who sows to please his sinful nature, from that nature will reap destruction; the one who sows to please the Spirit, from the Spirit will reap eternal life" (Gal. 6:7–8).

Ross nails the spiritual dynamic we should take away from this fascinating tale of romance in the workplace:

> The lesson is that, even though God's people may experience God's blessing on their endeavors, God will effectively discipline them by making them painfully aware of their unresolved sins. In short, we may say that they will reap what they have sown—even though they seem to be making progress by God's provision. God may wait patiently before disciplining his people, but discipline he will, often using means similar to the offense to correct them (Ross, 503).

C All My Children (29:31–35)

> **SUPPORTING IDEA:** *There's a wonderful theme in Scripture—God loves the unloved. He sees the agony of Leah, and she becomes the mother of the first tribal leaders of Israel.*

29:31–32. How often in Scripture God pays special attention to the unloved. Surely Jacob wanted his first son by Rachel, but the Lord saw to it that **Leah became pregnant**. Reuben reminds us of Ishmael, whose name also derived from a similar situation (Gen. 16:11). His name meant "see, a son," but phonetically it sounded like the Hebrew word for "he **has seen my misery**."

29:33–35. Obviously the Lord opened Leah's womb wide because three more sons came in rapid succession. *Simeon* means "hearing" or perhaps "one who hears" as Leah continued to explain her dilemma through the names of her sons. *Levi* connects with the Hebrew word **attached**, and *Judah* means exactly what Leah says in verse 35—**I will praise the LORD**. Then the text says **she stopped having children**—for a time. Of the names Kidner writes, "A verb begins the train of thought, and some of the Arabesques are freer than others. All of them reflect the immediate domestic tensions and triumphs; later, in the Blessing of Jacob (ch. 49), the names and their associated incidents will give rise to forward-looking oracles for the twelve tribes" (Kidner, 161).

The biblical portrait of Leah shows us a shy woman who perhaps lived most of her life in the shadow of her beautiful sister. But her sensitivity to spiritual things developed dramatically during these years of childbearing. Furthermore, the genes of Bethuel, seen so dominantly in both Laban and Rebekah, and then in Jacob, apparently did not reach Leah. We do see some diminishing of spiritual commitment in the next chapter, but generally Leah is the contented wife and mother as this present chapter ends. In the words of Phillips, "Leah was no longer fretting because her sister had so effectively monopolized Jacob's heart. Leah had found an outlet for her love in the Lord. She no longer needed people to make her happy, her joy and praise was in God. Having reached that high note in her spiritual life Leah ceased having sons. What need had she of further assurance? The Lord was better to her than a hundred sons" (Phillips, 243).

D Surrogate Mothers (30:1–24)

> **SUPPORTING IDEA:** *Any family that loses its dependence on the Lord can expect turmoil and chaos until it eventually becomes dysfunctional.*

30:1–8. In a society that considered children, especially sons, symbols of wealth and power, jealousy loomed as the inevitable result of Rachel's dilemma. Her illogical outburst, surely shouted in frustration at the moment, became a prophecy when she died while giving birth to Benjamin (35:16–19). Jacob, who disappeared from the scene after the wedding week narrative, responded angrily, reminding his love that he did not control the birth rate of his wives. How we want to read here that Jacob and Rachel held each other close and prayed that the Lord would grant them children. Instead, Rachel resorted to worldly methods used by Jacob's grandmother, although surely they both knew about the anguish that Ishmael's birth had caused.

Now we also see why Bilhah and Zilpah were introduced in chapter 29. They will enter the maternal wing of the patriarchal line. Obviously, as with Sarah and Ishmael, any children born to the female servants would belong to their owners. Names drawn from birth surroundings continued; *Dan* means "vindication" and *Naphtali* means "my struggle."

The words **as a wife** in verse 4 are interesting, since obviously Bilhah and Zilpah became mere concubines. Along with these two, Hagar and Keturah were also both wife and concubine in Genesis. Waltke says, "Each of these concubines is an auxiliary wife to the patriarch, not a slave, but subordinate to the wife who is her mistress. After the patriarchal period, the term *wife* is never used as a synonym for concubine" (Waltke, 411). Actually Zilpah never carried both titles, but her status in chapter 30 was exactly the same as Bilhah. In any case, the contest had begun, and these women were determined to create the first baby boom.

30:9–13. Imitation may be the most sincere form of flattery, but that is not exactly what Leah had in mind. She was still up four to two in bearing children, but she deemed that an insufficient lead in this marathon, so two more sons emerged: Gad, which is variously interpreted as either "good fortune" or "a troop" (probably the former), and Asher, who could have been nicknamed "happy" although the full name means "women will call me happy." The unwanted older sister, whose weak eyes attracted no suitors, was now the legal mother of six and the biological mother of four, well placed in the matriarchal driver's seat of the Jacobian camp.

30:14–16. Most commentators suggest that Reuben was seven or eight years old at this time and the reference to **wheat harvest** signals only a time of year, not the occupation of any family member. He found mandrakes, a type of wild fruit or vegetable, something like a child would find edible mushrooms and bring them home. The text does not indicate that Reuben understood the uses to which his mother would put this desirable plant. But Rachel immediately sensed the significance, and sister-strife edged up a notch.

Verse 15 suggests that Jacob had stopped sleeping with Leah because in actuality, she (Leah) stole Rachel's expected husband, not the other way around. Rachel's response indicates that Leah's matriarchal authority obviously did not cover Jacob's sexual behavior. Youngblood observes, "Apparently

Rachel, as Jacob's favorite wife, has the questionable privilege of deciding which of Jacob's wives or concubines would sleep with him on any given night" (Youngblood, 225).

So in the primitive bargain Rachel received the mandrakes and Leah received a night with her own husband! Leah had to say to him, **You must sleep with me**. Back to Waltke: "Just as Jacob's relationship with Laban has changed from 'flesh and blood' to 'wages,' so now his marriage to Leah is reduced to a commercial contract. Laban's degradation of Jacob to a shepherd under contract outside his home now strikes him from within his own family!" (Waltke, 413).

30:17–24. Although we have no record of Leah's prayer, it must have taken place because the text says **God listened to Leah**. A fifth biological son emerged. His name was Issachar, which sounds like the Hebrew word for "reward." But rather than acknowledging God's direct hand in the birth, Leah concluded that Issachar represented a present from God because she urged Jacob to sleep with Zilpah. Either her pregnancy or Rachel's ongoing permission must have brought Jacob to her bed again. We meet a sixth son whom she called Zebulun, a name related to the word **honor**. Finally, she figured, with eight sons on the roster, she would reclaim the role of number one wife and the respect of her husband.

The text tells us that **some time later she gave birth to a daughter and named her Dinah**. Jacob had other daughters (37:35; 46:7,15), and we will meet Dinah again under unfavorable circumstances in chapter 34. Any tricks with this name? No, because she would not be in the significant ancestral line and furthermore, "etymological word plays are the narrator's way of stressing the significance of the individuals who were important to the formation of the nation" (Ross, 513).

It had been some years since the birth of Naphtali, and Rachel was doubtless no longer saying, "I have won" (30:8). In fact, she may have given up the fight entirely, assuming the final score would be eight to two. But **God remembered Rachel; he listened to her and opened her womb**. We learn that Rachel had been praying quietly through the years for more sons. The mandrakes were forgotten (obviously they did not work), and Rachel gave credit where credit was due by saying, **God has taken away my disgrace**. So the eleventh son arrived. In reading Joseph's name, we recognize the person who will dominate the last eleven chapters of Genesis.

But what does the last line of verse 24 mean? The wording connects with the name *Joseph*, but it almost sounds as though Rachel was praying for yet another son after Joseph. The only logical conclusion is that, unlike his brothers, Joseph was named for an event that Rachel hoped would yet occur, not for the circumstances surrounding his own birth. Some interpreters have suggested a hidden wordplay in the words **taken away**, a prophetic indication of Joseph's kidnapping and slavery in Egypt, but that may be more than the text can handle.

E Curious Contract (30:25–43)

> **SUPPORTING IDEA:** *God's blessings may come in a strange way that allows us to think we designed them ourselves—but that would be a false conclusion.*

30:25–30. With eleven sons and a daughter in his tents, Jacob decided to head back to Canaan. The "work" and "serve" motif comes back into focus fourteen years after Jacob arrived in Paddan Aram. He had kept his part of the bargain, he had seen God add prosperity and posterity through those years, and he thought it was time to leave.

But Laban, considerably the richer because of Jacob's presence, implored him to stay because **I have learned by divination that the LORD has blessed me because of you.** Commentators are not agreed on what Laban wanted to say here. **Divination** is the attempt to discover hidden knowledge through incantation or other supernatural means. Our narrator contrasts the spiritual maturation of Laban and Jacob, since Jacob responded by saying, **the LORD has blessed you wherever I have been.** They came to the same conclusion, but Laban arrived along a different route that was forbidden in Israel after the Mosaic Law (Lev. 19:26; Deut. 18:10,14).

Since Laban's wealth had increased, he was willing to up the ante and pay Jacob whatever he asked. Jacob already had descendants; now he would like a piece of the prosperity. Presumably with that plan in mind, he responded with the question, **When may I do something for my own household?**

If we were reading contemporary fiction here, we would anticipate that Laban had some scheme in his pocket to outwit Jacob again. For these two, one-upmanship was a way of life. In chapter 27 Jacob deceived Esau; in chapter 29 Laban deceived Jacob; and now in chapter 30 Jacob will deceive Laban. Ross quotes Fokkelman: "What this repeating 'fraction' shows is: whenever people like Jacob and Laban mix with each other, there is no end to it. How is this to go on? Will the two take to an escalation of deceit, will they continue *ad infinitum*? What a prospect!" (Ross, 518)

30:31–36. When Laban asked the simple question, **What shall I give you?** he was not ready for Jacob's response. Jacob asked for **every speckled or spotted sheep, every dark-colored lamb and every spotted or speckled goat.** Everything else stayed with Laban. Although he uttered the right words (**Let it be as you have said**), Laban could not restrain himself from cheating. He removed all the animals that would have been Jacob's according to the bargain, gave them to his sons, and put distance between himself and Jacob. We can almost hear him muttering, "Now let my stupid son-in-law outwit me with his crazy plan."

Between Rachel's mandrakes and Jacob's trees, we can hardly fault Laban for his theological infancy. Morris says:

> Since the solid-colored animals were by far the more numerous, and since it was much less likely that they would bear striped and speckled offspring than those animals that were already striped and speckled—or brown among the sheep—this arrangement clearly was highly favorable to Laban and of very doubtful value to Jacob. Indeed, it was an act of pure faith on his part. He had put himself entirely at God's mercy. It would be up to the Lord to indicate, by a very unlikely set of circumstances, whether Jacob should prosper personally or not (Morris, 473).

But wait. In 31:10–12 Jacob will talk about a dream that essentially established the basic pattern for this plan. If that dream occurred before the bargain of chapter 30, Jacob was already acting in confident expectation of what God would do. That spiritual speculation, however, tarnishes immediately when we move into the next paragraph.

30:37–43. If the dream occurred before the bargain, and if Jacob was trusting God to come through on a plan that he had placed in Jacob's mind, all the human effort described in this section strips away the veneer of faith. The old peeled-bark prenatal influence trick is described in detail, and the chapter ends surprisingly with these words: **In this way the man grew exceedingly prosperous and came to own large flocks, and maidservants and men servants, and camels and donkeys.**

Although we do not learn it in this chapter, the only reason Jacob prospered was because of God's grace. Even at that, verse 40 seems to suggest that Laban changed the rules in the middle of the game. We read that some **streaked and dark-colored animals . . . belonged to Laban.** The point is that regardless of what Laban or Jacob did, God controlled the flocks and herds.

> **MAIN IDEA REVIEW:** *God allows families to behave in foolish and worldly ways and then often steps in to straighten out the mess.*

III. CONCLUSION

Belonging to God

George Wade Robinson, a Congregational minister, wrote the hymn "I Am His and He Is Mine" that appeared in 1876 in *Hymns of Concentration and Faith,* published by James Mountain, composer of the tune.

This meaningful hymn could have been Jacob's theme song. Its words teach us to look all around us for the creative hand and loving care of God.

When things have been made new in our hearts through faith in Christ, we have the opportunity to see the freshness and beauty of God's natural revelation—even in the birth of sheep and goats. Jesus often tried to get his disciples to understand their relationship with the Father through him. Robinson captured that thought in its spiritual bounty. Here is the last verse:

His forever, only His! Who the Lord and me shall part?
Ah, with what a rest of bliss Christ can fill the loving heart!
Heaven and earth may fade and flee, first-born light in gloom decline;
But while God and I shall be, I am His, and He is mine.

PRINCIPLES

- Monogamy has always been God's plan for marriage—for obvious reasons.
- The children of this world are wiser in their generation than the children of light.
- Jealousy is an ugly quality, especially among people who claim to serve God.

APPLICATIONS

- Never replace dependence on God with human schemes.
- Sometimes our most important ministry is to relatives who want to take advantage of us.
- List some of the ways God has blessed you in spite of yourself.

IV. LIFE APPLICATION

Jacob: Precursor to Postmodernism

Some would argue that the first twenty-first-century enemy of absolute truth is the spirit of postmodernism which began to build in the late 1900s. Among its other characteristics, post-modernism abandons absolute truth, preferring to create its own truth and approaching virtually every subject with freelance subjectivism. Christians believe that absolute truth is discovered in the absolute Word of God. Postmodernists believe truth is designed or created, and, therefore, what is true for one person may not be true for another, nor must truth synchronize with reality or rationality.

In his famous book *The Closing of the American Mind*, Allan Bloom complained that postmodern university students fear the danger of absolutism because it carries with it the ultimate curse—intolerance. He argues that virtually every entering college freshman is sure of one thing—all truth is relative.

At this point in his life, Jacob was struggling with absolutes, attempting to engineer his own world by his own schemes. After all, until he met Laban, it had always worked. Now maybe the old magic had returned. Although he mentioned God at various times, he hardly had a handle on sovereignty and still apparently believed he controlled his own destiny and that of his family.

Like us, Jacob had not yet seen the end of what God would do in his life. In some ways the story gets worse, and in other ways it gets better. But one issue of importance arises in forthcoming chapters: Jacob moves from a focus on himself to a focus on his Creator.

V. PRAYER

Father, keep us from our own schemes and always focusing on ourselves. Draw us into your truth and help us to commit our lives to you without reservation. Amen.

VI. DEEPER DISCOVERIES

A. Marriage Adoption (30:3)

We have already noted that this business of giving servant women to one's husband was common in the culture of the Semitic peoples. Some have suggested that Laban may have given his daughters these servant women to serve as backups against potential barrenness.

William LaSor's point of view develops the concept a bit further:

> Judging from the customs of the times . . . we have here what is known as a marriage adoption. No sons of Laban are mentioned at this time; they are mentioned later. According to the custom of the day, a man who had no sons of his own to look after him in his old age, and to take over the right of primogeniture and carry on the family and the family tradition, could marry his daughter to a young man under a marriage adoption contract, in which, in exchange for giving his daughter to this young man, he took the young man as his son and conferred upon him the rights of sonship. It is further stated in those marriage documents that should a son, a *true* son, be born to the man later, that son would take the place of primogeniture and the son-in-law (the adopted son) would lose it. I think that is what must have happened in the case of Jacob with Laban, because later on we come across a reference to Laban's son and Laban is sending Jacob off without the rights, or the title (LaSor, 34).

All of this makes sense from a strictly human point of view. But from the faith perspective that God wants to imprint upon the lives of the patriarchs, such behavior only brings sadness.

B. Magic Mandrakes (30:14–16)

References such as this pop up on occasion throughout the Bible and catch us by surprise. We are accustomed to the narrative text and the basic story line since Sunday school, but talking donkeys, left-handed judges, and angels stirring healing pools seem unusual biblical references. The mandrakes contained no special power. In spite of inbred superstition, all the children born to Leah and Rachel were a gift from God. But just a word more about mandrakes themselves. Wenham tells us:

> The mandrake (*Mandragora Autumnalis*) is a perennial Mediterranean plant that bears bluish flowers in winter and yellowish plumsized fruit in summer. In ancient times, mandrakes were famous for arousing sexual desire (cp. Cant 7:13) [Song of Solomon] and for helping barren women to conceive. These properties are certainly presupposed here and in Cant 7:13. Indeed, the word translated "mandrakes" is almost the same as . . . "love" (Prov 7:18; Cant 1:2; 4:10; 5:1) (Wenham, 246).

Phillips calls them "love-apples" and says, "The root can easily be pinched into the rough figure of a man. People thought the plant could excite passion and promote fruitfulness in a barren woman. Rachel was tired of waiting for God to make her fruitful. Maybe some love apples would help" (Phillips, 245).

C. Zebulun (30:20)

While Rachel had no luck with the love apples, Leah bore a sixth son and named him Zebulun, which may mean "honor" or "dwelling." Neither he nor his closest sibling Issachar stand out in the Book of Genesis. We read in Jacob's prophecy that "Zebulun will live by the seashore and become a haven for ships; his border will extend toward Sidon. Issachar is a rawboned donkey lying down between two saddlebags. When he sees how good is his resting place and how pleasant is his land, he will bend his shoulder to the burden and submit to forced labor" (49:13–15).

In the final division of the tribes by Joshua, Zebulun and Issachar were side by side in southern Galilee. Their territory stretched from Mount Carmel to the Jordan River, with Issachar on the south and Zebulun on the north. Note that Zebulun joined the seas (Mediterranean and Galilee). The territory of that tribe across the valley of Jezreel became one of the great trading routes of antiquity, the Via Maris. It stretched from Damascus in Syria to the Mediterranean Sea.

In later history the tribe of Asher located north of Zebulun was never able to dislodge the Canaanites in that area. Zebulun's people filtered north into the coastal areas of Phoenicia known today as Lebanon. The most notable Zebulunite in the Old Testament was the judge Elon, who led Israel for ten years (Judg. 12:11). Earlier in the Book of Judges, however, the great battle against Jabin and Sisera led by Deborah and Barak brought mention of people from Zebulun "who bear a commander's staff" as playing a significant role in that Israelite victory (Judg. 5:14). Later in Deborah's song she lauded the tribe by singing, "The people of Zebulun risked their very lives" (Judg. 5:18).

But perhaps the most important Zebulunic passage in the Bible appears in the little-known context of 1 Chronicles 12. There we read about his older brother, the tribe of Issachar "who understood the times and knew what Israel should do" (v. 32), a phrase which has picked up some popularity in leadership studies of recent years. And immediately following, "men of Zebulun, experienced soldiers prepared for battle with every type of weapon, to help David with undivided loyalty" (v. 33). So perhaps these boys of Leah were not as obscure as we think, giving birth to tribes that would stay on the cutting edge of what was going on and serve their king with singleness of heart. We could use more of both of these qualities in the church of today.

VII. TEACHING OUTLINE

A. INTRODUCTION

1. Lead Story: More Than Meets the Eye
2. Context: These chapters fall in the middle of the Jacob narrative, bringing him from young single manhood, to marriage, to father and prosperous rancher. Spiritually we see God's hand of sovereignty continuing to lead his people and bring about the fulfillment of his promises to Abraham.
3. Transition: Jacob disappoints us a bit after the vow at Bethel in chapter 28 by his manipulation of Laban, but this relationship is far from over. It will continue in chapter 31.

B. COMMENTARY

1. Kissing Cousins (29:1–14a)
2. Double Wedding (29:14b–30)
3. All My Children (29:31–35)

4. Surrogate Mothers (30:1–24)
5. Curious Contract (30:25–43)

C. CONCLUSION: JACOB: PRECURSOR TO POSTMODERNISM

VIII. ISSUES FOR DISCUSSION

1. What experiences do you see in these chapters which indicate that God was taking care of Abraham's grandson?
2. How might modern Christians behave like Laban? What would be their motivation? What do you see as the cure?
3. Why did God keep rescuing and blessing Jacob in spite of his scheming?

Genesis 31:1–55

On the Road Again

I. INTRODUCTION
The Perfect Gentleman

II. COMMENTARY
A verse-by-verse explanation of the chapter.

III. CONCLUSION
"Trust and Obey"

An overview of the principles and applications from the chapter.

IV. LIFE APPLICATION
Things Are Not Always What We Claim

Melding the chapter to life.

V. PRAYER
Tying the chapter to life with God.

VI. DEEPER DISCOVERIES
Historical, geographical, and grammatical enrichment of the commentary.

VII. TEACHING OUTLINE
Suggested step-by-step group study of the chapter.

VIII. ISSUES FOR DISCUSSION
Zeroing the chapter in on daily life.

Quote

"*W*hen a train goes through a tunnel and it gets dark,

you don't throw away the ticket and jump off. You sit still

and trust the engineer."

Corrie ten Boom

GEOGRAPHICAL PROFILE: MIZPAH

- Means watchtower or guard post
- Possibly located north of Mahannaim, east of the Jordan River
- Home of the judge Jephthah

Genesis 31:1–55

IN A NUTSHELL

*W*hen God blesses one of his children, not everyone will be pleased. Envy and greed can arise in the best of families to disrupt and destroy relationships.

On the Road Again

I. INTRODUCTION

The Perfect Gentleman

As I write commentary for these chapters, workers are still cleaning away the rubble of the World Trade Center Towers, and the Marines have set up a base in Afghanistan. For several months Americans have been attempting to make sense of this awful tragedy which killed more than twenty-five hundred and began a war whose magnitude is not measurable at this time.

On September 27, 2001, Bryant Gumbel interviewed Ann Graham Lotz and asked, "Why didn't God stop this or do something about this?" Ms. Lotz responded, "For years we have told God we didn't want him in our schools. We didn't want him in our government, and we didn't want him in our finances. And God was being a perfect gentleman and doing just what we asked him to do. We need to make up our minds—do we want God or do we not want him? We cannot just ask him in when disaster strikes."

Up to this point in his history, Jacob had been the perfect American. He reached for God in disaster or listened to direct revelation, but most of his life had been lived on a strictly human plane, dependent upon his own cunning. We have also noticed that Jacob had found a genetic rival of deceit in his Uncle Laban. Once again in this chapter the two demonstrate something that humankind has understood for thousands of years: in-laws do not always get along.

II. COMMENTARY

On the Road Again

> **MAIN IDEA:** *Jacob, although set on the right road at Bethel, still struggles with his service twenty-one years later. In earlier chapters it appeared that Jacob had acted on his own and called in God for emergencies. But now God is calling the shots. Jacob invokes his heavenly Lord no fewer than eight times in this chapter.*

A Called Home (31:1–21)

> **SUPPORTING IDEA:** *When God calls, we must not reject him. When he calls us as he called Jacob and we react as Jacob did, the promise still rings true: "I will be with you."*

31:1–3. By this time Laban was an old man, and his sons had begun to worry about their inheritance. This vagrant brother-in-law who had shown up unannounced and uninvited many years ago had prospered in flocks, herds, and people to a greater extent than their father, draining off some of their own assets. Jacob knew what they thought and also **noticed Laban's attitude toward him was not what it had been**. This is probably a reference back to 30:31 where Laban offered the ranch if Jacob would only stay in town. Nevertheless, both Laban and Jacob had contracts. It appears that neither wanted to be the first to break his word—so God intervened.

The Lord often uses the negative attitudes of other people (in this case Laban and his sons) to make us wonder whether it is time to move on. Pastors experience this with congregations; men and women in business and industry; and many who just think about relocating. Jacob was also encouraged by his wives (vv. 14–16), so he got ready to head southwest across the Euphrates River, out of Paddan Aram and back to Canaan.

31:4–9. Verse 4 is the first time in the Jacob narrative that we see Rachel named first, so we assume she had claimed the head wife role. This may also indicate that Jacob had now taken over the reins of his family, since Rachel was always his first choice. In addition, rather than being bantered about from wife to wife and from tent to tent as he was in chapter 30, Jacob had finally reached the decision point. He described the reason for leaving by attributing all of his success to God.

Waltke says:

> Jacob's twenty years of trial and the obvious presence of God to prosper him during the last years work a transformation in him. For the first time in this act, he emerges as a man of public faith, and he takes the leadership of his home. He acts promptly upon God's command to return to the Promised Land (31:3–4), bears witness first to his wives of God's presence and provision and then finally to Laban's whole family, and willingly undertakes the dangerous and difficult journey in obedience to God. For the first time, his wives follow his lead (Waltke, 422–23).

What did Jacob mean by saying that Laban changed his **wages ten times**? Any attempt to spiritualize this number falls flat. This specific number is unimportant; Jacob simply pointed out to his wives that Laban had cheated him at every opportunity and he would not take it any more. Verse 9 offers what we call today a *bottom line* in what appears to be technical terminology for transfer of property. In short, Jacob acknowledged that in spite of his own wits (rather than because of them) God had made him a wealthy man. In the next section he explained to his wives that he knew all this because of a dream.

31:10–13. The chronology here seems fuzzy. Did the dream occur some time earlier when this business of selective breeding began? Jacob merely said, **In breeding season I once had a dream**. This leaves us to wonder whether he meant a few months or a few years earlier. If all that Jacob announced in these verses took place earlier, then it would appear that God's command of 31:3 is a repeat of something Jacob had heard some time before. God had said at Bethel, "I will bring you back to this land" (28:15), but perhaps Jacob needed some prodding, some repetition of God's plan for his life.

31:14–21. One could hardly argue that the wifely response from Rachel and Leah put the focus on Jacob. They showed concern for what they had lost and how their father had treated them badly. According to Stevens, "They were already aware of a sense of alienation within the family. Laban had taken their dowry and used it for himself instead of making a heritage of it for them. Their future lay with their husband and children. They were ready to leave their family clan and join their husband's people. That was a normal marriage pattern in the culture of that day" (Stevens, 103).

So the caravan headed out with one minor glitch: **Rachel stole her father's household gods**. These were probably small portable idols that Rachel stole because she thought they would bring her protection and blessing. Or perhaps she wanted to have something tangible to worship on the long journey ahead. In any case, Rachel was not yet free of her pagan background (see Gen. 35:2; Josh. 24:2).

So Laban's genes that passed through Rebekah to Jacob had also passed directly to Rachel, and we have another deceiver on our hands. Apparently she was married to the right man. The very next verse tells us that **Jacob deceived Laban the Aramean by not telling him he was running away**. The word **deceived** in verse 20 can be literally translated "stole the heart" which might be stronger than deception since "elsewhere it involves taking away a person's ability to discern and act appropriately (2 Sam. 15:6; 1 Kgs. 12:27). The translations 'deceived' and 'outwitted' (NASB, NIV, RSV) lose the parallelism between Rachel's theft and Jacob's. Both steal from Laban: Rachel as means of divination, Jacob his ability to act rationally" (Waltke, 427).

The geography of verse 21 rises from the text to refocus our attention on the promised land. The Euphrates River was shallow enough at certain points during certain seasons to allow a tribe like this to ford. Jacob set his compass for a mountainous region close to the Jordan River just southeast of the Sea of Galilee known as Gilead. Morris spells it out:

> Its northern edges are nearly three hundred miles from Haran; so a long journey stretched ahead of them. It is possible, of course, that Jacob had already worked his flocks around to the south as far as possible as to have the advantage of a head start when he was ready to leave. . . . Once they began moving the flocks along, they would be able to make only fifteen or twenty miles a day. Thus, once they

started driving the cattle, it would take them probably ten days or so to reach the Mount Gilead region (Morris, 483).

ⓑ Missing Gods (31:22–35)

SUPPORTING IDEA: *When a family gives itself over to deceit and lies, they can never trust one another and will always live on the edge of strife.*

31:22–24. It took Laban three days to learn of Jacob's departure. He rushed southwest and arrived in Gilead in seven days rather than ten, obviously unencumbered by traveling herds and women on camels. Notice that the text refers to Laban no longer as the father of Rachel or Leah but simply as **Laban the Aramean** (Syrian).

God's message in Laban's dream seems strange unless we remember 24:50 where Laban and his father answered Eliezer's request for Rebekah by saying, "We can say nothing to you one way or the other." The dream warning also reminds us of God's protection of Sarah in his night message to Abimelech (20:3–7).

Who were these **relatives** whom Laban took with him for a military adventure? Probably as many family males as he could muster, perhaps even the whole clan. We should never doubt that in any physical contest Laban would have had the advantage. Possibly the Lord's words **either good or bad** could have legal ramifications as well. When Laban said in 31:29, "I have the power to harm you," that threat could be taken by Jacob in a variety of ways, all true and terrifying.

31:25–30. The uncle-nephew relationship had disappeared. Now we read military language like **captives**, **war**, and **harm**. Laban overstated the case, of course, but the contest between these two had been going on for a long time. In Laban's terms, he wanted to be the good father and grandfather, sending the family away with a great celebration. Likely Laban did not know that his daughters had already switched loyalties. He may have expected them and perhaps even his grandchildren to bolt back to his side immediately.

The question **What have you done?** in verse 26 is identical to what Jacob said to Laban on that fateful wedding night (29:25). Laban was clearly restrained in hand but not in the heart. He couldn't touch Jacob because of God's dream warning, but he could certainly bad-mouth his behavior and impugn his motives: **Now you have gone off because you longed to return to your father's house.** At this point Laban almost appeared to forgive Jacob's behavior, but there was still this business of the stolen gods.

31:31–35. Jacob spoke the truth when he replied **I was afraid.** But since he had no knowledge of the alleged theft, he invited Laban to search the camp and actually put to death anyone who might have stolen the gods. In fact, Jacob felt he had acted so honorably that he said, **In the presence of our relatives, see for yourself whether there is anything of yours here with me; and if so, take it**. If this were a novel, we would reach the climax as we watch Laban's tough guys tear through Jacob's camp searching everywhere for the missing idols. We would be led by the script to expect them to find the gods with Rachel, much in the way Joseph found his golden goblet in Benjamin's bag many years later.

But the family's third greatest deceiver had **put them inside her camel's saddle and was sitting on them**. To ensure their safety she told her father **I am having my period** as an excuse for why she could not get off her camel. Laban's frantic search for the idols, as well as Rachel's taking them in the first place, forces us to consider again the spiritual condition of the family into which Jacob had married. Griffith Thomas says:

> It is difficult to appraise anything like a spiritual value in the religion of Laban. It seems to have been mainly of an indirect and second-hand character, a mixture of truth and error, a blending of consciousness of the Divine presence with a belief in images. The superstitious use of household gods seems to have been a breach of the law of the second rather than of the first Commandment (Thomas, 286).

ⓒ Tough Bargain (31:36–44)

SUPPORTING IDEA: *How often the struggles of life burden us down. How often we must remind ourselves that "God has seen my hardship and the toil of my hands" (v. 42).*

31:36–37. When Laban's search for the stolen gods turned up no evidence, Jacob finally lost it. All those years of pent-up humiliation and subjugation to his uncle burst out, and he demanded a showdown. If Laban could find anything in the entire Jacobite camp that belonged to him, let him put it on the ground in front of both groups and render a judgment. The phrase **took Laban to task** offers a Hebrew word which speaks of quarrels and even legal disputes (13:7–8; 26:20–22). It can refer to pastures, wells, or, as here, possession of flocks. Waltke says, "He turns the table from being the accused to being the aggrieved party. Jacob's speech which summarizes his twenty years with Laban, is comprehensive and almost poetic. . . . The balance and parallelism create the effect of elevated rhetorical prose" (Waltke, 431).

31:38–42. Having begun the release of his emotions, Jacob could not restrain himself from reviewing the agonies of the past twenty years. From all we know about Laban, he would not sit quietly and listen to this condemnation if he could prove its inaccuracy. Jacob concluded with his own interpretation of God's dream message to Laban the previous night: **He rebuked you.**

So with this new interpretation, it had not been Laban against Jacob for the past twenty years but Laban against Jacob's God.

Kidner picks up on the shepherd metaphor of the passage: "The tale of hardships is an astringent corrective to romantic ideas of the biblical shepherd. This, and nothing idyllic, is the pastor's calling, reminiscent of the adversities of Paul in 2 Corinthians 11:26ff., or indeed of David, Amos or Jesus (Ps. 23:4,5; Am. 3:12; Jn. 10:11ff.)" (Kidner, 166).

The phrase **seen my hardship** in verse 42 appears only two other places in the Old Testament. Both describe the oppression of the Jews by the Egyptians (Exod. 3:7; Deut. 26:7).

31:43–44. Laban didn't yield an inch. Five times he used the words **my** or **mine** in his brief retort. He admitted nothing, answered nothing, and accepted no blame for Jacob's condemnation. Nevertheless, he conceded he had lost the battle and pleaded no contest by calling for **a covenant**, a peace treaty or a nonaggression pact similar to Abraham's treaty with the Philistines (15:8–21).

Ⅾ Witness Heap (31:45–55)

SUPPORTING IDEA: *Sometimes it becomes important for Christians to live in peace through simple nonaggression pacts with unbelievers.*

31:45–47. Jacob, fond of using stones for a variety of purposes, put up a pillar and asked his people to pile up additional stones. Laban named it in Aramaic **Jegar Sahadutha** but **Jacob called it Galeed**, using the language of the Hebrews. This symbolism reminds us that these men came from two different ethnic groups, two different religions, and two different cultures.

31:48–50. Following the building of the **Galeed** and ceremonial meal, Laban invoked the now famous **Mizpah** (*watchtower*) warning, giving the witness heap yet another name. The witness heap became a boundary line between the two families, and Laban warned Jacob not to **mistreat my daughters** because God is watching **even though no one is with us.** This was actually a denunciation and a negative curse.

Laban's hypocrisy surfaced in his demand that Jacob not take any wives beside his daughters, a guideline already broken with Zilpah and Bilhah. Let's not miss the fact that Laban called on Jacob's God on the assumption that Jacob was more likely to break this covenant. As Phillips puts it, "To Laban, then, the pillar was a boundary, a guarantee for the future, a guarantee that threw all the onus and stigma of the past on Jacob" (Phillips, 256).

31:51–53a. The boundaries were drawn. Laban would stay northeast of the line in Paddan Aram, and Jacob would stay in Canaan. Laban assumed they would harm each other if they didn't have this physical reminder to separate them, so he repeated his invocation to Jacob's God, this time in words that could not be misunderstood: **May the God of Abraham and the God of Nahor, the God of their father, judge between us**. However, Laban's polytheism creeps out in his use of the plural for gods. He actually said, or implied, "The gods of Abraham and the gods of Nahor" because the word **judge** appears in the plural, indicating that Abraham, Nahor, and their father worshiped different gods.

31:53b–55. Jacob ignored Laban's reference to multiple gods and took an oath **in the name of the Fear of his father Isaac**, the name he had used back in verse 42. Does this not seem a strange name for God? It appears only in these two verses (vv. 42,53) and has caused many scholars to wonder whether the Hebrew word actually means *fear*. Wenham argues that it does and says, "On the whole the traditional rendering, 'fear, dread of Isaac,' does not seem out of place here, for it is precisely his experience of this God that has scared Laban and discouraged him from wreaking revenge on Jacob" (Wenham, 278).

Waltke prefers "Awesome one of Isaac" and suggests that Jacob made a deliberate attempt to separate the God of Abraham from the God of Nahor (Waltke, 434).

With the treaty established and the witness heap built, the combatants became **relatives** once more so they ate and slept in the same campground. In the morning Laban kissed his grandchildren (v. 28), and **then he left and returned home**.

> **MAIN IDEA REVIEW:** *Jacob, although set on the right road at Bethel, still struggles with his service twenty-one years later. In earlier chapters it appeared that Jacob had acted on his own and called in God for emergencies. But now God is calling the shots. Jacob invokes his heavenly Lord no fewer than eight times in this chapter.*

III. CONCLUSION

"Trust and Obey"

Daniel B. Towner was singing in Brockton, Massachusetts, at a Moody crusade. During a testimony service he heard a young man say, "I'm not quite sure—but I'm going to trust, and I'm going to obey." Towner jotted down the words and sent them to his friend John Sammis, who wrote the chorus first and then added the five verses. Towner wrote the tune, and the hymn "Trust and Obey" was published in 1887.

> Not a burden we bear, not a sorrow we share,
> But our toil he doth richly repay;

Not a grief nor a loss, not a frown nor a cross,
But is blessed if we trust and obey.

The testimony of that young man describes Jacob throughout this chapter: "I'm not quite sure—but I'm going to trust, and I'm going to obey." God does not ask us to be calm and victorious in all the problems of life; he only asks us to trust him. And, like Jacob, many of us are slow to learn this important lesson.

Trusting God sometimes comes through the difficulty of circumstances, personal illness, emotional or social struggles, or relationships with other people. Certainly for Jacob, his twenty-year conflict with Laban had driven him into the arms of God.

PRINCIPLES

- God sometimes uses circumstances and other peoples' attitudes to indicate that a change is needed.
- God often uses difficult circumstances to mold leaders.
- Success is possible only because of what God has done.
- Deceit in families is harmful to individuals and to the family as a whole.

APPLICATIONS

- When God calls you to go somewhere, go, and go quickly.
- Even if your hard work pays off handsomely, give God the glory.
- If you must argue with relatives, let it end in a truce.

IV. LIFE APPLICATION

Things Are Not Always What We Claim

Laban and Jacob had been tricking each other for two decades. During that time Laban had specialized in lying on multiple occasions. But misunderstandings do not arise only from deliberate lies. Sometimes we simply say things we don't understand or even make statements that actually mean the reverse of what we intended. Have a look at some examples.

When we say about a certain person "he eats like a pig," we do not necessarily insult him. The pig is one of the cleanest of domestic animals and among the leanest, generally eating an average of three to four pounds of feed a day.

We might describe someone as "blind as a bat." In fact, bats are not blind. They are outstanding nocturnal hunters that can catch and eat as many as twelve thousand mosquitoes and other insects an hour. Most consume more than half their body weight—about nine grams—in gnats, moths, and other insects every night.

Or we might say of ourselves at times, "I'm as hungry as a horse." It implies we are ready to sit down and eat a huge meal—which horses do not do. They don't gorge; they graze. A typical recreational or light-working horse eats only about 2 percent of its body weight in good-quality feed every day (Loretta Lettner, *Reader's Digest,* May 2001, 150).

Jacob and Laban talked past each other like this on a regular basis. Even the very end had no real understanding, with Laban talking about multiple gods and Jacob holding fast to his monotheism. We certainly wouldn't want members of a church to disagree on something as important as monotheism, but we do argue a good bit about whose property belongs to whom and who did injustice to another. It would surely be safe to say that many church fights begin with conflict among relatives. So there are great lessons here for us. Jacob and Laban could have settled all their differences with much less turmoil and agony for the family had they taken time to understand each other and communicate clearly what they needed, expected, and were prepared to give.

Griffith Thomas focuses on the spiritual lesson of this chapter:

> We are often perplexed by the problems of sin and free will and we are baffled as we try to think out how God's will can possibly be done amid all the perverseness of human nature. But we can learn much from a story like this, as we observe each actor a perfectly free agent and yet see everything taken up into the Divine purpose and made to search far-reaching ends. We may well speak of God's providence—pro-vidence, his "seeing before hand" and making provision accordingly. It is this that gives quietness amidst perplexities, and enables the soul to rest in faith until all is made clear. God's providence is indeed the saints' inheritance (Thomas, 289).

V. PRAYER

Father, keep us from quarreling like Laban and Jacob. Help us to acknowledge others as better than ourselves as the New Testament admonishes us to do and to serve in such a way that we earn the accolade of Jesus, "Blessed are the peacemakers." Amen.

VI. DEEPER DISCOVERIES

A. Providence

The word *providence* does not occur in the Bible, but it represents a genuine biblical doctrine. There is no single Hebrew word that we can translate as *providence*. The Greek word *pronoia* seems to describe human foresight (Acts 24:2; Rom. 13:14). The doctrine of providence becomes the stage on which the drama of Genesis is played out. It deals with God's gracious outworking of his plan in the lives of his people, and ultimately in the salvation story of Christ and the cross.

If we had only Genesis 30 without 31, we would imagine Jacob construing some kind of magic formula to enhance his flocks. But chapter 31 shows us that all the success of Jacob's experiments depended upon God.

God's providence even orchestrates negative human emotions and actions to achieve his purposes. As the jealousy of Jacob's wives led to the birth of the tribes of Israel, so the jealousy of Laban and his sons led to Jacob's return to the land of his fathers. The folly of Rachel in stealing the household gods enabled Jacob to win his lawsuit.

Belief in the providence of God reminds us that the entire world and our individual lives are not determined by chance or fate but by God and his purposes, often being worked out behind the scenes.

B. Household Gods (31:19)

According to the Nuzi tablets, possession of household gods could strengthen one's claim to an inheritance, so Rachel may have had a material motive as well as a religious motive in snatching the idols and hiding them in her saddlebags. The word for "gods" here is *teraphim,* occurring fifteen times in the Old Testament. These idols were thought to provide protection for the family. They may have also been designed in the images of ancestors.

Sometimes in the Old Testament idols are associated with divination, or the foretelling of the future. Wenham suggests:

> Normally one must suppose that a father would have supplied his daughters with copies of the household gods to take with them, and according to Gen 35:2–4, others in Jacob's party had their own gods. But in this case, because of hurried departure, Rachel took Laban's teraphim. But what was the point of taking them? Greenberg suggests it was to insure fertility. . . . It might also be that she was rather less confident about leaving home than she sounded (vv. 14–16). The *teraphim* were thus a Saint Christopher for her (Wenham, 274).

VII. TEACHING OUTLINE

A. INTRODUCTION

1. Lead Story: The Perfect Gentleman
2. Context: Genesis 31 falls in the middle of the Jacob narrative which began in chapter 28 and ends with the emergence of Joseph in chapter 37. Our story carries the now prosperous shepherd Jacob and his family out of Paddan Aram to begin the journey back to Canaan.
3. Transition: Though out of Mesopotamia and headed back to his father's land, Jacob was still east of the Jordan River. As chapter 31 finds Jacob running from Laban, chapter 32 will find him running from Esau. Conflict with those he has deceived will follow Jacob all his life.

B. COMMENTARY

1. Called Home (31:1–21)
2. Missing Gods (31:22–35)
3. Tough Bargain (31:36–44)
4. Witness Heap (31:45–55)

C. CONCLUSION: THINGS ARE NOT ALWAYS WHAT WE CLAIM

VIII. ISSUES FOR DISCUSSION

1. What is your understanding of the role of Jacob's dream in his departure? When did it occur and how quickly did he act on it?
2. Describe Laban's religion. How did it differ from the faith of his son-in-law Jacob?
3. What lessons in trusting God can we draw from Genesis 31?

Genesis 32:1–33:20

In the Ring with God

I. INTRODUCTION
The Hanging Stove

II. COMMENTARY
A verse-by-verse explanation of these chapters.

III. CONCLUSION
"Rock of Ages"

An overview of the principles and applications from these chapters.

IV. LIFE APPLICATION
Lessons from a Hummingbird

Melding these chapters to life.

V. PRAYER
Tying these chapters to life with God.

VI. DEEPER DISCOVERIES
Historical, geographical, and grammatical enrichment of the commentary.

VII. TEACHING OUTLINE
Suggested step-by-step group study of these chapters.

VIII. ISSUES FOR DISCUSSION
Zeroing these chapters in on daily life.

Quote

"We shall not cease from exploration, and the end of all our exploring will be to arrive where we start and to know the place for the first time."

T . S . E l i o t t

GEOGRAPHICAL PROFILE: SEIR

- Both land of Seir and Mount Seir are alternative names of the territory inhabited by Esau and his descendants
- It is also called Edom (Josh. 15:1; Judg. 11:17)
- The mountainous country runs about one hundred miles long on both sides of the Arabah, which connects the southern part of the Dead Sea with the Gulf of Akabah
- Located in the valley of the Jordan River near Zarethan

Genesis 32:1–33:20

IN A NUTSHELL

As Jacob matures spiritually and emotionally, he learns to depend more on God and less on his own schemes.

In the Ring with God

I. INTRODUCTION

The Hanging Stove

*A*s the story appeared in *The Joyful Noise Letter,* a psychologist, an engineer, and a theologian were hunting when they stumbled upon a cabin where a potbellied stove was suspended in midair by wires attached to the ceiling. The psychologist theorized, "The lonely trapper has elevated his stove so he can curl up underneath and feel the warmth as if he has returned to the womb."

"No," said the engineer. "By elevating the stove, the man is simply distributing the heat more evenly in the cabin."

"Actually, lifting up fire has been a religious symbol for centuries," explained the theologian.

About that time the trapper returned, and the three hunters asked him to explain why he had suspended his stove in the air.

"I had plenty of wire," he replied, "but not much stove pipe."

Sometimes simplicity is best. Jacob had been through two decades of manipulation and treachery. His stove had been hanging in midair with some frequency. His plans had been held together with bailing wire more than once. But now he began to mature, journeying southwest at God's call. We discover in Jacob, as we did in his grandfather Abraham, a man of prayer.

II. COMMENTARY

In the Ring with God

> **MAIN IDEA:** Two spiritual themes dominate these chapters—revival and reconciliation. The former must precede the latter in individuals (such as Jacob and Esau), but in church congregations reconciliation often brings on revival.

 Prayer of Humility (32:1–12)

> **SUPPORTING IDEA:** These verses are best characterized by the phrase of verse 7, "in great fear and distress." In such a condition all true believers throw themselves upon God. He alone can relieve the distractions of life and the detractors of joy.

32:1–2. Genesis 32 offers us a record of how the intensely fervent prayer of a righteous person really does avail effectively before God. In this chapter Jacob prayed one of most devout and significant prayers of the Bible. He had just cut himself loose from Laban and would soon face Esau. God prepared him by giving him a vision of angels, opening his invisible world to Jacob's visible world. Jacob responded, **This is the camp of God!** He named the place **Mahanaim**, which means "two hosts" or "two camps." Perhaps he intended to designate the camp of angels and his own camp, or it could have been his own camp and the camp of Esau that he would soon encounter.

This place Jacob called Mahanaim later became a levitical city in Gad (Josh. 13:26) and then the capital of Ish-Bosheth's kingdom (2 Sam. 2:8–9). Here David sought refuge during Absalom's rebellion (2 Sam. 17:24). Most scholars assume this second camp was the army of God for protecting Jacob on his journey. But Waltke raises the honest question of the text and particularly the name *Mahanaim*:

> The name means either "two camps" or simply "camp" but the later reference to two camps (32:7–8,10) supports the dual number. If dual, its significance is ambiguous. Does it refer to God's camp and Jacob's camp? Does it foreshadow the meeting of Jacob's camp with Esau's? Does it refer to the two angelic camps, here and at Bethel? Or do the two angelic camps prompt him to divide his household into two groups (32:8,10), even as the dream of streaked, speckled, and spotted goats prompted him to draw up the terms of his flock contract (31:10–12)? Perhaps the narrator, who loves puns, means to evoke one or more of these connotations. In any case, the narrator employs the number two throughout the scene: two camps, two families, two meetings—one with God and Esau—and two brothers. We observed a similar pairing in the non-aggression pact between Laban and Jacob (Waltke, 441).

32:3–8. The angelic meeting apparently served as a wake-up call as Jacob made his way into Esau's territory. Had he thought of his brother during the past twenty years? We have no idea, but Esau had to become the focus of his attention now. He was scarcely one hundred miles north of Edom—time to send a friendly message to a rugged brother not known for his patience and forgiveness. He told the story of his twenty years in Haran and asked Esau for **favor in your eyes.** To his credit Jacob made a good start by introducing himself as **your servant.** He waved the white flag with every word of his message.

The messengers returned (a good sign), but they could only tell Jacob that Esau was on his way north **and four hundred men** were with him. According to 1 Samuel 22:2, 25:13 and 30:10,17, this was a standard number for a militia. Nothing in Esau's reply set Jacob's heart at ease.

The spiritual vision at the beginning of the chapter did not deliver Jacob from dependence on human resources. With the two-group plan still in mind, he divided his family and belongings, hoping to rescue at least 50 percent.

Rather than depending on the God of the angel camp to deliver him, Jacob seemed content to get out of this situation with at least half his belongings intact. Thankfully, God had a more positive game plan.

32:9–12. These verses contain Jacob's first recorded prayer and the only extensive prayer in the Book of Genesis. He approached God as the God of his father, the God who had made a covenant with his family. Jacob let the Lord know that he was familiar with the promises of God. This was no longer the God only of Abraham and Isaac but the LORD, **who said to me**, making the prayer personal.

Jacob showed the correct attitude for prayer—total dependence on God. He did not deserve God's help—and he knew it. In this moment of crisis his past sins came before him—deceit toward his father, trickery of his brother, arguments with his uncle. He finally saw himself as Jacob the deceiver who had no claim on God's grace and favor.

This prayer proceeded on the basis of personal relationship, family relationship, and covenant relationship. Jacob stood on solid theological ground to address God as he did. He prayed as a believer, concerned that God would reveal himself in power. Finally Jacob identified himself before God as **your servant**.

Jacob's prayer was also *based on a need for help.* What could be more direct and to the point: **Save me, I pray, from the hand of my brother Esau.** God knows what is in our hearts anyhow; we might as well tell him. Sometimes we find ourselves reluctant to form words that describe the sinfulness of our own character and the foolishness of our behavior. But God surely knows that, and he is pleased to hear us acknowledge it. In short, he wants us to know how much we need him even though he already knows it.

Jacob's prayer was also *based on God's promise.* Just as the Bible writers frequently recounted God's historic blessings in prayer, they also repeated his promises back to him. Jacob reminded God about those **descendants like the sand of the sea, which cannot be counted.** But all that seemed in jeopardy with Esau's four hundred tough guys on the horizon. Was this the end? Were God's promises empty dreams? One would think this recounting of God's promises would build confidence. But Jacob's guilt and fear had so controlled him that he found scant peace, even in something as great as the promises of God. Nevertheless, he did remember them and reminded himself of them at this point.

Griffith Thomas says of this prayer, "Like a stream that emerges into day after running for a long distance underground, Jacob's spiritual life comes out now after those years at Haran; and, though there is much to seek, we can see the clear marks of the work of God directing, deepening, and purifying his soul" (Thomas, 296).

B Plan for Pacification (32:13–21)

SUPPORTING IDEA: *Although gifts sometimes pacify a threatening and fearsome enemy, our expectation for deliverance should never be in the gifts, but only in God.*

32:13–16. When we do the math here, we count a total of 580 animals. This reminds us of how wealthy Jacob had become and how willing he was to part with some of that in order to settle the Esau problem. He divided them into five groups, each headed by servants, so Esau would receive this beneficence of incoming stock in five separate waves.

32:17–18. Jacob anticipated Esau's shock when he saw all this animal flesh moving in his direction, so he instructed the servants to say about the beasts, **They are a gift sent to my lord Esau.** In spite of the prayer of the night before, this plan had Jacob's fingerprints all over it. As Phillips puts it, "The principle Jacob employed was the same principle that lay behind the trespass offering, later to become a part of Israel's sacrificial system. The trespass offering taught that, if a man wished to get right with God, then he must necessarily get right with the person he had wronged. He must make restitution and add more than he stole" (Phillips, 260–61).

32:19–21. The word **pacify** comes from a Hebrew word that literally means "cover his face." The symbolism means to wipe the anger from one's face, which is exactly what Jacob had in mind. The word-play heightens when in verse 20 Jacob hoped that perhaps Esau would **receive me**, literally, "he will lift up my face." Kidner makes a good point here:

> Jacob's sacrificial terms unconsciously illustrate the gulf between man's thinking and God's. The pagan approaches his deity as Jacob now approached Esau . . . reckoning that "a man's gift maketh room for him" (Prov. 18:16). But in the Old Testament, a man's gift is first God's gift to him, before ever it is his to God (Lev. 17:11). As Jacob would soon discover, grace, not negotiation, is the only solvent of guilt (Kidner, 168).

C Outmatched at Peniel (32:22–32)

SUPPORTING IDEA: *Sometimes blessing comes only through prayer; but at times prayer requires intense spiritual struggle with physical side effects.*

32:22–28. The Jabbok River enters the Jordan River midway between the Sea of Galilee and the Dead Sea. Jacob's family crossed the Jabbok just east of where it enters the Jordan. All his possessions and people were gone, and **Jacob was left alone.** The Hebrew text reflects a significant word-play since the names *Jacob* and *Jabbok* and the word for *wrestle* all sound very much alike. Here Jacob's suffering in prayer became a turning point in his life. He stayed up all night wrestling with God's angel. This was a follow-up to his earnest prayer that we saw earlier in the chapter. During this wrestling match God changed Jacob's heart and prepared him to become Israel, the patriarch of the land.

Jacob had no way of knowing what was happening when the match began, nor does the text reveal to the reader anything other than a human match. But since we learn that Jacob's opponent was God himself, what could the text possibly mean when it says, **when the man saw that he could not overpower him?** Most commentators avoid this curious phrase. Waltke simply says, "Humbling himself, God has come to Jacob on some type of even terms" (Waltke, 446). Close to daybreak Jacob's opponent disabled him. Ross says, "The effect of this blow is clear: the assailant gave himself unfair advantage over the patriarch for he was more than a match for Jacob. The one that expected to take advantage of the other was himself crippled by a supernatural blow from his assailant" (Ross, 553).

Yet Jacob held on until he received a blessing, probably after realizing that his opponent was no common mortal. Remember that when Jacob answered the question about his name he was forced to say *deceiver*. Then a most unexpected thing happened as Jacob received a new name—**Israel**—literally meaning "he struggles with God."

The transformation pertained to the way in which Jacob prevailed. Always before he had prevailed over people through trickery. Now he prevailed with God, and so with humans, by his words, not by the physical gifts conferred on him at birth or acquired through human effort. His ambition to win had not been changed but oriented in the right direction.

32:29–32. As long as they were exchanging business cards, Jacob also wanted to know his combatant's name. But he received only the question, **Why do you ask my name?** We find it difficult to ascertain whether this was a mild rebuke ("Don't you know me by now?") or just a shrugging ("Forget the name—concentrate on the blessing"). In any case Jacob became the father of the nation of Israel, the people who struggle with God and with humanity. Jacob named the spot **Peniel** ("the face of God"), which became a town on the north bank of the Jabbok River four miles east of Succoth.

We should not dwell on the physical dimensions of this struggle, because the real key was the spiritual warfare. We do well to think about our needs and how God stands ready for us to call on him. This text reminds us to base our prayers on God's Word, our own unworthiness, a specific and clear need for help, and a remembrance of his promise.

Peniel became Jacob's third great spiritual landmark, following Bethel and Mahanaim. According to Griffith Thomas, at the first he learned of the divine presence, at the second the divine power, and at the third the divine favor.

"God desired and purposed to bring Jacob into this position of blessedness and power; and all the Divine dealings, from Bethel onwards, were intended to lead up to this. So it is now; everything that God has for us is expressed in terms of union and communion of which the New Testament is so full" (Thomas, 306).

Ⓓ Reunion in the Desert (33:1–11)

SUPPORTING IDEA: *In chapter 27 we wondered about Isaac's double blessing of Jacob and Esau and how that could possibly work. Now we discover how God turned human error into something that blessed both brothers.*

33:1–3. At last the fateful meeting took place. Jacob, never without a plan, arranged his family in precise order with his favorites at the rear, just in case Esau became violent. Morris suggests, "At least a secondary purpose was to have them meet Esau in climactic order" (Morris, 503). In the protocol of those days, a person approached a king by bowing seven times. And Jacob followed the pattern, not so much as subject to lord (surely he remembered the birthright), but in respect and recognition that Esau was, for all practical purposes, the king of Edom. This time Jacob took the leadership and stood in front of his family ready to take the first blows. But he wasn't ready for what happened next.

33:4–7. God had been at work in Esau's heart. The brothers embraced and wept at their reunion after twenty years. Waltke points out an interesting contrast between 25:34 and 33:4: "The narrator represented Esau's despising of his birthright with five terse verbs . . . he now represents the reconciliation with another five verbs" (Waltke, 454).

Esau seemed bewildered by the great company of people with Jacob. He asked, **Who are these with you?** All of Jacob's family members approached the king of Edom and demonstrated their submission. Kidner observes:

> The meeting is a classic of reconciliation. The stream of gifts and the demure family procession almost comically over-organized (as it turned out) give some idea of the load on Jacob's conscience and the sure grace of Esau's reply. Guilt and forgiveness are so eloquent in every movement of the mutual approach (3,4) that our Lord could find no better model for the prodigal's father at this point than Esau (Lu. 15:20) (Kidner, 171).

33:8–11. Then Esau asked a second question about the **droves** that had been sent ahead of the family party. Jacob answered, **To find favor in your eyes, my lord.** Esau toned down this **my lord** business by referring to Jacob appropriately as **my brother** and indicating that he didn't need any of the gifts. But Jacob, thrilled with Esau's response, was more than happy to dispose of the animals he had brought for his brother. He said, **For to see your face is like seeing the face of God, now that you have received me favorably.** Perhaps Jacob remembered Peniel (32:30) where he saw God's face and lived through it.

Notice the word **gift** switches to **present** in verse 11, now using the same Hebrew word which appeared for *blessing* in 27:35–36. Perhaps Jacob offered a blessing to Esau in exchange for the blessing he had stolen from his brother years before.

E Final Lap to Shechem (33:12–20)

> **SUPPORTING IDEA:** *We all know that home is where the heart is. Jacob finally returned to the place where his father and grandfather had dealt personally with God.*

33:12–15. Esau's offer was sincere. Four hundred fighting men could guarantee Jacob's safe arrival back in Shechem. Presumably Esau thought Jacob came to visit him, but Jacob had other intentions. He understood that the day-by-day existence of a farming community on the move was incompatible with the march of four hundred fighting men. At first glance we might think the reference to the animals and children offered a convenient excuse, but most likely it represented the reality of the different lifestyles these men and all their descendants had adopted.

Morris says, "Though he did not say so, Jacob no doubt also realized that he should be separate and independent from Esau, as far as the future accomplishment of God's plans for his children was concerned; and it would be better to establish such a separation from the beginning" (Morris, 506).

Esau wanted to at least provide an escort for his brother, but Jacob knew that was no longer needed. Once he freed himself from Laban, he had just one fear between Paddan Aram and Shechem—Esau. Now that problem had been taken care of, and he felt comfortable in moving on without a special guard.

33:16–20. So Esau headed back to Seir and thereby disappeared from Genesis except for the brief mention of Isaac's burial in 35:29. But then Jacob did a strange thing. He settled for a while in Succoth just west of Peniel on the Jordan River. We might see Succoth as a temporary resting place, a stop to catch his breath after the emotional encounter with Esau. But some interpreters see it as a failure to move directly into Canaan as God had commanded.

Griffith Thomas says, "Jacob had forgotten his vow at Bethel . . . and by making Succoth so evidently his home he was showing himself to be on a very low spiritual level in his forgetfulness of the claim of God upon him . . . he thus fails to rise to the full height of God's purpose. He had overlooked all of this, and was settling down, at any rate for a time, in earthly ease and prosperity" (Thomas, 313). How long he stayed in Succoth we do not know, nor can we agree with Thomas that his motives were entirely negative.

Some time later Jacob crossed the Jordan River and arrived at Shechem where Abraham had stopped so many years before (12:6). Jacob finally settled in the land to which he had prayed to return (28:21). He camped outside the city, bought some land and, in good patriarchal fashion, pitched his tent and **set up an altar** (see "Deeper Discoveries"). Here we observe that God had fulfilled all his promises and brought Jacob back to the land in safety and prosperity. There is a tone of closure in this passage: The wandering Jew, ill-treated in another country, had finally found his way home.

Sailhamer sets this narrative in national history:

> The picture of Jacob and Esau in these narratives curiously fore-shadows the relationship between the historical Israel of the Davidic monarchy and Esau's own descendants, Edom, as that relationship is depicted in the later prophetic books. Although often there was bitter resentment between the two nations, which God frequently used to chastise his disobedient people (e.g., 1 Kgs. 11:14; Obad. 1–18), in the end God's kingdom was to be extended even to include the land of Edom (Obad. 21) (Sailhamer, 212).

MAIN IDEA REVIEW: *Two spiritual themes dominate these chapters—revival and reconciliation. The former must precede the latter in individuals (such as Jacob and Esau), but in church congregations reconciliation often brings on revival.*

III. CONCLUSION

"Rock of Ages"

In 1776 the newly formed United States declared its independence; in England, Augustus Montague Toplady was writing hymns. The familiar "Rock of Ages" first appeared a year earlier in the *Gospel Magazine* that Toplady published. Only the first stanza appeared in 1775; the entire hymn in March of 1776 under the pretentious heading, "A Living and Dying Prayer for the Holiest Believer in the World." Toplady died three months before his thirty-eighth birthday. In 1866 as the steamer *London* sank in the Bay of Biscayne, the last human sounds heard from the helpless passengers were the words of "Rock of Ages."

This hymn reminds us of Jacob's fondness for rocks; he used them as a pillow, pillar, or monument. And this wandering Jew had finally learned something about the Rock of Israel. He could have applauded Isaiah's line, "Trust in the LORD forever, for the LORD, the LORD, is the Rock eternal" (26:4) and offered a loud amen to the words of Psalm 18:2: "The LORD is my rock, my fortress and my deliverer; my God is my rock, in whom I take refuge."

PRINCIPLES

- Jacob's behavior should remind us that God never abandons his promises.
- Biblical prayers show us that God's saints recounted verbally the things he had done for them as a foundation for what they needed.
- Our unworthiness should remind us that God has to deal with us as he did with Jacob before he can deal with our petitions.
- Whatever our needs, God knows them before we do and has a plan to provide for them.

APPLICATIONS

- God can transform your life, as he did Jacob's.
- Pray that God will keep us from our own schemes and tricks.
- Rather than try to work things out by our own plans, we should say like a little child struggling with a difficult toy, "Daddy, will you help me?"

IV. LIFE APPLICATION

Lessons from a Hummingbird

On the deck behind our Georgia home hang two hummingbird feeders with red liquid beckoning the little creatures to visit our home at will. And throughout spring, summer, and fall they come, displaying their feisty behavior and constant nervousness. Hummingbirds are among the smallest warm-blooded animals on earth and (although many refuse to acknowledge it) among the meanest. They have virtually no social behavior, and individual survival seems their only concern.

Although we think our little feeders allow them to survive, they get most of their energy sipping nectar from flowers—seven to twelve kilocalories of energy every day. One kilocalorie equals one thousand calories which, when translated into human terms, would mean an adult eating 204,300 calories a day—roughly 170 pounds of hamburger! A hummingbird must find as many as one thousand flowers a day to keep up its weight in nectar just to stay alive. During the breeding season the male broadtail hummingbird typically flies more than forty runs an hour to a feeder in order to drive off rivals. Seasonally they fly as far as two thousand miles.

Hummingbirds display amazing resilience, energy, and strength—but virtually no calm or trust. While we might admire their physical feats, if we lived either our spiritual or physical lives that way, we would be burned out in no time. The nervous, frantic, adversarial hummingbird offers no model for the Christian life.

Waltke argues that one of the theological lessons of Genesis 33 is submission: "Only in giving up his rights does Jacob fully become the family leader. Israel's role prefigures the role of Christ (Phil. 2:9–11). So also God gives up his Son who humbly gives up his rights to be equal with God, to reconcile the world to himself (see 2 Cor. 5:16–21; Phil. 2:6–8). Their model of servitude is an example to the church (Matt. 5:24; Phil. 2:5)" (Waltke, 457).

V. PRAYER

Father, forgive us for our frantic activities to defend and advance ourselves. Help us to learn the model of Jesus, whose spiritual strength lay not in control but in restraint. Amen.

VI. DEEPER DISCOVERIES

A. Angelic Encounters

In the Jacob narrative so far we have seen three encounters with angels and three specific namings to identify those places—Bethel (28:19), Mahanaim (32:2), and Peniel (32:30). At Bethel Jacob saw many angels climbing up and down the stairway (see 28:12); at Mahanaim the text says, "The angels of God met him" (32:1); but at Peniel the word *angel* never appears. Nevertheless, his opponent said, "You have struggled with God and with men and have overcome" (32:28).

The key passage, therefore, comes to us in the Minor Prophets where Hosea, referring to Jacob, says, "In the womb he grasped his brother's heel; as a man he struggled with God. He struggled with the angel and overcame him; he wept and begged for his favor. He found him at Bethel and talked with him there—the LORD God Almighty, the LORD is his name of renown!" (Hos. 12:3–5).

Some interpreters argue that this was a match with the preincarnate Son of God, a Christophany. But that argument can only be made from Hosea, not from the text of Genesis. Since angels are so popular in our day, we do well to remember the warning Griffith Thomas offers:

> Angels as they are brought before us in Holy Writ, are invariably depicted as the *servants* of the saints—their inferiors, not superiors. It is probably a mistake to think of angels as occupying an intermediate

place between men and God, as something more than the one and less than the other. It may have been this error that has led to the worshiping of angels and the thought of them as mediators between an impure humanity and a Holy God. Scripture, on the contrary, reveals them as always *ministers,* servants, of those who are higher than themselves in spiritual place and privilege, of those who are "heirs of salvation" (Heb. 1:14; 1 Pet. 1:12) (Thomas, 292).

B. "I Saw God Face to Face" (32:30)

In Genesis 16:13, Hagar received word from the Lord and said, "I have now seen the One who sees me." Now Jacob claimed to see God's face. But Exodus 33:23 says, "Then I will remove my hand and you will see my back; but my face must not be seen." Perhaps we best understand this in a referential symbolism. To experience a direct angelic encounter was to see God. Waltke says, "This unusual expression is used only of direct divine-human encounters, not necessarily of literal visual perception" (Waltke, 447).

In spite of all the divine contact with people in the Old Testament, John could say at the incarnation, "No one has ever seen God, but God the One and Only, who is at the Father's side, has made him known" (John 1:18).

C. El Elohe Israel (33:20)

This name of Jacob's altar at Shechem can mean "God, the God of Israel," or "Mighty is the God of Israel." Phillips considers this hypocrisy and criticizes Jacob for this altar:

> Just like so many of us who try to give backsliding the aura of religious respectability, Jacob erected an altar and called it El Elohe Israel ("God, the God of Israel"). It sounded very good but it was Jacob, not Israel at work, Jacob and not God. . . . No doubt Jacob intended his altar to be a testimony to the pagans round about him. If so, his intentions were soon brought to nothing by the behavior of three of his children (Phillips, 268).

Phillips has good intentions in making the point of separation (he also takes the position that Succoth was a terrible mistake). But the text does not seem negative at this point. Jacob invoked his new name, attached it to the God of his fathers, and appeared to raise the flag of genuine righteousness. I agree with Elliott who says of Jacob, "That he had a new and determined purpose is indicated in the name which he called the place of his altar, *El Elohe Israel, God, the God of Israel.* In his own mind, there was no doubt about it; this was his personal God who had brought him through" (Elliott, 173).

VII. TEACHING OUTLINE

A. INTRODUCTION

1. Lead Story: The Hanging Stove

2. Context: The Jacob story is winding down. He will make one more trip, back to Bethel, and soon the Genesis narrator will switch to Joseph. But for the moment, Jacob was where God wanted him—content, dependent, and focused on the true God.

3. Transition: The transition between chapters 31 and 32 occurs naturally as Jacob continues his journey south from Paddan Aram. But we are not prepared for chapter 34 that brings into focus a little-known personality—Dinah, Jacob's daughter.

B. COMMENTARY

1. Prayer of Humility (32:1–12)

2. Plan for Pacification (32:13–21)

3. Outmatched at Peniel (32:22–32)

4. Reunion in the Desert (33:1–11)

5. Final Lap to Shechem (33:12–20)

C. CONCLUSION: LESSONS FROM A HUMMINGBIRD

VIII. ISSUES FOR DISCUSSION

1. What areas in your life and family need revival and reconciliation?

2. If any conflict exists between you and a relative, how might you approach him or her with God's blessing to bring about a restoration of relationships?

3. Identify several lessons from Jacob's prayer in chapter 32 that can enhance your own prayer life.

Genesis 34:1–36:43

Nobody Knows the Trouble I've Seen

"*The* Christian sufferer need not know why the blow was struck. He wants to discover what God is doing in the face of it."

A u s t i n   F a r r e r

GEOGRAPHICAL PROFILE: EDOM

- The nation founded by Esau and his descendants, also called Seir
- Originally inhabited by Horites (Gen. 14:6)
- Conquered by David (2 Sam. 8:14)

GEOGRAPHICAL PROFILE: EPHRATH

- Burial place of Rachel
- The ancient name of Bethlehem or at least the area around Bethlehem
- Referred to in the messianic prophecy of Micah 5:2

PERSONAL PROFILE: HAMOR

- Literally means an "ass"
- A Hivite ruler of Shechem
- Father of Shechem, the man who raped Dinah

I N   A   N U T S H E L L

We have certainly seen Jacob's ups and downs, but these three chapters show the highest and lowest points of Jacob's life. He has to face rape and murder, and he moves immediately to purification and prayer. One thing we have learned from the lives of the first three patriarchs is that there are no heroes in the Bible except God.

Nobody Knows the Trouble I've Seen

I. INTRODUCTION

Guilt or Shame

Imagine an Iowa farmer driving across the cornfields at three o'clock in the morning. He knows exactly where the stop sign is a mile ahead, and considering the hour and his assurance that no one else could possibly be on the road at this time of night, he slows down, looks both ways, and slides through the stop sign. He places no one in danger, but he does break the law and therefore feels just a bit of guilt.

Consider the same situation in southern France. The driver sees a stop sign, has clear visibility over the countryside for miles, but drives on through without giving it a thought. If, however, a gendarme just happened to be waiting behind a tree and pulled over the French driver, he would be chagrined and shamed at being caught, but he would think he was not guilty of disobeying the stop sign.

Paul L. King has made a fascinating study on this phenomenon.

> Worldwide, people groups can be usefully divided into taxonomies of "guilt" and "shame" societies. "Guilt" societies are those whose members' consciences bother them when they violate rules, even when there is no chance that anyone else can discover their transgressions. "Shame" societies are those where conscience is not as big a factor as a sense of disgrace which a person experiences when offenses are brought to light. The usefulness of these categorizations is that they explain a lot about people's social behavior.

In this unpublished monograph entitled *Guilt and Shame,* King goes on to apply his principle of traffic to plagiarism, particularly in China where he has worked for a good portion of his adult life. He concludes, "Probably everyone of us tries to get away with something at one time or another. We cut corners. We take shortcuts. We bend or break the rules. However, the way people in a given society feel about individual wrong-doing affects the over-all shape of behavior in that society."

This fascinating sociological analysis, quite accurate from examples I have seen around the world, certainly applies to Jacob's family. In spite of his devious behavior, Jacob never seemed to feel guilt except when he experienced a direct confrontation with God. Even when he saw himself mirrored in the ugly behavior of Laban, there was little change in the way he set his moral standards.

Nor did this deficiency trouble Jacob unduly as God continued to overcome his blunders and mend his ways. But when the father eats sour grapes, the children's teeth are set on edge (Jer. 31:29). Jacob would soon experience in his children the fruits of his devious lifestyle.

II. COMMENTARY

> **MAIN IDEA:** God's care and blessing do not fall on perfect people but on struggling servants whose failures are obvious to others.

Nobody Knows the Trouble I've Seen

A Slaughter at Shechem (34:1–31)

> **SUPPORTING IDEA:** The intermarriage of Israel with the Canaanites presents a problem throughout the Old Testament and sets the stage for the New Testament condemnation of worldliness and carnality.

34:1–12. One need not be a skeptic to wonder why a chapter like this appears in the Bible. We flinch at the bloody carnage in Genesis 34. Some commentators see this passage so out of place that they argue it must have occurred much later in the history of Israel, at least later in the history of Jacob's family.

Ross indicates the options:

> If this event took place soon after Jacob's return to the land and before Joseph's sale into Egypt, the participants would be rather young. If Reuben was born to Leah in the eighth of Jacob's twenty-year stay with Laban, he would have been about fourteen at the return, making Simeon and Levi a couple of years younger, and Joseph possibly seven. According to Genesis 37:2, Joseph was seventeen when his first conflict with the brothers surfaced; and according to 41:46, he was thirty when he stood before Pharaoh (and thus thirty-seven after the seven years of plenty, when the brothers went to Egypt for food). If the rape of Dinah took place before Joseph was sold, the brothers would be in their early twenties; but if it took place after the sale, they could have been anywhere up to their early forties (Ross, 569).

This was not a national Canaanite war but tribal rivalry that raged around a specific incident. The issue of the chapter does not seem to be so much the rape of Dinah as the murder of the Shechemites. Whenever it took place, the principle is the same: sinful human behavior can easily get out of control. We see God in Jacob's altar at the end of chapter 33, and he speaks to Jacob again at the beginning of 35, but he makes no appearance in chapter 34.

Any parent of teenagers can sympathize with the problem of a daughter who wants to hang out with the wrong crowd, and that seemed to be the problem here. Dinah was not looking for a boyfriend or intending to engage in immorality; she just **went out to visit the women of the land.** It was an imprudent act on her part, but the text repeatedly emphasizes her role as Jacob's daughter, suggesting that her behavior was his responsibility.

Notice the rape comes first, and then the text says that Shechem **loved the girl and spoke tenderly to her.** Translations which portray Shechem's act as seduction miss the strength of the verb; the same one is used in Genesis 6:2 for sexual tyranny. This was, after all, the prince of the city who could take any girl he wanted and then order his father to **get me this girl as my wife.**

Jacob learned what happened but did nothing until his sons came home. Hamor wanted to negotiate a wedding, but Dinah's brothers **were filled with grief and fury.** The narrator says the rape took place **in Israel,** an anachronism referring to the nation in embryonic form.

Hamor opened dialogue not only for Dinah, but for general intermarriage that would break down any distinctions between the family of Jacob and the residents of Canaan. We must remember two things. First, both Abraham and Rebekah sent their sons out of Canaan to find wives precisely so this kind of thing would not happen. Second, all this discussion occurred while Dinah was still back at Shechem's house, presumably a captive.

Shechem (who apparently accompanied Hamor in this visit to Jacob's camp) wanted to know how much Dinah would cost. He said, **I'll pay whatever you ask me.** He even talked about a bonus, willing to add a **gift** to the **price** to sweeten the pot. Morris proposes, "Quite possibly it was this matter-of-fact, business-like attitude of Hamor and Shechem that infuriated Dinah's brothers beyond limit. Here these men were making a monetary offer for their beloved sister, just as though she were nothing but a harlot (v. 31) whose body could be purchased for the asking!" (Morris, 512).

34:13–23. Jacob dropped out of the conversation, and his sons took over. At this point in our analysis of the family, we should not be surprised to read that **Jacob's sons replied deceitfully.** They pretended that the only hindrance to intermarriage between Israelites and Canaanites was circumcision. They offered Dinah to marry among the Shechemites if **you become like us by circumcising all your males.**

That sounded like a good plan to Shechem, so he and his father went home to sell the idea to the rest of the city by attaching the rhetorical question, **Won't their livestock, their property and all their other animals become ours?**

We find it beyond belief that Jacob agreed to this horrendous plan. But apparently, after a short time of family leadership, he had once again receded into the background, unable to cope with the evil designs of his sons. We can hardly fault the Shechemites for anything other than mindless acquiescence to the wishes of their prince. The real sin was with Jacob's sons, who used the sign of a spiritual covenant with God as an act of treachery to exact revenge.

Griffith Thomas points out:

> Circumcision without faith in the covenant God could not be anything but carnal and earthly. And, worse still, they were about to employ the solemn seal of the Divine covenant for the purpose of wreaking their vengeance on these unsuspecting men. Their suggestion was therefore nothing more than a pretext to cover treachery. There was the appearance of piety with the reality of intended murder. Could anything be more truly terrible? What a light it sheds on the state of Jacob's home life! (Thomas, 323).

Jacob had other daughters, but none are named in the pages of Scripture (see Gen. 37:35; 46:7,15). Some commentators believe the reference to "brothers" in verse 11 pertains only to Simeon and Reuben who would have been the full brothers of Dinah, thereby excluding the other nine from this bargain. Both of these thoughts are purely speculation but worth considering.

34:24–31. The leaders of the city (**all the men who went out of the city gate**) bought into the plan, so **every male in the city was circumcised**. On the third day, while the entire male population was still disabled, Simeon and Levi began the slaughter, **killing every male**. They **looted the city**, took everything worth stealing, and **carried off all their wealth and all their women and children, taking as plunder everything in the houses**. As Phillips puts it, "The Holy Spirit lists each sordid detail (34:27–28), and each word falls like a lead weight of doom on the scales of the Holy One. Simeon and Levi had acted worse than Assyrian shock troops. Moses, who tells the story in all its naked horror, still feels the outrage and the shame of the deed even after the passing of over four hundred years" (Phillips, 271–72).

Finally Jacob felt the impact of this devastation, but he mentioned not a word about sin against a holy God. His concern was for himself and the possibility that the Canaanites might now **join forces against me and attack me.** Simeon and Levi protested lamely, **Should he have treated our sister like a prostitute?** Then this terrible chapter ends.

Sailhamer suggests that Simeon and Levi were excusable in this affair since "their motive had not been mere plunder but the honor of their sister"

(Sailhamer, 216). I think not. It seems quite questionable whether we can find any innocent party in this entire chapter, possibly even Dinah. Deception and deceit rule each verse, and Jacob, although he didn't reply to Simeon and Levi, never forgot or forgave their actions (Gen. 49:6–7).

🅱 Back to Bethel (35:1–15)

SUPPORTING IDEA: *When believers find themselves caught in the quagmire of sin and corruption, personal revival and purification are necessary. And for Jacob this means getting back to Bethel.*

35:1–5. God had seen enough. He intervened by sending Jacob back to Bethel to **settle there, and build an altar there to God**. The time had come to rid the family of the stench of Shechem and their shame, but three conditions had to be met before the trip could begin: **Get rid of the foreign gods you have with you, and purify yourselves and change your clothes**.

Up to this point the only foreign gods we know about were the household idols which Rachel stole from Laban. Now suddenly more idols appear, along with **the rings in their ears**, an indication that a significant portion of Jacob's family still clung to some form of the paganism they had learned in Paddan Aram. The purification dealt with complete washing of the body as both a literal and symbolical cleansing of the sin they left behind them. The change of clothes depicted a new life for the return to Bethel (Gen. 41:14; Lev. 15:18; 16:23–24).

Formerly peaceful shepherds and reasonably good neighbors, Jacob's family now carried the stigma of a pack of thugs who had to travel through alien territory. But at least they left behind the symbol of their idolatry (quite probably including items Simeon and Levi had sacked from Shechem) under the great oak at Shechem associated with Abraham's faith (12:6).

God's grace still reigned over the patriarchal family. We read that **the terror of God fell upon the towns all around them so that no one pursued them**.

35:6–8. Finally they arrived at Bethel. Jacob built another altar, calling it *God of the house of God* in remembrance of God's revelation to him there many years before.

The next verse startles us since Deborah has not been a major figure in the events of the Jacob narrative. She had come with Rebekah from Mesopotamia (24:59) and had very likely been Jacob's nursemaid from the day he was born. Morris considers her appearance here "proof that Rebekah herself was dead at this time" (Morris, 520), although the Scriptures never mention the death and burial of Rebekah. Some interpreters speculate that this information is omitted because of Rebekah's deceit of her husband Isaac. In honor of the beloved Deborah, the tree under which she was buried was named Allon Bacuth, "oak of weeping."

35:9–15. At first glance it appears our narrator simply rehearses what has happened to Jacob previously. But the early words of verse 9 dispel that notion. Instead, we see a repetition of God's dealing with Jacob during his first time at Bethel with some minor additions that represent an even deeper experience. God reconfirmed the change of his name, emphasized again the blessing of progeny by adding **kings will come from your body,** and repeated the promise of the land.

Jacob set up another **stone pillar,** but this time we have the first mention of a **drink offering** and the pouring of oil. Just as God reconfirmed Jacob's new name, Jacob reemphasized the name of the place as **Bethel,** a confirmation of his previous designation.

The theophany (appearance of God) of Genesis 35 completes the revelation of the Abrahamic covenant to Jacob. The first theophany was associated with God's covenant with Abraham in chapter 15; the second, with the expansion of that covenant in chapter 17.

C Birth at Bethlehem (35:16–29)

> **SUPPORTING IDEA:** *The Book of Genesis is full of births and deaths, with the message that God's work in the world continues even after his servants are buried.*

35:16–22. This section begins with the second transitional death of the chapter as Rachel experienced **great difficulty in childbirth . . . died and was buried on the way to Ephrath.** We remember Rachel's prayer for another son (30:24) but could hardly have guessed back then that Ben-Oni ("son of my trouble") would end her life. Jacob immediately renamed the boy **Benjamin** ("son of my right hand").

Ross points out:

> The naming was significant at this time. In contrast to the name of lamentation provided by Rachel in her suffering, Jacob's naming may have signified his sense of freedom from Laban and safe return to the God of Bethel—to the southern land of Canaan, for the completion of the tribes. Moreover, the lesson for Israel would be that the promise of progeny would continue after the nation settled in the land (Ross, 582).

For the first time **Ephrath** (Bethlehem) appears in the Bible. It was about twelve miles south of Rachel's actual burial place. The birth of Benjamin reminds us of another birth that would occur in Ephrath, or Bethlehem, hundreds of years later. Of course, Jacob found it necessary to erect a stone pillar which, at the time of the writing of this chapter, still stood. Notice the quick switch in name between verses 20 and 21. We read that **Israel moved on again**, this time **beyond Migdal Eder**. While there, **Reuben went in and slept with his father's concubine Bilhah**.

We have yet to see any positive behavior on the part of any of Jacob's sons. Later Jacob would say of his oldest son, "Turbulent as the waters, you will no longer excel" (Gen. 49:4). Let's keep track here. Simeon and Levi had already lost their leadership roles, now Reuben surrendered his, which brings us down to Judah. Just as he had nothing to say about the rape of Dinah, Jacob said nothing about Reuben's behavior with Bilhah.

35:23–26. We already know about Jacob's twelve sons. But since Benjamin has just been born and the tribal structure is complete, the narrator finds it useful to rehearse the list once again. They appear in order of social ranking of Jacob's wives and then secondly on seniority. We find this same sequence in Exodus 1:1–4.

The only thing that seems out of sync here is that the text says all these sons of Jacob **were born to him in Paddan Aram**. But we know that Benjamin was not. Waltke says, "The list of sons may idealize all the sons as participating in an exodus from exile in Paddan Aram to the Promised Land. . . . If so, the theological concern overrules the factual concern" (Waltke, 478). Quite possibly this list prepares us for the next paragraph by showing us the grandsons whom Jacob will formally present to his father Isaac. Presumably he had no intention of telling his father Isaac what a bunch of cutthroats he had raised.

35:27–29. Finally Jacob made it all the way home to Hebron, about twenty miles south of Jerusalem, back to that famous oak at Mamre where Abraham had lived years before. Some estimates suggest it had been sixty-five years since Jacob left home for Paddan Aram, and here we find the record of Isaac's death at the age of **a hundred and eighty**.

Morris reminds us that

> Isaac must have still been living at the time Joseph was sold into Egypt, but the writer found it appropriate to mention his death at this point. . . . Isaac's spirit, no doubt, was transported to Sheol, where the spirits of Abraham, Shem, Noah and others who had died in faith were resting and awaiting the coming redemption and resurrection (Morris, 524).

As a postscript to chapter 35, we read that Esau joined Jacob in the burial of Isaac. This introduces the descendants of Esau in the next chapter.

D East in Edom (36:1–43)

SUPPORTING IDEA: *We find the people of Israel and the people of Esau attempting to live in the same area of the world but struggling to maintain a peaceful coexistence. This chapter explains the wide expansion of Esau's descendants who parallel the descendants of Jacob.*

36:1–9. The careful reader will notice immediately the contradiction between the names of Esau's wives and what we have read in chapters 26 and 28. Here we learn that all of Esau's descendants came from three wives: **Adah daughter of Elon . . . Oholibamah daughter of Anah. . . Basemath daughter of Ishmael**. Their names are not nearly as important as the phrase **women of Canaan**. However, most commentators get so wrapped up in explaining the difference in the names that they miss Esau's great sin in choosing pagan wives.

Phillips reminds us, "Two things must be kept in mind—Esau's unsuccessful compromise and Esau's unceasing carnality. Esau's parents were godly people, and his marriage to pagan women distressed them greatly" (Phillips, 283).

The history of Edom continually intersected the history of Israel. This at least partially accounts for the details of this chapter. Furthermore, Edom was Israel's closest neighbor since Esau voluntarily moved all his people **as well as his livestock and all his other animals and all the goods he had acquired in Canaan**. An understanding of later Old Testament history requires that we fix the geography of Seir well in our minds. It lies southeast of the Dead Sea, south of Moab, an area which today represents the southern part of the kingdom of Jordan. Like Lot and Ishmael, Esau moved *away* from the promised land.

36:10–19. The list of Esau's descendants begins with the sons and reappears in 1 Chronicles 1:35–37. The sons also show up in the second list of this section as the **chiefs among Esau's descendants**. According to Waltke:

> In all likelihood the narrator has contrived this list in order to have twelve "grandsons" . . . counted as such by excluding Amalek the son of a concubine and by including the sons of Oholibamah. The sons of Oholibamah (wife of Esau) are placed on a line with the grandsons of Adah and Basemath by uniquely identifying her as a granddaughter, by placing her last, and by not listing her grandsons. Accordingly, the sequence of Esau's wives is given according to the descending number of their respective offspring: five, four, three. The list shows the transition of Esau from a family to a tribal arrangement (Waltke, 484–85).

36:20–30. First the sons, then the chiefs, now **the sons of Seir the Horite.** At first we see no logical reason for the inclusion of these verses. Yet the Horites became linked with descendants of Esau by intermarriage. Therefore they were blended into the tribal groups known as the Edomites. Ross notes, "Seven sons became chiefs, and from these seven came twenty-one sons and daughters (or tribes). Thus far a picture of Esau as a powerful overlord is emerging. Not only did his own sons become chiefs of clans, but the clans in the land were subjugated to him" (Ross, 586).

In this entire chapter we find only one anecdote, appearing in verse 24: **This is the Anah who discovered the hot springs in the desert while he was grazing the donkeys of his father Zibeon.** This little story distinguishes this Anah from his uncle, a pattern we have also seen regarding the two Lamechs (Gen. 4:17–24) and the two Enochs (Gen. 5:21–24).

36:31–43. Long before Saul took the throne of Israel, the Edomites had kings. The writer of Genesis wants us to know the power and extent of this monarchy. Waltke notes, "It is the only known non-dynastic king list among the national states of the ancient Near East, raising the question whether Edom should be considered a nation at this time. This king list shows the transition from a tribal arrangement to designated kingship" (Waltke, 486). This fact became important later when Saul, the first king of Israel, defeated the Edomites (1 Sam. 14:47).

MAIN IDEA REVIEW: *God's care and blessing do not fall on perfect people but struggling servants whose failures are obvious to others.*

III. CONCLUSION

Biblical Illiteracy

According to the American Bible Society, almost every American household has at least one Bible, but ownership does not bring familiarity. For many Americans the Sermon on the Mount was delivered by Billy Graham; Joan of Arc is the name of Noah's wife; and 80 percent of so-called born-again Christians believe that "God helps them who help themselves" is a biblical saying.

Research carried out by ABS, the Gallup Organization, and Barna Research supports the idea that Americans simply do not know what the Bible says.

- Less than one-half of Americans read the Bible every week.
- About one-third do not know that the Book of Isaiah is part of the Old Testament.

- About 40 percent erroneously believe that the entire Bible was written after Jesus' birth.
- The number of people who read the Bible at all has declined from 73 percent of the population in 1990 to just 59 percent at the end of the twentieth century. As the American flag represents patriotism, the Bible is a symbol of faith, a faith that is very broad but also very shallow.

We have seen that throughout the lives of Jacob and Esau, God has spoken often to Jacob, and yet Jacob repeatedly ignored his duties of spiritual leadership. Apart from a few emotional moments of acknowledging God's rule in his life, Jacob lived for himself, raising family with less concern for God's truth than their parents, grandparents, and great-grandparents. For his part Esau cared nothing about God's promises or God's covenant. He is a portrait of the secular man.

When surveys ask Americans about their favorite books of the Bible, Psalms comes in first and Genesis second. Yet the lessons of faith, covenant, sovereignty, and obedience—so crucial in the lives of the patriarchs—seem lost in a post-modern world.

PRINCIPLES

- Separation from wickedness and the world has always been God's plan for his people.
- Utilizing sacred symbols and rituals for evil purposes will bring God's judgment.
- Experiencing God up close doesn't guarantee that people will always remain faithful to him.

APPLICATIONS

- Get rid of all the idols in your life.
- Review God's promises often and with deep sincerity.
- Acknowledge that people from all nations will one day be in heaven. Work to accomplish the Great Commission of Jesus that promises this reality.

IV. LIFE APPLICATION

Nazi Trees

On December 4, 2000, forestry officials in Germany carried out a necessary but unusual task. They cut down trees that had been planted in the form of a swastika some sixty years before. When viewed from the air the trees were lighter in color than the forest around them, showing clearly the symbol of Nazi Germany more than half a century after the Third Reich had attempted to take over the world.

The continuing effects of evil represent one of the great realities of sin in the world. We have noted how the habit of deceit ran through Jacob's family. We have seen Isaac's weakness as a father reflected in Jacob as treachery, murder, and adultery ran rampant in the patriarchal family. We have noted that the sins of Simeon, Levi, and Reuben, unpunished at the time of their commission, came back to haunt them in Jacob's final blessing of the tribes.

We find it hard to believe that it took sixty years for people to notice those Nazi trees; perhaps officials refused to deal with the problem. But just as Jacob's family had to rid themselves of foreign gods and trinkets of evil, so we need to cut down the Nazi trees in our lives so sins of the past do not carry over into the present.

V. PRAYER

Father, thank you for the grace you displayed to Jacob and Esau, and to us as well. Help us to be people of the covenant who love your Word and raise our children to honor God. Amen.

VI. DEEPER DISCOVERIES

A. Hamor the Hivite (34:2)

The text indicates that Hamor the Hivite was "the ruler of that area." This may suggest that Shechem was something of an uncivilized part of the world at that time. If we place Jacob somewhere between 1800 and 1750 B.C., we find him in Shechem just about the time the city was under development. Waltke says:

> By about 1750 the city was enclosed within a free-standing mud brick wall 2.5 meters wide, sat on a stone foundation, and the buildings within were substantial structures, also with mud brick walls on stone foundations. However, at the time of Jacob, the walls were probably just beginning to be built; hence the term "area" (Waltke, 462).

Hamor first appears in Genesis 33 and 34 but is mentioned again in Joshua 24:32 in connection with the burial place of Joseph. The name comes up again in Judges 9:28 when Abimelech was scorned for his connection with "the men of Hamor, Shechem's father."

B. Reuben (35:22)

Although Reuben attempted to save Joseph's life in chapter 37, he never overcame the sin we read about here. When the sons assembled for Jacob's final blessing, the patriarch said to Reuben, "Turbulent as the waters, you will no longer excel, for you went up onto your father's bed, onto my couch and defiled it" (49:4). A firstborn son should be the natural leader of his brothers, but Rueben never earned that place. First Chronicles 5:1–2 tells us that because of this fling with Bilhah, Reuben's birthright was given to the sons of Joseph.

Assuming they had never spoken of the incident between Genesis 35 and Genesis 49, Reuben must have been shocked to hear Jacob's words about twenty years later. Perhaps even his own brothers didn't know what he had done. As we follow the behavior of the tribe of Reuben, we see the instability continuing when Dathan and Abiram joined the Korah rebellion in Numbers 16.

In the famous song of Deborah (Judg. 5) where Zebulun and Naphtali were praised for their role in the battle, Reuben was criticized for hiding among the sheep. The tribe of Reuben produced not one prophet, military leader, judge, or significant person throughout the history of the Old Testament. Long-term tragedy can result from a fleeting act of sin—tragedy that projects itself beyond the boundaries of our own lives.

C. Judah (35:23)

Of the twelve tribes Judah could perhaps be referred to as the most important, certainly since it formed the lineage for the birth of Messiah. The name *Judah* was common in the days of Jacob, however, and the naming of Leah's fourth son was no outstanding event. We see his role in the selling of Joseph in chapter 37 and his shame with Tamar in chapter 38. After the death of his wife, he committed incest with his daughter-in-law, who was disguised as a prostitute. From that union came twins whom Judah called Perez and Zerah. From the line of Perez ultimately was born the Christ of Nazareth, God's gift to the world. This shows that divine grace can overcome human frailty.

Judah's mention in the Genesis 49 blessing is considerably different from that of Reuben, Simeon, or Levi:

> Judah, your brothers will praise you; your hand will be on the neck of your enemies; your father's sons will bow down to you. You are a lion's cub, O Judah; you return from the prey, my son. Like a lion he crouches and lies down, like a lioness—who dares to rouse him? The scepter will not depart from Judah, nor the ruler's staff from between his feet, until he comes to whom it belongs and the obedience of the nations is his (49:8–10).

From the tribe of Judah came Elisheba, the mother of all the priests; Othniel, the first judge; Bezaleel, the builder of the tabernacle; and all the pious kings from David on down. The tribe of Judah led the march into the promised land. In the insurrection against David, Judah stood alone in backing their king.

VII. TEACHING OUTLINE

A. INTRODUCTION

1. Lead Story: Guilt or Shame
2. Context: Even though Jacob came back to Bethel and had a great spiritual experience there, the surrounding narratives reflect the ongoing struggle of his life which never let up until Joseph delivered him from the famine in Canaan by bringing him to Egypt. I can imagine Jacob wandering those dusty paths, always on the move, singing quietly to himself, "Nobody knows the trouble I've seen."
3. Transition: The break between chapters 33 and 34 introduces the horror of the Shechem story almost as an intrusion in the Jacob narrative. Although Jacob lives on for twelve more chapters, the actual narrative of his life ends at 37:1, and the Joseph story begins, moving Jacob into the background as a secondary player.

B. COMMENTARY

1. Slaughter at Shechem (34:1–31)
2. Back to Bethel (35:1–15)
3. Birth at Bethlehem (35:16–29)
4. East in Edom (36:1–43)

C. CONCLUSION: NAZI TREES

VIII. ISSUES FOR DISCUSSION

1. What might Jacob have done to prevent the massacre at Shechem?
2. How do you account for Jacob's consistent weakness as a spiritual leader in his own family, in spite of his occasional moments of revival?
3. If you were to explain to a child the reason for the inclusion of Genesis 36 in the Bible, what would you say?

Genesis 37:1–38:30

Joseph and His Brothers

I. INTRODUCTION

Favoritism in the Family

II. COMMENTARY

A verse-by-verse explanation of these chapters.

III. CONCLUSION

"To the Third and Fourth Generation"

An overview of the principles and applications from these chapters.

IV. LIFE APPLICATION

Recognizing God's Leader

Melding these chapters to life with God.

V. PRAYER

Tying these chapters to life with God.

VI. DEEPER DISCOVERIES

Historical, geographical, and grammatical enrichment of the commentary.

VII. TEACHING OUTLINE

Suggested step-by-step group study of these chapters.

VIII. ISSUES FOR DISCUSSION

Zeroing these chapters in on daily life.

Quote

"*F*elt weakness deepens dependence on Christ for strength each day. The weaker we feel, the harder we lean. And the harder we lean, the stronger we grow spiritually, even while our bodies waste away."

J . I . P a c k e r

Genesis 37:1–38:30

I N A N U T S H E L L

These two chapters introduce Joseph and demonstrate how and why God will direct his chosen people into the land of Egypt.

Joseph and His Brothers

I. INTRODUCTION

Favoritism in the Family

A number of years ago when I needed a kidney transplant, my Jewish nephrologist asked me a soul-searching question, "Do you know anyone who would give you a kidney?" I grew up in a wonderful Christian home with both my parents and three brothers and three sisters. I knew they loved me, but I must admit that when that question was asked, all sorts of strange thoughts went through my mind. Many of them had to do with how I had acted toward my brothers and sisters in earlier days. My parents did not spoil me, but I had acted spoiled in many instances. Now they reared their ugly memories in my mind.

I am humbled to write that my entire family expressed a willingness to share with me the needed kidney. As members of the same family, my brothers and sisters, as well as my mother and father, acted in a way that honored the Lord and showed great love for me. Not all families act in such a loving, accepting way. Neither do all Christians. And when a family fails to act like a family, terrible consequences occur. Sometimes these consequences are far-reaching.

A deplorable incident occurred in the life of Mahatma Gandhi. He said in his autobiography that during his student days he was interested in the Bible. Deeply touched by the reading of the Gospels, he seriously considered becoming a convert. Christianity seemed to offer the real solution to the caste system that was dividing the people of India. One Sunday he went to church to see the minister and ask for instruction on the way of salvation and other Christian doctrines. But when he entered the sanctuary, the ushers refused him a seat and suggested that he go worship with his own people. He left and never went back. "If Christians have caste differences also," he said, "I might as well remain a Hindu."

How do you act toward those who are different, toward those who have been placed in an awkward position by others, toward those who have been blessed by God in a unique way that requires us to submit to their leadership?

II. COMMENTARY

Joseph and His Brothers

> **MAIN IDEA:** *In circumstances filled with attitudes of favoritism, jealousy, hatred, greed, and selfishness, God acts sovereignly to protect and provide for his chosen family.*

A Jacob's Favorite Son (37:1–4)

> **SUPPORTING IDEA:** *Favoritism is always wrong and is especially harmful when displayed in a family.*

37:1–2a. The statement **Jacob lived in the land where his father had stayed, the land of Canaan** prepares the reader for the fact that Jacob would not always live in this land where his father Isaac had stayed and where his grandfather Abraham had come to live. It also gives the reader the historical backdrop for the start of the story of Joseph. This Joseph will be used of God to help fulfill the prophecy made to Abraham: "Know for certain that your descendants will be strangers in a country not their own, and they will be enslaved and mistreated four hundred years" (Gen. 15:13).

Once again in verse 2 the recurring expression used to divide the Book of Genesis, **this is the account of** (Heb. *toledot*), is found. This is the tenth and final main section of Genesis as divided by the author. What follows is the account of what happened to Jacob as developed in the lives of his sons although it is centered on his son Joseph.

37:2b. Joseph was Jacob's second youngest son, born to him by Rachel (Gen. 30:24), the wife whom he loved the most (Gen. 29:30). He is seventeen years of age, and we are introduced to him as a fellow shepherd with his brothers. Later we will learn that Joseph was treated differently from his brothers. He may not have had to serve as a shepherd as consistently as they (Gen. 37:12). His brothers are identified specifically as the sons of Bilhah and Zilpah, the two handmaids of Rachel and Leah, respectively, who functioned as additional wives to Jacob. Nothing is said of the sons of Leah, his first wife, or of Joseph's one full-brother Benjamin with whom Rachel had died giving birth (Gen. 35:16–18).

The omission of Benjamin can be understood since he was younger than Joseph and probably was still at home with his father. Perhaps the mention of only Bilhah and Zilpah is to emphasize that their sons had full standing in the family, or perhaps these brothers were the ones whose behavior was especially poor. Still the omission of a reference to the sons of Leah is strange since it becomes obvious they are with their brothers, but this exclusion remains unexplained.

While shepherding with his brothers, Joseph apparently observed some unethical or ungodly behavior and reported this upon returning to his father. Whether this was a wise or needful action the Scripture does not say. To call it tattling gives the impression of a poor motive or an unnecessary action. On the other hand, this behavior may have been a significant act that threatened the flock or Jacob's reputation among a people where he was without friend or ownership of land. What is important to note is that even as a young man of seventeen, Joseph was willing to speak against his brothers, although he must have been aware that this action could cost him dearly.

37:3. The Scripture states that **Israel** (the God-given name for Jacob; Gen. 32:28) **loved Joseph more than any of his other sons.** This is reminiscent of Jacob's attitude toward his now-deceased wife Rachel (Gen 29:30). It is also reminiscent of the treatment of Jacob by his mother Rebekah (Gen. 25:28). The reason given for Jacob's preferential treatment is that Joseph **had been born to him in his old age.** This was probably Jacob's stated reason, but the facts bear out that since Joseph had been born, so had Benjamin. In fact, Jacob would live for many more years during which time Joseph would be in Egypt and then Jacob himself would live in Egypt.

An evidence of Jacob's bias toward Joseph is shown in the special robe that Joseph was given. There has been much discussion of what exactly made this robe unique. The NIV speaks of **a richly ornamented robe.** Traditionally, this robe has been seen as a brightly colored, striped robe. This interpretation is based on the Greek translation of the Hebrew Old Testament whose translators were probably unclear about the exact meaning. It is used again in 2 Samuel 13:18 of a "garment the virgin daughters of the king wore," but this does not help in describing the actual robe, though it was obviously special.

When the Hebrew term is compared to cognate Semitic terms, the translations given are either a coat or tunic with long sleeves (NRSV), or a richly embroidered tunic as in the NIV. Either way, the coat distinguished Joseph as the favorite son of Jacob.

37:4. Combined with the earlier unfavorable report that Joseph had given to his father about them, the brothers despised Joseph because of their father's special treatment. In fact, they **could not speak a kind word to him.** These words are in antithesis with the "bad report" (v. 2b) that Joseph had spoken of them.

B Joseph's Dreams (37:5–11)

SUPPORTING IDEA: *When Joseph revealed his God-given dreams to his family, there was a less-than-enthusiastic response, as well as no recognition of divine prophecy on the part of his father and brothers.*

37:5–8. In Joseph's first dream he saw his brothers binding sheaves of grain in a field. Suddenly Joseph's sheaf rose and stood upright, while the brothers' sheaves gathered around Joseph's and bowed down to it. The result of revealing this dream to his brothers was the twice-repeated expression that **they hated him all the more.** They certainly did not believe the dream as divine prophecy but rather the wishful fantasy of a spoiled brother. The Scriptures never evaluate the wisdom of Joseph's revealing his dreams. Of course, the dream came true as can be seen in Genesis 42:6; 43:26; 44:14; and 50:18. Perhaps this dream was for Joseph's benefit alone, and he chose to reveal it to his brothers as a reaction to their hatred of him or even to provoke them. At this point Joseph may not have been acting as the servant whom he would become through many trials and tribulations.

37:9–11. In Joseph's second dream he saw the sun, moon, and eleven stars bowing before him. He told this dream to his father as well as his brothers. The interpretation of the sun, moon, and eleven stars are recorded in the words of Jacob, who asked, **Will your mother and I and your brothers actually come and bow down to the ground before you?** The subsequent reactions of the father and brothers are distinct in that **his brothers were jealous of him, but his father kept the matter in mind.** Perhaps this occurred because Jacob knew the Lord could speak in dreams (Gen. 28:12–16) and he also knew that the Lord's words in dreams came true (Gen. 35:7).

Since Joseph's birth mother Rachel had previously died (Gen. 35:19), the reference to his mother must be taken as a reference to his stepmother Leah, who bore six of the twelve boys (Gen. 35:23). Jacob never dealt with the jealousy of his sons. The next story will indicate how that jealousy bore fruit.

C Joseph's Journey into Slavery in Egypt (37:12–36)

SUPPORTING IDEA: *Through the jealousy and hatred of Joseph's brothers, God delivers Joseph into Egypt.*

37:12–17. Genesis 35:27 indicates that Jacob was living in Hebron at this time. He decided to send Joseph to the fields near Shechem to obtain a progress report on the brothers and the flocks. Shechem was located about sixty miles north of Hebron. This was the site of the slaughter of the Shechemites by Simeon and Levi years before (Gen. 34:25–26). At that time Jacob had been afraid to remain in the area (Gen. 34:30), but he still owned a small piece of land there (Gen. 33:19). When Joseph arrived at Shechem, he discovered that his brothers had moved to Dothan, about fifteen miles north of Shechem and seventy-five miles from Hebron. Joseph was persistent and faithful to his father's instructions and went to find his brothers.

37:18–22. Joseph's ten brothers (Benjamin was not part of the group) saw him in the distance. Referring to him as **that dreamer**, they decided to kill him. This reference to a dreamer may indicate that they were concerned about his dreams and therefore determined to act in such a manner as to prevent the possible fulfillment of the dreams. If so, they were acting in conscious rebellion against what they might have suspected was prophetic knowledge.

Reuben, Jacob's firstborn son (Gen. 29:32), apparently had second thoughts about this plan. He suggested that rather than taking an active role in killing Joseph, they should throw him into a cistern. The other brothers assumed that Joseph would then die "of natural causes" and their guilt would not be as severe over his death.

Later Reuben would remind his brothers of his warning about killing Joseph (Gen. 42:22). Reuben had plans to rescue Joseph and secretly restore him to his father (Gen. 37:22). This was probably not motivated by love but by a desire to make restitution to his father for his act of sleeping with his father's concubine Bilhah (Gen. 35:22).

37:23–27. Joseph was stripped of his robe that symbolized his special relationship with his father and thrown into the dry, empty cistern. As the brothers were eating, **a caravan of Ishmaelites coming from Gilead** approached. Traveling the east-west trade route that would now join the north-south trade route, these merchants used camels to carry their cargo of spices, balm, and myrrh. Without firstborn Reuben present, Judah acted as the ringleader of the brothers and suggested that they sell Joseph to the traders. This would not only release them of the guilt of killing him, but it would gain them a financial profit as well.

37:28. Joseph was sold for twenty shekels of silver. In later times in Israel, this was the value of a young male who had been dedicated to the Lord and was being redeemed (Lev. 27:5).

37:29–33. Reuben was upset when he returned, but there was nothing he could do, since the caravan had disappeared. To conceal their crime the brothers took Joseph's robe, dipped it in goat's blood, and took it to their father to make him think his favorite son had been killed and eaten by a wild animal.

37:34–35. The deceptive, hypocritical actions of Jacob's family are reminiscent of Jacob's actions in deceiving his father Isaac by the use of the skin of a goat (Gen. 27:16). In some fashion he now received what he had given. Jacob was more willing to believe the evidence for Joseph's death than he was to believe the revelations of Joseph's dreams, although God had also spoken to him in a dream.

37:36. In Egypt Joseph was sold by the Midianites **to Potiphar, one of Pharaoh's officials, the captain of the guard.** The story of Joseph will continue in Genesis 39. But first the author of Genesis develops the sordid story of Judah and Tamar.

Ⅾ Judah and Tamar (38:1–30)

> **SUPPORTING IDEA:** *The story of Judah and Tamar illustrates the ungodly culture of the land of Canaan and the need for Jacob's family to be protected from assimilation into this society.*

38:1–5. This story revolves around Judah; moreover, Jacob's name does not even appear in the chapter. This will be important later because Jacob will bless Judah, and the tribe of Judah will be given the right to rule (Gen. 49:8–12). Judah was the fourth son of Leah. He developed a friendly relationship with a Canaanite named Hirah from Adullam (a town southwest of Jerusalem; 2 Chr. 11:5,7). Judah voluntarily left his brothers, in contrast to Joseph, who was forced to leave. Judah married a Canaanite woman named Shua who bore him three sons named Er, Onan, and Shelah. The last son was born at Kezib, perhaps the town also known as Aczib (Josh. 15:44), which was three miles west of Adullam.

38:6–11. Judah's responsibility in this story continues. He **got a wife for Er.** In the patriarchal era parents were often involved in obtaining wives for their children (see Gen. 21:21; 24:3–4). Er, however, was disciplined by God, resulting in death, for an unrecorded act of wickedness. Apparently this act did not involve Tamar because she was left untouched. Judah then commanded his second-born son Onan to marry Tamar in order to **fulfill your duty to her as a brother-in-law to produce offspring for your brother.** This custom is suggestive of the later biblical law of "levirate marriage" as found in Deuteronomy 25:5–6 and practiced in Ruth 4:10. The purpose of this law was to produce a son for the dead brother so his name would not disappear and his son could inherit all of his father's property (see "Deeper Discoveries").

Onan, not wanting to share anything with a son who would not be regarded as his, practiced a form of birth control sometimes called "onanism." This method of birth control involved the withdrawal of the male sex organ from the body of the woman before ejaculation in order to avoid the fertilization of the egg. Onan revealed a selfish heart toward his dead brother, toward Tamar, and ultimately toward the Lord. God's plan included the multiplication of the descendants of Abraham and the birth of the seed whose offspring would bring deliverance from Satan.

This action by Onan was a persistent practice as signified in the English by the word **whenever**. The Lord regarded this as wickedness, so he put Onan to death like his older brother Er. Some people believe that any form of birth control is wrong, but this issue is not specifically addressed in this passage except in the context of levirate marriage.

Judah then instructed his daughter-in-law to live as a widow, but in her father's house, until his third son Shelah matured. This request that Tamar return to her father's house was a selfish act on the part of Judah and perhaps explains to some extent why his son Onan had developed into such a selfish person. But the Scriptures reveal that his real motive in asking Tamar to return to her father was to avoid the possible death of his last son. Obviously Judah was either unaware of the wickedness of his sons, or he assumed that Tamar was somehow responsible for their deaths, since he thought that Shelah **may die too, just like his brothers**. Judah's refusal to take responsibility for the welfare of his daughter-in-law shows a callous and irresponsible attitude toward someone who had married into his family.

38:12–26. After a long time during which Judah's wife died and Shelah matured, Tamar realized that Judah had no intention of giving Shelah to her as a husband. Hearing that Judah was going to Timnah, she decided to act to obtain a child from Judah's family. This was something that she obviously believed was her right (Gen. 38:14).

Tamar disguised herself as a shrine prostitute (Gen. 38:21). This required her to take a great risk. If she had been discovered engaged in such conduct, Judah could easily have had her killed. Having enticed Judah by way of her dress, although the formal approach seems to have been made by Judah to her (Gen. 38:15–16), Tamar demanded a pledge for the payment of a goat to be sent later. She received Judah's seal and its cord, as well as his staff.

Later Tamar found herself pregnant by Judah as a result of this act. Meanwhile, Judah's friend Hirah was unable to find any shrine prostitute to whom he could make the payment of a goat, so Judah gave up trying to find her to save himself embarrassment.

Three months later Tamar revealed that she was pregnant. Judah, in a fit of hypocritical indignation, ordered her burned to death for her sin. In later times in Israel, burning was the penalty for prostitution practiced by the daughter of a priest (Lev. 21:9). Tamar produced the items taken in pledge to reveal that it was Judah himself who was the father of her unborn child. A remorseful Judah declared that **she is more righteous than I, since I wouldn't give her to my son Shelah**.

The statement **he did not sleep with her again** shows that this act did not create a marriage between the two of them, nor should it have done so. We see perhaps some change in Judah from a man who sold his brother into slavery to one who acknowledged his sin and then one who determined not to pursue this sin further. It is possible this repentance later allowed Jacob not to exclude Judah from receiving a special blessing as happened with Reuben, Levi, and Simeon, Judah's three older brothers (Gen. 49:3–7).

38:27–30. Tamar gave birth to twins and called them **Perez** and **Zerah**. The midwife thought Zerah was going to be born first, but Perez ended up "breaking out" before him. The name *Perez* means "breaking out." *Zerah* can mean "brightness" or "scarlet." He may have received this name after the scarlet thread that had been tied around his hand when it appeared that he would be the firstborn. Perez became the person through whom the chosen line to David developed (Ruth 4:18–22) and of course, ultimately, to Christ (Matt. 1:1–16).

This story of Judah and Tamar is a rationale for the story of Joseph. It illustrates the need for Jacob's family to leave the corrupt and tempting culture of Canaan for a place where they could develop their culture without significant pressure from the surrounding people. Judah's morality of hedonistic willfulness would be contrasted with Joseph's self-control. We will see this illustrated in the next chapter of Genesis.

> **MAIN IDEA REVIEW:** *In circumstances filled with attitudes of favoritism, jealousy, hatred, greed, and selfishness, God acts sovereignly to protect and provide for his chosen family.*

III. CONCLUSION

"To the Third and Fourth Generation"

Max Jukes did not believe in Christ or in Christian training. He refused to take his children to church, even when they asked to go. He has had 1,026 descendants: 300 were sent to prison for an average term of thirteen years; 190 were public prostitutes; 680 were admitted alcoholics. His family, thus far, has cost the government more than $420,000. They made no contribution to society.

Jonathan Edwards lived at the same time as Jukes. He loved the Lord and saw that his children were in church every Sunday, as he served the Lord to the best of his ability. He has had 929 descendants: 430 were ministers; 86 became university professors; 13 became university presidents, 75 authored books; 7 were elected to the United States Congress; 1 was vice president of his nation. His family never cost the government one cent but has contributed immeasurably to the life of plenty in this land.

Jacob's family was faced with the threat that the third and fourth generations of the chosen family might be assimilated and permeated by the ungodly moral and spiritual culture of the Canaanites. God prepared to deliver them from this culture by sending Joseph on ahead to Egypt. Meanwhile, Judah gave a vivid illustration of what could happen if God did not intervene. How thankful we must be for those who have made godly decisions. We should also be grateful for a sovereign God who has his gracious, loving hand upon his people.

PRINCIPLES

- Favoritism is always wrong. Don't let it become part of your life or the life of your family.
- Jealousy nurtured in the heart can produce hatred that leads to violence and even murder.
- God's prophetic word will come true in God's sovereign plan and in his own time.
- God can use even our sin for his purposes and to fulfill his plan (Ps. 76:10; Rom. 8:28).
- Covering sin with additional sin is always unwise.
- Living by faith rather than by sight is God's means of assurance in times of crisis.

APPLICATIONS

- Be like Joseph and allow God to speak to you in any manner he chooses.
- Don't look to your ordinary dreams for God's revelation; look to the Word of God.
- Learn to trust God, in spite of acts of jealousy and cruelty from others.
- Don't be like the deceiving Jacob, who was eventually deceived by his own family.
- Don't be envious. Envy is a sin that breeds terrible actions.

IV. LIFE APPLICATION

Recognizing God's Leader

God has the right to choose whomever he wants to lead his people. This means believers must be careful about setting up qualifications that a person must have before he can be a leader. Age, position in family, and treatment by others are beyond a person's control and must not be held against anyone. Of course, ethical and moral qualifications cannot be compromised.

A fictitious pastoral search committee sent out the following letter:

Dear Church Member,

In our search for a suitable pastor, the following scratch sheet was developed for your perusal. Of the candidates investigated by the committee, only one was found to have the necessary qualities. The list contains the names of the candidates and comments on each, should you be interested in investigating them further for future pastoral placements.

Noah: Former pastorate of 120 years with not even one convert. Prone to unrealistic building projects.

Joseph: A big thinker, but a braggart, believes in dream-interpreting, and has a prison record.

Moses: A modest and meek man, but a poor communicator, even stutters at times. Sometimes blows his stack and acts rashly. Some say he left an earlier church over a murder charge.

Abraham: He took off to Egypt during hard times. We heard that he got into trouble with the authorities and then tried to lie his way out.

David: The most promising leader of all until we discovered the affair he had with his neighbor's wife.

Solomon: He has a reputation for wisdom but fails to practice what he preaches.

Elijah: He proved to be inconsistent, and is known to fold under pressure.

Hosea: A tender and loving pastor, but our people could never handle his wife's occupation. His family life is in shambles. Divorced and remarried to a prostitute.

Jonah: Refused God's call into ministry until he was forced to obey by getting swallowed by a great fish. He told us the fish spit him out on the shore near here. We hung up.

Jeremiah: He is too emotional, alarmist; some say a real "pain in the neck."

Amos: Comes from a farming background. Better off picking figs.

John: Says he is a Baptist but definitely doesn't dress like one. Would not feel comfortable at a church potluck supper because of his weird diet. Often provokes denominational leaders.

Peter: Has a bad temper, even has been known to curse. Had a big run-in with Paul in Antioch. Aggressive, but a loose cannon.

Paul: We found him to lack tact. He is too harsh, his appearance is contemptible, and he preaches far too long.

Timothy: He has potential but is much too young for the position.

Jesus: He tends to offend church members with his preaching, especially Bible scholars. He is also too controversial. Has had some popular appeal, but once his church grew to five thousand, he managed to offend them all, and then it dwindled down to twelve people. He even offended the search committee with his pointed questions. Seldom stays in one place for long. And, of course, he's single.

Judas: He seemed to be very practical, cooperative, good with money, cares for the poor, and dresses well. We all agreed that he is just the man we are looking for to fill the vacancy as our senior pastor.

Thank you for all you have done in assisting us with our pastoral search.

Sincerely,

The Pastoral Search Committee

People can misunderstand and misinterpret God's choice! Joseph was young, the son of Jacob's second wife, given special favors from his father, despised by his brothers, and not always out working with the flocks like the other boys. Yet God chose him. Joseph was true, honest, persistent, and a believer with faith. In the case of Joseph, character was far more important than age, success, finances, and social standing.

When it's time for you to find God's leader for your church, your city, your nation, what qualifications will you be looking for?

V. PRAYER

Father, help me to look past the things that people cannot control and to see your work in their lives. Make me a recognizer and encourager of your chosen leaders. Amen.

VI. DEEPER DISCOVERIES

A. Shechem (37:12)

Shechem was an important city in central Canaan. Abraham visited this site (Gen. 12:6). Jacob had lived in this area and had dug a well here (John 4:5–6). It was at Shechem that Dinah was raped and Simeon and Levi slaughtered the male inhabitants (Gen. 34:1–29).

B. Dothan (37:17)

Dothan was sixty miles north of Jerusalem and thirteen miles north of the city of Samaria. It was on one of the north-south trade routes that ran from Damascus to Egypt. It was just southwest of Ibleam, a city that protected one of three passes through the Carmel Mountain range. Later the prophet Elijah lived at Dothan (2 Kgs. 6:13).

C. Cistern (37:24)

A well has an underground source of water, while a cistern is a holding tank for water that is directed into it. Cisterns were often pear shaped. This made it possible to cover the small opening at the surface. Such a shape made them useful as holding cells for people or material (Gen. 37:22,28; Jer. 38:6–13; Zech. 9:11). Some cisterns were coated with a watertight plaster to keep water from escaping into cracks or porous walls. On behalf of God, the prophet Jeremiah warned, "My people have committed two sins: They have forsaken me, the spring of living water, and have dug their own cisterns, broken cisterns that cannot hold water" (Jer. 2:13).

D. Gilead (37:25)

Gilead was a fertile region east of the Jordan River and southeast of the Sea of Galilee. It was part of the territory claimed by Israel, specifically the tribe of Manasseh, before they crossed the Jordan River to occupy the land of Canaan during the time of Joshua (Num. 32:39–40).

E. Levirate Marriage (38:9)

Levirate marriage was part of the Mosaic Law (Deut. 25:5–6) which stated that if one brother died without leaving a male heir, one of his surviving brothers must marry the dead brother's widow. The first son of this latter marriage would take the name and privileges of the brother who had died. The purpose of this law was to produce a son for the dead brother so his name would not disappear and his son could inherit all of his father's property. The incident of Judah and Tamar in Genesis 38 predates the Mosaic Law. But the essentials of the later law seem to be part of early patriarchal custom.

Ruth 4:10 shows a later historical outworking of this law. It demonstrates that the "brother" could be the next closest relative (Ruth 3:12). Perhaps because Ruth was a Moabite, it was Boaz who spoke to the nearest relative in the city gate (Ruth 4:1; cp. Deut. 25:7).

In Matthew 22:23–32 this same law was used by the Sadducees to try to shame Jesus into admitting there could be no resurrection.

F. Shrine Prostitution (38:21)

The Canaanites used cult prostitution as a way of promoting fertility of the land and animals. The mother goddess, who went by the names Ishtar and Anat, was represented by young devotees who would dress in a veil as the symbolic bride of the god Baal or El (cp. Gen. 38:14). Positioning themselves at or near a shrine, these young women would service the men of the community prior to such activities as planting their fields or during the period of lambing. This was an ungodly practice that enabled sinful men to engage in adultery, all under the belief that it reenacted divine marriage and ensured fertility and prosperity for the fields and herds.

VII. TEACHING OUTLINE

A. INTRODUCTION

1. Lead Story: Favoritism in the Family
2. Context: Following the genealogy of Esau in Genesis 36, the account of Jacob and his son Joseph pick up the story last reported in Genesis 35. Now we will see what will happen to Jacob's sons in the land of Canaan.
3. Transition: Genesis 37:36 leaves Joseph in Potiphar's house in Egypt. Genesis 39 and following will narrate what became of Joseph in Egypt.

B. COMMENTARY

1. Jacob's Favorite Son (37:1–4)
2. Joseph's Dreams (37:5–11)
3. Joseph's Journey into Slavery in Egypt (37:12–36)
4. Judah and Tamar (38:1–30)

C. CONCLUSION: RECOGNIZING GOD'S LEADER

VIII. ISSUES FOR DISCUSSION

1. How much does a person's upbringing affect how he will direct his own family?
2. To what extent can a believer expect the law of retribution to remain in effect (see Gal. 6:7)?
3. Why does God seem to emphasize character above everything else for potential leaders?

Genesis 39:1–40:23

Not Fair!

I. INTRODUCTION
A Rotten Day

II. COMMENTARY
A verse-by-verse explanation of these chapters.

III. CONCLUSION
Faithful in All Circumstances

An overview of the principles and applications from these chapters.

IV. LIFE APPLICATION
Responding to Misfortune

Melding these chapters to life with God.

V. PRAYER
Tying these chapters to life with God.

VI. DEEPER DISCOVERIES
Historical, geographical, and grammatical enrichment of the commentary.

VII. TEACHING OUTLINE
Suggested step-by-step group study of these chapters.

VIII. ISSUES FOR DISCUSSION
Zeroing these chapters in on daily life.

"*Let* no man be sorry he has done good, because others

have done evil! If a man has acted right, he has done well,

though alone; if wrong, the sanction of all mankind will not

justify him."

Henry Fielding

Genesis 39:1–40:23

IN A NUTSHELL

Faithfulness to God does not ensure consistent fair treatment by others.

Not Fair!

I. INTRODUCTION

A Rotten Day

*H*ere are ten ways you can tell it's going to be a rotten day:

1. You start brushing your teeth with muscle relaxant cream.
2. You see the *60 Minutes* news team in your office.
3. You realize the hair spray you just used was really your new can of hair-removal spray.
4. You turn on the news and they're showing emergency routes out of the city.
5. You come out to find your car parked right where you left it, but there are no tires on it.
6. Your car horn goes off accidentally and remains stuck as you follow a group of Hell's Angels on the freeway.
7. Your boss tells you not to bother to take off your coat.
8. Your income tax refund check bounces.
9. You get passed on your morning jog by a little old lady with a cane.
10. You look down to see you have on one black shoe and one brown shoe and you remember seeing another pair just like them in your closet before you left home.

Joseph could tell us a thing or two about rotten days. He could tell us about unfairness, inequity, deprivation, and loneliness. But he can also show us that it is possible to live above the circumstances of life. It is possible to be faithful to God in the midst of a "rotten day."

II. COMMENTARY

Not Fair!

> **MAIN IDEA:** *Joseph displays godly character and discipline, in spite of being falsely accused and thrown into prison.*

A Faithful Employee (39:1–12)

> **SUPPORTING IDEA:** *Joseph is shown to be a faithful, God-honoring servant.*

39:1. On his arrival in Egypt, Joseph was sold to a man named Potiphar, who worked for the pharaoh of Egypt. Potiphar is called **the captain of the guard**, which was a very responsible position.

39:2–6a. Joseph rose through the various ranks of Potiphar's servants to become the chief steward in Potiphar's household. His rise in position was related to his relationship with the Lord. It is twice stated that **the Lord was with Joseph** and further that **the Lord gave him success in everything he did**. The fact that Joseph **lived in the house of his Egyptian master** would be significant when temptation came.

Potiphar was blessed **because of Joseph** in keeping with the Abrahamic promise that "I will bless those who bless you" and "all peoples on earth will be blessed through you" (Gen. 12:3). The blessing to Potiphar extended beyond what Joseph had immediate contact with to **everything Potiphar had, both in the house and in the field**. Because of this Joseph was in charge of everything. In the house Potiphar **did not concern himself with anything except the food he ate**.

39:6b-12. These verses describe Joseph's physical attributes. In his mid-twenties, he was successful, exercised great authority, was unattached, and was **well-built and handsome**. Besides the obvious sexual temptation that Joseph faced, the normal desire to respond to the feminine need for admiration and devotion may have been present. Many a man has responded in a chivalrous manner to a woman in need of attention, a woman whose husband may be too preoccupied or not available.

The words **took notice of** could be translated "looked with desire at." The sexual aspect is confirmed with the explicit command, **Come to bed with me!** Proverbs 6:20–35 and 7:10–20 warn a young man against the temptation that Joseph faced. But he refused to submit and argued from his proper view of responsibility, his proper view of marriage, and his proper view of sin. His view of responsibility was that **everything he [Potiphar] owns he has entrusted to my care**. His proper view of marriage involved the fact that the woman who was seducing him was someone's [Potiphar's] **wife**. His proper view of sin was that it was an action **against God**.

Finally, Potiphar's wife attempted to force Joseph to engage in sexual misconduct. She did this when no one else was around and when Joseph entered the house alone. Leaving his cloak in her hand, Joseph fled the house. While in the past this may not have been necessary with others nearby, apparently this time the wisest course for Joseph was to leave (cp. Prov. 5:8; 1 Cor. 6:18). The majority of the time the most sensible plan is for the believer to flee from temptation. Rarely should we try to challenge temptation by staying in its presence unless there is no way of escape.

🅱 Unfair Accusation and Imprisonment (39:13–20a)

SUPPORTING IDEA: *False charges, resulting in Joseph's imprisonment, are still under God's sovereign authority.*

39:13–18. A false charge of sexual molestation or attempted rape was the lot of this faithful servant of the Lord. Potiphar's wife, wounded by Joseph's rejection of her advances, turned on him. The unbelieving world doesn't always respect a desire for holiness and faithfulness. She developed a fictitious scenario using the cloak Joseph had left behind as "proof" for her charges. In the Joseph narratives this was the second time that a cloak or robe had caused him trouble! A garment could contain indications of status, rank, or office and therefore could be used to identify the owner as Joseph.

The fact that she referred to Joseph as **this Hebrew** indicates at least a prejudicial attitude if not anti-Semitism. She repeated this description to her household servants and later to her husband.

39:19–20a. The response of Potiphar was rather subdued in light of her accusations, although it is recorded that he **burned with anger.** Yet, rather than exercising the death penalty against Joseph, he had him thrown in prison, specifically the **place where the king's prisoners were confined.** Not much is known about the conditions in this prison. Joseph refers to it in Genesis 40:15 as "a dungeon," but this is the same word used in Genesis 37:24 for "cistern." It does appear from Genesis 40 that the prison was attached to the house of Potiphar, perhaps as a small, private, royal prison where the captain of the guard would live as well (see Gen. 40:3,7). For a man who had just acted righteously, such treatment must have been difficult to bear.

🅲 Faithfulness in Prison (39:20b-23)

SUPPORTING IDEA: *Rather than sulking about his unfair treatment, Joseph responds with faithfulness to the opportunities he receives.*

39:20b–21. Even while Joseph was in prison the Lord **showed him kindness and granted him favor in the eyes of the prison warden.** Joseph's character had not changed, although he had refused to give in to sin and had been unfairly treated. The Lord was able to honor him even while he was experiencing injustice. While nothing is said of Joseph's faith in God's earlier revelation through the dreams, one has to wonder if they were not part of what allowed Joseph to maintain an optimistic, faithful outlook on life. He knew that God was in charge and that God's will would be done.

39:22–23. The Lord blessed Joseph in prison. Joseph maintained his faith in the revealed promises of God, and he used his giftedness for others. This resulted in his becoming the trustee over the entire prison, responsible only to the warden.

D Faithful Interpreter of Dreams (40:1–23)

SUPPORTING IDEA: *Joseph is kind and helpful but gets nothing in return.*

40:1–4a. In God's providence Joseph became acquainted with the pharaoh's cupbearer and baker. Since the title **Pharaoh** was used as a proper name, his position is referred to as **king**. Both of these royal employees had offended their master and were put into the same prison where Joseph was confined. In the previous chapter we learned that Joseph was in charge of all who were held in prison. Now, apparently in some special manner, these two new prisoners were **assigned** to Joseph. Perhaps because they came from Pharaoh's household, the warden wanted them treated kindly or protected from some of the other prisoners. The investigation of the charges against them may have required isolation from others.

40:4b-8. Each of these royal servants had a dream on the same night, and each dream had a meaning of its own. While Joseph's two dreams had basically the same interpretation, these two were different. Joseph was sensitive enough to those under his care to discern that these two servants were dejected. Even with all he had been through, Joseph was not so preoccupied with his own troubles that he ignored the troubles of others.

The humility of Joseph is evident. He admitted that interpretations of dreams belong only to God as he asked, **Do not interpretations belong to God?** He had learned this through his own dreams. But in faith he still had to believe that the interpretations of his dreams that had been revealed to him years ago would come true some day. Joseph would insist in the next chapter as well that only God can interpret dreams (cp. Gen 41:16,25,28). Joseph asked the cupbearer and baker to **tell me your dreams**. He presented himself as the mediator through whom God would give the interpretation.

40:9–15. The chief cupbearer told Joseph his dream first. His dream consisted of a vine with three branches that budded, blossomed, and then ripened. He was then able to take Pharaoh's cup and squeeze grape juice into it and present the cup to Pharaoh. The interpretation was a positive one with the three branches representing three days until the cupbearer would be restored to his position as the cupbearer to Pharaoh. The restoration used the expression Pharaoh will **lift up your head**, which is a common Hebrew idiom (cp. Pss. 3:3; 27:6; 2 Kgs. 25:27; Jer. 52:31) meaning that the cupbearer would be released from prison and restored to his former position.

Joseph asked when this came true for the cupbearer that he would **remember me and show me kindness; mention me to Pharaoh and get me**

out of this prison. While Joseph was willing to carry on under the sovereign hand of God, he was not above using his skills to better his status. It must have been difficult for Joseph to be used by God in prison and yet not rescued from prison by this same God. Knowing what we know of the story, we understand it was not yet God's time for Joseph to be released. But that is from our perspective. It is always helpful to think of the perspective of the character of the story and how little he knew of the future.

40:16–19. Encouraged by the positive interpretation that the cupbearer received, the baker also shared his dream with Joseph. There were three baskets of bread on his head, just as there had been three branches containing grapes on the vine in the cupbearer's dream. But it was birds, not Pharaoh, who ate the baked goods out of the baskets in the baker's dream. The interpretation that Joseph passed on to the baker foretold that in three days Pharaoh would **lift off your head and hang you on a tree. And the birds will eat away your flesh.**

40:20–22. The reaction of neither the cupbearer nor the baker is recorded. What is recorded, however, is the accurate fulfillment of the interpretations of these dreams that Joseph had given. The **third day was Pharaoh's birthday**. At a feast given for all his officials, he **lifted up the heads of the chief cupbearer and the chief baker in the presence of his officials**. But what a contrast in their lifting up! The cupbearer's head was lifted up as he was restored to his former position, while the baker's head was hung or "impaled" (i.e., on a pole).

40:23. This verse states that **the chief cupbearer, however, did not remember Joseph; he forgot him**. How this must have disappointed and hurt Joseph. But God had not forgotten him. This was part of God's sovereign plan as we will see in the next chapter.

> **MAIN IDEA REVIEW:** *Joseph displays godly character and discipline, in spite of being falsely accused and thrown into prison.*

III. CONCLUSION

Faithful in All Circumstances

One of the reasons we admire Joseph is his faithfulness. D. Mennen in an article entitled "How the Wise Man Overcomes Temptation" states of Joseph, "In duty he was loyal, in temptation he was strong, and in prison he was faithful." What a life to imitate.

Joseph was not surrounded by his family, a church, or devout friends. He did not have a copy of the Scriptures since they were not yet written. But he did have the medium of prayer and the remembrance of the promises of God that had come to him in his dreams and perhaps in conversations with his father Jacob years before. For Joseph, knowing God and his character was enough for him to be loyal in duty, strong in resisting temptation, and faithful even in unfair circumstances.

PRINCIPLES

- Believers have no control over some experiences in life. But we can respond to unjust circumstances with faith and integrity.
- Faithful employees seek the best for their boss, not what might be easiest for themselves.
- The person who is faithful in the small things of life will ultimately be responsible for greater assets (see Luke 16:10).
- God's blessings do not insulate our lives from hardships or injustice.
- Our ability to overcome temptation depends more on character than on circumstances.

APPLICATIONS

- Do your work in such a way that you become indispensable to your employer.
- Believe that God will use you in his time and do not force your way into situations when you believe the time is right.
- Don't believe the lie that God is not aware of "secret" sin. Like Joseph, realize that every sin is against God, who knows all.
- Have "moral courage" to go along with God's sovereign work in your life.

IV. LIFE APPLICATION

Responding to Misfortune

What will be your response to unfairness, mistreatment, and misfortune? In the eyes of a skeptical world, the manner in which a believer meets difficulties by means of the grace of God is a powerful apologetic for faith in God. F. B. Meyer said, "The child of God is often called to suffer because there is nothing that will convince onlookers of the reality and power of true religion as suffering will do, when it is borne with Christian fortitude."

William Sangster, a well-known British pastor of the last century, was told by a doctor that he had progressive muscular atrophy; his muscles would gradually waste away, his voice would finally fail, and he would lose the ability even to swallow. He made the following resolutions and stuck by them for the rest of his life:

1. I will never complain.
2. I will keep the home bright.
3. I will count my blessings.
4. I will try and turn it to good.

Sangster devoted himself to the work of British home missions, figuring he could still write and he would have even more time for prayer. He wrote articles and books and helped organize prayer cells throughout England. He turned misfortune into triumph because he believed in the God of the Bible.

Some day we may also be called upon to face unfairness, mistreatment, or misfortune. Will we respond with faith and faithfulness or with complaint and compromise?

V. PRAYER

Lord, give us the grace to meet life's trials with confident faith in a sovereign God. May our response to unfairness or temptation be a clear testimony to your grace in our lives. Amen.

VI. DEEPER DISCOVERIES

A. Cupbearer (40:1)

The titles "chief cupbearer" and "chief baker" are found in extant Egyptian texts as well as the Bible. Most people understand what a baker is. But what did a cupbearer do? A cupbearer was a trusted servant who ensured the safety of the king by tasting all his master's food and drink to make sure it wasn't poisoned. In the postexilic period Nehemiah, as cupbearer, was a high-ranking member in a ruler's court (Neh. 1:11). The cupbearer in the Joseph narrative was the "chief cupbearer," indicating that the Pharaoh had more than one official with this responsibility.

B. Dreams (40:5)

In the Ancient Near Eastern world there is evidence that both Egyptians and Babylonians regarded dreams as very significant in predicting the future. "Experts" usually carried out the interpretation of dreams. Their interpretations were based on training they had received in dream literature that contained "keys" to dream explanation. A good understanding of the person who wanted his dream interpreted, as well as a knowledge of current events, would help to give a favorable interpretation. Among Egyptian and Babylonian literature there appears to be the belief that gods communicated through dreams but did not give the interpretation of these dreams. Explanation fell upon human interpreters. Joseph, of course, held a different view and consulted God for the interpretation of dreams.

VII. TEACHING OUTLINE

A. INTRODUCTION

1. Lead Story: A Rotten Day
2. Context: Genesis 37 gives the historical background to the entrance of Joseph into Egyptian slavery. Genesis 38 gives the cultural background to what staying in the land of Canaan might do to God's chosen family. Now Joseph is seen resisting the sinful seduction of his master's wife in Egypt and finding himself in prison as a result.
3. Transition: The correct interpretation of the dreams of the baker and cupbearer of the Pharaoh prepares the reader for the account of Pharaoh's dreams.

B. COMMENTARY

1. Faithful Employee (39:1–12)
2. Unfair Accusation and Imprisonment (39:13–20a)
3. Faithfulness in Prison (39:20b–23)
4. Faithful Interpreter of Dreams (40:1–23)

C. CONCLUSION: RESPONDING TO MISFORTUNE

VIII. ISSUES FOR DISCUSSION

1. How can a believer respond properly to unfair treatment?
2. Does God still speak through dreams today?
3. Does moving on from unfairness require an acknowledgement from the person who committed the abuse?

Genesis 41:1–42:38

Egyptian Politics

I. INTRODUCTION
Too Soon to Quit!

II. COMMENTARY
A verse-by-verse explanation of these chapters.

III. CONCLUSION
It Just "Happened" That Way!

An overview of the principles and applications from these chapters.

IV. LIFE APPLICATION
Just Keep On Keeping On!

Melding these chapters to life with God.

V. PRAYER
Tying these chapters to life with God.

VI. DEEPER DISCOVERIES
Historical, geographical, and grammatical enrichment of the commentary.

VII. TEACHING OUTLINE
Suggested step-by-step group study of these chapters.

VIII. ISSUES FOR DISCUSSION
Zeroing these chapters in on daily life.

Genesis 41:1–42:38

Q u o t e

"*N*ever think you could do something if only you had a different lot and sphere assigned to you. What you call hindrances, obstacles, discouragements, are probably God's opportunities."

H o r a c e   B u s h n e l l

I N   A   N U T S H E L L

*T*hese two chapters explain Joseph's dramatic change in fortune and his renewed contact with his brothers.

Egyptian Politics

I. INTRODUCTION

Too Soon to Quit!

*A*ccording to the *Encyclopedia Americana* and other biographical material, the following facts describe a man born February 12, 1809:

- Age 7—His family was forced out of their home on a legal technicality.
- Age 7—He had to go to work cutting trees, plowing, and harvesting to help support his family.
- Age 9—His mother died and his family lived almost in squalor.
- Age 12—His new mother, a widow with three other children, sought to have him receive some formal schooling, but he attended school less than a year.
- Age 22—He worked as a store clerk in a failing business, then joined the army for eight months.
- Age 23—He ran for the Illinois legislature.
- Age 24—He bought a store on credit with a partner.
- Age 25—He was elected to the Illinois House of Representatives (and again at ages 27, 29, 31).
- Age 26—His business partner died, leaving him with a huge debt that took years to repay.
- Age 27—He obtained a license to practice law.
- Age 28—Legend claims that after courting a girl for four years, she refused his proposal of marriage.
- Age 29—He was defeated for speaker of the state legislature.
- Age 31—He was defeated for elector.
- Age 33—He married.
- Age 37—On his third try he was elected to U.S. Congress.
- Age 39—He was defeated for reelection to Congress.
- Age 41—His four-year-old son died
- Age 46—He was defeated for U.S. Senate.
- Age 47—He was defeated for vice-presidential nomination.
- Age 49—He was defeated for U.S. Senate again.
- Age 51—He was elected President of the United States.
- Age 56—He died April 15, 1865.

That's the record of Abraham Lincoln, the sixteenth president of the United States. It is a brief history of a man whom most consider to be one of the greatest leaders in the history of this country.

What if Abraham Lincoln had quit at 22, or 31, or 49? We would have been deprived of the privilege of having one of the greatest presidents this country has ever known. God's timing is his timing and is seldom known to humans until after the fact. But it's always too soon to quit pursuing what is right and good.

II. COMMENTARY

Egyptian Politics

MAIN IDEA: *God's timing is perfect in Joseph's release from prison and in his appointment to a position from which he can be reunited with his brothers.*

A Pharaoh's Dreams and Joseph's Interpretation (41:1–32)

SUPPORTING IDEA: *Joseph correctly interprets the dreams of the Pharaoh of Egypt in an attitude of humility and dependence on God.*

41:1–4. Two years after Joseph had correctly interpreted the dreams of the cupbearer and the baker, Pharaoh, the highest ruler in Egypt, had a dream. His first dream was about seven well-nourished cows that were eaten by seven undernourished ones. The first set of cattle came **out of the river . . . and they grazed among the reeds.** In order to escape pesky flies and blazing sun, cattle often submerge themselves up to their necks in a body of water. When hungry, these cows came up out of the water and ate the reeds that grew along the bank of the Nile River. The twist to this story came when the undernourished cows, rather than eating the reeds, ate the other cows.

41:5–7. Pharaoh's second dream was about **seven heads of grain, healthy and good . . . growing on a single stalk.** These heads of grain were swallowed by seven **thin heads of grain.** The seven thin heads of grain were **scorched by the east wind.** In Egypt the *khamsin* wind (in Canaan it was called the *sirocco* wind) blew in from the desert (Hos. 13:15; Job 1:19) in late spring and early fall and could wither vegetation if it continued for very long (Jer. 4:11; Ezek. 17:10).

Pharaoh had two dreams. The significance of two may be related to the fact that Joseph dreamed two dreams as well. In Genesis 41:32, Joseph asserted that "the reason the dream was given to Pharaoh in two forms is that the matter has been firmly decided by God, and God will do it soon." Apparently the two dreams also indicated the immediacy of such events.

41:8. In the morning Pharaoh's **mind was troubled** for good reason. If these dreams were indicating anything about Egypt, they were dealing with two of his greatest assets—his cattle and his grain. In an attempt to figure out these two dreams, he sent **for all the magicians and wise men of Egypt**. The **magicians** may have been priests who claimed to have mystical knowledge (cp. Dan. 2:10–11). After telling them his dream, Pharaoh could find no one to interpret them for him. Perhaps their "dream books" did not deal with such symbolic action. But the actual symbols of his dream were common religious symbols in Egypt.

Keil and Delitzsch write, "For the cow was the symbol of Isis, the goddess of the all-sustaining earth, and in the hieroglyphics it represents the earth, agriculture, and food; and the Nile, by its overflowing, was the source of fertility of the land" (Keil and Delitzch, 1:349). Or if they depended upon some demonic power to interpret some dreams, this power was prevented by God so God's man could be brought into the picture.

41:9–13. At that moment the chief cupbearer, in an amazing statement before Pharaoh, stated, **Today I am reminded of my shortcomings**. He went on to explain that **a young Hebrew was there** [in prison] **with us . . . we told him our dreams, and he interpreted them for us, giving each man the interpretation of his dream. And things turned out exactly as he interpreted them to us**.

41:14. On the basis of this testimony, Pharaoh sent for Joseph, who was still in **the dungeon**. Before appearing before Pharaoh, Joseph **shaved and changed his clothes**. This was in keeping with the distinctive Egyptian practice of shaving one's beard. Other Ancient Near Eastern cultures treated the shaving of a beard as either an insult (2 Sam. 10:5) or a sign of deep grief (Isa. 15:2; Jer. 41:5). Normally, Joseph as a Hebrew would not have shaved (although as an unmarried man he might not have grown a beard yet), but this was a cultural, not a required, biblical practice at this time (cp. Lev. 19:27; Deut. 14:1).

41:15–32. Joseph interpreted both dreams of the Pharaoh and repeated his interpretation twice. He was faithful in giving the interpretation even though it was disturbing to the Pharaoh. But before he gave the interpretation, Joseph was careful and bold in declaring, **I cannot do it . . . but God will give Pharaoh the answer he desires**. Joseph realized where his ability came from. At the possibility of great risk to himself, he gave God the proper recognition.

Pharaoh first related both dreams to Joseph. Joseph declared that **the dreams of Pharaoh are one and the same. God has revealed to Pharaoh what he is about to do**. The dreams revealed seven years of abundance and then seven years of famine to follow. The famine would be so bad that **the abundance in the land** would **not be remembered,** just as the undernourished cows and thin grain did not appear to change in spite of their feast.

Ⓑ Joseph Becomes a Leader in Egypt (41:33–57)

SUPPORTING IDEA: *God raises Joseph up to a position of great authority in a foreign land under an ungodly ruler.*

41:33–36. Joseph gave Pharaoh some unsolicited advice! Such boldness had to come from his sense of God's presence and guidance. He certainly would not want to spend more years in jail for being insolent! But he was in a favorable position because he had answered Pharaoh's request. Joseph further advised that wise management could limit the harmful effects on Egypt and in fact that Pharaoh could profit from such an occurrence. The storing of one-fifth of the grain from each of the years of good harvest would supplement the grain from the years of poor harvest. The building of storehouses should be a part of this sensible plan (Exod. 1:11; 1 Kgs. 9:19).

41:37–57. Joseph was elevated to a position of authority and honor in Egypt. His exact title is not stated, but it may have been something like the modern "Secretary of Agriculture" (see "Deeper Discoveries").

Seven ceremonial steps were taken to proclaim Joseph's position and power: (1) a verbal appointment by Pharaoh, (2) the giving of a **signet ring**, (3) the dressing in **robes of fine linen**, (4) the placement of **a gold chain around his neck**, (5) his public display in a **chariot**, (6) the verbal charge to the Egyptians to **Make way!** before Joseph, and (7) the assignment of a new **name** to Joseph. The gifts of a signet ring, linen clothing, and a gold chain (Gen. 41:42) are three common items mentioned in Egyptian texts for similar use. These accessories signified Joseph's status and office. The bestowal of an Egyptian name completed the investiture ceremony, assuring a greater acceptance of Joseph by the Egyptian population.

The marriage of Joseph to **Asenath daughter of Potiphera, priest of On** is troublesome to some readers. Obviously, Joseph had little chance of obtaining a wife from among his own people. It is likely that he had little choice in who was presented to him as a wife. We know that Joseph was willing to suffer for living righteously, so we must assume that he believed this marriage would not offend his God.

At this time the priest of On officiated at all major festivals and supervised lesser priests who served the sun god Re in the temple city of Heliopolis. Only the priests of Ptah of Memphis were more influential at this time. Such a marriage allied his with a very powerful priestly family in Egypt. But apparently Joseph was not influenced negatively by such an arrangement. As we will see later, he remained true to his God.

Joseph had been in Egypt for thirteen years (Gen. 37:2; 41:46), but in only one day his fortunes changed dramatically! Biographies in Egyptians' tombs and literature from Egypt give other accounts of officials who were elevated from lowly status to high positions of authority. In a piece of literature called *Story of Sinuhe*, a man named Sinuhe fled the royal court and lived in exile for many years, finally returning and being honored. The story of Joseph can be seen as typical against such Egyptian background.

Ⓒ Joseph's Brothers Make Their First Journey to Egypt (42:1–38)

SUPPORTING IDEA: *God creates circumstances that bring Jacob's sons into contact with Joseph, the brother whom they had sold into slavery.*

42:1–5. Jacob sent his ten oldest sons from Hebron in Canaan to Egypt to buy food. God created the circumstances that would cause Jacob's family to begin the process of moving to Egypt. The famine provided the impetus. It became known that **there was grain in Egypt**, so Jacob sent all his sons except Benjamin to obtain food. Jacob's question, **Why do you just keep looking at each other?** contrasts their lack of leadership with what their younger brother Joseph had exercised the last seven years as an Egyptian government official.

Benjamin, Joseph's full brother, was not sent to Egypt because his father Jacob **was afraid that harm might come to him**. What is unstated is the implication that perhaps his other sons could not be trusted with Joseph's brother. Again Jacob was treating one son differently from the others. This action might have brought Joseph back to the minds of the brothers.

42:6–13. Of all the places in Egypt to which Joseph's brothers might have journeyed, and of all the people with whom they might have dealt, it was to Joseph that they came to purchase food. God's sovereignty is clearly seen here. Even if Joseph stationed himself at the most likely storage city on the route from Canaan, and even if Joseph insisted on seeing anyone coming from Canaan, it is still amazing that this meeting took place with all the possible variables present.

When the brothers arrived, **they bowed down to him with their faces to the ground**. This was a direct, though still partial, fulfillment of Genesis 37:10 where his father had asked Joseph, "Will your mother and I and your brothers actually come and bow down to the ground before you?"

Joseph's initial recognition and treatment of his brothers is detailed in Genesis 42:7–17. He **pretended to be a stranger and spoke harshly to them**. This included accusing them of being spies. The reason for such treatment is never explained, but it is possible that Joseph was testing the character of his brothers. They told the truth when they replied, **We are all the sons of one man. Your servants are honest men, not spies**. But their statement about honesty had to be limited to the purpose of their journey—not past history!

Although the brothers encountered Joseph several times, they did not recognize him. Not until Joseph revealed his identity did they know who he was. As Joseph continued to accuse them of evil intent, they revealed more and more about themselves, including the fact that there **were twelve brothers, the sons of one man, who lives in the land of Canaan. The youngest is now with our father, and one is no more**.

42:14–20. As a test Joseph declared that they would be thrown into prison and only one would be allowed to leave to bring the missing brother so he could learn if they were telling the truth. Of course, Joseph knew what they had told was the truth. It was a test to see if they would turn on one another as they did on him so many years before. He put them in **custody for three days**, probably so they would have time to come up with a plan and reveal to Joseph their true character.

On the third day Joseph communicated once more with his brothers. He discreetly revealed to them his religious commitment when he said **I fear God**. He amended his early request that they all remain, except one. Now he declared that all of them could return to their father, except one. A lone brother would remain to ensure that the missing brother Benjamin was brought to Egypt when they returned.

42:21–23. The first hint that the brothers might acknowledge their sin of some twenty years ago occurred when they discussed Joseph's proposal: **Surely we are being punished because of our brother. We saw how distressed he was when he pleaded with us for his life, but we would not listen; that's why this distress has come upon us**. The brothers interpreted the latest event theologically but declared that they were reaping what they had sown (Gal. 6:7). Reuben, the oldest, tried to avoid some responsibility by reminding them of his suggestion. Joseph was able to understand this discussion, although the brothers assumed he could not. Because he knew what they were saying, he had to turn away to weep.

42:24–26. Joseph required that Simeon remain behind as a hostage until the youngest brother Benjamin could return on the next trip. He may have chosen Simeon because of the attempt on Reuben's part to spare his life before (Gen. 37:21–22). Simeon was the next oldest. He had Simeon **bound before their eyes**. This may have reminded them again of what they did to Joseph some twenty years before when he was bound as a slave to prevent him from running away (Gen. 37:28).

Joseph realized that the famine would last for seven years, so he knew the brothers would need to return. He placed their payment back in their food shipment and sent them home, knowing they would now be faced with a great dilemma. Should they return to the one from whom it appeared they had stolen?

42:27–38. The very first night of travel home the brothers discovered that at least one of them had his money placed back in his sack of grain. **Their hearts sank and they turned to each other trembling and said, "What is this that God has done to us?"** They could have chosen to return at this point to make things right, but they must have sensed they would be at risk to return without Benjamin.

Upon returning home, Joseph's brothers explained to Jacob all that happened to them in Egypt. They told him that his son Simeon was required to remain in Egypt. Jacob's response to such news is not recorded. But when the sacks were emptied and each man's silver was found in his sack, **they and their father were frightened**.

Jacob refused to allow Benjamin to travel to Egypt even though Simeon was being held as a hostage. He accused the brothers: **You have deprived me of my children. Joseph is no more and Simeon is no more, and now you want to take Benjamin. Everything is against me!** Jacob was not responding in faith. He did not think the interpretation of Joseph's dreams had come from God, so he spoke as one who had nothing but his children to depend on. He accused them of letting him down again.

Reuben, acting as the oldest and perhaps also out of a sense of guilt (cp. Gen. 35:22), offered both of his sons as security for Benjamin's safety. But Jacob realized that putting Reuben's sons to death, while appearing to be a great sacrificial offer on Reuben's part, was not an option.

Again Jacob treated one son (Benjamin) with preferential treatment and refused to allow Benjamin to travel to Egypt to redeem Simeon.

MAIN IDEA REVIEW: *God's timing is perfect in Joseph's release from prison and in his appointment to a position from which he can be reunited with his brothers.*

III. CONCLUSION

It Just "Happened" That Way!

For many people a story like Joseph's is nothing but a series of coincidences. It just happened that way! The hand of God should not be given credit for any of this, they say, but fate rules as always. But the believer interprets life theologically. God had declared a plan for Joseph. We see the hand of a sovereign God in the timing of Joseph's release from prison, and in his appointment of Joseph to a position that would allow him to deal with his brothers.

PRINCIPLES

- God's timing is not always the same as our perception of what good timing should be.
- What we do in the name of the Lord should always result in giving credit to the Lord.
- Never allow the possibility of advancement or rewards to prevent you from being honest and giving good advice.
- Discernment sometimes requires a person to reveal information cautiously to another.

APPLICATIONS

- Wait patiently for God's timing in your life.
- Pray that God will place you in the right place at the right time for his divine appointments.
- Ask God to make you more patient and discerning before you speak.
- Always trust God's Word.

IV. LIFE APPLICATION

Just Keep On Keeping On!

When the circumstances of life put us in a place that we don't want to be, it's easy to give up. Day after day Columbus entered these words in the log of the Santa Maria: "This day we sailed on." They didn't *drift* on, but they *sailed* on. Not knowing exactly what lay ahead but believing they could accomplish something that would be of significance for their country, they sailed on. The result was the discovery of a new world.

Winston Churchill made a speech on October 29, 1941, to the students at his old school. It has been memorialized as his "Never Give In" speech. While some versions claim that all he said was "Never give in!" and then sat down, the official version is longer, though no less powerful. Part of his speech reads as follows:

> You cannot tell from appearances how things will go. Sometimes imagination makes things out far worse than they are; yet without imagination not much can be done. Those people who are imaginative see many more dangers than perhaps exist; certainly many more than will happen; but then they must also pray to be given that extra courage to carry this far-reaching imagination. But for everyone, surely, what we have gone through in this period—I am addressing

myself to the School—surely from this period of ten months this is the lesson: never give in, never give in, never, never, never, never—in nothing, great or small, large or petty—never give in except to convictions of honor and good sense. Never yield to force; never yield to the apparently overwhelming might of the enemy. We stood all alone a year ago, and to many countries it seemed that our account was closed, we were finished. All this tradition of ours, our songs, our school history, this part of the history of this country, were gone and finished and liquidated.

Very different is the mood today. Britain, other nations thought, had drawn a sponge across her slate. But instead our country stood in the gap. There was no flinching and no thought of giving in; and by what seemed almost a miracle to those outside these Islands, though we ourselves never doubted it, we now find ourselves in a position where I say that we can be sure that we have only to persevere to conquer.

As believers we can be sure that God's promises in his Word will remain true. All that the spokesmen of God have prophesied will some day be fulfilled. It is up to us never to give in, never give in, never, never, never, never—in nothing, great or small, large or petty—never give in except to convictions of honor and good sense (and if I could add to Churchill's words) and to the Word of God.

V. PRAYER

Father, when we are discouraged, keep us from giving up. Give us faith that your word will come true and your work in our lives is what we must live for beyond comfort and ease. Amen.

VI. DEEPER DISCOVERIES

A. The Nile (41:1–4)

The Nile River is the longest river in the world, stretching 4,160 miles from its sources in Equatorial Africa to the Mediterranean Sea. The name the ancient Egyptians had for the Nile was *Hapi*, which was also the name of the river god. This mention of the Nile in connection with Pharaoh's dream is the first of many references to the Nile River in the Bible. The importance of the Nile to the life of the Egyptians can hardly be overestimated. It affected nearly every aspect of Egyptian life, including religious and cultural identification and practices.

Egypt became the main breadbasket for much of the Ancient Near East because of the Nile River. The predictability and consistency of the annual flooding of the Nile allowed Egypt to become very fertile. The management of the waters of the Nile by the use of irrigation caused even more fertility. Cities that could store excess grain would typically be centrally located in each geographical region of Egypt. Storage of grain was possible because of prosperity. This was a wise practice because famine, though rare, was always a possibility.

B. Joseph's Position (41:37–57)

The titles of "Grand Vizier" and "Overseer of the Royal Estates" are both found in Egyptian documents and may have been bestowed upon Joseph (see 1 Kgs. 16:9; Isa. 22:15,19–21 for the use of the latter title in Israel's monarchial government). Many Egyptian nobles could claim to be second only to Pharaoh in some area of authority. From ancient inscriptions, titles such as "Great Favorite of the Lord of the Two Lands" and "Foremost Among His Courtiers" have been discovered. These indicate a claim to a special position in the Egyptian government.

Some scholars object to the idea that Joseph, a Semite and not an Egyptian, should be elevated to such a position in Egypt. But an Amarna letter (one of a series of letters written by Canaanite scribes detailing the relationship between Canaan and Egypt) dating from the fourteenth century B.C. has been discovered which possibly sheds light on such a practice. This letter was written to a person in a similar position with the Semitic name of Dudu (or Tutu). He was appointed "highest mouth in the whole country." So to be a Semite and to have a position of significant power is confirmed both within and outside of Scripture.

The Twelfth Dynasty of Egypt, which was ruling at this time, moved the Egyptian capital from Thebes to the northern site of Memphis. This coordinates with the visit of Joseph's brothers from Canaan. They would more likely have journeyed to a northern city in Egypt.

VII. TEACHING OUTLINE

A. INTRODUCTION

1. Lead Story: Too Soon to Quit!
2. Context: Joseph has been in prison for a number of years. Finally, he will get the chance to be redeemed from bondage though not exonerated for his alleged crime.
3. Transition: The sons of Jacob have now come and bowed down to Joseph in an unconscious fulfillment of Joseph's earlier dreams. Still, God must work it out so the entire family can move to Egypt in fulfillment of his promise to Abraham (Gen. 15:13).

B. COMMENTARY

1. Pharaoh's Dreams and Joseph's Interpretation (41:1–32)
2. Joseph Becomes a Leader in Egypt (41:33–57)
3. Joseph's Brothers Make Their First Journey to Egypt (42:1–38)

C. CONCLUSION: JUST KEEP ON KEEPING ON!

VIII. ISSUES FOR DISCUSSION

1. How can you convince a person that something is an answer to prayer when he believes it is just fate?
2. How can a believer give credit to God for his accomplishments?
3. Can you think of a circumstance that might cause you to conceal certain facts until more is known?

Genesis 43:1–45:28

Surprise! I'm Joseph, Your Brother!

I. INTRODUCTION
Shock! Surprise!

II. COMMENTARY
A verse-by-verse explanation of these chapters.

III. CONCLUSION
Patience Is Needed

An overview of the principles and applications from these chapters.

IV. LIFE APPLICATION
Family Reconciliation

Melding these chapters to life with God.

V. PRAYER
Tying these chapters to life with God.

VI. DEEPER DISCOVERIES
Historical, geographical, and grammatical enrichment of the commentary.

VII. TEACHING OUTLINE
Suggested step-by-step group study of these chapters.

VIII. ISSUES FOR DISCUSSION
Zeroing these chapters in on daily life.

Q u o t e

"*I*f your sorrow is because of certain consequences that have come on your family because of your sin, this is remorse, not true repentance. If, on the other hand, you are grieved because you also sinned against God and his holy laws, then you are on the right road."

B i l l y   G r a h a m

Genesis 43:1–45:28

I N   A   N U T S H E L L

*T*hese three chapters show the true character of the sons of Jacob through the testing devised by Joseph.

Surprise! I'm Joseph, Your Brother!

I. INTRODUCTION

Shock! Surprise!

A sole survivor of a shipwreck was washed up on a small, uninhabited island. He prayed feverishly for God to rescue him. Every day he scanned the horizon for help, but none seemed forthcoming. He eventually managed to build a little hut out of driftwood to protect him from the elements and to store his few possessions.

One day, after scavenging for food, he arrived home to find his little hut in flames, the smoke rolling up to the sky. The worst had happened; everything was lost. He was stunned with grief and anger. "God, how could you do this to me!" he cried.

Early the next day, however, he was awakened by the sound of a ship approaching the island. It had come to rescue him.

"How did you know I was here?" the man asked.

"We saw your smoke signal," they replied.

It is easy to get discouraged when things are going badly. But we shouldn't lose heart because God is at work in our lives, even in the midst of pain and suffering. Remember, next time your little hut is burning to the ground—it just may be a smoke signal that summons the grace of God.

II. COMMENTARY

Surprise! I'm Joseph, Your Brother!

> **MAIN IDEA:** *A patient Joseph takes time to test his brothers before revealing to them his true identity.*

A Jacob's Arrangement About Benjamin (43:1–14)

> **SUPPORTING IDEA:** *The continuing famine finally forces Jacob to send Benjamin to Egypt.*

43:1–2. Genesis 45:6 indicates that this second journey by Jacob's sons to Egypt occurred after two years of famine (with five more still to go). It can be presumed that their first journey was made after the first year of famine. A year had passed in which Simeon remained in an Egyptian prison, but Jacob refused to allow Benjamin to go to Egypt so Simeon might be released.

But the famine was so severe that after **they had eaten all the grain they had brought from Egypt**, Jacob commanded his sons to return **and buy us a little more food**.

43:3–14. Judah stepped forward as spokesman for the brothers. He had undoubtedly heard his father's previous refusal of Reuben's offer of surety. This role of spokesman and leader will be exercised more and more by Judah (see Gen. 43:8–10; 44:14–34; 46:28). His father, at his deathbed blessing, would confirm Judah's role as leader of the family (Gen. 49:8–10).

Judah again explained to his father the stipulations that **the man** (that is, Joseph) had placed on them before they had left Egypt. Jacob, now referred to as Israel (see Gen. 43:8,11), responded by asking, **Why did you bring this trouble on me by telling the man you had another brother?** Jacob had earlier referred to this situation of requiring Benjamin to travel to Egypt in the words, "Everything is against me!" (Gen. 42:36). He had also stated, "My son [Benjamin] will not go down there with you" (Gen. 42:38). The lack of faith by Jacob in God's sovereignty is clear. He believed Joseph was dead and that it was now up to him to protect his son Benjamin.

After explaining to their father that they had been questioned directly about their family, specifically if their father was still alive and if they had another brother, they sought to show Jacob that they had answered direct questions and had not volunteered any additional information. But the story, as related in Genesis 42:13, indicates that they had given this information in response to an accusation of being spies.

Judah again stepped forward in a leadership role and sought to guarantee the safety of Benjamin. He requested that Jacob **send the boy along with me and we will go at once, so that we and you and our children may live and not die. I myself will guarantee his safety; you can hold me personally responsible for him**. His guarantee involved bearing **the blame before you** [Jacob] **all my life**. At the end of the previous chapter Reuben, the firstborn, had offered surety for Benjamin. Jacob had refused Reuben's offer. Now the famine had forced Jacob to reconsider sending Benjamin, but he did not reconsider Reuben's offer.

This may have been because Reuben had shown himself unworthy and disloyal to his father in the incident of Bilhah (Gen. 35:22). Later Jacob would speak of Reuben in these terms: "Turbulent as the waters, you will no longer excel, for you went up onto your father's bed, onto my couch and defiled it" (Gen. 49:4). Simeon, the second born, was in an Egyptian prison; and Levi, third born, had proven himself to be lacking in self-control (Gen. 34:25; 49:5–7). Judah had acted improperly in the incident with Tamar, but he had repented and now apparently had come back to be part of his father's family.

Jacob agreed to allow Benjamin to go to Egypt out of necessity. But he insisted that they take a gift, a customary practice when approaching a person of high rank. Israel (that is, Jacob) was not poor, although he lacked grain. God had blessed him materially, so he declared firmly that they should take **some of the best products of the land . . . a little balm and a little honey, some spices and myrrh, some pistachio nuts and almonds** (see "Deeper Discoveries"). He also insisted they take the silver that was found in their sacks after the first journey to Egypt as well as silver for the new purchases.

The phrase **perhaps it was a mistake** showed that Israel did not contemplate the providence of God in all these affairs. He had allowed the emotion of his losses to overwhelm him and dictate his theology. But he then stated this desire: **May God Almighty grant you mercy before the man so that he will let your other brother and Benjamin come back with you.**

The phrase, **as for me, if I am bereaved, I am bereaved,** contains a note of resignation that does not seem to imply faith. For Israel the element of faith was not strong except for his previous comment on the Lord's granting them mercy before the Egyptian authority.

Ⓑ Jacob's Sons Back in Egypt (43:15–44:34)

> **SUPPORTING IDEA:** *Joseph tests his brothers in two different ways to determine their true character.*

43:15–25. Upon their arrival in Egypt, the brothers **presented themselves to Joseph**, although of course they did not yet know him as Joseph. Apparently without allowing a conversation, but noticing that Benjamin was with them, Joseph gave instructions to the steward of his house: **Take these men to my house, slaughter an animal and prepare dinner; they are to eat with me at noon.** Whether Joseph had made this plan in advance is unstated, but surely he must have thought about what he would do if his brothers returned.

The brothers imagined that they **were brought here because of the silver that was put back into our sacks the first time. He wants to attack us and overpower us and seize us as slaves and take our donkeys.** If this was Joseph's desire, he would not have sent them to his home. They attempted to convince Joseph's household manager that they had not stolen the payment for the grain they had bought on their former trip. He responded with the assurance, **It's all right. . . . Don't be afraid. Your God, the God of your father, has given you treasure in your sacks; I received your silver.**

The steward's statement shows that Joseph had shared his religious background with him and that the return of their money was to be regarded as a divine gift, not an error on the part of the Egyptian. As further evidence that they were not being threatened, **he brought Simeon out to them**.

Furthermore, the steward **gave them water to wash their feet and provided fodder for their donkeys**. All this was further evidence of grace and generosity. Still wanting to assure themselves of avoiding Joseph's wrath, **they prepared their gifts for Joseph's arrival at noon**. This refusal or inability to accept grace and generosity characterized these brothers even after their father died.

43:26–34. When they presented their gifts to Joseph and **bowed down before him to the ground**, in a second fulfillment of his dream of long ago (see Gen. 37:10; 42:6), Joseph responded with questions of concern about them and their **aged father**.

Joseph then looked for Benjamin, who was **his own mother's son** and therefore his full brother. He pronounced a blessing upon him by stating, **God be gracious to you, my son**. This emotional time proved too much for Joseph. So **deeply moved at the sight of his brother, Joseph hurried out and looked for a place to weep**. Benjamin may have been up to sixteen years younger than Joseph. Joseph had been in Egypt for twenty-two years, so he would have last seen Benjamin when he was very young. This is why Joseph asked, **Is this your youngest brother, the one you told me about?**

Joseph threw a lavish banquet for his brothers. But the brothers were fed at a separate table in Joseph's house, **because the Egyptians could not eat with the Hebrews, for that is detestable to Egyptians**. Joseph of course was not a true Egyptian. But at this point, to his brothers and perhaps to many of the servants, he was as Egyptian as anyone. The Egyptians considered all other peoples uncultured, so they would not associate with them, especially in the intimate action of eating.

To the amazement of the brothers, they were seated in the order of their ages. Benjamin, the youngest, was given five times as much food as the others, and Joseph answered part of the blessing he had pronounced upon his brother. Joseph had never had a chance to show Benjamin any love since he was so much younger than Joseph. This also served as a test to determine how the older brothers would react to favoritism shown to their younger brother. Evidently, this test was passed. **So they feasted and drank freely with him**. Although they ate at an adjacent table, the **portions were served to them from Joseph's table**, so there was a communion and conversation between the brothers.

44:1–5. Again Joseph had their payment money for the grain placed in the food shipment, and he also placed his own silver cup in Benjamin's sack. He then instructed his servant to pursue the Hebrew men, and he even gave him the words he was to use in questioning his brothers. Joseph was preparing to test their loyalty and character again.

44:6–13. Before getting far the brothers were arrested (at Joseph's command) and accused of stealing his silver cup with the question originally phrased by Joseph in verse 4, "Why have you repaid good with evil?" The words of this question would be restated later in reference to their earlier treatment of Joseph with Joseph then insisting that "you intended to harm me, but God intended it for good" (Gen. 50:20).

When confronted, the brothers sought to assure the servant that stealing was never their practice. If the stolen cup could be found among their possessions, they said, whoever **is found to have it, he will die; and the rest of us will become my lord's slaves**. This is how certain they were that they were innocent of Joseph's charge. Before a search was conducted, Joseph's servant agreed to this procedure, except he changed it slightly by saying, **Whoever is found to have it will become my slave; the rest of you will be free from blame**.

A search, starting with the oldest and proceeding down to the youngest, revealed the silver cup in Benjamin's sack. The silver that had been placed in each sack is not mentioned. The cup was the focus. Rather than sending Benjamin back as was agreed upon in the servant's statement, all the brothers **tore their clothes . . . and returned to the city**. This time they would not leave a younger brother, a favorite of their father, to become a slave. This shows they had changed since selling their brother Joseph into slavery about twenty-two years before.

44:14–34. The brothers found themselves before Joseph a third time. This time they did not bow but threw themselves on the ground before him. Then Judah stepped forward as the leader and spokesman for the group. While claiming innocence for the stolen property, he admitted that **God has uncovered your servants' guilt**. His conscience must have been bothering him. He was willing to admit that there was a reason God may have delivered them into bondage. He regarded this as divine discipline. Judah did not argue on the basis of the arrangement the servant had declared (v. 10) or on the basis of what the brothers had declared previously (v. 9). Rather, he suggested that all of them would become Joseph's slaves.

Joseph protested such a strong penalty and demanded only the slavery of **the man who was found to have the cup** (that is, Benjamin). Again we see the brothers being treated with kindness and grace and yet not noticing or at least not understanding it.

Judah then begged Joseph to accept his life in the place of Benjamin. He reminded Joseph that their old father Jacob would die if anything happened to Benjamin. He admitted that Jacob believed that Joseph had been **torn to pieces** and that now Jacob's life was **closely bound up with the boy's** [Benjamin's] **life**. Judah asked to be a substitute for Benjamin because he could not stand to see **the misery that would come upon my father** if Benjamin did not return home. Judah did not try to hide the brothers' guilt or blame their actions on anyone else.

Joseph had tested his brothers by framing Benjamin and allowing his other brothers to go free if they so chose. How the other brothers reacted is not stated, but the fact that all the brothers returned (v. 13) seems to indicate that they were united in their commitment to their father and to Benjamin. Judah's intervention on their behalf showed the great love he had for his father and the loyalty he had to Benjamin. It also demonstrated that the brothers were not willing to repeat the act they had committed against Joseph many years before. They were not perfect, but they were showing signs of repentance and change.

Joseph Reveals Himself to His Brothers (45:1–24)

SUPPORTING IDEA: *In an act filled with great emotion, Joseph finally reveals his true identity to his brothers.*

45:1–3. The urgent pleas by Judah on behalf of Benjamin and his father caused Joseph to break emotionally. Unable to restrain himself any longer, Joseph ordered his attendants out and revealed his true identity to his brothers: **I am Joseph! Is my father still living?** What a shock! He disclosed his identity in an atmosphere of such intense emotion that the weeping by Joseph was heard by his household and reported to Pharaoh's household. First, Joseph wanted his brothers to know who he was and then he wanted to be reassured of his father's welfare. He said nothing about his treatment by his brothers twenty-two years before.

His brothers were **terrified at his presence**. All the gracious and generous treatment by Joseph was forgotten. Their minds could not comprehend what this revelation might mean since all they apparently could remember now was their brutal treatment of him.

45:4–15. Joseph repeated his assertion that he was their brother Joseph. This time he added, **the one you sold into Egypt**. But this was done for confirmation purposes only. He went on to assure them that they were not to be distressed or angry with themselves for selling him into slavery. Joseph had interpreted the circumstances theologically. He realized that **it was to save lives that God sent me ahead of you**. Four times he would state that God was behind the events of his life.

Joseph also revealed to his brothers the knowledge he had that the present famine would last for another five years. His brothers were reassured again that Joseph harbored no ill will toward them. He believed that God had overruled their evil plan in order to guarantee that the family of Israel would survive.

He urged them to bring their father Jacob back with them and to make plans to live in Egypt. Joseph, in anticipation of his brothers' repentance, had already made plans for where they could live (Goshen) so they could **be near** him. In order to encourage Jacob to make the move, even at his advanced age, he was to be told **about all the honor accorded me** [Joseph] **in Egypt**. Part of the Abrahamic covenant, especially the promise of a great name, was being fulfilled in Jacob's son Joseph, because **God has made me lord of all Egypt** (see Ps. 105:16–22).

Embracing first his brother Benjamin and then all the brothers, Joseph then kissed them all and wept for joy. **Afterward his brothers talked with him**, and Joseph explained his unbelievable journey of the last twenty-two years.

45:16–24. When informed of the situation with Joseph's family, Pharaoh was pleased that he was able to honor and assist Joseph in some way. He also insisted on Jacob and his family's moving to Egypt. Pharaoh promised Jacob's family **the best of the land of Egypt** and provided carts to help them make the journey.

Joseph also gave them **provisions for their journey** along with new clothing. Benjamin received a large amount of silver as well as five sets of clothing (cp. Gen. 43:34 where Benjamin's table portions were five times more than the brothers' portions). In addition, ten extra donkeys were loaded with the **best things of Egypt** and another ten with **grain and bread and other provisions** for his father's journey to Egypt.

Then Joseph sent his brothers on their way. But as they were leaving, he reminded them, **Don't quarrel on the way!** Joseph probably knew his brothers well enough to recognize that accusations and recriminations could travel with them on the way back. In addition, his special treatment of his full-brother Benjamin could be a source of jealousy. Their explanation to their father of how Joseph was alive when they had presented him "proof" of Joseph's death years before could also spark quarreling. Joseph wanted them to enjoy their good fortune and not dwell on the past.

D Jacob Hears That Joseph Is Still Alive (45:25–28)

SUPPORTING IDEA: *Jacob, disbelieving at first, is finally convinced that Joseph is alive.*

45:25–28. At first Jacob was unable to believe the amazing news that his long-lost son Joseph was still alive and held an important position in the government of Egypt. But when he was assured by the evidence of Joseph's generosity, he finally believed and made plans to move to Egypt.

MAIN IDEA REVIEW: *A patient Joseph takes time to test his brothers before revealing to them his true identity.*

III. CONCLUSION

Patience Is Needed

Joseph exercised great patience and discernment with his brothers. He did not need to test them persistently before declaring who he was, but he did. He knew people well enough to realize that there is a difference between repentance and remorse. He wanted to be assured that his brothers realized that what they had done to him was wrong and that they would not do the same to his younger brother Benjamin. But once he knew their heart, he revealed himself and experienced a joyful reconciliation.

PRINCIPLES

- Belief in the sovereignty of God allows the believer to be forgiving rather than vindictive.
- Theology should be based on the revealed Word of God and not on the emotions and circumstances of life.
- True repentance involves a change of attitude and action, not just tears and regret.
- Leadership means speaking up and taking a stand.
- Believing God's Word will come true can help us be patient with the circumstances of life.
- Reconciliation is possible when people are willing to confess, forgive, and be forgiven.

APPLICATIONS

- Look beyond sinful motives and actions to see the sovereign hand of God at work.
- Don't quarrel with your brothers on the journey!
- Don't be in such a hurry to make a decision today; discernment sometimes comes over time.

IV. LIFE APPLICATION

Family Reconciliation

Our families and churches are full of many broken relationships that beg to be mended. But reconciliation requires the conviction that something is wrong, the confession of that wrong, and the forgiveness that must be offered and accepted.

A father and his teenage son had a stormy relationship. So the son ran away from home. His father began a journey in search of his rebellious son. Finally, in Madrid, in a last desperate effort to find him, the father put an ad in the newspaper. The ad read, "Dear Paco, meet me in front of the newspaper office at noon. All is forgiven. I love you. Your father."

The next day at noon in front of the newspaper office eight hundred "Pacos" showed up. They were all seeking forgiveness and love from their fathers.

Joseph didn't require that his brothers make the first move in seeking forgiveness. Even before their repentance Joseph had treated them generously and graciously when he had every right to treat them with bitterness and vengeance. He wanted to be reconciled. Once he knew their hearts were ready, he revealed the truth to them. He held nothing against them but desired to hold them close and to see his father again.

What are you prepared to do to repair a relationship? What is your desire—to be vindicated or to be reconciled? May we be like Joseph, seeking reconciliation.

V. PRAYER

Lord, make me willing to wait for the truth. Keep me from vengeance and let me seek reconciliation. Amen.

VI. DEEPER DISCOVERIES

A. Balm, Honey, Spices, Myrrh, Pistachio Nuts, and Almonds (43:11)

Balm is an oil or gum exuded by the fruit or stems of certain small trees. It is used for medicinal purposes (see Jer. 8:22; 51:8). Myrrh is an aromatic gum (Ps. 45:8; Prov. 7:17; Song 3:6; 5:13) secreted from the leaves of the cistus rose. Its oil was used in beauty treatments (Esth. 2:12) and to perfume the body after death (John 19:39–40). In New Testament times it was mixed with wine and drunk for pain relief (Mark 15:23). Because of its value myrrh was one of the third gifts (beside gold and frankincense) brought to the baby Jesus (Matt. 2:11). "Honey" can refer to either the substance produced by bees or to the sweet syrup made by boiling grape or date juice into a thick syrup. Pistachio nuts are mentioned only here in the Bible. These nuts grow on a small, broad-crowned tree found in Asia Minor, Syria, and Canaan.

Of all these gifts, only balm, honey, and nuts were native to Canaan. The spices and myrrh were imported and thus quite costly. Jacob hoped that all these gifts would buy favorable treatment in Egypt.

B. Goshen (45:10)

Goshen was the eastern region of the Nile River delta, northeast of the Egyptian capital city of Memphis. It was linked closely with the land and city of Rameses (Gen. 47:6,11). It was the most fertile part of Egypt because of moisture from the yearly flood and the productive soil that was annually deposited here. It was a good place to raise cattle (Gen. 46:34; 47:6).

In the Book of Exodus the Hebrews were still living in Goshen. The Hebrews left Egypt from this region of the land (Exod. 8:22; 9:26; 12:37).

VII. TEACHING OUTLINE

A. INTRODUCTION

1. Lead Story: Shock! Surprise!
2. Context: The sons of Jacob have already journeyed once to Egypt, but they had to leave Simeon there as surety for their return with Benjamin. Because of the prolonged famine, Jacob is now forced to let Benjamin travel to Egypt to see "the man."
3. Transition: As a result of the shocking news that Joseph is still alive, and with the tremendous gift of provisions that Joseph has sent to his father, Jacob now makes the journey to see the son he thought he had lost over twenty-two years before.

B. COMMENTARY

1. Jacob's Arrangement About Benjamin (43:1–14)
2. Jacob's Sons Back in Egypt (43:15–44:34)
3. Joseph Reveals Himself to His Brothers (45:1–24)
4. Jacob Hears That Joseph Is Still Alive (45:25–28)

C. CONCLUSION: FAMILY RECONCILIATION

VIII. ISSUES FOR DISCUSSION

1. What is the difference between remorse at getting caught and true repentance?
2. How does a person develop a deep conviction about the sovereignty of God when surrounded by evil people and unfair treatment?
3. Can you forgive a person before he or she asks you for forgiveness?

Genesis 46:1–47:31

Family Relocation

Genesis 46:1–47:31

Quote

"*P*rovidence is God acting anonymously."

Paul   Harvey

IN A NUTSHELL

*J*acob leaves the land of promise in response to his son's invitation and by God's encouragement, but he makes plans to be returned to this land some day.

Family Relocation

I. INTRODUCTION

"Keep Playing"

*W*ishing to encourage her young son's progress on the piano, a mother took him to a Paderewski concert. After they were seated, the mother spotted a friend in the audience and walked down the aisle to greet her. Seizing the opportunity to explore the wonders of the concert hall, the little boy eventually explored his way through a door marked "NO ADMITTANCE."

When the house lights dimmed and the concert was about to begin, the mother returned to her seat and discovered that the child was missing. Suddenly, the curtains lifted and spotlights focused on the impressive Steinway on stage. In horror, the mother saw her little boy sitting at the keyboard, picking out "Twinkle, Twinkle Little Star."

At that moment the great piano master made his entrance, quickly moved to the piano, and whispered in the boy's ear, "Keep playing." Then Paderewski reached down with his left hand and began filling in the bass part on the piano. Soon his right arm reached around to the other side of the child as he added a running obbligato. Together, the old master and the young novice transformed a frightening situation into a wonderfully creative experience. The audience was mesmerized.

That's the way it is with God. What we can accomplish on our own is less than noteworthy. We try our best, but the results aren't exactly graceful, flowing music. But with the hand of the Master, our life's work can be beautiful. Next time you set out to accomplish great feats, listen carefully. You can hear the voice of the Master, whispering in your ear, "Keep playing." Feel his loving arms around you. Know that his strong hands are there to help you turn your feeble attempts into a true masterpiece.

God doesn't call the equipped; he equips the called. And he'll always be there to love you and to guide you on to great things. Your worst days are never so bad that you are beyond the reach of God's grace. And your best days are never so good that you are beyond the need of God's grace.

Jacob did not expect to see his son Joseph again, but now he would because God did not "stop playing." God will make something out of our lives if we remain faithful to him.

II. COMMENTARY

Family Relocation

MAIN IDEA: *Jacob exercises faith as he prepares to leave the land of promise and again when he arrives in Egypt.*

A Jacob Travels to Egypt (46:1–4)

SUPPORTING IDEA: *Jacob's journey to Egypt receives God's blessing because this is part of his plan to fulfill his promises to Abraham.*

46:1–4. At Beersheba, as Jacob traveled toward Egypt, God reassured him that he would bless him, even in Egypt. This move to Egypt was part of the Lord's wonderful plan. The Abrahamic covenant was repeated to Jacob as he left the land of promise. He was told that he would die in Egypt but that God would bring his descendants back to the promised land some day.

There have been many questions about whether Jacob's trip to Egypt was God's "perfect will" or his "permissive will." Abraham had traveled to Egypt many years before to avoid a famine in Canaan (Gen. 12:10). God had planned that Egypt would be the place of sustenance for his people (Gen. 45:7). Once God gave the nation of Israel the land of promise, Egypt would become a forbidden place since the provisions of Egypt would then be seen as substituting for the Lord's care (Jer. 42:13–22). In later Scripture Egypt became an image of bondage and defiance of the true God (Ezek. 29:1–7), but at this point such a concept was not in Jacob's mind.

Jacob seemed hesitant to leave the land of promise, even though he must have had a great desire to see Joseph. Jacob offered a sacrifice **to the God of his father Isaac.** This seems to indicate that Jacob was acknowledging the calling of his family. Furthermore, he was probably seeking God's approval to leave the land of Canaan. When Jacob had left the land of promise to go to Haran many years before, God had appeared to him in a vision and reassured him that he would return to this land and that his descendants would possess the land. In Genesis 28:21 Jacob had promised that when he returned safely "to my father's house, then the LORD will be my God."

Now, once again, Jacob was preparing to leave the land of promise. He wanted to acknowledge God and perhaps to hear from him. He may have remembered the prophecy to Abraham that his descendants would be enslaved in a foreign land (not identified as Egypt; Gen. 15:13). Jacob may have been wondering if this journey was the right thing to do.

God spoke to Jacob **in a vision at night** and declared, **I am God, the God of your father. . . . Do not be afraid to go down to Egypt, for I will make you** a great nation there. I will go down to Egypt with you, and I will surely bring you back again. And Joseph's own hand will close your eyes. This was the sixth time that God had revealed himself to Jacob. He assured him that this journey was in accord with his will for Jacob and his family.

B Jacob's Family and Possessions (46:5–27)

SUPPORTING IDEA: *Jacob's entire family that goes into Egypt consists of only seventy persons. They are listed in detail so God's promise of a great nation can be validated later.*

46:5–7. When Jacob went into Egypt with his family, he used the **carts that Pharaoh had sent to transport him.** With the family came **their livestock and the possessions they had acquired in Canaan.** In contrast to Abraham who left his extended family behind, Jacob brought **his sons and grandsons and his daughters and granddaughters—all his offspring** since all of these were now members of the covenant.

46:8–27. In a detailed listing, Jacob's entire family is accounted for in their relocation to Egypt. The expression in verse 8, **these are the names of the sons of Israel . . . who went to Egypt,** is repeated exactly in Exodus 1:1 when the story of the exodus is introduced. Thus the journey into Egypt and the journey out of Egypt are closely tied together. God fulfills his promises.

The sons and grandsons of Jacob are listed in chronological order. But they are also arranged according to their mothers: Leah, then Leah's handmaid Zilpah, Rachel, and then Rachel's handmaid Bilhah.

Leah was the mother of Reuben, Simeon, Levi, Judah, Issachar, and Zebulun. The number of their descendants was thirty-three sons and daughters (v. 15).

Zilpah, the servant of Leah, was the mother of Gad and Asher. There were sixteen members of this branch of the family (v. 18).

Rachel was the mother of Joseph and Benjamin. These two sons and their children were fourteen in number (v. 22). It is noted in the listing that Joseph's two sons **were born to Joseph by Asenath daughter of Potiphera, priest of On.** This is the second time that a foreign woman has been mentioned in the listing, although the first time no proper name was given (see v. 10).

Finally, Bilhah was the mother of Dan and Naphtali. This branch of the family was seven in number (v. 25). By adding the numbers given by the author of Genesis (33 + 16 + 14 + 7), the grand total of seventy descendants of Jacob is reached. This number included Dinah and Serah but not the wives of any sons including Joseph, although his wife's name is mentioned (v. 19). It is possible that Dinah and Serah were the only two unmarried women of marriageable age who entered Egypt with Jacob.

The difficulty about the exact number of people who entered Egypt with Jacob is complicated by the fact that three different numbers are given in Scripture. Here in Genesis 46:26 the number is given as sixty-six who actually traveled to Egypt. But this number does not include Jacob or his son's wives. In Genesis 46:27 the number is seventy because Jacob, Joseph, and Joseph's two sons, Ephraim and Manasseh, are added in. The number seventy is found in the Hebrew text (and again in Exod. 1:5 and Deut. 10:22), but the Septuagint as well as the New Testament Book of Acts has seventy-five.

In Genesis 46:20 the Septuagint adds five other males, including a son of Manasseh (Machir), two sons of Ephraim (Sultalaam and Taam), and one grandson for both Manasseh (Galaad) and Ephraim (Edom descended through Sutalaam). In Acts 7:14 the number is stated as seventy-five and refers to the "whole family," which apparently included these five other males. In Genesis 46:27 the Septuagint also adds, "And the sons of Joseph who were born to him in Egypt were nine persons. All the souls of the house of Jacob who entered Egypt were seventy-five." These nine added to the sixty-six also produced the number of seventy-five.

The difficulty with both verses in the Septuagint is that Manasseh and Ephraim could hardly have been older than seven and five, respectively, when Jacob entered the land of Egypt. If these two sons did have the sons and grandsons whom the Septuagint attributes to them, they would have had difficulty fathering them all by the time their grandfather Jacob died. At this point Manasseh would have been about twenty-five and Ephraim about twenty-two years of age. While four grandsons of Jacob have been included in Genesis 46:12,17, these apparently were alive at the time of Jacob's entrance into Egypt. Surely many other grandsons were born after he began to live there.

Some scholars, not wanting to give any credence to the Septuagint translation, have speculated that the seventy-five descendants of Jacob included five surviving wives of Jacob's sons. Whatever solution is used, our view of inspiration demands that we recognize the truth of both Genesis 46:27 and Acts 7:14.

C Jacob's Reunion with Joseph (46:28–30)

> **SUPPORTING IDEA:** *Jacob is reunited with his son Joseph, an event that strengthens his faith.*

46:28–30. Judah, the son who had exhibited an ability as spokesman and leader (Gen. 37:26–27; 43:3,8; 44:18), was given the responsibility of making contact with Joseph. Jacob obviously believed that Joseph would come through on his promise to provide a place for them to live (see Gen. 45:10–11).

Joseph could have requested that his father come and visit him (and even bow down to him; Gen. 37:10), but Joseph was the one who initiated contact. He **had his chariot made ready and went to Goshen to meet his father Israel.** What a reunion! **As soon as Joseph appeared before him, he threw his arms around his father and wept for a long time.**

After this reunion Jacob declared that he was **ready to die, since I have seen for myself that you are still alive.** Years before when Joseph had shared his dream with his father about the sun and moon and eleven stars, his father had rebuked him (Gen. 37:10). But Genesis 37:11 also notes that Jacob "kept the matter in mind." Surely Jacob realized now as he and his sons thanked Joseph for what he had done for them that this was a fulfillment of prophecy.

D Jacob Appears Before Pharaoh (46:31–47:12)

SUPPORTING IDEA: *Jacob demonstrates that he has something to offer one of the most powerful men on earth.*

46:31–34. Joseph prepared his family for their meeting with Pharaoh, the ruler of Egypt. He instructed his family to tell Pharaoh that they were shepherds. Joseph did this so Pharaoh would allow them to settle in Goshen, an area suited for the raising of sheep and cattle.

Joseph also stated that **all shepherds are detestable to the Egyptians.** The word **detestable** could be translated "an aversion." This aversion was probably based on social custom since Egypt did have large flocks and herds (Exod. 9:3,19). In fact, Pharaoh even requested that Joseph have some of the Israelites look after his own livestock (Gen. 47:6). But plant agriculture was the foundation of Egyptian society. The Egyptians were highly skilled in organizing fields, irrigation, and the collection and storage of harvested food. Apparently, those who spent time with animals were considered inferior and perhaps even crude as compared to those who grew crops.

47:1–6. Five of Joseph's brothers were chosen to represent the entire family. They did as Joseph had instructed them to do in their answers to Pharaoh. They told Pharaoh that they had **come to live here awhile, because the famine is severe in Canaan and your servants' flocks have no pasture.** The length of time the Israelites planned to spend in Egypt was probably the five years left in the famine. Little did they realize that God's word to Abraham about enslavement (Gen. 15:13) was about to come true for them and their descendants.

Pharaoh allotted to Jacob's family the region of Rameses, called **Goshen** (Gen. 47:6; see also Gen. 45:10; 46:28). This area was perfect for raising herds and flocks as well as for cultivating the soil.

47:7–10. After the brothers had worked out the living arrangements, **Joseph brought his father Jacob in and presented him before Pharaoh.** Note the statement that Jacob **blessed Pharaoh**. To bless someone is "to endue with power for success, prosperity, fecundity, longevity, etc." (Oswalt, 132). Blessing is usually conveyed from the greater to the lesser (for example, father to son, king to subject). Jacob expressed faith in God's promises and acted on the promise that "all peoples on earth will be blessed through you and your offspring" (Gen. 28:14).

Pharaoh questioned Jacob about his age. Jacob answered, **The years of my pilgrimage are a hundred and thirty. My years have been few and difficult, and they do not equal the years of the pilgrimage of my fathers**. He used the word **pilgrimage** to refer to the itinerant nature of his life and that of his forefathers. It had been an earthly pilgrimage and a landless pilgrimage, waiting for the fulfillment of the promise of a land.

47:11–12. Joseph was able to settle his father and brothers in Egypt, giving them food and property (which they had never had in Canaan except by way of promise) **in the best part of the land, the district of Rameses**. This was done **as Pharaoh directed**. Joseph was a man of great benevolence, but he was also a man under the authority of Pharaoh. He did not use his God-given talents to undermine the person whom he served, even though this man was not a believer in the true God.

🄴 Pharaoh Prospers During the Famine (47:13–26)

SUPPORTING IDEA: *Through Joseph's hard work Pharaoh experiences great prosperity in fulfillment of Jacob's blessing.*

47:13–26. Joseph became the trustee and distributor of all food supplies that allowed the Egyptians to live during the time of severe famine. Pharaoh was able to add to his wealth because of the need for food in Egypt and Canaan. After money ran out, livestock (vv. 15–17), land and slaves (vv. 18–21), and finally a fifth of all future harvests (vv. 23–26) were given in payment to Pharaoh. As Pharaoh blessed Jacob and his family by giving them land and provisions, God blessed Pharaoh by giving him land and affluence. In the Book of Exodus, when another Pharaoh arose who did not know Joseph or the blessings Pharaoh had received through him, the Egyptians would begin to experience the curses that come upon those who curse Abraham's descendants (see Gen. 12:3).

🄵 Jacob Nears the End of His Life (47:27–31)

SUPPORTING IDEA: *As Jacob realizes that he will not return to the promised land in his lifetime, he makes plans to be returned there after he dies.*

47:27–31. Jacob lived in Egypt for seventeen years. There is no record that he made any attempt to return to Canaan after the famine ended. Perhaps it was because he believed God's promise that Joseph would close his eyes when he died (Gen. 46:4)—and Joseph was still in Egypt! But as Jacob neared the end of his life, he made plans to fulfill God's promise that he would be brought back to Canaan some day (Gen 46:4).

He called for Joseph because he recognized that only Joseph among all his sons would have the authority and the means to be able to carry out his desire. If he wanted his body carried back to Canaan, it would need to be mummified by the processes the Egyptians had developed. He made Joseph promise by having Joseph place his hand under his thigh (see "Deeper Discoveries"). For Jacob kindness and faithfulness on Joseph's part would result in Jacob's not being buried in Egypt but being carried out of Egypt to the place where his fathers rested (that is, the promised land). Jacob was not looking for a grand funeral that Joseph could have easily provided in Egypt. He was looking for God's promise to be fulfilled.

MAIN IDEA REVIEW: *Jacob exercises faith as he prepares to leave the land of promise and again when he arrives in Egypt.*

III. CONCLUSION

A Mature Faith

It is not always easy to trust God. In Mark 9:23 a father was told by Jesus that "everything is possible for him who believes." And the father exclaimed, "I do believe; help me overcome my unbelief!" (Mark 9:24).

In the life of Jacob, something similar was occurring. God challenged Jacob throughout his life to have faith in the promises and presence of his God. But Jacob struggled, deceived, and lost faith. But God was not finished with him yet; he did not give up on his chosen man Jacob. Now at the age of 130, Jacob trusted God for his promises and journeyed to Egypt. He believed that Joseph would be there for his death and that his body would be returned to the promised land.

Jacob had come a long way from the "heel catcher" and the one who manipulated and deceived to get what he wanted. At the end of his life, his faith had matured and he trusted God in a deeper way. He had become Israel because he had struggled with God and with others and had overcome (Gen. 32:28).

PRINCIPLES

- Nonacceptance by peers may be God's way of preventing our conformity to an ungodly lifestyle.

- God is not limited by geography but is with us wherever we go, if we go in his will.
- People who belong to the Lord have nothing to fear from human leaders.

APPLICATIONS

- Don't be afraid to confirm God's leading in the midst of puzzling circumstances.
- Believers are on a pilgrimage that will end in the promised house of our Father (John 14:2).
- Trust God's Word as a sure and certain guide for life.

IV. LIFE APPLICATION

"You're Bad Luck!"

Many Christians as well as unbelievers wish one another "good luck!" But luck is not part of God's plan. There is no good luck or bad luck for the Christian. There is only the sovereign plan of Almighty God.

A man looked up from his hospital bed and said to his wife, "You've always been with me when I've had trouble. When I lost my shirt in a poor investment, you were there. When I had the car wreck, you were with me. I got fired, and you supported me. Now that I think about it, I've come to the conclusion that you're bad luck!"

But Joseph had a different theological interpretation of the events of life. In Genesis we have no record of God's speaking directly to Joseph except through his two dreams. But Joseph believed that God was in charge, and he lived accordingly. We also see that Joseph experienced the natural consequences of man's actions, both good and evil. Joseph was hardworking and honest. Some people might say that he made his own "luck." But his reunion with his father and the joy of living again as a united family was not luck but the blessing of God.

For the Christian one of the most important biblical doctrines is the sovereignty of God. We should not look at life as one lucky or unlucky break after another but as one sovereignly planned moment after another. What an exciting way to live!

V. PRAYER

Sovereign Lord, ruler of everything, help me to believe you love me and that you are in charge of every moment of my day. Give me an attitude of "good faith" rather than "good luck." Amen.

VI. DEEPER DISCOVERIES

A. Beersheba (46:1)

This city lay on the southern border of Canaan. Abraham had planted a tamarisk tree at Beersheba, where he called upon the name of the Lord (Gen. 21:33). Later Isaac also built an altar here and called on the Lord after God had appeared to him (Gen. 26:24–25). Perhaps Isaac's altar was still present when Jacob arrived and offered sacrifices to "the God of his father Isaac" (Gen. 46:1).

B. Put Your Hand Under My Thigh (47:29)

This strange practice also occurred in Genesis 24:2 when Abraham made his chief servant, possibly Eliezer, promise that he would not get Isaac a wife from among the Canaanites but only from among Abraham's own people. Here it occurs between a father and his son.

This practice was similar to today's courtroom custom of swearing on a Bible. In the ancient patriarchal world, the placing of a hand under a thigh close to the circumcised male sex organ connected the oath to the divine presence. For Abraham and his descendants, circumcision was a constant reminder of God's presence.

The placement of a hand under the thigh also might have emphasized the ties of family kinship. Promises made by placing the hand near the organ of procreation tied this oath to the continuation of Abraham's line through Isaac, Jacob, and their descendants. If anyone violated an oath made in such a manner, the other descendants would carry out appropriate judgment.

VII. TEACHING OUTLINE

A. INTRODUCTION

1. Lead Story: "Keep Playing"
2. Context: These chapters conclude the incident that started when Joseph's brothers first came to Egypt to obtain food. Now Jacob and his entire extended family will travel to Egypt to obtain food and be reunited with Joseph.
3. Transition: God has promised Jacob that Joseph will close his eyes when he (Jacob) dies. But God has also promised Jacob that he will return to the land of promise. The final chapters of Genesis will give the closing days of Jacob's life and show the faith that he and his son Joseph had in the promises of God about the land of promise.

B. COMMENTARY

1. Jacob Travels to Egypt (46:1–4)
2. Jacob's Family and Possessions (46:5–27)
3. Jacob's Reunion with Joseph (46:28–30)
4. Jacob Appears Before Pharaoh (46:31–47:12)
5. Pharaoh Prospers During the Famine (47:13–26)
6. Jacob Nears the End of His Life (47:27–31)

C. CONCLUSION: "YOU'RE BAD LUCK!"

VIII. ISSUES FOR DISCUSSION

1. What promises of God do Christians have the most difficult time trusting God to perform?
2. How could Jacob bless Pharaoh? What did Jacob have that Pharaoh didn't possess?
3. How do you justify Joseph's being involved with a pagan government and bringing great wealth to an unbelieving ruler?

Genesis 48:1–50:26

Blessings and Burials

I. INTRODUCTION
Did You Ever Wonder Why?

II. COMMENTARY
A verse-by-verse explanation of these chapters.

III. CONCLUSION
Faith to the End

An overview of the principles and applications from these chapters.

IV. LIFE APPLICATION
The Will of God

Melding these chapters to life with God.

V. PRAYER
Tying these chapters to life with God.

VI. DEEPER DISCOVERIES
Historical, geographical, and grammatical enrichment of the commentary.

VII. TEACHING OUTLINE
Suggested step-by-step group study of these chapters.

VIII. ISSUES FOR DISCUSSION
Zeroing these chapters in on daily life.

"*G*rief and tragedy and hatred are only for a time. Goodness, remembrance and love have no end."

George W. Bush

Genesis 48:1–50:26

IN A NUTSHELL

*T*hese three chapters show how thirteen tribes that would inherit Jacob's blessings came to be and why each of the thirteen was assigned unique roles.

Blessings and Burials

I. INTRODUCTION

Did You Ever Wonder Why?

*M*ost of us wonder about the oddities of life at one time or another. Well, did you ever wonder . . .

- why people spend so much for those little bottles of Evian water? Try spelling Evian backwards: NAÏVE.
- why we say something is out of whack? What's a whack?
- why the man who invests your money is called a broker?
- why croutons (stale bread) come in airtight packages?
- if lawyers are disbarred and clergymen are defrocked, doesn't it follow that electricians can be delighted, musicians denoted, cowboys deranged, models deposed, tree surgeons debarked, and dry cleaners depressed?
- if Lipton Tea employees take coffee breaks?
- what hair color they put on the driver's licenses of bald men?
- if American mothers feed their babies with tiny little spoons and forks, do Chinese mothers use toothpicks?

In Scripture there are many things that cause the reader to wonder why. In this passage there are a number of whys, some of which are answered while we are left to wonder about others.

II. COMMENTARY

Blessings and Burials

> **MAIN IDEA:** *God acts to bring about his own sovereign purposes even when this violates human custom and tradition.*

A Jacob Blesses Joseph's Sons (48:1–20)

> **SUPPORTING IDEA:** *Just as Jacob, the younger son of Isaac, had received the blessing, so did Ephraim, rather than Manasseh, receive a special blessing from Jacob.*

48:1–2. Joseph, recognizing that his father was about to die, took his two sons, **Manasseh and Ephraim**, to see their grandfather one last time and perhaps also in anticipation of a final patriarchal blessing.

48:3–7. Jacob repeated the Abrahamic covenant that he had been given many years before at Bethel (Gen. 28:13–15). But in this repetition of the covenant, the numerous descendants and land are emphasized. It is in this context that Jacob adopted Joseph's two sons as his own. This would guarantee a separate inheritance in the land for them that would be equal to Jacob's other eleven sons. He specified that Joseph's sons, who had been born before Jacob entered the land of Egypt, would be adopted. But if any more sons were born to Joseph, they would not receive a separate inheritance. Jacob had always showed favoritism to Joseph when he was younger. This may have been an attempt to honor Joseph for providing deliverance for the family.

48:8–11. Jacob told Joseph to bring his two sons to him **so I may bless them**. To bless a person meant to request that God's favor would rest upon him. In Genesis 47:7,10 Jacob blessed Pharaoh after the king of Egypt had blessed the Israelites with land and provisions.

48:12–14. Jacob planned to pronounce a patriarchal blessing on both of Joseph's sons. Joseph had arranged his two sons so Manasseh, the older son, would encounter Jacob's right hand and receive the prime blessing. But in a surprising move, Jacob reached out with his right hand and placed it on Ephraim's head while crossing his arms so his left hand rested upon Manasseh's head.

48:15–16. Joseph was blessed by his father in a poetic blessing (for other poetic blessings in Genesis, see 9:26–27; 14:19–20; 27:27–29; 27:39–40; 48:20; and 49:2–27). This blessing of Joseph essentially involved the blessing of his two sons.

48:17–18. When Joseph saw Jacob put his right hand on Ephraim's head, **he was displeased**. Joseph may have been displeased because he felt his father was showing favoritism to the younger son just as Joseph as the second youngest had been shown favoritism years before. Or perhaps Joseph was displeased that his father was not thinking clearly any more or that his nearly blind condition was confusing him (Gen. 48:10). In any case Joseph sought to "correct" his father.

48:19–20. Jacob refused to be corrected by Joseph. He informed Joseph that this was no mistake but a purposeful action that would reflect God's plan for these two boys. The fact that the younger would be greater is similar to Genesis 25:23 where Rebekah was told that "the older [Esau] will serve the younger [Jacob]."

The declaration that **his descendants will become a group of nations** may find its fulfillment in the time of the divided kingdom when Ephraim's descendants were the most powerful of any tribe in the north. The name *Ephraim* was often used to identify the entire Northern Kingdom (e.g., Isa. 7:2,5,8–9; Hos. 9:13; 12:1,8).

Jacob's proclamation, **In your name will Israel pronounce this blessing: "May God make you like Ephraim and Manasseh,"** contains a reversal of the birth order when giving the names of Joseph's sons and putting the younger first. By including both of his grandsons, Jacob seemed to indicate that they would receive an inheritance as sons and would be regarded by others as being significantly blessed.

B Joseph's Double Portion (48:21–22)

SUPPORTING IDEA: *Joseph is identified by his father as the one to whom the double portion will be given in the promised land.*

48:21. Using the name **Israel**, Jacob declared to Joseph that he was about to die but that he believed God would be with Joseph and take him back to the promised land. The Hebrew word for **you** and **your** is in the plural. Like Jacob, Joseph would return to the land after his death. But his descendants would return to the land en masse four hundred years later.

48:22. Joseph was also given a double portion of the land. This is clearly stated in 1 Chronicles 5:1: "The sons of Reuben . . . his rights as firstborn were given to the sons of Joseph." This occurred because Jacob saw him **as one who is over your brothers.** Joseph was not the oldest son of Jacob, but he was used to provide for the rest of the family as the oldest son often did. As a result Jacob gave him **the ridge of land** that Jacob **took from the Amorites with my sword and my bow.**

A number of interesting concepts occur in this verse in the Hebrew. The word in the original language for **ridge of land** is the same as the place-name *Shechem*. This is where Joseph would later be buried (see Gen. 33:19; Josh. 24:32; John 4:5). This Hebrew term can also be translated "shoulder" or "portion" in the sense that Jacob gave Joseph a portion [more] than his brothers— that is, a double portion.

This extra portion was identified as that which Jacob had taken **with my sword and my bow.** This may refer to the incident in Genesis 34:25–29 when Simeon and Levi looted the city of Shechem, since Jacob purchased the burial plot from the sons of Hamor, the father of Shechem, for a hundred pieces of silver (Gen. 33:19). In any case, it is clear that Jacob was granting to Joseph special privileges, probably not as a sign of favoritism as he did early in his life but as an honor for what Joseph had done for the family.

C Jacob Blesses His Sons (49:1–28)

SUPPORTING IDEA: *In the longest poem in Genesis, Jacob addresses each of his sons and pronounces on them prophecies about the future.*

49:1–2. Although Jacob was near death (Gen. 48:1–2), he called for his sons to tell them **what will happen to you in days to come.** Often called the "Blessing of Jacob," this poem addressed each of the sons directly, although the fulfillment of the prophecies would be through the various tribes that descended from them. Most of the prophecies were based on the characteristics of each of Jacob's sons as evidenced in his behavior.

49:3–4. Reuben, Jacob's firstborn son, was recognized as one who deserved to receive a special blessing and prophecy because of his position. This blessing normally included roles of leadership and priesthood as well as a double portion of the birthright. But because of the **turbulent** nature of Reuben, evidenced by his immoral act of sleeping with his father's concubine Bilhah (Gen. 35:22), he lost his legal status as firstborn. This act of Reuben was a premature claim to his inheritance, and now he had lost it all. He would not enjoy preeminence over the other tribes.

The rights of leadership would be given to Judah. The priesthood would ultimately go to Levi, and the double portion had already been given to Joseph (the firstborn son of Rachel). Although Reuben had tried to redeem himself in his effort to protect Joseph from death (Gen. 37:21–22), he still lost his position. Later, in Judges 5:15b, the tribe of Reuben struggled with indecision. Throughout the rest of the Old Testament the tribe of Reuben, that would choose to live on the eastern side of the Jordan River (Num. 32), did not play a leadership role. Nothing redeeming is ever stated of Reuben. No significant judge, king, or prophet ever came from this tribe.

49:5–7. Simeon and Levi are dealt with together because they shared the same characteristics of violence and anger and the same violent history in killing the men of Shechem (Gen. 34:25). As a result, their future would be identical. These two tribes would be scattered when they entered the promised land so that neither would have a centralized, independent tribal territory. Jacob may have realized that to allow a large group of these men to live together would pose a real threat to the other tribes. Obviously, the leadership role that should have gone to the second born or third born was not given to either Simeon or Levi because of their behavior.

49:8–12. The blessing on Judah, Jacob's fourth-born son, is the most theologically significant of all the blessings reiterated in this chapter. Judah's trait was that of a lion's cub, a picture of sovereignty, strength, and courage. Although Judah had started down the wrong path with his family (Gen. 38), he had repented and then shown leadership (Gen. 43:3–10). Judah was declared to be the royal tribe and identified as the one through whom the future rulers, King David and the Messiah, would come.

Jacob said of Judah, **The scepter will not depart from Judah, nor the ruler's staff from between his feet**. The scepter was a symbol of royal command, so Judah was given the right to rule **until he comes to whom it belongs** ["or *until Shiloh comes; or until he comes to whom tribute belongs*"] **and the obedience of the nations is his**. The NIV notes the difficulty in translating part of this verse. Shiloh may be a proper name of a person, that is the Messiah, who would ultimately arise in Judah and bring victory and peace to

Israel (Num. 24:17). Because Christ is never referred to by this name, it may be best to translate it not by a proper name but as in the NIV text. This prophecy does not contain a promise of uninterrupted rule by Judah but rather the right to rule by Judah.

Genesis 49:10b–12 describes the conditions that would occur once the great leader of Judah, the Messiah, ruled. A settled, abundantly prosperous life is implied by the fact that one would attach animals to vines and branches (since there would be so many) and wash his clothes in wine (since it would be so abundant). Finally, the ruler is described: **His eyes will be darker than wine, his teeth whiter than milk.** This is a picture of strength, health, and power.

49:13. Jacob's next son Zebulun was not described by his character. Rather, his future territory was denoted by the fact that he would **live by the seashore and become a haven for ships; his border will extend toward Sidon.** Zebulun never obtained "seaside property." He was landlocked, since the tribe of Asher was between him and the Mediterranean coast. But this tribe was within ten miles of the Mediterranean Sea and able to "feast on the abundance of the seas" (Deut. 33:19) and so fulfilled this prophecy. Zebulun's northern border pointed in the direction of Sidon on the Phoenician coast.

49:14–15. Issachar, Jacob's sixth son, is referred to as **a rawboned donkey lying down between two saddlebags.** This is probably not a character trait of Issachar. Rather, it refers to the land he obtained in lower Galilee, including the eastern portion of the Valley of Jezreel. This valley was located between the low hills of Galilee (including Mt. Tabor) and the hills where Manasseh would live (including Mt. Gilboa). Jacob recognized **how good is his resting place and how pleasant is his land, he will bend his shoulder to the burden and submit to forced labor.**

This probably does not refer to any situation that caused Issachar to become a slave to one of his brothers or even to a foreign invader. In time all the tribes of Israel in this region were forced to submit to foreign nations (2 Kgs. 15:29; Isa. 9:1). The expression seems to depict how Issachar would embrace an arduous, agricultural way of life and not seek political dominance.

49:16–18. Jacob's next son Dan would exercise a measure of leadership because he would be a judge in Israel and would **provide justice for his people as one of the tribes of Israel.** The name *Dan* was connected originally with vindication (Gen. 30:6), but here the name is connected with justice. Although the biblical record only records Samson as a judge from this tribe, it must have exercised this role in other ways. But the tribe of Dan is also said to **be a serpent by the roadside, a viper along the path, that bites the horse's heels so that its rider tumbles backward.** This tribe would be treacherous and would end up leading Israel into idolatry (Judg. 18).

Genesis 49:18 seems to be a cry of the heart from Jacob in the midst of his prophecy. Recognizing what some of his children would do in the future caused him to cry out, **I look for your deliverance, O LORD.**

49:19. Jacob's son Gad would choose to live east of the Jordan River (Josh. 13:24–27). This land would contain the north-south major route called "the King's Highway." As a result Gad would experience being **attacked by a band of raiders**, but he would **attack them at their heels.** While he would encounter military attacks, Gad would be effective in counterattacking (for example, Jephthah against the Ammonites in Judg. 11–12).

49:20. The next son, Asher, would live along the coast of the Mediterranean Sea. This tribe's food would **be rich**; he would **provide delicacies fit for a king.** Not only would Asher live in an area with fertile farmland (the lowlands of the Carmel range north along the coast) and abundant rain, but he would have the opportunity to trade for goods from other sections of the Mediterranean world. The character of Asher is not mentioned—only his future prosperity.

49:21. Jacob's son Naphtali is said to be **a doe set free that bears beautiful fawns.** The tribe of Naphtali would live north and west of the Sea of Galilee in a rugged, isolated, but fertile area. Apparently this tribe would exhibit a freedom and beauty that would be different from the other tribes.

49:22–26. Joseph received an abundant blessing that had already been anticipated in the blessing given to Joseph in Genesis 48:15–16 and to his two sons Ephraim and Manasseh in Genesis 48:20. The name *Joseph* means "may he add" (Gen. 30:24) while the name of his son *Ephraim* means "twice fruitful" (Gen. 41:52).

The tribe of Joseph known as Ephraim became prosperous and fruitful as they dealt with invaders from their central hill-country position in the middle of what becomes known as Samaria. The land of Ephraim had good rainfall and abundant harvests. Joshua was from the tribe of Ephraim. In later years this tribe would contend with Judah for the leadership role. When the nation divided into north and south, Ephraim gave its name to the northern territory (Isa. 7:2,5,8–9; Hos. 9:13; 12:1,8).

The tribe of Joseph known as Manasseh was subdivided into two half tribes. They were located on each side of the northern portion of the Jordan River. This area also experienced good rainfall and abundant crops.

49:27. Jacob's final son Benjamin is referred to as a **ravenous wolf.** In the time of the judges, this tribe would hold off the other eleven tribes (Judg. 20) until they were finally ambushed and nearly annihilated because they were defending an immoral group of people from their tribe. In the time of the monarchy, Saul, a Benjamite and a great warrior, was chosen as Israel's first king (1 Sam. 9–10).

49:28. Although some tribes did suffer punishment for the sins of their fathers, each received **the blessing appropriate to him**. The fact that each retained a place in Abraham's chosen family and enjoyed the national promises given to Abraham was in itself a major blessing.

D Jacob's Death and Burial (49:29–50:14)

SUPPORTING IDEA: *Even in his death Jacob's faith is evident.*

49:29–32. Jacob charged his sons to bury him in the patriarchal tombs at Machpelah (see Gen. 47:30). His first wife Leah was buried there. He chose to be buried with her and his father (Isaac) and mother (Rebekah) and grandfather (Abraham) and grandmother (Sarah). Throughout her life Jacob had favored Rachel. Now perhaps he recognized the value and position of his first wife Leah. He believed this land where he wanted to be buried would some day be part of the land of the nation of Israel.

49:33–50:3. When Jacob died, he was embalmed in accordance with Egyptian practice. If he had not been embalmed, there would have been no way to transport his body back to Canaan.

50:4–14. Joseph and his brothers transported their father's body back to Canaan as he had requested. The people of Canaan misinterpreted the event. They thought the Egyptians were holding **a solemn ceremony of mourning**. The clothing, the coffin, and maybe even the language may have led to this assumption. But the reality was that this was a Hebrew patriarch who was being buried in the land he believed he owned by faith.

E Joseph's Brothers Revisit Their Sin (50:15–21)

SUPPORTING IDEA: *The forgiveness offered by Joseph is finally accepted by his brothers.*

50:15–18. With their father now dead and buried, the brothers began to fear that Joseph would take revenge against them. They had never truly believed that Joseph had forgiven them. Joseph wept, perhaps because of their inability to understand forgiveness or perhaps because he realized he should have reassured them before now that his forgiveness was genuine. In the busyness of his life as minister of agriculture, he may not have had much time with his brothers.

50:19–21. Joseph reminded them that such an action was not his to perform, even if he wanted to do so. He again stated the principal that all the events of his life had been planned by the Lord and that evil intentions had not prevented God's plan from being accomplished. They had meant harm to him, but God had used it for good. To reassure them Joseph demonstrated his forgiveness again by promising to provide for them and their children.

F Joseph's Death (50:22–26)

> **SUPPORTING IDEA:** *As Joseph is about to die, he once again displays his faith in the promises of God.*

50:22–23. This paragraph summarizes the rest of Joseph's life. Joseph was thirty-nine when his father Jacob moved to Egypt. His father lived for another seventeen years in Egypt. Now fifty-four years later Joseph died at 110. Joseph had lived long enough to see his grandchildren and some great-grandchildren.

50:24–26. Like his father before him, Joseph asked to be buried in Canaan. Realizing that his brothers would not have the resources to travel to Canaan immediately, he requested that he be brought back when the nation returned at the time of the future exodus (see Gen. 15:12–16). Hebrews 11:22 reads, "By faith Joseph, when his end was near, spoke about the exodus of the Israelites from Egypt and gave instructions about his bones."

The fulfillment of this request is found in Exodus 13:19 and Joshua 24:32. Joseph's act of faith was rewarded long after he died. No doubt many Egyptians tried to convince Joseph that he should be buried in Egypt where he had made such a great name for himself. But Joseph was more interested in what God had to say than in what humans said.

> **MAIN IDEA REVIEW:** *God acts to bring about his own sovereign purposes even when this violates human custom and tradition.*

III. CONCLUSION

Faith to the End

It is sometimes difficult to understand why things happen as they do. Even as believers we find it difficult to understand why God chooses certain purposes and brings them about a certain way. But God is sovereign. He acts in keeping with his character but not always in harmony with human custom and tradition. Both Jacob and Joseph demonstrated they understood that their responsibility was to exercise faith—faith to the very end of life.

PRINCIPLES

- God is in control of circumstances, and he works providentially to accomplish his purposes.
- God acts according to his own purpose, not necessarily in line with human tradition or custom.
- Believers must never settle for this land with its power and affluence as home; we are citizens of a heavenly home.

APPLICATIONS

- Can you appreciate the depths of forgiveness, or are you like Joseph's brothers who feared and expected revenge after many years?
- Are you prepared to interpret life theologically, based on the promises of God, or naturally, based solely on the processes of life?
- It's always appropriate to cry out to God for help.

IV. LIFE APPLICATION

The Will of God

Joseph had a quiet confidence that he was in God's will—that the Lord had placed him in Egypt for a purpose. The following poem expresses the need for all believers to find confidence and security in the will of God.

The Will of God will never take you
Where the Grace of God cannot keep you,
Where the Arms of God cannot support you,
Where the Riches of God cannot supply your needs,
Where the Power of God cannot endow you.

The Will of God will never take you
Where the Spirit of God cannot work through you,
Where the Wisdom of God cannot teach you,
Where the Army of God cannot protect you,
Where the Hands of God cannot mold you,

The Will of God will never take you
Where the Love of God cannot enfold you,
Where the Mercies of God cannot sustain you,
Where the Peace of God cannot calm your fears,
Where the Authority of God cannot overrule you.

The Will of God will never take you
Where the Comfort of God cannot dry your tears,
Where the Word of God cannot feed you,
Where the Miracles of God cannot be done for you,
Where the Omnipresence of God cannot find you.

—Author Unknown

V. PRAYER

Father, may I live my life in such a way that it will open the door for future blessing for my children and their children. May I continue to trust your Word throughout my life so faith will be the dominant characteristic of my being. Amen.

VI. DEEPER DISCOVERIES

A. Typology (Joseph)

Many Bible readers have seen similarities between the life of Joseph and the life of our Lord Jesus Christ. Rejected by his brothers, sold for silver, suffered for the good of those who betrayed him, offered forgiveness to those who didn't deserve it—these and many other parallels between Christ and Joseph are obvious.

The hermeneutical methodology of recognizing such similarities is called typology. A type is an event, character, or institution which has a place and purpose in history but which by divine design can correspond to a later event, character, or institution (the antitype). The value of typology lies in recognizing that God has foreknowledge. He can design and record in a specific manner an earlier event, character, or institution to resemble a later one. This helps the reader of Scripture to see God's hand in all of history.

B. Twelve or Thirteen Tribes?

Jacob had twelve sons from his two wives and two concubines. The Scriptures continually speak of twelve tribes but since the two sons of Joseph were adopted as sons by Jacob, there were actually thirteen tribes. The granting of a double portion to Joseph meant there would no longer be a tribe of Joseph but two Joseph tribes: Ephraim and Manasseh. Later, the males of the tribe of Levi would become a substitute for the firstborn of the other tribes (Exod. 32:25–29; Num. 3:11–13). Only twelve tribes would inherit a tribal territory, since the Levites received designated cities and towns scattered throughout the land of Israel. In the twenty-nine lists of the tribes of Israel found in the Old and New Testaments, never are more than twelve names listed. Often it is the name of Levi that is missing, although the tribe of Dan that became so idolatrous is left out on occasion.

C. Laying On of Hands (48:14)

Jacob's placing of his hands on the sons of Joseph is the first of many biblical instances of the "laying on of hands." In Scripture there are probably five reasons why hands were laid on a person: (1) identification with a sacrifice (Lev. 1:4), (2) for healing (Mark 5:23), (3) when arresting a person (Acts 5:18), (4) impartation of the Spirit (Acts 8:17), and (5) the transference of spiritual power or a promise to another person such as in ordination (1 Tim. 4:14). It is the fifth reason that relates to Genesis 48 where Jacob symbolically transferred blessing that he had received from God to Joseph's sons.

VII. TEACHING OUTLINE

A. INTRODUCTION

1. Lead Story: Did You Ever Wonder Why?
2. Context: These final chapters in Genesis wrap up the story of both Jacob and Joseph. They show how God is faithful to his people and how his people still believe in the promises given to Abraham.
3. Transition: This story of the children of Israel moving to Egypt for preservation prepares the reader for the Book of Exodus. God will bring the people who have become a great nation out of the land of Egypt to deliver on his promises.

B. COMMENTARY

1. Jacob Blesses Joseph's Sons (48:1–20)
2. Joseph's Double Portion (48:21–22)
3. Jacob Blesses His Sons (49:1–28)
4. Jacob's Death and Burial (49:29–50:14)
5. Joseph's Brothers Revisit Their Sin (50:15–21)
6. Joseph's Death (50:22–26)

C. CONCLUSION: THE WILL OF GOD

VIII. ISSUES FOR DISCUSSION

1. How does a patriarchal blessing work? Is this the same as God speaking, or is God "forced" to uphold the words of a man?
2. Why was it so important to both Jacob and Joseph where their bodies would be buried? Should a believer today be concerned about where he is buried or even if he is buried (or cremated)?

3. Why is it sometimes hard to accept the forgiveness of another person?

4. If you had to predict what your future family will be like and what they will experience based on your character or behavior, what would it be like and would you be proud of it?

Glossary

angel—A messenger from God, either heavenly or human, who delivers God's message of instruction, warning, or hope

atonement—God's way of overcoming sin through Christ's obedience and death to restore believers to a right relationship with God

circumcision—The removal of the foreskin of the male sex organ as a sign of inclusion among the covenant people of Israel

covenant—A contract or agreement expressing God's gracious promises to his people and their consequent relationship to him

creation—God's bringing the world and everything in it into existence from nothing

election—God's gracious action in choosing people to follow him and obey his commandments

evil—Anyone or anything that opposes the plan of God

fall, the—The result of the first human sin which marred the image of God in humans and created an environment for and a tendency toward sin for all people

firstborn—The oldest son born into a Jewish family or the first offspring of livestock. The firstborn were dedicated to God in a special sense

holy—God's distinguishing characteristic that separates him from all creation; the moral ideal for Christians as they seek to reflect the character of God as known in Christ Jesus

Holy Spirit—The third person of the Trinity; the presence of God promised by Christ and sent to his disciples at Pentecost representing God's active presence in the believer, the church, and the world

idolatry—The worship of that which is not God

image of God—That in human nature which reflected God at creation but was marred in the fall by sin and is being restored as Christians are molded into the image of Christ

monotheism—Belief in only one God

original sin—The disobedience of Adam and Eve that plunged humankind into sin and has been followed by every person (except Jesus Christ) choosing to sin

Pentateuch—First five books of the Hebrew Bible: Genesis, Exodus, Leviticus, Numbers, Deuteronomy

providence—God's care for and guidance of his creation against all opposition

righteousness—The quality or condition of being in right relationship with God; living out the relationship with God in right relationships with other persons

Sabbath—The seventh day of the week corresponding to the seventh day of creation when people in the Old Testament were called on to rest from work and reflect on God

sacrifice—According to Mosaic Law, an offering to God in repentance for sin or as an expression of thanksgiving; Christ as the ultimate Sacrifice for sin

Satan—The personalized Evil One who leads forces opposed to God and tempts people

sin—Actions by which humans rebel against God, miss his purpose for their lives, and surrender to the power of evil rather than to God

temptation—The pull toward sin that all humans experience; it comes from Satan, not God

Trinity—God's revelation of himself as Father, Son, and Holy Spirit unified as one in the Godhead and yet distinct in person and function

Bibliography

Anderson, J. Kerby. *Moral Dilemmas*. Nashville: Word, 1998.

Arnold, Bill T. *Encountering the Book of Genesis*. Grand Rapids: Baker Books, 1998.

Barker, William P. *Everyone in the Bible*. Westwood, N.J.: Fleming H. Revell, 1966.

Barnhouse, Donald Grey. *Genesis: A Devotional Exposition*. Grand Rapids: Zondervan, 1973.

Boa, Kenneth, and William Kruidenier. *Romans*. Vol. 6 of The Holman New Testament Commentary. Nashville: Broadman & Holman, 2000.

Boice, James Montgomery. *Genesis*. Vol. 2. Grand Rapids: Zondervan, 1985.

Bramer, Stephen J. *The Bible Reader's Joke Book*. Unpublished manuscript.

Brown, Colin, ed. *The New International Dictionary of New Testament Theology*. Vol. 1. Grand Rapids: Zondervan, 1967.

Bruce, F. F. *The Epistle to the Galatians*. Grand Rapids: Eerdmans, 1982.

Butler, Trent C. *Luke*. Vol. 4 of The Holman New Testament Commentary. Nashville: Broadman & Holman, 2000.

Calvin, John. *Commentaries on the First Book of Moses Called Genesis*. Grand Rapids: Eerdmans, 1948.

Dyer, Charles, and Gene Merrill. *Old Testament Explorer*. Nashville: Word, 2001.

Elliott, Ralph H. *The Message of Genesis*. Nashville: Broadman, 1961.

Hinckley, Karen C. *The Story of Stories*. Colorado Springs, Colo.: NavPress, 1991.

Kaiser, Walter C. *Toward an Exegetical Theology*. Grand Rapids: Baker Book House, 1981.

Keach, Benjamin. *Preaching from the Types and Metaphors of the Bible*. Grand Rapids: Kregel, 1972 (first published in 1855).

Kidner, Derek. *Genesis*. Downers Grove, Ill.: InterVarsity Press, 1967.

LaSor, William S. *Great Personalities of the Old Testament*. Westwood, N.J.: Fleming H. Revell, 1959.

Lea, Thomas D. *Hebrews & James*. Vol. 10 of The Holman New Testament Commentary. Nashville: Broadman & Holman, 1999.

Lewis, C.S. *Mere Christianity*. New York: The Macmillian Company, 1952, 1960.

Matthews, Kenneth A. *Genesis*. Vol. 1 of The New American Commentary. Nashville: Broadman & Holman, 1996.

MacArthur, Jr., John. *God*. Wheaton, Ill: Victor Books, 1993.

Morgan, Robert J. *On This Day*. Nashville: Thomas Nelson, 1997.

Bibliography

Morris, Henry M. *The Genesis Record.* Grand Rapids: Baker Book House, 1976.

Packer, J. I. *Knowing God.* Downers Grove, Ill.: InterVarsity Press, 1973.

Patterson, John. *The Goodly Fellowship of the Prophets.* New York: Charles Scribner's Sons, 1954.

Philips, John. *Exploring Genesis.* Chicago: Moody Press, 1980.

Pick, Heron. *Dictionary of Old Testament Words for English Readers.* Grand Rapids: Kregel, 1977.

Ross, Alan P. *Creation and Blessing.* Grand Rapids: Baker Book House, 1988.

Ross, Alan P. *Genesis.* The Bible Knowledge Commentary. Wheaton, Ill.: Victor, 1985.

Ryrie, Charles Caldwell. *The Ryrie Study Bible.* Chicago: Moody Press, 1978.

Sailhamer, John H. *Genesis.* Vol. 2 of The Expositor's Bible Commentary. Grand Rapids: Zondervan, 1990.

Sauer, Erich. *The Dawn of World Redemption.* London: The Paternoster Press, 1956.

Schaeffer, Francis A. *Genesis in Space and Time.* Downer's Grove, Ill.: InterVarsity Press, 1972.

Stevens, Sherrill G. *Genesis.* Vol. 1 of Layman's Bible Book Commentary. Nashville: Broadman, 1978.

Thomas, W. H. Griffith. *Genesis.* Grand Rapids: Eerdmans, 1953.

Towns, Elmer. *History Makers of the Old Testament.* Wheaton, Ill.: Victor Books, 1989.

Tozer, A. W. *The Knowledge of the Holy.* New York: Harper & Brothers, 1961.

Waltke, Bruce K. *Genesis.* Grand Rapids: Zondervan, 2001.

Watts, J. Wash. *A Distinctive Translation of Genesis.* Grand Rapids: Eerdmans, 1963.

Wenham, Gordon. *Genesis 16–50* in Word Biblical Commentary. Dallas, Tex.: Word, 1994.

Wilkinson, Bruce H., and Larry Libby. *Talk Thru the Bible Personalities.* Atlanta: Walk Thru the Bible Ministries, 1983.

Wilmington, Harold L. *Wilmington's Survey of the Old Testament.* Wheaton, Ill.: Victor Books, 1987.

Wilson, William. *Old Testament Word Studies.* Grand Rapids: Kregel, 1978.

Wiseman, Donald J., and Edwin Yamauchi. *Archeology and the Bible.* Grand Rapids: Zondervan, 1979.

Westermann, Claus. *Genesis 12–36.* Minneapolis: Augsburg, 1981.

Young, Edward J. *An Introduction to the Old Testament.* Grand Rapids: Eerdmans, 1949.

Youngblood, Ronald F. *The Book of Genesis: An Introductory Commentary.* Grand Rapids: Baker, 1992.